Victorian Culture
and Society

Other titles in *The Essential Glossary* series

Forthcoming

Victorian Culture and Society
The Essential Glossary

Adam C. Roberts

Department of English, Royal Holloway,
University of London

A member of the Hodder Headline Group
LONDON
Distributed in the United States of America by
Oxford University Press Inc., New York

First published in Great Britain in 2003 by
Arnold, a member of the Hodder Headline Group,
338 Euston Road, London NW1 3BH

http://www.arnoldpublishers.com

Distributed in the United States of America by
Oxford University Press Inc.,
198 Madison Avenue, New York, NY10016

The advice and information in this book are believed to be true and
accurate at the date of going to press, but neither the authors nor the publisher
can accept any legal responsibility or liability for any errors or omissions.

British Library Cataloguing in Publication Data
A catalogue record for this book is available from the British Library

Library of Congress Cataloging-in-Publication Data
A catalog record for this book is available from the Library of Congress

ISBN 0 340 80761 X (hb)
ISVN 0 340 80762 8 (pb)

1 2 3 4 5 6 7 8 9 10

Typeset in 10/12pt Minion by Phoenix Photosetting, Chatham, Kent
Printed and bound in Great Britain by MPG Books Ltd, Bodmin, Cornwall

What do you think about this book? Or any other Arnold title?
Please send your comments to feedback.arnold@hodder.co.uk

Contents

Introduction

This Glossary is designed to be of use to students of the Victorian period at all levels, as well as to more general readers or people with an interest in nineteenth-century culture. Its main emphasis is on the literature, and many entries are geared so as to provide contextual and background information for readers or students of Victorian fiction, poetry, prose or drama. But it also contains a good proportion of entries on historical, political, economic, art-historical, cultural and general topics. Of course it cannot, given the necessary constraints of size, make any claims to absolute comprehensiveness. It stands alongside (rather than pretending to supersede) a number of other excellent guides to the period, amongst which I might single out four as especially good: John Belchem and Richard Price (eds), *The Penguin Dictionary of Nineteenth-Century History* (Harmondsworth: Penguin 1994); Herbert Tucker (ed.), *A Companion to Victorian Literature and Culture* (Oxford: Blackwell 1999); Paul Schlicke (ed.), *The Oxford Reader's Companion to Dickens* (rev. edn, Oxford: Oxford University Press 1999); and John Sutherland, *The Longman Companion to Victorian Fiction* (Harlow: Longman 1988). Readers of *Victorian Culture and Society – The Essential Glossary* will see for themselves the extent to which this book is built upon the achievements of these scholars, as well as many others. It differs from them in range and accessibility: the many hundreds of alphabetical entries and the index provide for short-cuts to a wide range of information about the period. A conscious attempt has been made to give a flavour of Victorian culture as well as including necessary but sometimes drier factual information, dates, figures and statistics. To this end I have tried to quote as generously as possible from original sources, and in these cases I use a system of 'author plus short title' citation to identify the provenance of these quotations; the full title and publication details can be found in the Bibliography at the end of the volume.

The present book can be used in several ways. The reader who wants to know the names of Victoria's nine children, or the poets laureate of the period, or the specific details of the Crimean War, or exactly what the 'Corn Laws' were, or the precise difference in nobility between (Alfred, Lord) Tennyson (a baron) and Lord Alfred Douglas (son of a marquis), can easily check the information herein. Other entries provide not only factual information, but also a degree of critical assessment: entries on writers and artists, and entries on specific novels, poems, plays and paintings, contain both specific detail and interpretative angles. Some entries are short and factual. Some are longer, essay-like accounts of larger topics of particular importance for the Victorians (such as LAW AND LEGAL INSTITUTIONS, PHOTOGRAPHY or WORK). Cross-references to other entries are indicated, as above, by small capital letters for the entry heading or related words. Also within each entry, birth and death dates are given for all figures not accorded an entry of their own. Speaking broadly, the Victorian period is taken as 1837–1901, although some entries include data from outside those dates if I have considered them of importance to a proper understanding of the era.

That era remains one of the most fascinating in western cultural history. It is almost a cliché to talk of the richness and range of Victorian achievements, and to instance the startling contrasts of the culture that produced those achievements (extreme riches and extreme poverty, enormous human energies liberated and enormous effort put into repression of human energies); but the cliché has its roots in truth. Here is a short passage written by a pair of Victorian brothers – neither one famous – in 1861, that expresses their absolute confidence in their own age:

> We are living in the nineteenth century, an age destined to be rendered glorious in the page of history. Great indeed is our birthright, for we are children of the brightest day that has ever dawned upon the world, with tools forged by our forefathers at our hand, wherewith we may carve for ourselves an immortal name. Wonderful and vast are the resources of our time, and truly astounding are the discoveries and inventions which have been made and are being made every day.

What is most remarkable about this passage is not its fizzing self-belief, which was common enough across the period. What is remarkable is that it forms the opening paragraph of a 70-page *Guide to the Art of Illuminating and Missal Painting, by W. & G. Audsley, Architects*. That so resounding an assertion of cultural supremacy could preface an otherwise purely functional guide to a technical aspect of book illustration, complete with 'eight pages of lithographic illustrations', speaks to the ubiquity of the cultural force it embodies. That none of the readers of the brothers' book would have considered it out of place, that nobody would quarrel with what today seems an arrogant appropriation of glory, says as much as the statement does itself. The Victorian age believed in itself in a way that subsequent ages have been unable to match. Writing this glossary has brought home to me again some of the reasons for that self-confidence – the extraordinary richness and diversity of the Victorian cultural achievement. If this book has taken care not to overlook the less appealing aspects of the Victorian world-view, it also celebrates the many successes of that most vibrant period.

Adam C. Roberts

Acknowledgements

I should like to thank the English department and the Library of Royal Holloway, University of London, my workplace, for various assistances afforded during the writing of this project. Elena Seymenliyska and Eva Martinez at Hodder Arnold have been very supportive. I would especially like to thank Melissa Thompson, who read through an early draft and made many corrections and suggestions for improvement. Any mistakes that remain are, of course, my responsibility.

Albert, Prince (1819–1861)   Francis Charles Augustus Emmanuel Albert was born in Coburg, Germany, the second son of the Duke of Saxe-Coburg-Gotha. He married VICTORIA in 1840, becoming not King but Prince Consort, which position he maintained through his life. Initially he was regarded with a degree of suspicion by many Britons as a foreigner whose energetic enthusiasm for his adopted country was seen by some as an attempt to usurp his wife's position as head of state. He won over many, however, with his dedication to the bourgeois Victorian ethics of hard work, family and philanthropy, played an important role in advocating the arts and sciences, and was especially interested in the GREAT EXHIBITION of 1851. He died in 1861 of typhoid, occasioning his widow much grief. The gaudy Albert Memorial (in Hyde Park) was one manifestation of the country's sentiment; the many pubs, streets and squares named after him are another.

Alice's Adventures in Wonderland (1865) and _Through the Looking-Glass and What Alice Found There_ (1871) by Lewis Carroll   The 'Alice' books are the most loved, and studied, examples of Victorian CHILDREN'S LITERATURE; works of superb invention and charm, beautifully illustrated (by John Tenniel, 1820–1914), they also open themselves to a variety of critical and theoretical interpretations. The first book was a version of Carroll's handwritten and self-illustrated _Alice's Adventures Underground_ (1863–4), produced as a gift for Alice Liddell, the daughter of Henry Liddell, the Dean of Christ Church, Oxford. By the time the book appeared in print Carroll had become estranged from the Liddell household, for unknown reasons.

Alice's Adventures in Wonderland (1865) starts with Alice falling down an Oxfordshire rabbit hole into a surreal world beneath. By alternately drinking a shrinking potion and eating an elongating cake she undergoes a series of alternate diminishments and growths in her stature; she meets various talking animals, experiences a number of adventures, takes tea with a Mad Hatter and a March Hare, and finally ends up in the palace grounds of the Queen and King of Hearts, with their playing-card retinue. She attends a trial, in which the Knave of Hearts is arraigned for stealing some tarts, finally objecting to the topsy-turvy logic of the wonderland realm ('"No, no!" said the Queen. "Sentence first – verdict afterwards." "Stuff and nonsense!" said Alice loudly' (Carroll, _Alice's Adventures_: 107)), at which point the whole environment dissolves and is revealed as a dream.

Delightful as _Wonderland_ is, Carroll's sequel, _Through the Looking-Glass and What Alice Found There_ (1871) is the richer, more profound and more perfect work. Where _Wonderland_ adapts fairy tales and card games to its purposes, _Looking-Glass_ takes its organising principle from chess; its parodies are drawn from literature rather than nursery rhyme, and the premise of Alice passing through the mirror in her house into a weirdly comical but often alarming inverted world is brilliant. On the other side of the mirror Alice meets live chess pieces and sees the landscape outside the mirror-house divided up like a chess board. It becomes clear that her journey through this land is that of a pawn across this board, flying over the first square (in a railway carriage), encountering the sheep-like white queen and the alarmingly violent red queen, as well as the sleepy white knight, until eventually she reaches the final rank and is promoted to Queen Alice. She captures the red queen and checkmates the king, ending the game – which is again revealed to have been a strange dream.

Further reading

Alice's Adventures in Wonderland and Through the Looking-Glass (1865, 1871; edited by Hugh Haughton 1998) by Lewis Carroll (Charles Dodgson).

All The Year Round (1859–1893)   Dickens' weekly journal took up where Household Words had left off in 1859; continuing the same mix of serialised fiction, articles, occasional reviews, poetry and, most importantly, a 'Dickensy' overall tone. Dickens' own novels *A Tale of Two Cities* (1859) and *Great Expectations* (1860–1), and Wilkie Collins' *The Woman in White* (1860) were serialised in the first two and a half years of the journal's run, and fiction by Elizabeth Gaskell, Charles Reade (1814–84) and Bulwer Lytton (1803–73) followed. Circulation in Britain was steady at around 100,000 copies a week (Dickens reckoned this 'several thousands' higher than *The Times*), although special Christmas supplements containing seasonal fiction written by Dickens in collaboration with other writers sold upwards of 300,000 copies. In America the journal was massively popular; reaching perhaps as many as three million readers regularly. After Dickens' death in 1870 the journal was edited by his son, Charles Dickens Jr (1837–96), until it ceased publication in 1893.

Anderson, Elizabeth Garrett (1836–1917)   Born Elizabeth Garrett in Suffolk, she studied medicine privately and set up a medical practice in the east end of London in 1865, becoming the first woman doctor in England. She married James Anderton in 1871 and had three children, but continued to be active in feminist and women's movements to her death.

Anglo-Chinese Wars. *See* **Opium Wars.**

Annuals   Annuals were lavishly produced one-off books, expensively bound in tooled cloth or leather, often with gilt-edged paper, containing stories and poems and a high proportion of steel-engraved illustrations. The first annual was introduced to Britain from the continent by the illustrator Rudolph Ackermann (1764–1834) in 1823, who published the first of the *Forget-me-not* series. Others followed upon the success of this anthology, *Friendship's Offering* (still published today as *Friendship's Garland*), *The Keepsake* (which appeared between 1828 and 1857) were perhaps the most popular, but many others also appeared, *Heath's Book of Beauty*, *Iris* and *The Amulet* to name only a few. At one point in the 1850s, 63 annuals were on the market. They were designed for specific audiences; usually as gift books issued once a year (hence the name) at Christmas or Easter, and with a readership made up chiefly of well-to-do women, and were often edited by 'ladies', who commissioned a number of submissions from famous names, and filled out the rest of the books with low-paid hack work. Southey, Lamb, Coleridge, Elizabeth Barrett BROWNING, DICKENS and TENNYSON all contributed to annuals, although the form was widely looked down upon, regarded as mediocre and cliché ridden.

Anti-Semitism The term was coined in 1879 by Wilhelm Marr (1818–1904) to describe hatred of, or discrimination against, Jews. Such discrimination, of course, goes back many centuries before this date; but 'scientific' anti-Semitism, if that phrase can meaningfully be invoked, only emerged with the pseudo-scientific racial theories of the century's end. Before then, anti-Semitism drew on the cruder (and equally offensive) popular traditions that also informed Shakespeare's Shylock. DICKENS' wicked Jew Fagin in OLIVER TWIST (1837–9) remains one of the most potent embodiments of this racist tradition, although Dickens himself, compared to many of his friends, was relatively free of this particular prejudice. Jewish friends pointed out to him the 'great wrong' that Fagin had done Jews generally, and Dickens attempted to make amends by creating a benign and eloquent Jewish character, Riah, in *Our Mutual Friend* (1864–5). Literary representation of Jews in during the century are varied; from the caricature sinister hypnotist Svengali in George Du Maurier's *Trilby* (1894) at one end of the scale, to the sympathetic and sensitive portraits of Jews in George ELIOT's *Spanish Gipsy* (1868) and *Daniel Deronda* (1876).

Through the 1860s the notion of RACE as, broadly, a common cultural and historical inheritance was being replaced by the notion of race as a determinist and essential biological category, and anti-Semitism became more focused.

A crucial moment in the development of nineteenth-century European anti-Semitism was the French DREYFUS AFFAIR in the 1890s. The affair prompts Marcel Proust's (1871–1922) fictional Monsieur de Guermantes to shun his former friend, the cultured French Jew Charles Swann, justifying his own anti-Semitism in terms of class and nation. Previously, he tells friends 'I would have been prepared to vouch for Swann, I would have answered for his patriotism as my own.'

I have always been foolish enough to believe that a Jew can be a Frenchman, I mean an honourable Jew, a man of the world. . . . Well, now [Swann] forces me to admit that I was mistaken, since he has taken the side of this Dreyfus (who,

3

guilty or not, never moved in his world, whom he wouldn't ever have met) against a society that had adopted him, had treated him as one of its own.

(Proust, 1996: 90–1)

The point, for de Guermantes, is that Swann's support of Dreyfus proves 'that they're all secretly united and are somehow forced to give their support to anyone of their own race, even if they don't know him personally'. This perception of Jews as a separate nation within the nation-state mutates very easily into a sense of Jews as a hostile force, like a cancer, within the body of the fatherland. It is a very short step from this to the murderous state-sanctioned anti-Semitism of the twentieth century.

Arnold, Matthew (1822–1888), poet and essayist   Arnold's career falls with remarkable neatness into two phases: an earlier period when he established an enduring reputation as a poet, and a later when he shifted his allegiances more to prose and became, with CARLYLE and RUSKIN, one of the three most influential 'sages', or public thinkers, of the age with regard to cultural issues. The division is instructive: disillusionment with the first, 'poetic' phase, in so far as Arnold found himself unable to write the sort of poetry he felt ought to be written, led him on to the prolific production of critical writings from 1853 onwards. Although he continued writing verse until 1867, most of his major poetry was written before 1853.

Arnold was born in Laleham-on-Thames, west of London, the eldest son of the eminent Thomas Arnold (1795–1842), who is most famous as, from 1828, headmaster of Rugby School. The pressures of growing up under the shadow of so overwhelming a pater took their toll on the young Arnold and emerge in various ways in his verse – for instance, in *Sohrab and Rustum* (1853), in which a strong warrior son is killed in combat by his stronger father. Arnold graduated from Oxford in 1844 with a second-class degree, and worked for a time as the Private Secretary to Lord Landsdowne. He also travelled abroad, most significantly to Switzerland in 1848. It was here that he met the woman referred to in his poetry by the pseudonym 'Marguerite'. It is hard to determine precisely what happened with Marguerite, but it seems likely that Arnold fell in love with her, and that something (possibly Arnold's own consciousness of their differences in social caste) prevented marriage. He returned to Switzerland the following year, and again met Marguerite, but her presence in his poetry is an entirely valedictory one, as in 'Parting' and 'Farewell', and the famous 'To Marguerite – Continued', where Arnold asks himself why the lovers should be separated, and replies:

> A God, a God their severance rul'd!
> And bade betwixt their shores to be
> The unplumb'd, salt, estranging sea.

(ll. 22–4)

1849 saw the publication of Arnold's first collection of poetry, *The Strayed Reveller, and Other Poems*, which was favourably received. In 1851, still (to judge from his verse) melancholy over the unsuccessful affair with Marguerite, Arnold married Lucy Wightman, daughter of Sir William Wightman, Justice of the Queen's Bench. Wealthy enough not to work, Arnold nevertheless believed that it was proper and character-building for a man to work; accordingly he became a government Inspector of Schools. This was demanding work, with onerous responsibilities and long distances to travel across the country; the strain of this job almost certainly contributed to the heart attack that eventually killed him.

The lengthy title poem of *Empedocles on Etna, and Other Poems* (1852) was particularly well received, and Arnold's reading public were all the more puzzled when he excluded it from his collected *Poems* of 1853. In fact, Arnold had decided, as his preface to the 1853 volume explained, to suppress *Empedocles on Etna*; not because it was a badly written work, or because it had in some artistic sense 'failed', but simply because Arnold judged the *effect* of the work to be too negative. In the story of a philosopher wracked with misery and finally committing suicide, Arnold had delineated a subject in which the suffering found no vent in action. For Arnold, the prime directive for any poetry was not 'Is this poem well written?' but 'Will this poem *do good?*'. He insisted that all art must 'animate' and 'ennoble' its readership, and art that failed to do this was – no matter how beautiful it might be – deplorable. His views, published in various essays, became extremely influential throughout the period.

Arnold's own problem was that he was not particularly skilled at producing animating and ennobling works of poetry; his genius lay in the evocation and dissection of melancholy, as with the bleak but lovely Marguerite poems, or *Tristram and Iseult* (1852), another work influenced by his unhappy love affair. Arnold found increasing pleasure in writing prose, a medium he claimed to prefer as more immediately communicative than verse. From 1857–67 he was the elected Oxford Professor of Poetry. In his later life he published a great deal of critical prose, including *On Translating Homer* (1861), *Essays in Criticism* (1865). *On the Study of Celtic Literature* (1866), and his most famous book, CULTURE AND ANARCHY (1869). During his later years he expended a great deal of energy examining religious and dogmatic questions, with works such as *St Paul and Protestantism* (1870) and *God and the Bible* (1875). His personal life was not entirely happy, with three of his children predeceasing him, although he did eventually (1884) become Chief Inspector of Schools, and he was widely acclaimed as the nation's most influential spokesman on issues of culture. He died of a heart attack at the age of 66, at Liverpool docks, awaiting the boat on which his daughter was returning from America.

Architecture   Victorian architecture represents the most obvious material inheritance of the Victorian age; British cities are still shaped by the architectural achievements of Victorian culture. Twentieth-century architectural theory moved, largely, away from the more ornate, busy and adorned styles prevalent in the nineteenth century, and yet only those areas of British cities bombed flat in the Second World War have been purged of the ubiquitous Victorian style. Most Britons walk through mostly Victorian streets, and many live and work in Victorian buildings.

In terms of the private architecture of houses and apartments the Victorian norm is now our ideal. The stuccoed excesses of Regency architecture, epitomised by John Nash's (1752–1835) Georgian façades with their mock-classical pillars and pediments, was no longer in favour by mid-century; 'mid-Victorians', as Karen Chase and Michael Levinson argue, came 'to revile the "fakery"' of this style, with stucco ornaments concealing the '"truth" of structure beneath the pretence of classical dignity'. Victorian architecture laid plain the materials from which houses were built, although arranging their features in artfully mannered ways, 'red brick, sash windows, prominent gables, and high chimneys' (Chase and Levinson, 1999: 427). According to Chase and Levinson, this embodiment of domestic space embodied the rejection of 'blandness' in favour of 'the assertions of an articulate wall. The colour and ornament were one indication of house pride,' and the 'brazenly protruding doorway' (extending through 'muscular columns' or, later in the century, through 'elaborate glass awnings') was another. This domestic architectural aesthetic remains, arguably, our most significant material inheritance from the Victorians. Middle-class houses are now our urban palaces, and the working-class terraced houses (what Andrew Saint has called, 'shrunken versions' of the middle-class house, 'built for profit and rented out', quoted in Matthew, 2000: 259) are now the middle-class norm.

On the other hand, when we think of Victorian architecture we are more likely to think of the grander, public building projects. The most famous of these is undoubtedly Charles Barry's (1795–1860) Palace of Westminster (1840–70), built after the destruction of the old Houses of Commons and Lords by fire in 1834. This Gothic masterpiece (or monstrosity, depending on one's opinion) was in its day the world's largest functioning building.

John Ruskin's influential advocacy of Gothic architecture, especially churches, in his *The Seven Lamps of Architecture* (1849), was an expression of a wider cultural taste in mid-century. What is especially interesting about Victorian Gothic is the way archaic designs are used to embody up-to-date engineering advances, such as the then state-of-the-art heating and ventilation system Barry installed in the Palace of Westminster, or the University Museum at Oxford (1854), designed as a Gothic space and yet built entirely out of iron and glass. From 1850 through to the 1870s there was a near-explosion of church and cathedral building, with designs often influenced by Ruskin's ideas, although church styling towards the end of the century tended to move away from the Gothic ornamentation towards a cleaner, more classical style.

City redesign gathered momentum from the 1840s, with slum clearances and embankment work shoring up riversides in many cities, and urban design was facilitated by a series of laws passed in 1870 that made clearance easier. In 1884 a royal commission urged widespread slum clearance, and city councils replaced derelict housing stock with new developments. The creation of public parks was also part of this process, such as the creation of Prince's Park and Birkenhead Park on the banks of the Mersey in Liverpool (1842–7), or the extensive landscaping that surrounded the relocated Crystal Palace at Sydenham, south London, in 1854. On the other hand, the relatively piecemeal nature of these reforms has given British cities a markedly less coherent urban design than is found in the main cities of Europe.

Arrangement in Grey and Black No 1: The Artist's Mother (1872), by James McNeill Whistler   The American painter Whistler (1834–1903), who had been settled in London since 1859, exhibited his iconic portrait of his old mother at the Royal Academy in 1872. He had begun titling his works with pseudo-musical terminology in the 1860s (his portrait of two young women wearing white, 1865–7, is called *Symphony in White No 3*, and an 1872 landscape of the Thames at night is titled *Nocturne in Blue and Silver: Cremorne Lights*). His 'arrangement' portrait of his mother, on the other hand, is a much less fluid composition: the model sits stiffly in a chair in profile, her hands in her lap and her feet on a stool. Her formal black dress makes a bulky, toppling skittle-shape in the left-lower centre of a composition otherwise wholly dominated by verticals and horizontals – the vertical rectangle of dark curtains to the left, the horizontal rectangle of a picture hanging on the wall behind the subject upper-centre, two vertical lines of part of another picture and the chair legs on the right, two horizontal lines of skirting board and footstool in the lower portion. Yet despite the mannered artificiality of the pose, the picture expresses a sense of vivid personality in the frozen profile of the old woman; it manages to achieve both formal precision and human warmth.

Arthurian literature   A rich cycle of stories is associated with the legendary (possibly historical) King Arthur: his elevation to the throne by drawing the sword from the stone, his unification of the kingdom, the various adventures of his chivalrous knights 'of the Round Table', his unhappy marriage to Guinevere and his eventual death fighting his son Modred constitute the 'matter of Britain'. It is this body of myth and story most particularly linked to the national and geographical construction of 'Britishness'.

Arthurian literature had enjoyed enormous popularity in the mid- and late Middle Ages, culminating in Malory's prose collection of Arthurian tales, *Le Morte D'Arthur* (1485). Through the Renaissance the tales dropped in popularity, but the early nineteenth century witnessed a renaissance in interest in Arthurian myth. In August 1839 the Earl of Eglintoun held a quasi-Arthurian chivalric tournament on his Ayrshire estate, in which men dressed in armour and women in medieval dress, and jousting and other suitable events were undertaken. However, it rained continuously, and the contemporary press made great comic capital out of the image of men in fifteenth-century dress holding nineteenth-century umbrellas over their heads.

Edward Bulwer-Lytton (1803–73) published a 12-book epic poem *King Arthur* (1848–9); it is mostly stodge but it does attempt an interesting synthesis of myth, history and allegory. Matthew Arnold wrote a small-scale *Tristram and Iseult* (1852), dramatising the mournful love triangle of the Arthurian knight; Algernon Swinburne also wrote on Tristram, although his *Tristram of Lyonesse* (1882) is epic in ambition, and erotically passionate in execution. Swinburne also wrote a lengthy balladic Arthurian *Tale of Balen* (1896). But the century's most significant Arthurian poet was Tennyson, who published a wealth of shorter works on an Arthurian theme (such as the beautiful 'The Lady of Shalott' (1832), the stately 'Morte D'Arthur' (1833) and the autobiographical, valedictory 'Merlin and the Gleam' (1889)). But his major intervention in this genre was his own epic *Idylls of the King*, written in erratic instalments from 1833 through to the century's end. The bulk of this 12-book epic appeared in parcels of specific 'idylls', *Idylls of the King* (1859) containing four of them, *The Holy Grail and Other Poems* (1869) and *Gareth and Lynette and Other Poems* (1872) containing more. The publication of *Balin and Balan* (1885) completed the process of putting all the poems into print, although the sequence as we now have it was not published until 1891.

Further reading

Camelot Regained: the Arthurian Revival and Tennyson 1800–1849 (1990) by Roger Simpson.

Aurora Leigh (1856)   Elizabeth Barrett Browning's 11,000-line, blank verse epic was designed as 'a true poetical novel – modern, and on the level of the manners of the day'. The story centres on Aurora Leigh herself, born in Italy to a Tuscan mother and English father. Orphaned at 13 she moves from Italy to England to stay with her aunt, where she meets her cousin Romney Leigh, an idealistic young would-be social reformer. She spends most of her time in books: 'I read much . . . The world of books is still the world . . . And both worlds have God's providence, thank God.' Romney proposes marriage, but Aurora cannot accept: 'What you love/Is not a woman, Romney, but a cause:/You want a helpmeet, not a mistress, sir,/A wife to help your ends'. Romney then proposes to the socially inferior Marian Erle, a London seamstress, by way of building a bridge between the classes, although on the wedding day Marian fails to turn up at the church and Romney goes in search of her. Returning to Italy Aurora encounters Marian in Paris, and goes with her to her home ('a room/Scarce larger than a grave, and near as bare') where Marian tells her story. Lured onto a ship with the promise of a better life in Australia, Marian was kidnapped, taken off the ship at the first French port of call, drugged and raped. Turned loose, she had to fend for herself; she worked as a maid to a Parisian woman, but lost this job when her pregnancy became obvious. She contemplated suicide, but thought instead of 'the sinless babe that should be' and found work. Aurora takes Marian with her on to Italy, where Romney comes to visits them. He reports that Leigh Hall, in which he had established a Utopian socialist community, has been burnt to the ground by one of the inmates. Romney declares that he has come to marry Marian, but Marian demurs ('I do not love you, Romney Leigh.') We then discover that Romney is blind, having lost his sight in the fire at Romney Hall, and Aurora is moved to confess 'weeping bitterly . . . I love – /I love you, Romney.'

B

Ballad   Ballads are narrative poems deriving from an oral folk or popular tradition, usually expressed in short rhyming stanzas (often abcb) with refrains and other devices to make memorisation easier. The ballad form was transferred into the printed, literary mainstream through the success of a number of collections of original pieces. Thomas Percy (1729–1811) claimed to have 'collected' a large number of original English ballads in *Percy's Reliques of Ancient English Poetry* (three vols, 1765), although many of these were 'augmented' and 'improved' by Percy himself, or else derived from literary rather than oral tradition. The success of Percy inspired other collections, most notably Walter SCOTT's *Minstrelsy of the Scottish Borders* (three vols, 1802–3), which assembled Scots ballads under three headings: 'Historical Ballads', 'Romantic Ballads' and 'Imitations of the Ancient Ballad'. Scott's own subsequent poetic career drew on the poetics implied by this sort of collection. More significantly, one of the main strands of Romanticism saw a self-conscious move towards the ballad form – as, for instance, in Wordsworth and Coleridge's collection *Lyrical Ballads* (1798). Valorisation of the ballad form expressed a belief that such poetry, deriving from the historically rooted oral traditions of ordinary people, was more 'authentic' than literary compositions. Allied to that was a belief that ballads were amongst the most primitive, and therefore originary, forms of human literature. MACAULAY, for example, believed that the histories of Ancient Rome were based on now-lost oral poetry; he wrote a series of ballads that aimed to reproduce in English what these lost Roman ur-ballads might have been like, and *The Lays of Ancient Rome* (1842) were very successful because of (rather than despite) their simplicity, their rocking-horse rhythms and highly coloured simplified narratives. F.W. Newman translated Homer into ballad form, the metre (that of TENNYSON's 'Lady of Shallot') and the vocabulary deliberately archaic after the manner of Percy's *Reliques*, in the belief that Homer would have appeared this way to Ancient Greek audiences: Matthew ARNOLD's witty and devastating riposte to this belief, in his essays 'On Translating Homer', marks an important fault-line in Victorian poetics, between deliberately archaic simplicity on the one hand, and 'classical' poise and sophistication on the other (*see* TRANSLATION).

Victorian scholarly work on ballads culminated in Francis James Child (1825–96), an American scholar based at Harvard, whose enormous collection *English and Scottish Popular Ballads* (five vols, 1882–98) remains the standard collection. Victorian poets continued imitating and utilising the ballad form, such that almost no examples can be found of a poet who did not write at least a few poems in this form. SWINBURNE is one of the most skilled balladeers of the period; his three series of *Poems and Ballads* (1866, 1878, 1889) contain many original poems that precisely and evocatively capture the swing and urgency of original ballads.

The form was so ubiquitous as to occasion widespread PARODY; the point of which was almost always to derive humour from the gap between contemporary life and the implied archaism of the ballad form, as in this example from Robert Fuller Murray:

> The lady stood at the station bar,
> (Three currants in a bun)
> And oh she was proud, as ladies are
> (And the bun was baked a week ago.)

(Murray, 'A Ballad of Refreshment', *The Scarlet Gown*, 1891)

At the same time ballads continued to do what they had always done: to function as the literature of ordinary people. When Samuel Maunder (1785–1849) defines the form as 'a tale in verse of a simple and popular character . . . generally in most esteem by the lower classes' (Maunder, *Scientific and Literary Treasury*, 1848: 67) he pinpoints an important social bias. In the words of Victor Neuburg, 'ballad literature maintained a vigorous life in nineteenth-century streets' printed 'in broadside form, on one side of a sheet of flimsy paper' (Neuburg, 1977: 123). An enormous number of these productions were hawked on the streets by street-sellers ('three yards a penny!' was one cry). It was this subculture that a writer like Rudyard Kipling (1865–1936) could utilise to powerful serious effect. The poems in his *Barrack-Room Ballads and Other Verses* (1892) are written in the idiom of cockney working-class soldiers, and elide the skill and subtlety with which they are constructed under the gloss of their 'primitive' form, allowing them to work more powerfully at evoking 'plain feeling'.

Moreover, as *The Princeton Encyclopedia of Poetry and Poetics* points out, ballad metre (sometimes called 'common metre') is 'more or less the same as English hymnal metre' except that 'the beat is slightly more regular' (Preminger *et al.*, 1974: 64). Critical work on the rich corpus of English HYMN texts is only just beginning, but the inter-relations between the way these work inhabit popular ballad forms on the one hand, and the complex dialectic between Church, spiritualism and populism on the other, is one of the most interesting aspects of ballad writing in the nineteenth century.

Bank holidays   Holidays in Great Britain had traditionally been taken on Good Friday, Christmas Day (although not as regularly in Scotland, where New Year was the more widely observed celebration) and the first day in May. The Bank Holidays Act of 1871, and the Holidays Extension Act of 1875, added a number of statutory holidays to the British working year, including: Boxing Day (in Scotland, New Year's Day); Easter Monday; Whit Monday and the first Monday in August.

Bible   Although the religious complexion of the Victorian society was various, splintered across Anglican, evangelical and Nonconformist fault-lines (*see* religion), one uniting factor was the ubiquitous centrality of the Bible. No reading of Victorian literature whatsoever can afford to be ignorant of the King James translation of the Bible (the so-called 'Authorized Version' of 1604–11). Quotations, references and allusions to stories and situations from this text were instantly familiar across the range of Victorian society. The dissemination of the Bible to all classes of society was achieved through cheap or free printings of the text, often handed out by such figures as the urban missionaries of Ellen Raynard's Bible Society, founded in 1857.

Biblical scholarship, drawing on work done in Germany, was one of the most significant academic cultures of Victorian Britain. William Smith's *Dictionary of the Bible* (three vols, 1863) drew on the expertise of 68 of the most eminent divines and scholars of the day. Dissatisfaction with the accuracy of the King James translation represented a continuing debate throughout the period; 1841 saw the publication of a *Holy Bible: with 20,000 Emendations*, and motions were put before Parliament on several occasions to secure a new translation. Eventually it was spiritual rather than secular impetus that revised the Bible. The Anglican Convocation of Canterbury agreed to instigate re-translation in 1870, and the Revised Text appeared in 1881 (the New Testament) and 1885 (the Old). Important scholarly studies of the original text appeared in the same period: Westcott and Hort's New Testament in 1881, and H.B. Sweete's edition of the Septuagint in 1887.

The Higher Criticism challenged the legitimacy of the Bible on several fronts, but this scepticism did not percolate very far into the Victorian mainstream. Bishop Colenso of Natal translated the Bible into Zulu for his parishioners, but in doing so found himself unable to accept the literalism of the holy book; he published a lengthy and bizarre critique of the Bible in 1862–3, attacking Biblical chronology with elaborate mathematics, and this led to his being deposed from his bishopric. Biblical scholars in Britain were mostly embarrassed by Colenso's amateur methods, and more sophisticated Bible criticism became more common as the century wore on – for instance, in the discussion that stemmed from the *Essays and Reviews* brouhaha. But most Victorian Christians would have echoed Martin Tupper's (1810–89) clunkily expressed faith in the book:

> Yea, spite of all the learned zeal to prove the Bible false,
> Their reckonings and disputings, and their eager hunt for errors, –
> In spite of all their casuistry, discoveries, statistics,
> And every sceptic effort of apostates, clerk and lay,
> The Bible is but stablished by its gainsayers and assailants
> And all its difficulties die, though galvanised to life.
>
> (Martin Tupper, 'Of the Bible', 1869)

Birth   Birth was a precarious business for Victorians, with infant mortality at a monstrously high rate throughout the period. Calculated as the number of children who died before the age of one year per thousand live births, this rate averaged 149 across England through 1838–54, although some areas were much worse than others. In Liverpool in 1841 the infant mortality rate was 256 per thousand, and only half of children born reached the age of ten. In Glasgow in 1871 the infant mortality rate was 170 per thousand, and 40 per cent of children died before the age of ten (Woods, 1996: 329–30). Every year, throughout the Victorian period, perhaps as many as 100,000 children died before their first birthday. Working-class and poorer areas suffered dreadful levels of infant mortality, but the affluent classes were by no means safe from it: for example, DICKENS' third daughter, Dora, was born in 1850 and died a few months later. 'R.C. Ansell's analysis of infant mortality rates for the professional and upper classes in 1874 showed that 8 per cent died during their first year, which compared with 14 per cent for the population of England as a whole between 1840 and 1900' and higher rates in poorer districts (Jalland, 1996: 121) (it is now no higher than 0.09 per cent for any portion of society). This rate of infant mortality stayed stubbornly high until the very end of the century; only after 1899/1900 did it start to come down. In other words, if you were born into an average English family in mid-century you had a 70 per cent chance of reaching your tenth birthday; if you happened to be born into a poor family in Liverpool your odds were cut to 50:50.

Partly this massacre of innocents can be explained by poor understanding of hygiene and obstetric medicine. But even after medical science had made important advances in this regard, the infant death rate remained high. There were probably several reasons for this. Most births were attended only by midwives, almost all of whom were women without any medical training at all. Dickens' Sairy Gamp, from *Martin Chuzzlewit* (1843–4), is a satire on midwifery that contains a grain of truth: garrulous, drunk and incompetent, Mrs Gamp is hilarious until one remembers that she has undoubtedly been responsible for dozens of births fatal (via infection and exsanguinations) to mother and child alike. Ideologies of motherhood also played a significant role in infant death: well-to-do mothers often preferred not to breast-feed, passing their babies to wet nurses. Nutrition was very poorly understood, and children doubtless died through inadvertent malnutrition, being given gruel or whey when their metabolisms still required a high-calorie high-fat diet.

Boer War (1899–1902)   Sometimes called 'the Anglo-Boer War', or 'the South African War', this conflict was fought between the British and the Boers, white settlers in South Africa of Dutch provenance. In fact, there were a number of wars fought between these two peoples in the nineteenth century, notably in 1846–7 ('the War of the Axe'), 1880–1 (sometimes called 'the Transvaal War' or 'the First Anglo-Boer War') and 1899–1902. The phrase 'the Boer War' usually refers to this last conflict.

The British had annexed the Dutch settlements at Cape Colony in 1815, but continuing friction between British rulers and predominantly Dutch settlers led to a substantial population of Boer 'voortrekkers' (or 'front-runners') leaving the colony and founding two new republics further inland in 1835 and 1843. These republics were eventually granted limited autonomy as Transvaal (1852) and Orange Free State (1854). For a while these nations co-existed with the British Imperial presence, but the discovery of diamonds in the Transvaal in 1867 and gold in Orange Free State in 1886 upset the political status quo. Britain annexed the Transvaal in 1877, and the Boer President Stephanus Johannes Paulus Kruger (1825–1904) led a military revolt against this rule in 1880. After the British were badly defeated at Majuba Hill in February 1881, GLADSTONE restored Transvaal's independence at the Conference of Pretoria that same year.

Tensions continued throughout the 1880s and 1890s, with the British government believing that the whole of South Africa needed to be taken into the Empire if British interests were to be protected. Actual conflict followed when Kruger pre-emptively declared war in October 1899, following British military aggression (particularly the Jameson Raid in 1896, in which a group of British opportunists associated with Cecil Rhodes (1853–1902) attacked the Transvaal), and months of negotiation. At this point Boer soldiers outnumbered British four to one, but Britain eventually shipped in more troops than had been sent overseas at any time since the Napoleonic Wars.

> What the British government expected in 1899 was a short campaign which might involve 75,000 troops, result in – at worst – a few hundred casualties, cost about £10m, and be successfully completed within three to four months. In the event, the war lasted for two years and eight months, cost £230m, involved a total of 450,000 British and Empire troops, and resulted in the deaths of some 22,000 soldiers on the British side, about 34,000 Boer civilians and combatants, and an unknown number of the African population which has been estimated at not less than 14,000.
>
> (Saunders and Smith, 1999: 617)

In the early stages of the war the Boers enjoyed the upper hand. Fighting rapid engagements and guerrilla battles, they were used to life in the saddle, were expert with the latest Martini-Henry and Mauser rifles, and inflicted a series of defeats on the British: during 'black week' in December 1899 the British lost successively the Battles of

Magersfontein, Stormberg and Colenso. A new British commander, Lord 'Bob' Roberts (1832–1914), brought better tactics to play, using his superior numbers to steam-roller through the country. He relieved the sieges of Ladysmith, Kimberley and Mafeking in early 1900, defeated the Boers at Paardeberg and went on to annex both the Orange Free State and the Transvaal by September 1900. Subduing the country, however, was a much more onerous business. The British decided on a scorched-earth policy, destroying Boer farms and cattle, and confining the civilian population in concentration camps. These camps were intended as purely incarcatory, but unsanitary conditions and overcrowding resulted in several tens of thousands of deaths, mostly of women and children, a fact that clouded Anglo-Afrikaans relations throughout the twentieth century. Pinning down the mobile Boers eventually required an enormous, and enormously expensive, network of guard towers and fences covering the whole country (some 8,000 blockhouses were eventually built, with 3700 miles of wire fencing, guarded by 50,000 troops). Peace was negotiated in April 1902, with the Boer states reverting to Crown control, but the British government agreed to their eventual self-government.

At the beginning of the war, the climate in England – fuelled in part by the patriotism of Victoria's Diamond Jubilee in 1897 – inspired a number of jingoistic literary responses to impending conflict. Algernon Swinburne published a sonnet in *The Times* called 'The Transvaal' (11 October 1899) in which he urged the chastisement of the Boer in rabid terms: 'scourge these dogs, agape with jaws afoam,/Down out of life. Strike, England, and strike home.' Alfred Austin (1835–1913), the Tory poetaster who had been made Laureate by the Tory administration, published 'To Arms!' (23 December 1899), also in *The Times*: 'comrades in arms ... force the foe from covert crag,/And chase them till they fall,/Then plant for ever England's Flag/Upon the rebel wall!' As the war stretched into the new century, military frustration and high casualties took the shine off this level of enthusiasm. Kipling's 'The Lesson: 1899–1902 Boer War' (published in *The Times*, July 1901) declared sourly that 'conclusively, comprehensively and several times and again,/Were all our most holy illusions knocked higher than Gilderoy's kite'. His version of the battle between the mounted Boer farmers and British foot-soldiers was: 'we have spent two hundred million pounds to prove the fact once more,/That horses are quicker than men afoot, since two and two make four'. The war produced no great art, although the understated melancholy of Thomas Hardy's 'Drummer Hodge' (December 1899) perhaps approaches greatness, mixing English and Afrikaner terms to evoke a mood both particular and timeless:

> They throw in Drummer Hodge, to rest
> Uncoffined – just as found:
> His landmark is a kopje-crest
> That breaks the veldt around;
> And foreign constellations west
> Each night above his mound.

Further reading

'Southern Africa 1867–1886' and 'Southern and Central Africa 1886–1910' by Shula Marks in *The Cambridge History of Africa: Volume VI, From 1870–1905* (1985), edited by Roland Oliver and G.N. Sanderson; 'Southern Africa 1795–1910' by Christopher Saunders and Iain R. Smith in *The Oxford History of the British Empire: Volume III, The Nineteenth-Century* (1999) edited by Andrew Porter.

Book illustration   New inventions in the field of the technologies of book illustration, and an overall reduction of cost, meant that the nineteenth-century became the first great age of the illustrated mass book. Where illustration (hand-painted, or wood-blocked) had previously been a relatively expensive process, three technical innovations made wood- or metal-engraved illustration much commoner. These were, first, the replacement of the old hand-press with faster power presses, such that by 1850 'the laborious hand-press was almost a thing of the past' (Goldman, 1994: 40); second, the invention of electrotyping in 1839 led to the ability to transfer images to press-plates much more efficiently; and, third, the development of PHOTOGRAPHY had several consequences for book illustration, with photographs acting as artists' models in the process of making engraving plates and, later in the century, photographs being used as illustrations in their own right.

DICKENS' relationship with his illustrator 'Phiz' (Hablot Knight Browne) is perhaps the paradigmatic example of the power of 'text plus illustration' in the Victorian period. It is difficult to disengage Dickens' written words from Phiz's distinctive and charming illustrations. Browne would draw the illustrations, and would hand the sketches to Robert Young, who would engrave them onto steel plate and print them, delivering them to the printers so that they could be bound in with the text for the monthly parts. Engraved steel plates are good for about 15,000 impressions; when the print run was higher than this figure, Young had to engrave two, and sometimes three or four, versions of the same image. By mid-century, lithography, a process of chemically fixing images onto metal such that greasy ink adheres to the outlines of the image, became popular; the process was invented by the German Alois Senefelder (1771–1834) in 1796, but did not become general until the 1840s and 1850s. Lithographic plates can produce many more copies than steel plates before quality deteriorates, although the images are not as sharply defined.

The illustrations that John Tenniel (1820–1914) produced for Lewis CARROLL's ALICE books are almost as intimately wedded to the text they embroider as Phiz's for Dickens (although Carroll has had and continues to attract a wealth of other illustrators). Tenniel was in demand: he provided copy for the illustrated magazine PUNCH on a weekly basis, and had recently produced 60 images for R.H. Barham's *Ingoldsby Legends* (1864), and others for Dalziel's *Arabian Nights* (1865). His work on Carroll's two books remains his most famous. Tenniel was only one of a crowd of gifted professional illustrators, including Richard Doyle (1824–83), John Leech (1817–64), Charles Keene (1823–91) and George du Maurier (1834–96). PRE-RAPHAELITE artists such as DANTE GABRIEL ROSSETTI, John MILLAIS and Arthur Hughes (1832–1915) also produced illustrations for their own and others' published texts. The whole century was a rich period for illustration, but the decades of the 1860s and 1870s marks an especially high point.

RUSKIN saw a higher aspect in these engraved illustrations. He called his lectures on the art of engraving *Ariadne Florentina* (1872) because, like the figure of Ariadne from Greek myth, engravers re-enact the primordial pattern-making impulse of scratching a surface to make it a sign. Ruskin reads engravings as miniature mazes, their multiple inter-crossing lines mapping out labyrinthine spaces. He goes on to claim that 'to engrave is, in final strictness, "to decorate a surface with furrows" . . . a ploughed field is the purest type of such art: and is, on hilly land, an exquisite piece of decoration' (Ruskin, *Ariadne*: 322). This earthy, almost primal connection perhaps explains the unflagging delight that can be derived from the variety and number of intricate beautiful book illustrations.

Further reading

Victorian Illustrated Books 1850–1870; the Heyday of Wood-Engraving (1994) by Paul Goldman.

Boxer Rebellion   The 'Boxers', or 'Yihetuan', were a Chinese group more properly known as 'The Society of Righteous and Harmonious Fists', who practised a form of martial art that they believed, erroneously, rendered them impermeable to gunfire. They began attacking foreigners in China in 1898, but the so-called 'Boxer Rebellion' dates from June 1900, when the Imperial government set Boxers upon foreign traders and missionaries in Peking and Tientsin, killing several hundred and massacring many more Chinese Christian converts. By August an international military expedition had arrived to relieve the foreign enclaves in the two cities, and brutal reprisals were experienced across the north of China. Peking was widely looted and the Imperial Palace destroyed. Reparations of more than $300 million were later extracted from China for the episode.

Brontë, Anne (1820–49), novelist   Anne Brontë's reputation has never properly emerged from shadow of her more notable sisters, CHARLOTTE and EMILY BRONTË. As a child, together with Emily, Anne created the imaginary world of Gondal, and wrote poetry and prose stories set in this place. She worked as a governess at Blake Hall, in Yorkshire, in 1839, and spent 1841 to 1845 as a governess for the Robinson family at Thorp Green Hall in the same county. Her experience with the spoiled Robinson children informed her first, semi-autobiographical, novel *Agnes Grey* (1847), in which Agnes endures various vicissitudes as a governess and eventually marries a pleasant young man. The book, although not charmless, seems insipid and passive besides Charlotte and Emily's fiction. Anne's second and last novel, *The Tenant of Wildfell Hall* (published, as was *Agnes Grey*, under the male pseudonym 'Acton Bell' in 1848) is an epistolary novel. The chief correspondent, Gilbert Markham, relates the story of the tenant of the title, a widow called Mrs Graham, who lives with her young son Arthur. It transpires that this woman's real name is Helen Huntingdon, and that she is not widowed but still married to the violent and alcoholic Arthur Huntingdon (a figure based, in part, on Anne's own drunk brother Branwell Brontë). Helen had been cajoled into marriage with the impossible Arthur, and fled the marriage after much abuse. Arthur of course discovers his wife's whereabouts, but falls from his horse and is nursed by his again-dutiful wife until his death. She goes on to marry Gilbert Markham. By 1845 Anne had left the employment of the Robinsons and was again living with her two sisters and her father at Haworth, a small town in West Yorkshire. After the relative success of *The Tenant of Wildfell Hall* Anne travelled to London in company with Charlotte and met members of the literary world, but she was already suffering from tuberculosis. She succumbed rapidly to the disease and died in 1849, without having had so much as a suitor.

Brontë, Charlotte (1816–1855), novelist The oldest of the Brontë sisters, Charlotte was also the most controlled and significant literary talent. One of a family of five daughters and one son, Charlotte was four when her father Patrick Brontë took up his position as perpetual curate at Haworth, West Yorkshire. Her family life was not affluent, but the companionship of her sisters provided a rich literary and cultural environment. The daughters of the family were all sent to the stark Clergy Daughters' School at Cowan Bridge (fictionalised as the appalling Lowood in *Jane Eyre*); Charlotte endured this school's puritanical regime, but blamed its harshness for the death of her two elder sisters in 1825. The remaining children continued their education at home. Charlotte collaborated with her tempestuous brother Branwell in the creation of an imaginary kingdom, called Angria, and the composition of stories set in this realm; Anne and Emily invented a rival world called Gondal. During 1831–2 Charlotte picked up a little further education at a school in Roe Head, to which she returned in 1835–8 as teacher. She worked as a governess 1841–2, and afterwards travelled to Brussels to study languages with Emily. Emily returned to England at the end of 1842, but Charlotte returned for a further year. Despite her dislike of the country, and her anti-Catholic prejudices, she was drawn to Brussels by her unrequited love for the prim Belgian M. Heger. Back in England, still hurting from the non-affair, she gathered together poems by all three sisters and published them as *Poems by Currer, Ellis and Acton Bell* (1846), the pseudonyms that the three sisters were later to use in the publication of their novels. The volume was not a great success.

Her first novel *The Professor*, based obliquely on her experiences in Belgium, did not attract a publisher. But Emily's *Wuthering Heights* and Anne's *Agnes Grey* were accepted by the minor London publisher Thomas Newby in 1847 (and published the following year). Spurred on, Charlotte completed Jane Eyre. It was issued by Smith, Elder in 1847, and was a great success, helped in part by speculation as to the real identities of the author. Milking this publicity, Newby encouraged Charlotte and Anne to visit London in 1848, and circulate in the literary world.

The year from late 1848 to mid-1849 was an especially traumatic period for Charlotte Brontë. Her brother Branwell died of alcohol abuse and her sister Emily of tuberculosis in September and December 1848 respectively, and Anne succumbed to tuberculosis in the summer of 1849. Charlotte was finishing *Shirley* during this period, a polished novel set in the Yorkshire of the Napoleonic Wars. By 1849, when this novel was published, the 33-year-old Charlotte was the only Brontë child left alive. She befriended Elizabeth Gaskell the following year (Gaskell went on to write her biography in 1857), and worked on her most autobiographical work *Villette*. This novel was published in 1853, and in 1854 Charlotte married the Rev. Arthur Bell Nicholls, who had been her father's curate since 1845. The marriage was placid and loving, if not passionate, and Charlotte died a few months later, in 1855, probably of complications arising from pregnancy. Her earlier novel *The Professor* was published posthumously in 1857.

Brontë, Emily (1818–1848), novelist and poet   For some readers, Emily is the most interesting, because the most spontaneously passionate, of the Brontë sisters. She spent a higher proportion of her life at home in Haworth parsonage in Yorkshire than did her sisters, staying with her father Patrick Brontë, a perpetual curate. Apart from brief periods at school, a time as a governess in 1837 and a truncated trip abroad to study languages with Charlotte in 1842 she did not leave Haworth, and a sense of rootedness in the landscapes of the Yorkshire moors permeates all her writing. She wrote some juvenilia with her sister Anne (set in the imaginary world of Gondal), but otherwise her enormous contemporary reputation depends upon one novel – WUTHERING HEIGHTS (1847) – and a number of shorter poems. Contemporary readers did not know what to make of the dark passion, the violence and the deliberate vigorous crudity of this novel, dismissing it as merely morbid. After her death, Charlotte published a 'Biographical Notice' (1850) to explain away the 'horror of great darkness' that seems to find manifestation in the work. Her poetry, exclusively short lyric pieces, is also very highly regarded, in part because it gives voice to a similar turbulently dark mood:

> The night is darkening round me
> The wild winds coldly blow
> But a tyrant spell has bound me
> And I cannot cannot go
> The giant trees are bending
> Their bare boughs weighed with snow
> And the storm is fast descending
> And yet I cannot go

> Clouds beyond clouds above me
> Wastes beyond wastes below
> But nothing drear can move me
> I will not cannot go

> (Written ?1837, first published 1902)

A poem such as this expressively catches the way strength of purpose, or will, can be as imprisoning as it is liberating; but more striking, perhaps, is the minimalist starkness of the landscape evoked, the Emily Dickinson-like desolation of the cosmos emptied out of extraneous paraphernalia (even to the level of punctuation) to leave only the starkness of petrified essence.

Emily died of 'consumption', which is to say tuberculosis, in 1848 after a short illness during which she is supposed to have refused treatment – a fact that sets a marvellous cope-stone on her life for one sort of Emily Brontë fan. Many such readers and critics apprehend Emily as a visionary, and see her works as a locus for a semi-mystical dynamic of power, for passion and a Lawrentian 'erotics of darkness'. That many critics have little sympathy for this sort of approach does not negate the very broad popularity it still enjoys. More fertile, though, are readings that see Emily Brontë negotiating subjectivity and female identity through masculine Victorian discourses. In particular the 'strength' of Emily Brontë's writing, seen both in terms of its fascination with strength of body and will aligned to the 'strength' of the land, and also in the fact that it is 'strong' literature – powerful, effective and lasting – this 'strength' exists uneasily in certain gender networks, in a society where 'strength' was seen as a specifically masculine quality. Her French teacher in Brussels, M. Héger, said that 'she should have been a man – a great navigator' (Cosslett, 1996: 28) and a number of interesting critical works have explored the problematic of gender as expressed through her writing.

Further reading

Emily Brontë (1971) by Winifred Gérin.

Browning, Elizabeth Barrett (1806–1861), poet   Properly, Elizabeth Barrett Barrett until her marriage to Robert Browning in 1846, and Elizabeth Barrett Browning afterwards (a state of affairs that, conveniently, means that the initials 'E.B.B.' apply throughout her life). The first four decades of her life were largely determined by her patriarchal, over-protective father, Edward Moulton Barrett, whose wealth came from investments in Jamaican plantations. Elizabeth, the eldest child, spent her often sickly childhood reading, becoming highly educated in classic and modern literatures and writing poetry of her own. She wrote two mini-epics in the manner of Alexander Pope when still a teenager, *The Battle of Marathon* (published 1820) and *An Essay on Mind* (1826). A fall from a horse when she was 15 injured her spine, left her bedridden for a year, and presaged an adulthood dominated by invalidity. In 1832 the family moved to Sidmouth, where she worked on a translation of Aeschylus's *Prometheus Bound* (published in 1833). The abolition of SLAVERY in British dominions in 1834 brought financial disaster to Edward Barrett, whose estates had depended on slave labour; in 1835 the family moved from their spacious estate to a house on Wimpole Street in London. Here her health deteriorated. After a blood vessel burst in her chest (this, at any rate, was the diagnosis by the imprecise physicians of her day) she travelled to Torquay to convalesce. Here tragedy struck: Edward, the eldest of her brothers, drowned in the sea, to her lasting grief. Her health continued to decline, probably due to a combination of physical ailments, her addiction to laudanum (heroin) and what today would be called anorexia. In 1841 she returned to Wimpole Street, barely venturing out of her bedroom, her state of health delicate in the extreme. At the same time, her reputation as one of the finest poets in the country had been forged with the publication of *The Seraphim and Other Poems* (1838), and a collected *Poems* (1844) dedicated to her father.

In 1845 she began corresponding with Robert Browning, a younger poet whose own reputation was still, at this stage, small. Browning seems to have decided to fall in love with her before even meeting her. During 1845–6 they met most days, and also wrote to one another daily, and often several times a day. The snag was Elizabeth's father. Perhaps slightly unhinged by the deaths of his wife in 1828 and of his son in 1840, he had become a domestic tyrant, refusing to allow any of his offspring to marry. To overcome this difficulty Elizabeth and Robert married in secret in 1846, and afterwards ran off together to the continent. Her health was apparently not so delicate after all, and she travelled by coach over the Alps to Italy, where they set up house together in Florence. After several miscarriages she gave birth to her only child, Robert Wiedemann Barrett Browning, in 1849.

By now her reputation was so high (much higher than her husband's) that her name was openly mentioned as a possible successor to the post of poet LAUREATE on the death of William Wordsworth in 1850, although in the event TENNYSON was appointed. A second collected *Poems* (1850) included her rather gnashing but nonetheless powerful anti-slavery poem 'The Runaway Slave at Pilgrim's Point'. Her love poems to Robert, *Sonnets from the Portuguese*, also appeared in print in 1850; the title was a deliberate mis-direction, to make readers think that the works were translations rather than the painfully intimate pieces they actually were. This collection contains, perhaps, Barrett Browning's most famous single poem, sonnet 43 'How do I love thee? Let me count the ways'. *Casa Guidi Windows*, a political poem, written for the cause of Italian liberation, appeared in 1851; Casa Guidi was the house the Browning's inhabited in Florence, and the poem urges Italy to resist Metternich's military occupation, 'Will, therefore, to be strong, thou Italy!/Will to be noble! Austrian Metternich/Can fix no yoke unless the neck agree'. Her major work was the verse-novel AURORA LEIGH (1857), a bold experiment in 'realist' topic (class injustice, rape, female emancipation) allied to a formally ambitious blank verse. It was very popular. Less so was the sometimes stridently political poetry of *Poems Before Congress* (1860). After her death in 1861, a posthumous publication, *Last Poems* (1862), met with great acclaim.

In her own day Barrett Browning fitted a certain pre-existing Victorian aesthetic category, 'the poetess', a writer of sentimental, affective, sometimes gushing poetry. She resisted such categorisation vigorously by adopting political themes, by working with strenuous intellectual engagement with large questions, and by experimenting (like her husband, but to a lesser degree) with poetic form and tone. These aspects of her work were regarded with suspicion, or even hostility, by critics in her own day, although they are now what most critics find appealing. Above all, it was her resolution (despite her deep classical learning) to write poetry that was *contemporary*, that marked out her work as distinctive: *Aurora Leigh* in particular, is full of up-to-date observation and characterisation, and works through its theme thoroughly, that

> Nay, if there's room for poets in this world
> A little overgrown (I think there is)
> Their sole work is to represent the age,
> Their age, not Charlemagne's.

> (*Aurora Leigh*, Book 5, ll. 200–3)

Browning, Robert (1812–1889), poet   According to a still-influential tradition of Victorian criticism, Browning contends with TENNYSON for the title 'greatest Victorian poet'. Isobel Armstrong, for instance, divides the verse of the period between that written by 'the mythic poetics of the Tennyson group' and 'the dramatic poetics of the Browning group' (Armstrong, 1993: 37). Browning's life falls into three main periods: the years of his youth, before his courtship of and marriage to ELIZABETH BARRETT BROWNING in 1845–6; the years of the marriage, 1846–61; and late Browning 1861–89. Most critics treat the first two of these, but the latter was actually the most prolific in terms of poetic output.

Raised in south London, Browning's family were financially comfortable and he was never troubled with having to earn his own living. His first published poem, *Pauline* (1833), dramatises his own youthful struggles with religious faith and doubt, and his hero-worshipping of Shelley. It was little noticed, although his next work, a lengthy poetic-drama based on the life of the Renaissance alchemist, *Paracelsus* (1835), brought him some public attention. After meeting the actor-manager William Macready (1793–1873) Browning was persuaded that he ought to write for the stage; but of the seven theatrical tragedies he wrote over the next few years only one was performed and it was not a success. He published a long-gestated epic poem, *Sordello*, in 1840, a version of the life story of a medieval Italian poet; but the poem was greeted with astonishment, incomprehension and even outrage. Jane Carlyle (1801–66), for example, declared she had read through the whole thing and had never worked out whether Sordello was a man, a city or a book (Sordello is, in fact, a man). With *Sordello* Browning established a reputation for obscurity and poetic affectation that dogged his career, although the poem was to some extent rehabilitated in the twentieth century by the enthusiastic endorsement of Ezra Pound (1885–1972). Learning from his setbacks, this period also saw Browning experimenting with the form of the shorter poem, and his is the most significant claim to having invented the DRAMATIC MONOLOGUE, in some senses the most important Victorian poetic form. Two collections of his shorter pieces, *Dramatic Lyrics* (1842) and *Dramatic Romances and Lyrics* (1845), contain some of the most famous poems of the age, amongst them 'My Last Duchess', 'Soliloquy of the Spanish Cloister' and 'The Bishop Orders His Tomb'. These two collections appeared, together with Browning's unperformed plays, in a series of eight pamphlets called *Bells and Pomegranates* (1841–6).

In 1845 the famous romance with the bedridden Elizabeth Barrett began, and for two years the poets met and exchanged letters every day. Barrett's overprotective father would not permit marriage, so the two were wed in secret 12 September 1846 and ran away to the continent, settling in Florence at the house (still preserved as a Brownings museum) Casa Guidi. The marriage produced one child: Robert Wiedemann Barrett Browning, known as 'Pen' (1849–1912). Barrett Browning's reputation far outshone that of her husband, and Browning himself was content largely to support his wife's poetic compositions. He did publish a curious religious piece, *Christmas Eve and Easter Day* (1850), and collected together 50 shorter poems in what is seen today as his most important collection, MEN AND WOMEN (1855). But popular and critical success eluded him, and Browning was more involved in raising his son, and later in nursing his ailing wife. She died in June 1861 and Browning returned to Britain.

A collected *Poetical Works* (three vols, 1863) went some way to establishing Browning's currency as a great poet, and his reputation was further enhanced by the publication of a collection of dramatic monologues, *Dramatis Personae* (1864), including 'Caliban Upon Setebos' and 'Mr Sludge the 'Medium'. But it was the 12-book epic THE RING AND THE BOOK (published in four instalments, 1868–9) that really cemented Browning's reputation with Victorian readers. For the first time in his career, Browning became celebrated. Although he never matched Tennyson's sales Browning was increasingly lionised, and a Browning Society (still extant) was formed in London in 1881 dedicated to the dissemination and explication of his works. In September 1869 Browning proposed marriage to the beautiful and eligible Lady Ashburton, but her rejection stung him deeply and he reacted with hostility. The 1870s, however, was his most productive decade, including a series of long poems. *Balaustion's Adventure* (1871) is a sunny and positive poem set in Ancient Greece and including an adaptation of Euripides' *Alkestis*, in which the hero Herakles brings back a much-loved wife from the dead – a drama that presumably had personal significance for Browning. *Prince Hohenstiel-Schwangau* (1871) is a long blank-verse dramatic monologue spoken by a sort of NAPOLEON III; *Fifine at the Fair* (1872) is longer still, written in iambic hexameter rhymed couplets; in dense and difficult poetry the poem explores the mind-set of an adulterous Don Juan, justifying himself to his virtuous wife. *Red Cotton Night-Cap Country* (1873) retells a grisly true-life story about a Frenchman who is thwarted in love, mutilates and eventually kills himself. *Aristophanes' Apology* (1875) is a sequel to *Balaustion's Adventure*, packed with classical learning and allusion, and contains a direct translation of Euripides' *Herakles*. *The Inn Album* (1875) is a sort of novel-in-blank-verse, and the collection of works in *Pacchiarotto and How He Worked in Distemper* (1876) constitutes an attack on Browning's critics. In 1877 Browning published a translation of Aeschylus's *Agamemnon* that he boasted was 'literal at every cost save actual violence to the language', although reviewers found it stylistically strained and distorted. Browning also published a number of collections of shorter poems: *Dramatic Idylls: First Series* (1879), *Dramatic Idylls: Second Series* (1880), *Jocoseria* (1883) and *Ferishtah's Fancies* (1884). The remarkable and challenging poetry of *Parleyings With Certain People of Importance in their Day* appeared in 1887, and Browning, still hale at 76, supervised his 16-volume *Poetical Works* in 1888–9. His final collection of short lyrics and dramatic monologues, *Asolando*, was published on 12 December 1889. Browning was visiting Italy; he died later in the same day in Venice, his body being returned to England for burial in Westminster Abbey.

In his own day Browning was highly regarded for the content of his writing, and had something of a reputation as a sage (the title of a contemporary study – *Browning as Religious and Philosophical Thinker* – is revealing). His friend Frederick Furnivall (1825–1910) founded the Browning Society on the grounds that 'Browning is the most thought-full poet alive' (quoted in Irvine and Honan, 1974: 500). Nowadays Browning's thought is rarely studied in these terms; its religious and moral certainties seem stolid, 'Victorian' in a bad way, and its famous optimism – epitomised if slightly unfairly by the sentiment 'God's in his heaven/And all's right with the world' (*Pippa Passes*, Part 1, ll. 227–8) – is out of tune with modern-day ironic gloom. But in the areas of poetic form and style, Browning's literary achievements remain vital and exciting, as well as being enormously influential. Formally he is the most influential dramatic monologuist in English, capable of 'creating characters' by giving the reader their speeches as vivid and fully realised poetry, whilst also capable of exploring the ironic subtleties of language and discourse with great deftness. More than this, the boldness of the formal conception of *The Ring and the Book* (12 monologues from 10 different perspectives, telling the same story over and over) epitomises a relativism that appeals greatly to many modern sensibilities.

The Victorian word for his style, 'Browningese', was applied pejoratively in the nineteenth century as indicative of confusion, obscurity, over-compactness and a general lack of euphony. Lines such as 'Irks care the crop-full bird? Frets doubt the maw-crammed beast?' ('Rabbi Ben Ezra', l. 24) perhaps lack charm, but Browning's compression certainly forces out a high quotient of apothemic utterance, where reso-nant or complex situations are given forcefully economical utterance: 'Ah, but a man's reach should exceed his grasp,/Or what's a heaven for?' ('Andrea Del Sarto', 1855, l. 97); 'How sad and bad and mad it was – /But then, how it was sweet!' ('Confessions', 1864); 'Still more labyrinthine buds the rose' (*Sordello*, 1:476). This last sentiment might figure as the motto for the very many critical studies of the complex and shift-ing fictions Browningese creates, and particular of their self-referential and ur-decon-structivist language self-awareness. The brilliancy and precision of Browning's observations of the natural world, and the vigorous inventiveness of his use of lan-guage continue to astonish.

Further reading

The Book, the Ring and the Poet: a Biography of Robert Browning (1974) by William Irvine and Park Honan; Browning's Hatreds (1993) by Daniel Karlin.

Brunel, Isambard Kingdom (1806–1859)   An energetic and brilliant engineer, Brunel worked in the first instance for his father Marc Isambard Brunel (1769–1849), helping build a tunnel under the Thames, which was completed in 1843, and initiat-ing work on the Clifton Suspension Bridge near Bristol. His most famous work was for the Great Western Railway company (*see* TRANSPORTATION: RAILWAYS), particularly his construction of a line from London to Bristol. Beginning in 1833, Brunel supervised the construction of a range of brilliant engineering solutions to the geographical problems of laying a flat line over the hilly, river-laced landscape between the two cities. He also engineered and built a number of enormous ships: the *Great Western* (completed in 1838) was the largest wooden ship in the world; the *Great Britain* (1845) was an iron ship with a screw propeller; and the *Great Eastern* (1858) was a colossal iron ship, which helped lay the first transatlantic cable. Dedicated to his work to the point of obsession, this problem-afflicted last project helped destroy Brunel's health, contributing to an early death.

Cameron, Julia Margaret (1815–1879)   Cameron is probably the most signifi-cant British PHOTOGRAPHER of the nineteenth century; certainly she is the one whose genius is most distinctive. Born in Calcutta in 1815 the daughter of James Pattle (an official in the East India Company), Julia was one of five sisters. She married Charles Hay Cameron, a senior member of the Supreme Council of India, in 1838, and moved in the highest echelons of Anglo-Indian society. The couple had six children. In 1848, her husband retired (he was many years older than his wife), and the family moved to England. There Cameron moved in an artistic set, meeting and befriending TENNYSON, CARLYLE, BROWNING, ROSSETTI and Edward Burne-Jones (1833–98).

In 1860 Cameron and her husband moved to the Isle of Wight, and it was here that she took up photography. Records of her tend to stress her eccentricity. Edith Ellison recalled in 1907 knowing her as a child: 'clad in the never-failing wrapper, stained – as were her hands and eager face – with the chemicals she used in her work, her hair falling any way but the right way ... Garibaldi thought she was a beggar when she kneeled before him, her stained hands upraised, begging to be allowed to take his picture' (quoted in Harker, 1983: 5–6).

Her preference was for intimate portrait; instead of the more usual three-quarter-length portrait she usually took close-up images of her sitter's face. Her skill with contrast and tone means that these faces seem unusually vivid and defined. Her striking portraits of Carlyle and Tennyson are especially good. She herself talked of photography in spiritual, almost religious, terms. In an autobiographical fragment, *Annals of My Glass House* (1874), she recalled taking Carlyle's portrait:

> ... when I have had such great men before my camera my whole soul has endeavoured to do its duty towards them in recording faithfully the greatness of the inner as well as the features of the outer man. The photograph thus taken has been almost the embodiment of a prayer.
>
> (Quoted in Harker, 1983: 59)

Such vocabulary ('soul', 'faithfully', 'prayer'), in attempting to impose a religious value on the 'truthfulness' of photographic mimesis, is part of a broader attempt on Cameron's part at raising the reputation of photography as an art. Most critics argue that in this regard Cameron was not struggling to overcome gender prejudice as such, since there was no standing precedent governing the reception of man or woman in the field, but rather the general suspicion that tends to greet any new form of art. She returned to India, to Ceylon (modern Sri Lanka), with her husband in 1875, and died there in 1879.

Further reading

Julia Margaret Cameron (1983) by Margaret Harker.

Carlyle, Thomas (1795–1881) Carlyle is perhaps the best known 'Victorian sage' – that strange, unofficial grouping of writers and thinkers whose essays, pamphlets and books had such direct impact upon thought and culture in the later nineteenth century. We might bracket him with Matthew Arnold, John Ruskin and John Stuart Mill in this capacity, except that of all of these Carlyle was by far the most idiosyncratic: passionately individual to the point of oddity, deeply and imaginatively romantic.

Carlyle was born into a serious, devout and dutiful Presbyterian family in Dumfriesshire. He was so poor that, winning a scholarship to Edinburgh University in 1809, he had to walk the 80 miles to the city. After working as a teacher, he taught himself German in order first to study, and then to earn money translating Schiller, Goethe and German philosophy. He wrote a life of Schiller for *The London Magazine* (1823–4), and translated Goethe's *Wilhelm Meister's Apprenticeship* (1824) and *Wilhelm Meister's Travels* (1827), as well as compiling a four-volume anthology of German writing, *German Romance* (1827). He, together with Coleridge, was the chief channel by which German Romantic thought and writing found its way into mainstream British culture during the nineteenth century. He married Jane Baillie Welsh in 1826, and the two of them lived for two years in Edinburgh, afterwards moving to a remote farmhouse in Craigenputtock in Scotland from 1828 to 1834. They moved full-time to London, where Carlyle resolved to earn a living writing and lecturing, in 1834.

His first major work, *Sartor Resartus*, appeared in instalments in *Fraser's Magazine* 1833–4, and was greeted by select admiration and more widespread bafflement and condemnation; one old subscriber to the journal wrote to the editor threatening to cancel his subscription if there was 'any more of that damned stuff'. The book is a work of fictionalised autobiography and unconventional philosophy, written in a jarring and peculiar style, and styled as the biography of a fictional German writer of a history of clothes. Its title, Latin for 'the tailor retailored' ('retailored' in the sense of having the rips in his clothes patched over) refers to a spiritual allegory in which clothes are the trappings and institutions of the world covering the naked spirit beneath. The tailor, in other words, is 'man' in his social and political role; and this book 'retailors' him in the sense of radically critiquing contemporary life. A central series of chapters sees Carlyle moving from doubt to indifference to what he calls 'The Everlasting Yea', in which state he, quoting Goethe, realises that 'doubt of any kind cannot be removed except by an action'. Carlyle adjures his readers to '*do the duty which lies nearest thee*', but more important even than duty is work: 'be no longer a Chaos, but a World, or even Worldkin. Produce! Produce! Were it but the pitifullest, infinitesimal fraction of a Product, produce it, in God's name!'. Carlyle's book vigorously advocates the supercession of the old Greek philosophical precept 'know thyself' with the Carlylean, Victorian one: '*know what thou canst work-at*' (Book 2, Chapter 7).

Carlyle's writing style is one of the most distinctive aspects of his genius. A character in George Meredith's (1828–1909) novel *Beauchamp's Career* (1876) describes it as follows:

. . . a style resembling either early architecture or utter dilapidation, so loose and rough it seemed; a wind-in-the-orchard style, that tumbled down here and there an appreciable fruit with uncouth bluster; sentences without commencements running to abrupt endings and smoke, like waves against a sea-wall, learned dictionary words giving hand to street-slang, and accents falling upon them haphazard, like slant rays from driving clouds.

(Quoted in Gross, 1998: 521)

Carlyle's reputation as a historian was established by his enormous *A History of the French Revolution* (1837), which configured the events in France as epic prose-poetry. As an attack on 'sham' society, and an extended demonstration that any culture that comes to be governed by blind custom, hypocrisy, falsehood and indifference will necessarily fail bloodily, this is less as history as we understand the term and more a moral text for the time. Something similar is true of *Past and Present* (1843), which contrasts the organic harmony of life in England in the Middle Ages, in the representative community of the abbey at Bury St Edmunds, with the alienation of life in the Industrial Revolution, where the 'cash-nexus' had become the sole point of connection between human beings.

A famous biographical incident associated with the composition of *The French Revolution* encapsulates the complex of Byronic Romanticism and dutiful Victorian work ethic embodied by Carlyle. He had completed the first volume of this work after much labour, and had lent the manuscript to John Stuart Mill, whose servant inadvertently burnt it. After agonising for a night, Carlyle resolved to write it all out again: "'*shall* be written again," my fixed word and resolution to [my wife]. Which proved to be such a task as I never tried before or since.' But whilst shouldering this duty with Victorian forbearance, and ultimately with success, Carlyle's sense of himself was melodramatically Romantic:

I was very diligent, very desperate . . . always heavy-laden grim of mood; sometimes with a feeling . . . of Satan's stepping the burning marl . . . Generally my feeling was, 'I will finish this Book, throw it at your [the public's] feet; buy a rifle and spade and withdraw to the Transatlantic Wildernesses – far from *human* beggaries and basenesses!'

(Carlyle, *Reminiscences*, 1881: 92–3)

This sort of grouchy misanthropy, present to one degree or another throughout his career, became increasingly pronounced as he grew older. A late conversation with his friend Robert Southey (1774–1843) illustrates Carlyle's sometimes apocalyptic pessimism:

We sat on the sofa together, our talk . . . the usual one, steady approach of democracy, with revolution (probably *explosive*) and a *finis* incomputable to man, – steady decay of all morality, political, social, individual ... [until] noble England would have to collapse in shapeless ruin, whether forever or not none of us could know. Our perfect consent on these matters gave an animation to the Dialogue, which I remember as copious and pleasant. Southey's last word was in answer to some tirade of mine about universal Mammon-worship ... to which he answered, not with levity, yet with a cheerful tone in his seriousness, 'It will not come, it cannot come to good!'

(Carlyle, *Reminiscences*, 1891: 398)

The gloomy joy at this imagined prospect is immensely expressive of Carlyle's view of the contemporary scene. His later life sees a calcification of political opinion into a rigid and, to modern sensibilities, rather repellent anti-democratic dogma, where increasing the franchise is intemperately attacked (*Shooting Niagara – and After?*, 1867), and great leaders of, to use an anachronistic term, quasi-fascist mould are valorised (*Oliver Cromwell*, two vols, 1845; *Frederick the Great*, six vols, 1858–65). The racism of his 'Occasional discourse on the nigger question' (1849) is especially unpalatable. After his wife's death in 1866 he wrote little, and lived a largely reclusive life, until his own death in 1881.

Further reading

Thomas Carlyle: Modern Critical Views (1986) edited by Harold Bloom; Moral Desperado: A Life of Thomas Carlyle (1995) by Simon Heffer.

Carroll, Lewis (1832–1898), children's writer and mathematician   Charles Lutwidge Dodgson, desiring a pseudonym under which to publish his children's writing, anglicised his middle name and Latinised his given name. As 'Lewis Carroll' he wrote the finest nonsense, and arguably the finest children's novels, in English. Dodgson himself was a shy, conservative (and Conservative) individual. Born the third of 11 children in the rectory at Daresbury, Lancashire, his mother, Frances Lutwidge, taught him abiding religious principles, and his father Charles Dodgson taught him mathematics and literature. He attended Rugby School from 1846, and entered Christ Church, Oxford, in 1851 to read classics and mathematics (this was also the year his mother died). Closely tied to his home, he returned often, and helped produce home magazines with titles such as *Rectory Umbrella* and *Rectory Magazine* with his brothers and sisters, which showcased his love for word puzzles, acrostics, parodies and the like. On graduating in 1854 he stayed in Christ Church to lecture in mathematics. He was ordained into the Church of England as a deacon in 1861, but had no ambitions to rise higher in the church hierarchy, possibly because the pronounced stammer that appeared when he was nervous made sermons almost impossible. This stammer disappeared when he was in the company of children, with whom he loved to pass time, either giving them Bible talks (assisted by a mechanical Humpty Dumpty doll) or else amusing them with stories.

His friendship with the young daughters of the Dean of Christ Church, Henry Liddell – and with Alice Liddell in particular – led to the writing of a children's fantasy *Alice's Adventures Underground*. This was published, with illustrations by John Tenniel (1820–1914), as ALICE'S ADVENTURES IN WONDERLAND (1865). A sequel, *Through the Looking-Glass and What Alice Found There* was published in 1871. These two examples of polite-carnivalesque CHILDREN'S LITERATURE, with (like Grimms' tales) dark and violent undertones, are Carroll's main achievement as a writer, although his lengthy nonsense poem *The Hunting of the Snark* (1876) approaches the same levels of brilliant absurdity. His other children's novel *Sylvie and Bruno* (1889–93) is very dull indeed by comparison.

Carroll's other claim to Victorian fame was as a PHOTOGRAPHIC portraitist. An enthusiastic amateur in this field, he took many pictures of young girls, sometimes naked, as well as striking portraits of Tennyson's two curly-headed sons, Hallam and Lionel. Other words included his lively mathematical work, *Euclid and his Rivals* (1879), and various collections of poems, collected in *Rhyme? and Reason?* (1883). He never married. Carroll retired from Christ Church in 1881 but continued living in the college until his death, of bronchitis, in 1898. Several of his nonce-word formulations ('galumphing', 'mimsy', 'brillig', and others) have entered the language, and the *Alice* books are amongst the most-quoted Victorian texts in modern times.

But there is no avoiding Carroll's distasteful, to modern sensibilities, fascination with little girls. This dominated his life, and also informs his best writing, although it remains questionable to what extent it is a merely sexual, though repressed, obsession. Mrs Liddell famously insisted that Carroll break off his friendship with Alice; the relevant pages of Carroll's diary are razored out, and biographers have speculated about an inappropriate advance, proposal of marriage, or something more lurid still. As far as the written works go, Valentine Cunningham puts it well, if severely, when he talks of 'not only the whimsy but also the chaos of Alice's fausse-naïve encounters', together with 'their horror, violence and implicit sexual danger. It's a nightmare being enmeshed in the sadistically disarranged games and tangled logics of the clerical child-lover with the blackened hands (black from photographic chemicals: he wore gloves in public)' (Cunningham, 2000: 685). The present-day climate of extreme outrage at the very thought of child abuse is not one in which is it is easy to discuss the motivations of this (to quote Cunningham again) 'active-repressed paedophile'. Certainly Carroll himself always denied any sexual component to his relations with children, or to any aspect of a sexual life at all; for instance, he advocated (a very Victorian touch, this), the contemplation of difficult problems in mathematical logic as a mental distraction should one be awoken in the night by 'impure thoughts'. The fact that we do not know precisely why Mrs Liddell forced Carroll to break off his friendship with Alice also fuels prurient speculation, although this probably had as much to do with class snobbery as with any perceived sexual danger. Ultimately, it is the sheer strength of Carroll's repressive mechanisms, allied to a ludic and heroically inventive imagination, that forges a truly great literature, that is as appealing in its creative warpings to adults as children.

Catholic Emancipation (1828) A range of legal and constitutional penalties against Roman Catholics dated from 1688, the so-called 'Glorious Revolution', when a Catholic monarch (James) was prevented from occupying the throne because of his religious beliefs. In the early nineteenth century it was still the case that the oath that had to be taken by members of parliament excluded Catholics from being MPs or holding other political office, such as town councillors. In 1807 Sydney Smith campaigned for the rights of dissenters (i.e. non-Anglican Protestants), and the ensuing climate of partial tolerance enabled a bill for Catholic Emancipation to be presented to Parliament in 1808, although it was defeated 281 votes to 128. A pressure group, the Catholic Board, was founded in 1811 to campaign on the issue, although another Emancipation Bill was defeated in committee in 1813, and the Board was dissolved by government order in 1814. Further bills were defeated in 1819, 1821 and 1825; in the latter two cases the bills passed the Commons, but were defeated in the Lords.

There were only 60,000 Catholics resident in Britain. However, the majority of the population of Ireland (still a part of the United Kingdom throughout the nineteenth century) was Catholic, although the official church of the province was Anglican. Accordingly the campaign for Catholic Emancipation was inextricably linked with nationalist movements in Ireland. Daniel O'Connell (1775–1847), the Irish radical, was elected Member of Parliament for County Clare, but could not, as a Catholic, take his seat in the House. With Ireland seemingly on the verge of open rebellion, the Duke of Wellington decided to force Emancipation through Parliament, and after a stormy ride the Catholic Emancipation Act became law in 1829: Catholics were made eligible for parliament and all offices of state except Monarch, Lord Lieutenant and Lord Chancellor. The Act helped focus Catholic and Irish confidence, but also contributed to a resurgence of anti-Catholicism in Britain. Oxford and Cambridge retained their insistence on the XXXIX ARTICLES, and it was not until 1911 that George V, assuming the throne, refused to take the anti-Catholic Coronation oath.

Further reading
Catholic Emancipation: A Shake to Men's Minds (1992) by Wendy Hinde.

'Celtic literature' The term is most associated with MATTHEW ARNOLD, who used it to describe Irish, Welsh and Scottish literatures in his book *On the Study of Celtic Literature* (1867). This work, and the debate it engendered, was largely behind Oxford University's decision to establish a Chair of Celtic Studies. Arnold speaks persuasively of a distinctively northern European 'celtic' literary aesthetic, something epitomised by OSSIAN (a writer Arnold considered valuable aesthetically despite not being authentic). Despite a tendency towards essentialist definition of 'celtic', Arnold's interest at least rescued 'Irish literature' from the reputation of being either a predominantly comic literature, after the manner of Thomas Moore (1779–1852), or else a literature governed by tweeness – as in Irish poet William Allingham's (1824–89) hideous 'The Fairies': 'Up the airy mountain/Down the rushy glen/We daren't go a hunting/For fear of little men;/Wee folk, good folk,/Trooping all together;/Green jacket, red cap,/And grey cock's feather!' (1850). Samuel Ferguson (1810–86) attempted more serious poetic recasting of Celtic legend in *Lays of the Western Gael* (1865) and his epic *Congal* (1872). Aubrey de Vere (1814–1902) mined a similar vein with his *The Foray of Queen Maeve* (1882).

By the end of the century literature of what was known as the 'celtic twilight' was very popular. William Butler Yeats (1865–1939) published a collection of stories entitled *The Celtic Twilight* in 1893, illustrating a supposed Irish fascination with faded myths, fairies, ghosts and spirits. Douglas Hyde (1860–1949) wrote a *Literary History of Ireland* (1892) and his translated *Love Songs of Connacht* (1893) contributed to the sense of 'Irish revival'. Decades later the great Irish novelist James Joyce was to dismiss this whole genre of 'celtic twilight' literature as 'the cultic toilet'.

Celtic literature remains a vibrant area of academic culture, and culture more generally, but it should not be forgotten that the category is founded on essentialist and racist assumptions. David Fitzpatrick connects British attitudes to 'the Irish' with racist opinions about coloured races, quoting Lord Salisbury's opinion that the Irish were like the Hottentots in being incapable of self-government, and Sydney and Beatrice Webb who honeymooned in Dublin in 1892 and reported 'the people are charming but we detest them, as we should the Hottentots – for their very virtues' (quoted in Fitzpatrick, 1999: 499). The exuberance and creativity of 'the Celt' is necessarily connected to a perceived emotional immaturity, savagery and childlike-ness in this particular ideological construction, and accordingly it cannot be straightforwardly endorsed.

Chambers's Journal (1832–1938) Robert Chambers (1802–71) was an Edinburgh-based publisher whose firm specialised in producing books relating to Scottish history and culture. He founded *Chambers's Edinburgh Journal* in 1832, a periodical that included a variety of articles on literature, science and the arts with a populist spin. The name was changed to *Chambers's Journal* in 1854, by which time circulation was around the 80,000 mark. The *Journal* was published weekly, 16 close-printed double-columned pages without illustration priced at 1½d. The tone was mostly informative, although some articles were more jocularly phrased.

A typical mid-Victorian edition of the *Journal* (picked at random) is No. 125, published Saturday 24 May 1856. The front-page masthead announces *Chambers's Journal of Popular Literature, Science and Arts, Conducted by William and Robert Chambers*. The lead article is an introduction to the work of French writer Alexander Dumas, entitled 'The Literary Leviathan'; this is followed by 'Mistakes About Snakes', a piece of popular biology; 'The Painter and his Pupil: a Flemish Story' is short fiction; 'Testimonials to Character' is a serious article on the difficulties of relying upon letters of reference, suggesting that a system of officially sponsored Certificates ought to replace such testimonials. 'Curiosities of Our Post-Office' is a humorous account of life in an Irish village; 'College Life in Finland' is translated and excerpted from a French book about that country. Three short articles (on 'Thermometers', including conversion charts from Centigrade to Fahrenheit, on 'Inns of Court' and on 'Cold') and a poem ('Castles in the Air', by 'H.M. junr') conclude the issue.

Chartism   Active throughout the late 1830s and the 1840s, Chartism was a widespread movement for democratic reform in England, Wales and Scotland dedicated to the promulgation of the 'People's Charter', a document created in May 1838. The Charter was largely drawn up by William Lovett (1800–77), a cabinet-maker and radical reformist, and was published by the London Working Men's Association, which he had founded. Other prominent radicals of the day, and several liberal MPs, were among the signatories. The Charter called for six points of political reform:

1. universal male adult suffrage
2. vote by secret ballot
3. the abolition of property requirements for MPs
4. payment of salary to MPs
5. equalised electoral districts
6. annual general elections.

It can be observed that all but the last of these demands were eventually realised.

Chartism derives from the climate of political debate surrounding the Reform Act of 1832, and in particular the widespread sense that reform had been limited to the affluent middle classes, and that the majority of the population had been ignored, or even 'betrayed'. What distinguishes Chartism, apart from the sheer size of its support, its national character and its predominantly working-class complexion, was that – unlike Revolutionary politics on the continent – it was committed to reform within the framework of the constitution. The movement included two wings. One was moderate, a 'moral force Chartism' associated with Lovett, that denounced violence and preached a religiously influenced ideology of education, self-help and temperance. The other was the more radical 'physical force Chartism' associated with Feargus O'Connor (1794–1855). The charismatic O'Connor advocated a more confrontational approach, sometimes including the application of a sometimes violent 'physical force'. *The Northern Star* (1837–52), Chartism's national newspaper, was owned by O'Connor.

A mass petition was presented to Parliament in 1839 urging the Chartist case. It was rejected. Further petitions followed in 1842 and 1848 (the 1842 petition was signed by three million individuals). Mass meetings of Chartists could assemble as many as

200,000 people. Throughout the 1840s, as economic hardship began to bite, many Chartists became frustrated with the apparent impotence of lawful agitation; one popular slogan promised 'peaceably if we can, forcibly if we must'. In the winter of 1839/40 some Chartists attempted an (abortive) insurrection, and in 1842 local industrial action was coordinated into a general strike predicated on the demand that the Charter be passed as law – again, unsuccessfully. In 1848, with revolution sweeping across Europe, Chartists attempted and failed to organise revolution in Britain. Indeed, many historians see the success of Chartism at mobilising and thereby to some extent venting working-class anger as a prime reason why revolution did not spread to Britain in this year. By the 1850s Chartism had mostly dissipated as a coordinated political force, although many influential Chartists and popular radicalism in general continued throughout the century.

Most affluent and middle-class observers were suspicious of, or downright hostile to, the threat to social stability they saw represented in Chartism. The narrator in Tennyson's 'Locksley Hall' (written 1838–9, published 1842) looks with alarm at working-class agitation:

> . . . all order festers, all things here are out of joint:
>
> . . . .
>
> Slowly comes a hungry people, as a lion creeping nigher,
> Glares at one that nods and winks behind a slowly-dying fire.

Dickens' *Barnaby Rudge* (1841) represents London being savaged by rioting mobs; the historical recollection of the Gordon Riots (1780) functioning in this case as a cipher for the terror that followed the French Revolution – a frequent point of reference for middle-class fears of what Chartism might lead to. That even so populist-minded a writer as Dickens could denounce Chartism shows how thoroughly the bourgeoisie were alarmed:

> It is unnecessary for us to observe that we have not the least sympathy with
> physical-force Chartism . . . apart from the atrocious designs to which these
> men, beyond all question, willingly and easily subscribed . . . they have done too
> much damage to the cause of rational liberty and freedom all over the world.

(Dickens, 'Judicial Special Pleading', *Examiner*, 23 December 1848)

On the other hand, some writers were more sympathetic to the Chartist cause. Charles Kingsley's *Alton Locke: Tailor and Poet* (1850) tells the story of the eponymous hero who falls in with the physical-force Chartists and wins a reputation as a radical poet. Jailed for involvement in a riot, and subsequently caught up in the events of the failure of the 1848 petition, Locke falls sick and is nursed back to health by the woman he loves, Eleanor, who converts him to moral-force Chartism. They emigrate to America together, where Alton dies.

It is significant that Kingsley cast his Chartist hero as a poet. Recent scholarship has begun unearthing the extensive and rich tradition of Chartist and working-class radical literature, largely poetry. Literary Chartism was profoundly influenced by the example of radical Romantic Percy Bysshe Shelley (1792–1822), and especially his *Queen Mab* (published in 1813 with a series of lengthy, politically inflammatory *Notes*, which were sometimes circulated independent of the poem). Anne Janowitz talks about 'the poetic exuberance of Chartist poetry', adding that 'Chartism was the first movement in the name of the working class to render explicit and democratise the links between cultural and political efficacy' (Janowitz, 1998: 134–5). Allen Davenport (1775–1846) looked forward to a reformed future:

> A day when every working man shall know,
> Who is his truest friend and who his foe –
> A day of union and of moral might –
>
> . . . .
>
> A day when working men of every state,
> Shall feel as brothers in their common fate.

> ('The Poet's Hope', quoted in Janowitz, 1998: 115–16)

Thomas Cooper 'the Chartist' (1805–92) published an epic poem in Spenserian stanzas, *The Purgatory of Suicides* (1846) dedicated to CARLYLE, and listing the many individuals driven to self-destruction. Despite the rousing radical rhetoric ('slaves toil no more! Why delve, and moil, and pine,/To glut the tyrant-forgers of your chain?') the enormous parade of suicides makes for a peculiarly depressing read. Ernest Jones's (1819–69) *The New World* (1850, 1857), another epic, is more heartening: although it surveys the world as under the yoke of oppression and tyranny, it ends with a powerful peroration: 'Grandly and silently the People rose!/None gave the word, they came together brought/By full maturity of ripened thought.'

Further reading

The Chartist Experience (1982) edited by James Epstein and Dorothy Thompson; *Lyric and Labour in the Romantic Tradition* (1998) by Anne Janowitz.

Child labour   Children – cheap to employ and easy for a foreman to intimidate – worked in a wide range of early Victorian jobs, and in the first decades of the century there was no legislation preventing employers from exploiting children in this way. Anthony Ashley Cooper, seventh Earl of Shaftesbury (1801–85), a Tory aristocratic politician, campaigned over many years for legislation to ameliorate the lot of working children. His first success was the Factory Act of 1833, prohibiting the employment of children under the age of nine in textile mills, and limiting the work of those aged nine to thirteen to 48 hours a week. He also passed the Coal Mines Act of 1842, preventing the employment of children under the age of ten in coal mines. The 'Ten

Hours Act' of 1847 was sponsored by another campaigner, John Fielden (1784–1849), and limited the number of hours that could be worked by any person under the age of 18 to 58 hours a week, and no more than 10 hours in any one day. Later in the century, the Gangs Act of 1867 and the Education Act of 1876 prevented the employment of 'gangs' of children in agricultural work.

Children's literature   Literature produced to be read by children was, before the nineteenth century, limited, piously didactic and – usually – dull. More detailed recent scholarship has perhaps modified this view in a few subtle ways, but it remains broadly true. Works such as James Janeway's *A Token for Children* (1671), Isaac Watts' *Divine Songs for the Use of Children* (1715) and Maria Edgeworth's *Moral Tales* (1801) seem especially stern and forbidding to modern sensibilities. A more sheerly entertaining literature begins to emerge in the first decades of the century, with German Johann David Wyss's (1743–1818) *The Swiss Family Robinson* (first translated into English in 1814) an important milestone. This tale of a family shipwrecked on a desert island is mildly diverting. The fairy tales collected by the Grimm brothers were increasingly available in English translation from the 1820s, and by the 1850s such tales constituted an established sub-genre of children's literature, as is evidenced by Thackeray's good-humoured send-up of fairy-tale conventions in his *The Rose and the Ring* (1855). Other sub-genres emerged through the 1850s: adventure stories for boys such as Robert Ballantyne's (1825–94) *Coral Island* (1857), which was perhaps the most popular boy's adventure story of the century, although it is now mostly known as the text against which William Golding's (1911–1993) *Lord of the Flies* (1954) was written. School stories, such as Thomas Hughes's (1822–96) still-popular *Tom Brown's Schooldays* (1857) were also popular, as were family sagas, such as the American author Louisa May Alcott's (1832–88) *Little Women* (1868), and animal tales like Anna Sewell's (1820–78) *Black Beauty* (1877). These last three titles are still in print today, where other popular Victorian works for children now seem dated. George Sargent's *Roland Leigh, the Story of a City Arab* (1857) led a small vogue for stories of ragged but virtuous child-heroes. Hesba Stretton's (1832–1911) *Jessica's First Prayer* (1867) was a female variant of this, in which street-child Jessica's innate goodness shines through her adversities and leads to her being adopted by a well-to-do guardian. Alexander Strahan (1834–1914) founded a religiously toned magazine for youngsters called *Good Words for the Young* in 1864. *The Water Babies* (1863), by the ultra-religious Charles Kingsley harks back to the fairy-story tradition, but is still in thrall to a moralistic tradition.

In a sense the two most significant children's novels of the century are Lewis Carroll's Alice's Adventures in Wonderland (1865) and Robert Louis Stevenson's *Treasure Island* (1883). These two, very different, works shared one important feature: a refusal to subordinate the story to a didactic or moralistic end. In Carroll's case this is an odd feature, for he was a moralistic individual, and other of his works for children (such as *Sylvie and Bruno*, 1889–93) are quite didactic. But in Alice, and its 1871 sequel THROUGH THE LOOKING GLASS, Carroll's sheer exuberance of imagination produces energetically rhizomatic books that invite children simply to enjoy. Stevenson's case is more straightforward; a novelist of genius, he applied the same approach to his adult as to his children's works. *Treasure Island*, and later *Kidnapped* (1886), are superb novels, accessible to children because focused on a youngster's adventure and written clearly, but equally enjoyable for an adult audience.

The later decades of the century saw a number children's classics published: Richard Jefferies' (1848–87) semi-autobiographical tale of a boyhood in Wiltshire, *Bevis* (1882), is evocative and often beautiful. Francis Hodgson Burnett (1849–1924) enjoyed enormous success with *Little Lord Fauntleroy* (1886), although its tale of a velvet-suited golden-curled young American who discovers that he is in line to inherit an earldom is quite annoying, and not nearly as good a book as her later *The Secret Garden* (1911). KIPLING's *Jungle Books* (1894–5) are unsentimental and atmospheric animal tales. Edith Nesbit (1858–1924) began a prolific career as a children's author with *The Story of the Treasure-Seekers* (1899); *Five Children and It* (1902), *The Phoenix and the Carpet* (1904) and *The Railway Children* (1906) followed, although this now leads us out of the Victorian age. Beatrix Potter (1866–1943) is likewise too late for us, although her first book, *The Tale of Peter Rabbit*, was published in 1901, and represents an important moment in the *Alice* tradition of books in which illustration is as important as text.

Cholera   This unpleasant disease is fatal in more than 50 per cent of cases if untreated. The symptoms include violent diarrhoea, resultant severe dehydration and accompanying cramps, and a blue colour in the body's extremities. It appeared first in Britain in the 1830s, and there were a number of severe epidemics in the 1840s and 1850s. The worst of these occurred between the summer and mid-autumn of 1849, during which time 15,000 Londoners and 20,000 people from elsewhere in the country died of the illness. Combating infection was made harder by a lack of understanding of its infectious vector. Health campaigner Edwin Chadwick (1800–90) argued that its spread was air-borne, a miasma attendant upon rotting rubbish. John Snow (1813–58) provided more effective medical evidence by drawing up epidemiological maps of infection that demonstrated the relationship between groups of infected people and certain water supplies. Snow elegantly demonstrated the force of his argument when he halted an infection in Soho by removing the handle of the Broad Street pump. The German scientist Robert Koch (1843–1910) identified the water-borne cholera bacillus as the infectious agent in 1884. It is now understood that the bacillus passes on via infected faeces that find their way, through inadequate sewage disposal, orally into other human beings.

Christian Socialism   A variety of Protestant religious belief, allied to MUSCULAR CHRISTIANITY. It is particularly associated with Frederick Denison Maurice (1805–72), a

UNITARIAN turned Anglican, whose book *The Kingdom of Christ, or Letters to a Quaker concerning the Principles, Conceptions and Ordinances of the Catholic Church* (1838) is usually taken as inaugurating the 'Christian Socialist' movement. Maurice argued that Christ had come not to found a religious sect, but rather a kingdom embracing all men and women. In such a kingdom there would be no rich and poor, no class distinctions, no oppression, and everybody would live according to the word of God. This linkage of almost radical notions of social justice with religious doctrine attracted many, including J.M. Ludlow (1821–1911) and Charles KINGSLEY (1819–75). Kingsley contributed many essays to the short-lived *The Christian Socialist: a Journal of Association* (1850–1), which expressed many core beliefs of the movement. Christian Socialists supported the cause of moral-force CHARTISM, agitated for legislation, education and sanitation, and founded the Society for Promoting Working Men's Associations.

Christmas   At the beginning of the nineteenth century, Christmas was a relatively unimportant religious festival; many people worked on Christmas day – a fact reflected by practice in Scotland where, until recently, Christmas was a normal working day and it was the New Year that was the important festival. It is true that the roots of Christmas celebration go back far in British culture; in the Middle Ages 12 days and nights of feasting took place at mid-winter, combining Christian rituals with traditions based distantly on the ancient Roman festival of Saturnalia, a pagan celebration for the Roman god of agriculture, and the Germanic winter festival of Yule. But the seventeenth-century rise of Puritanism had discredited the licentiousness of the celebration. Oliver Cromwell (1599–1658) had particularly disapproved, and had effectively outlawed Christmas festivity. Christmas was celebrated through the eighteenth and into the nineteenth century, but it was often a low-key affair. By the 1840s, however, general attitudes were shifting. Queen VICTORIA's new husband, the German Prince ALBERT, had brought the custom of Christmas trees from his homeland. The first 'Christmas card' appeared early in 1843, invented by Henry Cole (1808–82) and bearing a design by the painter John Callcott Horsley (1817–1903) of three generations of a Victorian family sitting down to Christmas dinner, flanked by images of charitable living. The ancient habit of singing special seasonal hymns, Christmas carols, was undergoing a revival. But it was the Christmas stories of DICKENS, particularly his 1843 masterpiece *A Christmas Carol*, that had the greatest impact on Christmas in Britain and America.

Dickens places the moral of his story right at the beginning; unusually, perhaps, but effectively. After establishing Scrooge's hard-hearted dedication to money, and his callous disregard of his clerk's wellbeing, he has Scrooge's cheerful nephew make a brief appearance. In reply to Scrooge's denial of Christmas and Christmas spirit, the nephew makes a little speech underlining the point of Christmas from Dickens' point of view, and the point of *A Christmas Carol* too:

I am sure I have always thought of Christmas time, when it has come round – apart from the veneration due to its sacred name and origin, if anything belonging to it can be apart from that – as a good time; a kind, forgiving, charitable, pleasant time: the only time I know of, in the long calendar of the year, when men and women seem by one consent to open their shut-up hearts freely, and to think of people below them as if they really were fellow-passengers to the grave, and not another race of creatures bound on other journeys. And therefore, uncle, though it has never put a scrap of gold or silver in my pocket, I believe that it has done me good, and will do me good; and I say, God bless it!

(Dickens, *Christmas Books*: 10)

Circulating libraries   Victorian books were expensive items: three-volume novels might retail at between £1 and 30s., at a time when a working-class weekly wage might be calculated in shillings (*see* MONETARY VALUE). Circulating libraries were the most popular mode of more affordable access to books. For an annual fee, usually a guinea, readers could borrow as many books as they could read. A number of circulating libraries were well established by the 1840s and 1850s, the most significant being Mudie's. Established by Charles Edward Mudie (1818–90) in 1842, it began to grow after relocating to New Oxford Street in 1852, thereafter swiftly dominating the market. By the 1860s it had no competitors of any size except for the circulating library of W.H. Smith (est. 1860), which, being based chiefly in RAILWAY stations, did not compete directly. Libraries were established in the major cities, but also in holiday resorts (particularly Bath and seaside resorts), and as the railway network spread so libraries appeared throughout the whole country. By 1861 Mudie claimed to be buying some 180,000 volumes a year, and his decision to stock a book could make or break a title (as with the 430 copies of THACKERAY's *Henry Esmond* ordered in 1852). This purchasing power gave Mudie's tremendous influence over the publishing market, and Mudie's strong views on the proper moral tone he considered fiction ought to strike had a direct effect on the literary scene. MEREDITH's 1859 novel *The Ordeal of Richard Feverel* was deemed unacceptable by the library, without whose purchases the book flopped. Meredith himself believed it took his reputation ten years to recover. (Horsman, 1990: 3). DICKENS rarely published triple-decker novels, preferring the technique of SERIAL PUBLICATION, whereby novels were issued in weekly or (more usually) monthly instalments at a few pennies or a shilling. An exception is *Great Expectations*, which came out in three volumes in 1861, perhaps specifically to appeal to the circulating libraries: Mudie's purchased 1400 copies of the first edition.

Further reading

Mudie's Circulating Library and the Victorian Novel (1970) by Guinevere Griest.

Class   If we define class, with the *Oxford English Dictionary*, as 'a division or order of society according to status, a rank or grade of society', we may be tempted to see the parallels between Victorian times and our own; for all that politicians sometimes advocate a 'classless society' our world is still stratified along class lines: a small 'upper class' or aristocracy, a larger 'middle class' (often divided into a slightly wealthier 'upper-middle' and a 'lower-middle') and a 'lower' or 'working class'. But the comparison is misleading, for at least class today is not – as it was for the Victorians – an all-consuming determinant of social life. When examining the Victorian attitude to class it may be better to think in terms of (to quote the title of Thomas Robertson's popular play from 1867) *Caste*. Marrying across class boundaries was frowned upon; moving from one class to another inhibited in both direction. On the one hand, there was a refusal to accept that upper class or bourgeois individuals who fell into poverty had been socially diminished (the category 'shabby genteel', no longer in general currency, was used for such individuals; the upper classes also put great effort into 'looking after its own', with many charitable trusts dedicated to relieving the poverty of 'distressed gentlefolk'). On the other hand, individuals who were born into the working class and who acquired money were not perceived as genuinely higher class. There are a number of scornful words, such as 'arriviste' and 'parvenu', to describe such individuals.

The many anxieties of class in this period produced at least one work of great art. DICKENS, himself the grandson of a servant and somebody never quite genuinely accepted into the highest circles, wrote in *Great Expectations* (1861) an enduring masterpiece of the awkwardness, the comedy and the agony of moving in classes into which one has not been born. On the other hand, the certainties of class, and in particular the certainty of upper-class superiority produced nothing but the banality of SILVER-FORK or YOUNG ENGLAND culture.

One thing that is not so acute today as it was in the Victorian period is the super-sensitivity to relative seniorities and inferiorities within broader class bands. Richard Altick captures this well:

> Menial domestic servants, of whom there were no fewer than a million in 1850 . . . belonged to the working class, but farm stewards and housekeepers – positions Dickens' paternal grandparents had had at Lord Crew's Staffordshire home – ranked higher. . . . A skilled handloom weaver like Silas Marner, though out of work, clearly outranked a comparatively well-paid but rough 'navvy' (itinerant construction worker, member of the gangs that built canals and railways). A consumptive piecework tailor employed in a sweatshop still was better than a road mender.
>
> (Altick, 1973: 34–5)

Similar internal gradations could be sketched out for the middle classes. For the gradations within the upper class, *see* PEERAGE. A novel such as Dickens' *Bleak House* (1852–3) provides a complete panorama of social class, from the aristocratic Sir Leicester Dedlock at the top all the way down to Jo the crossing sweeper at the very bottom.

ARNOLD's anatomy of his time, CULTURE *and* ANARCHY (1869) saw the tripartite class structure as entrenched and dangerously uncultured, with upper-class 'barbarians' addicted to intellect-free blood sports, middle-class 'philistines' living with minds narrowed by prudery and religion, and the working-class 'masses' undifferentiated. But Karl MARX anatomised the Victorian class-system more hopefully; he argued that the middle-class burghers, investors and industrialists – the 'bourgeoisie' – had taken effective control of the country from the upper classes, and that in turn the working classes would wrench power from them, but that this bloody time would lead eventually to a true classless society. The words he wrote with Friedrich Engels (1820–95) in their *Communist Manifesto* (1848) still have the power to stir the blood: 'in place of the old bourgeois society, with its classes and class antagonists, we shall have an association, in which the free development of each is the free development of all'.

Classical myth and legend   The school and university education system of the Victorian period was rooted in a thorough working-through of Ancient Greek and Latin literature; accordingly, one sign of an educated individual during this period was a familiarity with the myths and legends of the classical world. In the words of Samuel Maunder, writing in 1848, 'the study of the classics has a most salutary influence on the intellectual development of modern students' (Maunder, 1848: 143). Many writers, particularly of poetry, take such knowledge for granted in their readership. Most of the poets of the period worked strenuously at classical mythic and historical subject: ARNOLD afterwards suppressed his *Empedocles on Etna* (1852) as not classical enough, but he thought highly (although he has found no like-minded companions in posterity) of *Merope* (1858), his scholarly exercise in the form of Attic tragedy. His most famous poem, 'Dover Beach' (written 1851, published 1867), touches readers today despite, just as it once touched Victorian readers *because*, it invites us to compare contemporary mournfulness with Sophocles' verse – a game made more involving by the fact that it is not clear which Sophoclean quotation is being alluded to. TENNYSON wrote on a Homeric theme with great, languid beauty in 'The Lotos Eaters' (1832), and found in Greek myth a vehicle for exploring his own grief at the death of his friend Hallam in 'Tithonus' and 'Ulysses'. BROWNING's commitment to the classics was much more extensive, from youthful works such as 'Artemis Prologises' (1841), and in the work of his 'Greek decade', the 1870s: the long poem *Balaustion's Adventure* (1871) combined a recreation of Greece of the fifth century BC with a direct translation of Euripides' *Alcestis*; even longer was *Aristophanes' Apology* (1875), which explored in exhaustive length and detail both Athenian fifth-century society and the plays of Aristophanes, as well as including a complete translation of Euripides' *Heracles*. Browning's translation of the *Agamemnon* was published in 1877. Numerous shorter works also reworked classical themes – Numpholeptos (1876),

'Pheidippides' (1879), 'Echetlos' and 'Pan and Luna' (both 1880), and 'Ixion' (1887), and the complex late work *Parleyings with Certain People* (1887). In all these cases Browning found in the classics a medium for his own concerns with the difficulties of expressing the truth, mirrored for him by the difficulties of his self-taught readings in complex Attic Greek, as well as a means of articulating questions of violence and transmission. SWINBURNE found in the classics neither Arnoldian calm, nor Browningian grotesqueness and force, but rather a liberating (for him) sexualised passion and vigour. His energetic *Atalanta in Calydon* (1865) works very much better than Arnold's *Merope* as a modern Attic tragedy (although his later *Erechtheus*, 1876, is almost as dull as the Arnoldian original); but it is in the sado-masochistic shorter poems, often on a lesbian theme, that his classicism is most startling: 'Itylus', 'Hymn to Proserpine' and 'Anactoria' (all 1866).

Further reading

The Victorians and Ancient Greece (1980) by Richard Jenkyns.

Clothing   As Pamela Horn points out, 'clothes served as indicators of social status, and their subtle nuances had to be weighed up carefully'. Nor was 'fashion' a purely female preserve.

> Mrs Humphry in *Manners for Men* (1898) warned that those who did not
> dress well would never be a social success. The man who committed 'flagrant
> errors in costume . . . will not be invited out very much . . . If he goes to a
> garden party in a frock-coat and straw hat, he is condemned more universally
> than if he had committed some crime'.

(Horn, 1999: 43–4)

As the century proceeded, fashions became more elaborate and changeable. This produced its own mini-reaction – for instance, a work such as

> Mrs Haweis' *The Art of Dress* (1879), which declared that 'we can hardly find a
> modern dress which is not throughout in the worst taste and opposed to the
> principles of good taste . . . some dresses tire the eye as much as a wriggling
> kaleidoscope'.

(Quoted in Briggs, 1990: 261)

Nevertheless 'fashion' became an increasingly important social concern as the century progressed.

Women's fashions were more mutable through the century than men's. In the 1830s a bell-shape was deemed fashionable for women's skirts, and was achieved by the wearing of multiple petticoats, sometimes half a dozen or even a dozen, a weighty and uncomfortable practice. The invention of artificial crinoline in the 1850s rendered this practice redundant; petticoats stiffened with whalebone, and later steel, allowed the dimensions of the fashionable skirt to swell to enormous proportions, a vogue that reached its peak in the 1860s. New chemical dyes enabled dressmakers to work with gaudier and more colourful fabrics. By 1870 this fashion, much derided by writers and commentators, was superseded by a tighter skirt, often bunched at the back to cover a bustle. This new shape, in which the bustle-enhanced rear was balanced by large hair (or a wig) bunched at the back of the head, emphasised what was known as 'a Grecian bend' in the female figure. To emphasise the waist and enhance this curve, tighter and tighter corsets and high heels became popular. Bustles passed from fashion towards the end of the 1870s, enjoying a resurgence in the mid-1880s before passing away entirely; skirts became tighter, in many cases restricting the ability to walk properly. These tight clothes emphasised a certain fashion (known as 'the Princess line'); but in the 1880s and 1890s many women, some but not all of whom could be described as NEW WOMEN, rejected the impracticality of these fashions for a more 'rational' dress: looser skirts, no laced-up corsets or artificial enhancements of the figure and more muted colours. This movement gained currency from widely expressed medical opinions on the unhealthiness of tight-laced corsets and the greater weight of the older fashions. A Rational Dress Society was formed in 1881 to promote healthy and comfortable clothes.

For men, the fashions were generally more sober and restrained. A GENTLEMAN of the latter third of the century would most likely wear either a frock-coat (a more formal, longer jacket to be worn with a top hat) or a morning coat (shorter and lighter, to be worn with a bowler hat); both would be made from black, dark grey, light grey or blue cloth. Tweeds, browns and greens were not properly worn in the city, but might be worn in the country. By the end of the century the frock-coat was seen as old-fashioned and over-formal except for certain occasions. Lounge suits, comprising trousers, waistcoat and jacket cut from flannel or serge, came into vogue from the 1860s onwards: these might be worn for leisure pursuits for higher-class men, or as 'best wear' for those from the working class.

Clough, Arthur Hugh (1819–1861), poet Clough was the second son of a Liverpool cotton trader who emigrated with his family to South Carolina in 1822, but who sent his sons back to England to be educated. After attending Rugby School from 1829, Clough became friendly both with the headmaster, Thomas ARNOLD, and with his son Matthew. He went up to Balliol, Oxford, in 1837, and although graduating with only a second-class degree in 1841 he obtained a prestigious fellowship at Oriel in 1842. But Clough's time at university had been marked by an involvement in the Oxford Movement, at least to the extent of exploring degrees of RELIGIOUS DOUBT and uncertainty. In 1848 he resigned his tutor's position at Oriel, unable to continue to subscribe to the XXXIX ARTICLES as was a requirement of the position. Soon afterwards he published his long poem *The Bothie of Toper-na-Fuosich* (1848; he later changed the title to the meaningless *The Bothie of Tober-na-Vuolich* after he discovered that the Gaelic name he had first used referred to female genitalia). This work was based on the undergraduate reading parties to remote Scottish cottages with which Clough had been familiar in his university days, but it was the tone of the piece rather than its content that made a splash in the literary scene: accomplished, urbane and above all *modern*. A second long poem, also in supple hexameter verses, was more sophisticated still: *Amours de Voyage* was serialised in the American *Atlantic Monthly* between February and May 1858. This epistolary verse-novel explores the consciousness and opinions of an intelligent, slightly world-weary English traveller abroad, his abortive love affair and his observations. It is formally loose, inclusive rather than tightly controlled, but the overall timbre of the piece is very likeable.

Despite writing some notable shorter poems, including the often-anthologised 'Say not the struggle naught availeth' (1853), the witty 'The Latest Decalogue' (first published posthumously in 1862) and the verse-drama of spiritual indecision *Dipsychus* (1862), poetry was not really Clough's first calling. He worked as Professor of English Literature at the relatively new London University for a few years, worked for a year in Boston, and eventually settled into what amounted to a civil service position as an examiner in the Education Office in 1853. The following year he married Blanche Smith, but deteriorating health sent him on a tour of the Mediterranean. Hoping for renewed health he instead contracted a malarial infection and died in Florence. His widow brought out a number of posthumous publications, including *Poems* (1862), *Letters and Remains* (1865) and a two-volume *Poems and Prose Remains* (1869). Arnold's fine elegy for his friend was the poem 'Thyrsis' (1866).

Collins, Wilkie (1824–1889), novelist   William Wilkie Collins (in his twenties he dropped the William) was one of the most prolific and successful SENSATION novelists of the period; many contemporary critics see great merit in his work, but his reputation has resisted reflation in the present age. Born in the bohemian London household of his artist father and educated privately, Collins worked for a while as a clerk to a London tea merchant, and studied for the law (he was called to the bar in 1851, but he never practised). His first novel, a historical romance of ancient Rome called *Antonina*, had a long gestation period, and was published in 1850. The work was popular, but not such a success as *Basil: a Story of Modern Life* (1852), a book John Sutherland has described as a 'sexually superheated melodrama' (Sutherland, 1988: 141). His early works drew from melodramatic fiction as well as the traditions of the novel; in a preface to *Basil* he declared that 'the Novel and the Play are twin-sisters in the Family of Fiction'. In the same year began his lasting and profitable friendship with DICKENS; Collins contributed to *HOUSEHOLD WORDS* and later collaborated with Dickens on a play, *The Frozen Deep* (1856).

His first masterpiece was *The Woman in White* (1860), a mystery thriller written adventurously as a series of individual testimonies (Collins got the idea from watching a court case in 1856). The huge success of this novel stands at the head of the 1860s vogue for sensation fiction. Collins followed it with *No Name* (1862), *Armadale* (1866) and *The Moonstone* (1868), as well as 15 other novels of varying though generally diminishing quality. He died whilst his last novel *Blind Love* was being serialised in THE ILLUSTRATED LONDON NEWS; Collins' friend, the novelist Walter Besant (1836–1901), fulfilled Collins' deathbed request to complete it, and it was published in 1890. Collins is sometimes credited with inventing the modern detective novel, on the strength of Sergeant Cuff, the detective who appears to try and solve the jewel theft in *The Moonstone*; although 'detective fiction' as such is more usually concerned with the solution to murder mysteries (as with Inspector Bucket in Dickens' ante-dating *Bleak House* (1852–3) – a much better contender for the title 'first British detective novel').

Condition of England novel. See **Social problem novel**.

Conservative. See **Tory**.

Consols   The commonly used abbreviation for 'Consolidated Annuities', the Government Securities of Great Britain. A number of government investment funds had been consolidated into a single stock in 1751; investment in these annuities paid 3 per cent annual interest (hence the alternate name for the consols, 'the three-per-cents'), such that £10,000 invested produced an annual income of £300. This may seem small returns to modern sensibilities, but the attraction of the Consols was that this money was effectively guaranteed, where investment on the open market, for instance in railway stock, was notoriously insecure. Many wealthy people secured their money in this form, and a great many characters in Victorian fiction (especially well-to-do spinsters and widows) derive their income thereby.

Contagious Diseases Acts   The Contagious Diseases (Not Relating to Animals) Act was passed in 1864, with two later acts passed in 1866 and 1869. The aim of this legislation was to prevent the spread of sexually transmitted diseases by giving the authorities the legal power to detain any women suspected of carrying such a disease for up to nine months in a 'lock hospital'. The particular rationale of the act was the wide incidence of gonorrhoea and syphilis in the armed forces: up to one-third of serving soldiers, and one-eighth of serving sailors were infected with one or both of these diseases. But the emphasis on criminalising only women embodied in the acts was fiercely opposed by women's rights activists, prominent amongst them Josephine Butler (1828–1906), whose active campaigning at the head of the Ladies' National Association led to the repeal of the acts in 1883.

Copyright   At the start of the Victorian period laws of copyright were ineffective and piracy was widespread. According to an act of 1709 an author was allowed a share of his or her own writing (prior to that time copyright had been asserted by printers rather than writers) for a 14-year period, renewable for another 14 years at the end of that time if the author was still alive. However, even this limited protection was largely unenforced.

The barrister and author Thomas Noon Talfourd MP (1795–1854) began campaigning for a more effective copyright bill in 1837, supported by his friend DICKENS – whose novels were very extensively pirated both in rival editions and unauthorised stage dramatisations. The Copyright Amendment Act eventually became law in 1842: it established textual copyright for a period of 42 years (or seven years after the author's death, whichever period was longer) and made prosecution for infringement of copyright easier. Legislation to ensure author's copyright abroad took longer to establish. Dickens toured America in 1842 speaking out (amongst other things) in favour of international copyright agreements, although there was a certain hostility from the American press to the idea. An act of 1844 (superseding an unused act of 1838) protected the copyright of authors in number of signatory countries. In 1852 an Anglo-French convention was signed, protecting the rights of British authors over the Channel. In 1887 Britain signed to the Berne Convention, establishing reciprocal copyright arrangements between many countries.

Corn Laws   Laws were enacted following the end of the Napoleonic Wars in 1815 to protect British cereal farmers from being undercut by cheaper foreign imports following the renewal of foreign trade after the war blockade. The 1815 act prevented imports unless they were priced at 80/- or more per quarter – which is to say, unless the imports were more expensive than home-grown corn (from 1815 through to the end of the century the price of corn never rose higher than 74/6 and the price more usually fluctuated between 40/- and the mid-60/-s). Although popular with farmers, this bill was resented by many in the general population, for it kept cereal prices, and therefore bread prices, high. In 1828 the act was modified, so that foreign corn could be imported duty-free if the home price reached 73/-; when the price was between 60 and 72 shillings a sliding scale of duties was imposed on imports. Although proponents of LAISSEZ-FAIRE economics disapproved of any intervention in the market, and although farmers objected to the lowering of the 80/- tariff, this was seen by many as a reasonable compromise. But opposition to the laws continued. The Anti-Corn Law League was founded in 1838, and CHARTISTS and other radicals campaigned against the laws; during the general election of 1841 with the very effective slogan 'cheap bread!' PEEL changed the duty on corn in 1842, with a duty of 20/- on foreign imports when the domestic price was 51/- a quarter, dropping to the nominal figure of one shilling when the price rose to 73/-. In 1846, after the continuing pressure of famine in Ireland and hardship at home, Peel finally repealed the Corn Laws, leaving only a notional one-shilling tariff on all cereal imports (this was abolished in 1869). Historians have seen this 1846 repeal as a canny move by an aristocracy adapting to popular pressures instead of succumbing to popular revolution: in the words of Norman Gash this repeal 'in spectacular manner removed from [the aristocracy] the odium of a class monopoly at no cost to themselves in either money or status' (Gash, 1983: 350).

Cost of living. *See* **Money: monetary value.**

Cotton Panic, the One consequence of the American Civil War (1861–65) was a blockade that prevented cotton from the southern states reaching Europe. The textile works in northern England (which imported up to 80 per cent of their raw cotton from America) suffered a prolonged economic slump. The majority of the half-million workforce faced lay-off or sharply reduced pay, but despite the incentive offered by the Confederate states that the cotton trade would be resumed should Britain recognise its independence, these workers refused, to their credit, to support the slave-owning states. The Panic (also known as the 'Cotton Famine') produced an especially generous PHILANTHROPIC response: the Manufacturers Relief Committee raised £130,000 for the relief of distressed cotton workers in a short space of time.

Crime and punishment The century saw a general reduction in violent and capital punishment for crimes against property, and a corresponding reduction in those crimes themselves. The older so-called 'Bloody Code' had been partly relieved in the eighteenth century by the more humane policy of transporting convicts to British dominions overseas, initially to America. When American Independence interrupted this policy in 1776, convicts were imprisoned in decommissioned warships, known as 'Hulks', moored in Thamesmouth. In 1787 transportation was resumed (Australia replacing America as the destination), but the Hulks continued to be used, indicating a shift of attitude towards prisons and incarceration. The Hulks remained in use until 1857, despite their dreadful conditions and high mortality rate. They loom, for instance, over the brilliantly evocative opening chapters of DICKENS' *Great Expectations* (1860–1).

Older prisons were slowly superseded by newer prisons built to embody certain ideological beliefs concerning crime, punishment and rehabilitation. Pentonville prison, opened in 1842, was modelled on American institutions, and established a regime of quasi-military discipline, solitary confinement, silence, reduced diets and repetitive, useless labour. Ten new prisons on the same model were built throughout Britain in the following decade, although it was not until 1877 that all British prisons were integrated into a unitary government-funded organisation. Solitary confinement and hard labour remained the dominant prison ideology throughout the century, until mounting criticism of its dehumanising tendencies led to the passage of the Prison Act of 1898, relaxing the system.

Transportation was not discontinued until 1868, by which time approximately 160,000 convicts had been shipped out to the Australia colonies. About a quarter of these were of Irish birth. The rationale for transportation was partly that it was a more humane approach to crime than incarceration, giving the criminal the chance to redeem him- or herself; although a weightier consideration was doubtless that it proved 'surprisingly efficient in satisfying colonial demand for domestic and outdoor service, compensating for Australia's lack of slaves' (Fitzpatrick, 1999: 513). Certainly for many, pressured by famine in Ireland, state-assisted relocation was an attractive proposition. A quarter of a million Irish emigrants (many state assisted) willingly joined the transported convicts in resettling in Australia.

In general, though, punishments became less violent and more humane as the century wore on. During the eighteenth century, capital punishment was on the statute books for a bewilderingly large array of crimes (some 200 offences), but PEEL saw a number of acts through Parliament from 1824–9 effectively restricting the death penalty to murder and treason (a law formally restricting capital punishment to these crimes was passed in 1861). Executions continued, but much reduced in frequency: 'in 1817–20 there were 312 executions in England and Wales; between 1847 and 1890 the annual number was always less than 25, with 1871 the lowest year (3)' (Matthew, 2000: 132). After 1832 the corpses of executed people were no longer given over to be dissected, and public executions were ended in 1868.

Other gestures towards more humane punishment included the abolition of public floggings of women (in 1817) and of men (in 1835), although the lesser corporal punishment of public whipping continued until 1862, and private corporal punishment for adults and children continued into the twentieth century. Flogging was not abolished in the army until 1881, and later still in the Navy.

At the same time, policing in Britain was established on a systematic footing. Peel's Act of 1829 established a London Metropolitan POLICE force, and the City of London created its own force, distinct from the metropolitan police, in 1839. Similar schemes were established in most British cities through the 1830s and 1840s, although the principle of professional full-time policemen took longer to spread to the English and Welsh counties. Government legislation finally mandated the creation of county constabularies nationwide in 1856.

Crimean War (1854–1856)   Fought between Russia on the one hand, and an alliance of Britain, France and the Ottoman Empire (modern-day Turkey) on the other; after 1855 Sardinia joined the allies. The ostensible cause of the war was a dispute over access to the holy places in Palestine between Catholic and Greek Orthodox priests. France, which regarded itself as the protector of the Catholic interest, intervened in the Ottoman Imperial treatment of the situation; Russia, claiming to represent the Greek Orthodox Church, declared that the concessions France had obtained were an insult to Russian honour. Events escalated, and war followed. Historians agree that the actual cause of the war was a desire on the part of the allies to prevent perceived Russian expansion into the Mediterranean. Public opinion in Britain was vehemently anti-Russian, and the Czar was a particular hate figure.

The war was fought on the Crimean peninsular, in the Black Sea, and Russia was defeated at the battles of the Alma, Balaclava and Inkerman. The preponderance of public houses in England called 'The Alma', and the knitted head covering now called the 'balaclava' (originally designed to help British soldiers through the bitterly cold winter) indicate how completely the British in particular entered into the spirit of war. The Battle of Balaclava saw the famous Charge of the Light Brigade (25 October 1854), celebrated by TENNYSON in his poem of the same title. The Light Brigade, a troop of 673 horse, was ordered to retrieve some captured British cannons; misinterpreting the order they charged at the main concentration of Russian artillery, losing 107 men and 397 horses, and with 134 men wounded. Tennyson's poem, in energetically trotting dactyls ('Half a league, half a league,/Half a league onwards,/All in the Valley of Death/Rode the six hundred') celebrates this disaster as a sort of triumph: 'when can their glory fade?/O the wild charge they made!'. This war is also famous for Florence Nightingale (1820–1910) who worked as a nurse. The reputation she gained through her work with the many sick and wounded enabled her, on her return to Britain, to raise the prestige of the nursing profession; her books *Notes on Hospitals* and *Notes on Nursing* (both published in 1859) promulgated a number of sensible practices to do with hygiene and care, and quickly became standard texts.

The war ended in allied victory, sealed with a peace treaty (the Treaty of Paris, 1856, brokered by NAPOLEON III), but before this outcome the public mood had turned bitter. The sense was that the war had been mismanaged, both by the military high command and by the government of Lord Aberdeen (followed, after 1855, by Palmerston's administration). The majority of British casualties died not on the battlefield but of cholera and other diseases. In fact, British public opinion began shifting fairly early in the war, when the expected swift victory did not arrive. Writing for *The Times*, Irish reporter William H. Russell (1823–1907) highlighted various instances of mismanagement. Troops were ordered to abandon their equipment upon landing in the Crimea, to expedite their deployment, these materials never being recovered; men wounded at the battle of the Alma were left lying in the field after the battle. Disease took so heavy a toll that there were even worries the army itself would disintegrate; of 53,000 men mustered for the campaign, only 14,000 were healthy enough to fight, and only 2000 were judged to be in 'good health'. From the large scale to the small: coffee beans were sent out to the troops green, needing to be roasted and ground, but soldiers were not provided with the equipment to do either of these things. *The Times* attacked this 'total disorganisation', and the abdication of responsibility by the political establishment:

> . . . there are people in government who would rather the expedition were wholly unsuccessful . . . than that one iota of the official system, of patronage, of seniority, and of all that semblance of order, that has kept up the illusion of military strength . . . should be rudely swept away or reformed.

> (*Times*, 19 February 1854)

DICKENS, writing *Little Dorrit* at this time (it was published in 20 monthly instalments, from December 1855 to June 1857), picked up on this climate of opinion. Although there are no specific references to the war in that novel, critics have traditionally taken it as Dickens' attack on the government's mismanagement of the campaign. The book expresses this disillusionment in the form of the Circumlocution Office, whose dogma is 'how not to do it', and the abdication of political responsibility for all the ills in society implied by Dickens' original title for the book, 'Nobody's Fault'.

Poetic responses to the war tended to be less contentious. Alexander Smith and Sydney Dobell, two poets associated with the SPASMODIC school of verse, published a series of conventionally patriotic *Sonnets on the War* in 1855. Tennyson's major work of the period was *MAUD* (1855), in which the narrator, after killing his beloved's brother and causing her own death of grief, goes mad only to recover his senses by abandoning his selfish woes in the greater cause and going off to fight in the Crimea:

> . . . the heart of a people beat(s) with one desire;
> For the long, long canker of peace is over and done,
>
> . . .
>
> It is better to fight for the good than rail at the ill;
> I have felt with my native land, I am one with my kind.

(Tennyson, Maud, Part III, ll. 49–57)

This sort of jingoism met with critical disapproval; a review of the poem in *Tait's Edinburgh Magazine* (September 1855), for example, deplored the notion that 'the slaughter of 30,000 Englishmen in the Crimea' could be presented as the answer to society's problems, and insisted that the phrase 'the long, long canker of peace' was both morally and factually wrong ('thirty years of intermitted war – absolute peace we have *not* had during the interval'). Tennyson changed the line to 'the peace, that I deemed no peace' in subsequent editions. Edward Bulwer Lytton (under the pseudonym Owen Meredith) published his long poem *Lucile* in 1860; a tale whereby an Englishman, Vargrave, and a Frenchman, Luvois, compete over the love of the beautiful French woman of the poem's title; the Englishman marries his (English) betrothed instead, but his rivalry with the Frenchman is not resolved until 20 years later. Luvois has become a French general in the Crimean War, and Lucile a Florence Nightingale-style nurse; Vargrave's son is wounded and nursed back to health, and effects a reconciliation between the two men.

Further reading

Crimea: the Great Crimean War 1854–1856 (1999) by Trevor Royle.

***Culture and Anarchy*, by Matthew Arnold (1869)**   Arnold's last lecture as Oxford Professor of Poetry was entitled 'Culture and Its Enemies'. It was published in the *Cornhill Magazine* in July 1867, and was followed by five more articles on the same topic under the general title 'Anarchy and Authority'. Arnold revised these articles and published them in book form under the title *Culture and Anarchy* in 1869. The book became a great talking point, and remains one of the most important statements of Victorian cultural values.

In essence, the book is an elegantly written polemic in favour of 'culture' as the core aspect of society. In this (and despite Arnold's inclusive definition of the term to mean 'making the will of God prevail') is found the book's revolutionary thesis: by placing culture rather than 'religion', 'tradition' or 'family' at the heart of society Arnold stands at the head of a tradition that sees a social secularisation taking place by slow degrees through the nineteenth and twentieth centuries. We may say, running the risk of simplification, that, before Arnold, the Church and the class-based structures of the village and town were the central institutions of British society; Arnold inaugurates a change whereby the school and university, the literary and artistic worlds, usurp that place. Latterly popular media such as film, TV and music, and 'celebrity' more generally, have in turn usurped the literary and artistic as the core culture – a development to which Arnold would certainly have been hostile.

By culture Arnold means more than 'a smattering of Greek and Latin', although his aesthetics are deeply embedded in the classics. His definition of culture is 'the best that has been thought and said in the world', that which is ennobling and empowering in art, knowledge and craft. Without 'culture' at the heart of a society, he argues, anarchy is inevitable. In Steven Marcus's words 'culture is not merely intellectual, or a passion for intellectual goods and truths, but is decidedly moral and social as well . . . in this particular sense culture is analogous to religion' (Arnold, *Culture*: 172). Arnold himself sees poetry, rather than religion *per se*, as the closest correlative of culture: 'it is thus by making sweetness and light to be characters of perfection that culture is of like spirit with poetry' (Arnold, *Culture*: 37). The key phrase 'sweetness and light', taken from Swift's satirical *Battle of the Books* (1704), gives a flavour of Arnold's technique in the book: it is at once compelling, because difficult to disagree with, and also imprecise. 'Sweetness' approximates to 'beauty' and 'light' to 'reason, intelligence'; and 'making sweetness and light prevail' involves cultivating a national idiom of creative art and thought, fed by an enlightened education system. But Arnold holds patrician notions of 'beauty' and 'reasonableness'; these are not negotiable terms in his opinion, and must indeed be strictly enforced by arbiters of cultural taste. So, he has no time for 'popular literature', because it did not (he thought) ennoble and elevate its audience; and although he asserts a desire 'to rise above the idea of class to the idea of the whole community' (Arnold, *Culture*: 64) he also requires 'an adequate centre of authority' to compel the primacy of these values.

The first two chapters of *Culture and Anarchy* ('Sweetness and Light' and 'Doing As One Likes') explore the ways this sense of 'culture' can enrich national life. The third chapter, 'Barbarians, Philistines, Populace' anatomises the contemporary malaise, as Arnold saw it, rooting the problem in the CLASS system. His influential labels still have cultural currency. The Philistines were originally a Biblical tribe who habitually harassed the Israelites, and whose name was sometimes applied to people with an insufficiency of, or hostility to, liberal culture and enlightenment. For Arnold it is the British middle classes who are philistinical, because their attitude to art was wholly habitual and conventional, governed by notions of 'respectability' rather than intrinsic merit, and above all because of their 'inveterate inaccessibility to ideas'. For Arnold the 'Philistines' are people 'who prefer to [sweetness and light] that sort of machinery of business, chapels, tea-meetings, and addresses from Mr Murphy and the Rev. W Cattle, which makes up the dismal and illiberal life on which I have so often touched' (Arnold, *Culture*: 68). Above them in social rankings were the aristocracy, which Arnold sees characterised by a love of field sports, physical prowess and external grace, and whom he names Barbarians after the historical Barbarians who 'reinvigorated and renewed our worn-out Europe'. The savagery as well as the grace implicit in the label makes it a distinctly double-edged compliment. The working-class Arnold dubs 'Populace', 'raw and half-developed . . . half-hidden amidst its poverty and squalor' (Arnold, *Culture*: 71). Our life can only be improved by a properly 'acculturated' society; and the middle and upper classes are exhorted to assume the proper cultural authority they have abdicated.

Chapter 4 is called 'Hebraism and Hellenism', and meditates upon this cultural dialectic as the 'two points of influence' between which 'move our world' (Arnold, *Culture*: 87): Hebraism with its religious dedication to proper conduct and obedience, and Hellenism's commitment to truly perceiving and enjoying the world. 'The governing idea of Hellenism is *spontaneity of consciousness*: that of Hebraism, *strictness of conscience*.' For Arnold these two noble impulses must be properly balanced. The two last chapters, 'Porro Unum Est Necessarium' and 'Our Liberal Practitioners', stress the importance of discipline and liberty in turn.

Arnold's was not the first statement of concern about the erosion of 'high culture' but it was the first to strike a genuinely national note, and the first to link that decline with a turning-away from reason and rational standards. The eloquence and penetration of Arnold's book gave it an influence throughout the twentieth century. Indeed, in the words of Gerald Graff from 1994,

> *Culture and Anarchy* established the categories and the grammar through which we think about cultural crisis . . . so pervasive has Arnold's influence been on the terms of cultural diagnosis that since its publication (the book) has virtually been rewritten every decade.

> (Arnold, *Culture*: 186)

Further reading

Culture and Anarchy: an Essay in Political and Social Criticism (1994) by Matthew Arnold, edited by Samuel Lipman, with commentary by Maurice Cowling, Gerald Graff, Samuel Lipman and Steven Marcus.

Daily Telegraph   Nowadays an Establishment, Conservative paper, at its founding in 1855 the *Telegraph* was a Liberal paper with Radical touches. It was the first daily newspaper to be issued at the low price of 1d., and this feature, combined with its vigorous and colourful style, brought it a wide circulation.

Darwin, Charles (1809–1882)   Darwin was born and raised in affluence in the south of England, the son of a doctor. He spent seven years in a Shrewsbury school, studied medicine at Edinburgh and afterwards Christ's College, Cambridge; but he later claimed that his formal education taught him nothing ('all I have learnt of any value has been self-taught', quoted in Ridley, 1994: 4) and that at school and university he was largely idle. His amateur interest in botany and zoology was enough, in 1831, to win him a place as naturalist aboard the research vessel HMS *Beagle*. This five-year voyage took him throughout the Atlantic, Pacific and Indian Oceans, and during it he assembled an enormous amount of natural historical data. He returned to England in 1836 and lived for a while in London arranging his collections. By 1842 he had moved to Down House in Kent with his wife (he married his cousin Emma Wedgwood in 1839). His health deteriorated, and he avoided the London scientific scene, spending time instead with his rapidly increasing family – he eventually had ten children.

Darwin wrote up his experiences as a naturalist on the *Beagle* in several forms. The most accessible was *The Voyage of the Beagle*, which was published first in 1839 as *Journal of Researches into the Geology and Natural History of the Various Countries visited by HMS Beagle*, and heavily revised as *A Naturalist's Voyage* in 1845. This, and several other *Beagle*-related publications, were wholly descriptive and taxonomic. More theoretical was his *The Structure and Distribution of Coral Reefs* (1842), which advanced a hypothesis to explain how such reefs had grown in deep water. In the early 1850s he published four scholarly monographs on cirripedes derived from his time on the voyage.

Of course, Darwin's name is now mostly associated with the theory of EVOLUTION; but this theory as such was not his own invention, and had in fact been explored by a wide number of nineteenth-century thinkers, as he himself acknowledges. Darwin's breakthrough was to identify a plausible mechanism for evolution – natural selection, whereby organisms less fitted to their environment tend to die out without passing on their attributes to offspring, and organisms better fitted tended to thrive and have more children, carrying their positive adaptations onwards. After much delay, and chivvied along by friends, Darwin finally published the ORIGIN OF SPECIES in 1859. The extraordinary fuss that this volume created seems to have upset the rather thin-skinned Darwin; in the maelstrom of religious and popular hostility that followed publication he was content to allow others to argue his case for him, especially his vigorous young friends Herbert Spencer (1820–1903) and Thomas Huxley (1825–95).

In *The Variation of Animals and Plants under Domestication* (1867) Darwin revisited his theory, and tried to provide a mechanism for the hereditary principle that underlies natural selection. His hypothesis, the 'theory of pangenesis', was that every cell in an organism produces 'gemmules' that circulate through the body, perhaps in the bloodstream, to accumulate in the reproductive organs, and so be transferred into the offspring. This theory is wrong, and has been superseded by the current theory of DNA, which was derived from the German biologist August Weismann's theory of germ plasm first advanced in 1883, a year after Darwin's death.

Darwin returned to evolution again with *The Descent of Man, and Selection in Relation to Sex* (1871), an account of the possible evolutionary line from lower animals to human beings. The following year saw another, more anthropological work, *The Expression of the Emotions in Man and Animals* (1872). Five botanical studies followed, and Darwin's last work was on worms, a lifelong interest. Indeed, *The Formation of Vegetable Mould through the Action of Worms* (1881) is a work of considerable charm, despite its unprepossessing subject matter, and sold the most of all Darwin's writings, better even than the *Origin of Species*.

The impact Darwin's ideas have had on world culture is difficult to overstate. Sigmund Freud (1856–1939), in 'A Difficulty in the Path of Psychoanalysis' (1917), suggested that 'the universal narcissism of men, their self-love' has suffered three devastating crises from the researches of science; first on a cosmologic level, when the Copernican theory of the cosmos overturned the Ptolemaic, and second, biologically, with Darwin. (The third 'psychological' blow Freud claimed for his own theories.) 'To himself [man] attributed an immortal soul, and made claims to a divine descent which permitted him to break the bond of community between himself and the animal kingdom ... [Darwin] put an end to this presumption on the part of man' (Freud, 1953–6: 140–1).

Through the last four decades of the nineteenth century, Darwinian ideas spread through almost all cultural and social discourses. Spencer applied the notion of 'struggle for life' to politics, and the field of what is known as Social Darwinism has had a lengthy, and pernicious, life. The profound impact of Darwin's thinking on cultural forms has been widely remarked. The best study in this field is Gillian Beer's *Darwin's Plots: Evolutionary Narrative in Darwin, George Eliot and Nineteenth-Century Fiction* (1983), a work that details the impact not just of Darwin's ideas, but the forms and underlying logic of the *Origin*, and naturalist narratives.

Further reading

Darwin (1991) by Adrian Desmond and James Moore; *A Darwin Selection* (1994) edited by Mark Ridley.

David Copperfield (1849–1850), by Charles Dickens DICKENS' eighth novel was his most autobiographical, a first-person narrative that incorporated in minimally altered form an account Dickens had written of his own childhood experiences of misery and abandonment working in a blacking factory in London. It remained Dickens' 'favourite child' amongst his writings. It was issued in 20 monthly parts from May 1849 to November 1850; each monthly instalment carried the title *The Personal History, Adventures, Experience and Observation of David Copperfield the Younger, of Blunderstone Rookery (Which He Never Meant to be Published on Any Account)*. When the complete work was published in single-volume form the title had been shortened to *The Personal History of David Copperfield*. The book was brilliantly illustrated by Hablot 'Phiz' Browne (1815–82).

David recalls his idyllic childhood with his beautiful but unworldly mother, a paradise that is shattered when his mother marries again to the brutish Murdstone. Sent to school, David is miserable, but he sinks lower when his stepfather sends him to do menial work in Murdstone and Grinby's warehouse. He runs away and treks through Kent, and is eventually taken in by his eccentric and severe but essentially kindly aunt Betsey Trotwood. Educated at a better school at Canterbury, David is much happier; afterwards he is articled as a sort of apprentice to the kindly lawyer Mr Spenlow and falls in love with his daughter Dora. David changes his mind about a career in the law, and becomes first a parliamentary reporter and then a successful novelist (as Dickens had done before him), and marries the pretty-but-dim Dora; the practical incapability of this loving but basically childish married couple is brilliantly and hilariously evoked. Dora dies in childbirth, and after a period of grieving David marries the much more dependable Agnes, daughter of his old Canterbury schoolmaster, Mr Wickfield. Tied intimately in with this central plot are several colourful and brilliant narratives: the improvident, larger-than-life comedy of Mr Micawber, the insinuating and mock-humble villainy of Uriah Heep (who tries to wreck Mr Wickfield's life and has sexual designs upon Agnes until Micawber unmasks him), the seduction of innocent, beautiful working-class Emily – a friend from David's youth – by another of his friends, the upper-middle-class Steerforth. Dickens orchestrates all these plotlines brilliantly, bringing them to a resounding climax in a stunning storm scene off the coast of East Anglia. As a *Bildungsroman*, or novel of individual development and growth (a relatively new genre in the Victorian period), David learns to steer a path between the over-stern attitudes of Murdstone, the carelessness of Micawber, and the destructive looseness of Steerforth. The novel was greatly praised in its own day for its wealth of memorable characters, although perhaps its greatest triumph is its careful, vivid and profound evocation of childish experience and the adult retrospective vision of childhood.

Death and mourning We moderns tend to condescend to the Victorians because of their prudishness and repressed narrow-mindedness about human sex and sexuality; but our own narrow-minded and (in a manner of speaking) prudish attitude to death paints us in a very poor light compared to them. Mourning was more ritualised in the nineteenth century than it is today, with a specific code of behaviour and specific forms of dress (a carefully delineated diminution in the amount of black an individual ought to wear over particular time periods after the death). Pat Jalland argues that these mourning rituals 'provided opportunities for the bereaved to express their sorrow in a manner that made the grieving experience easier to endure and to complete, aiding an ultimate return to a more normal way of life' (Jalland, 1996: 193). The most celebrated example of mourning, however, rather contradicts this general truth; VICTORIA put on mourning when her beloved husband Albert died in 1861; she never dressed in anything but widow's clothes afterwards.

Arguably the Victorians had greater need for efficiently therapeutic mourning processes, since they were much more intimately acquainted with death than most western moderns. Mortality rates were, by present-day standards, dreadfully high; the average life expectancy 'improved from the mid-thirties to the upper forties and the low fifties by 1911. It is now 75 years' (Woods, 1996: 330). The averaging implicit in this figure is a little distorting; in the latter half of the century between 15 and 20 per cent of all deaths were of children under the age of one, and 25 per cent of all deaths were of children under five years (*see* the entry on BIRTH). If you survived childhood you had a reasonable chance of living into later middle age. But, nevertheless, air-borne and water-borne disease killed on average 13 people per thousand in the population per year from 1848–54 (by 1971 that figure had been reduced to one-seventh of one person per thousand), and all diseases taken together killed 22 people per thousand over that period. If the death toll in many Victorian novels strikes us today as excessive it is good to bear in mind John RUSKIN's opinion that the large number of deaths in DICKENS' *Bleak House* (1852–3) is actually 'a representative average of the statistics of civilian mortality in the centre of London' (quoted in Schlicke, 1999: 154). Most deaths happened at home rather than in hospital, something reflected in the ubiquitous 'deathbed scene' of the period's fiction. Indeed in literature, generally speaking, the emphasis was not on sudden or meaningless death, but on a considered, drawn-out deathbed scene, replete with reflection and, often, a summary of lived values.

> It was pre-pondered death that preponderated: the long deaths of KINGSLEY's Alton Locke (1850), THACKERAY's Colonel Newcombe (1855), TROLLOPE's Septimus Harding (*The Last Chronicles of Barset*, 1867), ELIOT's Mordecai Cohen (*Daniel Deronda*, 1876) all represent different values; but across a quarter of a century they represent in common an established mode of making values tell.
>
> (Joseph and Tucker, 1999: 117)

Further reading

Death in the Victorian Family (1996) by Pat Jalland; 'Passing On: Death' by Gerhard Joseph and Herbert F. Tucker in *A Companion to Victorian Literature and Culture* (1999) edited by Herbert F. Tucker.

Decadence   Speaking generally, art has been called 'decadent' by its critics when perceived to be degenerating or falling away from previous high standards. In the Victorian period, 'decadent' literature is broadly cognate with the FIN DE SIÈCLE and SYMBOLIST movements from the last decades of the century. Writers as varied in style and approach as SWINBURNE, PATER and WILDE, and artists as unalike as Aubrey Beardsley (1872–98) ROSSETTI, and Edward Burne-Jones (1833–98). As a very loosely conceived 'school' it was thought to have originated in France, evident in the work of Charles Baudelaire (1821–67) and Paul Verlaine (1844–96), who wrote one poem beginning 'je suis l'Empire à la fin de la décadence ...'. By the 1880s and the 1890s 'asethetic' artists in Britain were being identified with what the *Athenaeum* called 'the *décadents* and the *décadentisme*, a malady of the hour' (24 July 1886).

If the variety of artists brought under this pejorative judgement is striking, what they have in common is a disinclination to be bound by the moral and literary conventions of Victorian culture at large, and a belief in the validity of individual and transgressive impulses – in other words the sense, encapsulated in the phrase 'L'art pour l'art', that art is to be judged on aesthetic not moral grounds. Some of these figures were interested in the notions of decay (social and cultural as well as personal) from which we derive the term 'decadence'. But Swinburne, Pater and Wilde, to instance only three, had little interest in decay as such, although they were interested in sexual transgression, in 'aestheticism' as a philosophy of art, and in the primacy of 'beauty' (something that can look, to one's enemies, like mere hedonism). As a shorthand it can be useful to think of 'decadence' as ornate, atmospheric literature much concerned with sex, death, extreme states, languor, colour and pleasure.

Depressions. *See* **Economic cycles**.

Detective fiction   The precise origins of detective fiction are unclear. Many examples of Gothic fiction deal with crimes, secrets and their uncovering, although none includes those elements now considered constitutive of a 'detective' novel: a criminal milieu, a specific crime, and a policeman or private detective working through to a solution such as the revelation of the murderer, of the *modus operandi*, or of some other 'key' to the narrative.

The fiction of police detection shadowed the development of a department of criminal detection itself. France, historically ahead of Britain in the development of a professional police force, was also the home of the century's most famous detective: Eugene Vidocq (1775–1857). Vidocq's *Memoirs* (1828) contains stories of his dogged pursuit of Parisian criminals in which clues are deciphered, disguises adopted and gangs infiltrated. As British police forces were established through the 1830s and 1840s there was a correlative increase of public interest in stories of criminals (NEWGATE novels) and inevitably with criminal apprehension. In 1843 *Chambers's Journal* (Vol. 12: 54) reported that 'intelligent men have been recently selected to form a body called the "detective police"' and that 'at times the detective policeman attires himself in the dress of ordinary individuals'. Such detectives appear in a number of PENNY DREADFULS through the 1840s, although the first mainstream literary representative of a detective policeman is Inspector Bucket in DICKENS' *Bleak House* (1852–3). John Sutherland asserts that 'the first out-and-out detective story in English is Wilkie Collins' *The Moonstone* (1868)', adding that 'it is with Collins that the uncovering of crime becomes a pseudo-scientific exercise involving the application of superior powers of intellect and deduction' (Sutherland, 1988: 181). This claim can be contested, however, particularly in the light that the crime being investigated in this novel is theft rather than (as in almost all modern-day crime novels) murder, and that the solution to the mystery involves the sub-rational levels of hypnotic suggestion; Bucket, on the other hand, solves a murder mystery by the ordinary practice of his craft.

Many later Victorian writers wrote detective novels, or included detective sub-plots in their narratives. Mary Elizabeth Braddon's *Aurora Floyd* and *Eleanor's Victory* (both 1863) utilise detective elements; Trollope's *He Knew He Was Right* (1869) includes a private detective. But the most famous, and by far the most influential writer of Victorian detective fiction was Arthur Conan DOYLE, whose short stories and novellas centred on the GENTLEMAN private detective Sherlock Holmes continue to excite a large body of fans and followers.

Devotional literature   Strictly, devotional literature is instrumental, designed to be of use to the religious individual in his or her spiritual contemplation or religious practice. More broadly conceived, Christian literature enjoyed a great deal of popularity throughout the period. Most poets wrote works that expressed and explored questions of RELIGIOUS DOUBT and CERTITUDE, and some talented writers limited themselves purely to works of a religious or devotional character. In particular, several of the clerics and academics associated with the OXFORD MOVEMENT created significant bodies of devotional literature. John Keble (1792–1866) wrote many religious poems, and his collection *The Christian Year: Thoughts in Verse for the Sundays and Holy days Throughout the Year* (1827) was enormously popular. John Henry NEWMAN's poetry, particularly the poems collected in *Lyra Apostolica* (1836) and the long poem *The Dream of Gerontius* (1865), is a body of sensitive devotional meditation in verse. Sarah Flower Adams (1805–48) wrote a verse-drama, *Vivia Perpetua* (1841), set in first-century Rome in which a pagan converts to Christ and is martyred, but she is better known for her composition of HYMNS, particularly 'Nearer, My God to Thee' (from *Hymns and Anthems*, 1841) which was played as the *Titanic* sank. Another hymnist and composer of devotional poetry, John Mason Neale (1818–66) published many collections. Many of Christina ROSSETTI's lyrics are devotional. Frances Ridley Havergal (1836–79) put out a well-received collection of enthusiastic religious poems in *The Ministry of Song* (1871). Coventry Patmore (1823–96) published a number of devotional poems, and collections of religious essays and aphorisms, including *Religio Poetae* (1893) and *Rod, Root and Flower* (1895). Perhaps the greatest devotional poet of the age was barely published in the century; Gerard Manley HOPKINS made distinctive and experimental poetry that also captures a complex sense of religious faith.

Dickens, Charles John Huffam (1812–1870)   Charles Dickens was born on Friday 7 February 1812 in Portsmouth, where his father was working as a naval pay clerk. In January 1815, when Dickens was not yet three, the family moved to Kent, where Dickens grew up. He was taught to read and write by his mother, and attended a local day school. In 1822 the family moved again to London, the city with which Dickens is most closely associated. His father John Dickens was a kindly man without the skill to manage the family finances, and got into debt, once even going to prison over non-payment. With the aim of helping this situation the 12-year-old Charles was taken out of school and sent to work in a blacking factory on the Strand. This experience was deeply traumatic for the young boy; he felt himself demeaned and humiliated as well as abandoned and miserable. Although he only worked in the factory for a few months, afterwards being put back into school, the event marked him throughout his life. As an adult he kept it secret from all but his very closest friends; but his novels return to the figure of the orphaned or abandoned child in an attempt to work through the trauma.

In 1827 Dickens finished school and was engaged as a law clerk, planning to become a lawyer himself, but instead changed jobs and began work as a parliamentary reporter. Whilst working as a journalist he began writing short stories and sketches that were published in various magazines, the first appearing in 1833 when he was 21. He wrote these stories under the pseudonym 'Boz', a childhood nickname, and they were successful. A collection of them was published in 1836 as *Sketches by Boz*, and a publisher commissioned Dickens to write the words to accompany a series of illustrations by a popular artist called Robert Seymour (1798–1836), *The Posthumous Papers of the Pickwick Club*. The project was supposed to concern the sport of hunting, and the publishers thought that people would buy monthly instalments of the novel chiefly because of the pictures. But Dickens' writing was so superb that *The Pickwick Papers* became a nationwide sensation, catapulting its author to fame.

He had married Catherine Hogarth (1816–79) in 1836 on the prospects of *Pickwick*, and in 1837 the first of their ten children was born. Dickens moved into a house at 48 Doughty Street, London (which is now maintained as a museum to Dickens). He wrote a number of novels very quickly, often writing two at once, and issued them in monthly or weekly instalments. *OLIVER TWIST* (1837–8) and *Nicholas Nickleby* (1838–9) were both big successes, and *The Old Curiosity Shop* (1840–1) became something of a craze. People followed the instalments in much the same way, and with the same passion, that they follow soap operas today; in *Curiosity Shop*, for instance, people thronged the docks in New York as the ship came in carrying the latest instalment of the novel, shouting to people aboard to tell them what had happened in the tale.

A historical novel, *Barnaby Rudge* (1841–2), followed. Dickens' next novel, *Martin Chuzzlewit* (1843–4), was less successful, but 1843 saw the first of his famous 'Christmas Stories', *A Christmas Carol*. Most present-day critics see the next novel, *Dombey and Son* (1846–8) as marking a change in Dickens' career. Where before he had been content to be a popular entertainer, after *Dombey* he concentrated increasingly on writing complex works of literary art. His popularity continued to grow, but the later novels DAVID COPPERFIELD (1849–50), *Bleak House* (1852–3), *Hard Times* (1854) and *Little Dorrit* (1855–7) are more complex and sophisticated, as well as being more serious, than the earlier, jollier works. In the 1850s Dickens started editing a weekly journal called HOUSEHOLD WORDS, which increased his audience still further. Although his public life was going from strength to strength, his private life was less happy; he separated from his wife Catherine in 1858, after more than 20 years of marriage, and began a secret relationship with a beautiful young actress called Ellen Ternan (1839–1914). He was now living in a large house in the country, Gad's Hill in Kent. His next novel, *Great Expectations* (1860–1) is considered by some to be his best work. But his health was failing, partly because he refused to live life at anything except the most rapid and energetic pace. He undertook several series of public readings from his novels that were highly successful, although exhausting for Dickens himself. *Our Mutual Friend* was issued in monthly instalments between 1864 and 1865. He began writing his fourteenth novel, *The Mystery of Edwin Drood*, in 1870 and completed about half of it before he died, suddenly, of a stroke. He was 58.

It is difficult to overstate the centrality and importance of Dickens to the Victorian literary scene, to the development of the novel as a whole and of popular culture. An entertainer of genius he was also the most stylistically and formally gifted writer in English for centuries.

Further reading

The Oxford Reader's Companion to Dickens (1999) by Paul Schlicke.

Disraeli, Benjamin (1804–1881)   This entry is divided between Disraeli's political and literary life.

Political   Disraeli came from a financially secure middle-class family of Italian Jewish extraction. He grew up in London, but elected not to go to Oxford University (having been baptised into the Anglican faith his Jewishness would have been no bar) instead pursuing a career in the law. After working for a time as a clerk in a solicitor's office he tried, in 1824, to make a fortune for himself in the city. Some speculators were investing heavily in South American states, and Disraeli became involved in this world; when the market crashed in 1825 he incurred large debts that were to trouble him for many years. In 1825, he teamed up with the publisher John Murray (1778–1843) to establish a right-wing daily newspaper called *The Representative*. Conceived as a rival to *The Times*, this project collapsed soon after being set up. Disraeli published his first novel *Vivian Grey* anonymously in 1826 to pay off some of the debts incurred by this failure, but the success of the book encouraged him to write a continuation in 1827. Other reasonably successful literary work followed in the 1820s and early 1830s, and Disraeli spent 1830–1 in lengthy travels around the Mediterranean and Near East. His political ambitions led him to fight, unsuccessfully, two by-elections in Wycombe, Buckinghamshire (1832), one in Marylebone (1833) and one more in Taunton (1835); only in this last case was he an official Tory candidate. In 1837 he was finally elected MP for Maidstone, Kent. His maiden speech, however, underscored the hostility of many people to him as a flamboyantly dressed, extrovert outsider: he was shouted down by fellow MPs, and forced to abandon his speech. 'Though I sit down now,' he concluded, 'the time will come when you will hear me' (Partington, 1992: 246).

In 1839 he married the wealthy Mary Anne Lewis (1792–1872), whose husband had died the previous year. Despite this financial good fortune, Disraeli's extravagant lifestyle meant that he owed various creditors as much as £30,000 in 1841. His energy and political vision, however, was paying off in the House of Commons. In the early 1840s, he inaugurated the movement that became known as Young England, initially as an umbrella for all youthful Tories and without a specific ideological programme, although later the movement became more of a vehicle for Disraeli's own Romantic, nostalgic 'One England' nationalism. He split with Robert Peel (Tory Prime Minister, 1841–6) over the issue of repealing the Corn Laws. By supporting the continuation of these Laws in 1846 Disraeli courted popularity with the important agricultural component of the party. Although the Corn Laws were repealed nevertheless, Tory disaffection with Peel compelled him to resign.

The fall of Peel, however, ushered in two decades of Liberal dominance of British politics: Liberal Prime Ministers were in power from 1846 to 1865 with only two brief interludes of (minority) Conservative government. Lord Derby (1826–93) became effective leader of the party, but Disraeli led the party in the Commons; and with Derby's retirement in 1868 on grounds of ill-health it was Disraeli who became Prime Minister. In the interim he had been largely responsible for turning around the fortunes of the Conservatives, partly by seizing the initiative on the question of Parliamentary Reform, so that the Tories went from being an unpopular anti-Reform party to sponsoring the most significant Reform Act of 1867. Disraeli's ideological position in the 1860s and 1870s sometimes seems contradictory: he vigorously supported the Empire, although on occasion he had referred to British colonies as 'a millstone round our necks' (quoted in Jenkins, 1996: 73); he supported the established Church of England and opposed Irish home rule ('in internal politics,' he wrote in 1861, 'there is only one question now, the maintenance of the Church' (Jenkins, 1996: 69)) despite his continuing attachment to his Jewish heritage. In his novel *Tancred* (1847) he asserts that Christianity is nothing if it is not Judaism completed.

The election of November/December 1868, and its resounding Liberal victory, meant that Disraeli had been Prime Minister for only ten months; but throughout the following six years he displayed a genius for opposition, attacking GLADSTONE on financial, foreign policy and personal fronts ('you behold,' he told the House of Commons in 1872, gesturing to the government front bench, 'a range of exhausted volcanoes'), accusing the Liberals of seeking to disintegrate the Empire. In the 1874 election Disraeli brought the Conservatives their first majority government in decades. His second term as Prime Minister saw him supporting a range of reforms on factory, housing and trades union law. In 1875 he arranged the purchase of the Suez Canal for Britain. In 1876, in increasing ill-health and losing his ability to dazzle the Commons, Disraeli accepted ennoblement as the first Earl of Beaconsfield. Gladstone's Liberals won the election of 1880 with a large majority. Lord Beaconsfield, as he now was, continued as leader of the Conservative Party, but died a year later.

Disraeli's contribution to the Conservative Party was partly practical and partly ideological. Practically speaking, he brought the party, in the 1870s, out of the doldrums of opposition and gave it the experience and appetite for power (it was in government for most of the 1890s and for large portions of the twentieth century). Ideologically Disraeli's blend of sentimental nationalism, traditional identity of party with Church and Crown and jingoistic enthusiasm for Imperial expansion gave the Tories a consistent set of political principles that lasted well into the twentieth century.

Literary Disraeli's father was Isaac D'Israeli (1766–1848), a literary historian and anthologist: his six volumes of *Curiosities of Literature* (published between 1791 and 1834) were highly diverting anthologies of quotation and literary history, and remained popular throughout the century. Young Benjamin experimented in a variety of literary forms, including poetry, verse-drama, satire and prose writing of various length, but apart from his unsuccessful and uncompleted epic poem *The Revolutionary Epic* (the first three books only were published in 1834) it is as a novelist that he established a major literary reputation. His first novel was *Vivian Grey* (1826), a SILVER-FORK romance of fashionable contemporary aristocratic life in which Disraeli's own young life is reworked in a much more romanticised, fanciful form as literature. It was so popular that Disraeli wrote and published a continuation in 1827, and although he later dismissed it as 'puerile' it is far from dull. Three similar novels followed, *The Young Duke* (1831), *Contarini Fleming* (1832) and *Alroy* (1833); in all, the main character is a sensitive, idealistic young man, and the treatment is romantic and colourful. *A Year at Hartlebury, or the Election* (1834) appeared pseudonymously; it was probably written by Disraeli together with his sister Sarah, but he was so successful at suppressing knowledge of his authorship that it was only discovered to be his by scholars in 1979. The eponymous heroine of *Henrietta Temple* (1837) falls in love with a rather implausibly marvellous young nobleman of an ancient and now reduced Catholic line. *Venetia* (1837) is based only loosely on the later life of Byron;

the brilliant poet Marmion separates from his traditional English bride Lady Annabel Herbert, goes off to America where he becomes a general in the American revolutionary army, and afterwards lives in Italy. His daughter Venetia comes to Italy with her mother and effects a reconciliation between them. These early works are often gushing and sometimes over-written, but they carry off a sentimentalised romanticism with brio.

Disraeli's became an MP for the first time in 1837, and the new workload reduced his output of fiction. He published a verse-play, *The Tragedy of Count Alarcos* (1839), in which the villainous count of the title schemes against and eventually murders his virtuous wife (it was first performed in 1868, when Disraeli was Prime Minister). The three novels by which Disraeli was best known are: *Coningsby* (1844), Sybil (1845) and *Tancred, or The New Crusade* (1847). All three are political novels, and to a certain extent they function as propaganda for Disraeli's Young England beliefs. But they are also powerful and effective pieces of fiction, and John Sutherland is of the opinion that *Sybil* 'contains the most graphic depictions of working-class wretchedness to be found anywhere in the Victorian novel' (Sutherland, 1988: 188). *Coningsby* is a *roman-à-clef* following the career of the protagonist, through various vicissitudes, into Parliament. *Sybil* is a 'condition of England' novel, whose virtuous young Tory hero disguises himself to travel amongst the poorest of society, and which culminates in the violence of a Chartist riot. *Tancred*, although also addressing contemporary social problems, is more mystical-religious in form; its hero is a young English aristocrat who travels to the Middle East and has a conversation with God, via His 'Angel of Arabia', in Sinai, afterwards becoming caught up in the wars of the region. *Tancred's* message is one of the unification of Judaism and Christianity, to be symbolised by the hero's marriage with the beautiful Jewess Eva, although this last union does not happen in the novel. Disraeli later said that he wrote this 'Young England' trilogy because he believed that it was his best way of influencing public opinion to accept his political views; and although the political minutiae and ideological slant are sometimes indigestible there is much more to these books than mere propaganda.

He published no more fiction for over 20 years, devoting his energies increasingly to his political life. His next novel, *Lothair* (1870), again took an English aristocratic, idealistic hero with political ambitions through a series of circumstances, this time associated with Protestant–Catholic relations and Garibaldi's military campaign to unify Italy. Although reviewers were not impressed the book was an enormous popular success, going through eight editions in 1870 alone. This popularity owed much to the lightness of Disraeli's wit. The 'Lothair-mania' that swept Britain and the USA, and the 1870 collected edition of all of Disraeli's novels, re-ignited his literary reputation, which in part explains the unprecedentedly large advance of £10,000 that Longman paid for *Endymion* (1880). This novel revisits the 1830s and 1840s in vividly realised historical style, but again describes a sensitive, well-bred young hero who follows a winding narrative path to political success. Only a few chapters of Disraeli's last novel, *Falconet* (the title character, a humourless but driven politician, was a fictionalisation of Gladstone), were completed before his death in 1881. Disraeli's pleasant witticism 'when I want to read a novel, I write one' may have been uttered on the publication of *Daniel Deronda* (1876), but equally may be apocryphal appropriation from an 1878 edition of Punch (*see* Partington, 1992: 249, 531).

Further reading

Disraeli and Victorian Conservatism (1996) by Terence Jenkins.

Dodgson, Charles Lutwidge. *See* Lewis Carroll.

Domestic fiction   A type of Victorian novel focusing, as its name suggests, on family life, the home, ordinary life and ordinary drama. John Sutherland argues that it is 'scarcely a "school"' so much as 'a well defined anti-type, which gave the Sensation novelists of the 1860s a sense of their identity' (Sutherland, 1988: 192–3). Nonetheless the large number of Domestic novels attests to their continuing popularity throughout the Victorian period: Trollope's *Barchester* series (from *The Warden*, 1855, to the *Last Chronicle of Barset*, 1867) avoided the melodramatic excess of 'good hero versus evil villain' found in many other novels. Many writers specialised in Domestic tales, amongst them the prolific Charlotte Yonge (1823–1901) and Margaret Oliphant (1828–97), whose many-volumed 'Chronicles of Carlingford' are set, like the *Barchester* series, in a quiet provincial town. The great masterpiece of un-sensational Domestic fiction is certainly Eliot's *Middlemarch* (1872).

Doyle, Arthur Conan (1859–1930)   Doyle's education (at Stoneyhurst public school and Edinburgh University) prepared him for a career as a doctor, and he practised medicine from 1882 to 1890 before his literary pursuits became remunerative enough for him to devote himself solely to writing. His first success was *A Study in Scarlet* (1887), a short novel introducing the super-cerebral mystery-solver Sherlock Holmes. Another Holmes story, *The Sign of Four*, followed in 1890: many critics regard this as the archetypal Holmes tale – a mystery surrounding an attractive young woman, her vanished father and mysterious gifts of pearls. Holmes acts as unofficial detective, using his own distinctive (and, strictly speaking, flawed) logical deductive approach (in Chapter 6 he states his famous dictum: 'when you have eliminated the impossible, whatever remains, *however improbable*, must be the truth'). Other Holmes novels followed, although the bulk of the 'Sherlock Holmes' work was published as short fiction in the *Strand* magazine. Although the works were (and remain) extraordinarily popular, Doyle himself quickly grew tired of the character. He wrote Sensation fiction (such as *The Mystery of Cloomber*, 1888), and historical novels (*Micah Clarke*, 1889, and *The White Company*, 1891). When the public still clamoured for Holmes, Doyle killed the character off in 1893, although he later brought him back, improbably, to life in 1901. His writing career continued prolifically into the twentieth century.

Drama   For some students of the history of British theatre the Victorian age is a null period, between the vigorous eighteenth-century tradition that produced Sheridan (1751–1816) and the twentieth-century renaissance in British theatre. Theatre was massively popular throughout the period, both as 'serious' entertainment for discerning playgoers, and as mass entertainment (melodrama, music hall and travelling shows). But few plays written in the nineteenth century are still performed today, and not until Wilde's and George Bernard Shaw's (1856–1950) plays in the late 1880s and 1890s did writers of theatrical genius appear. It is not immediately clear why this should be. Shaw himself (in the theatre reviews collected in *Our Theatre in the Nineties*) attacked the artificiality of Victorian stage-plays, their removal from real-life concerns. In a way, Victorian theatre is at its best when this artificiality is pushed to its extremes, as is the case in melodrama – Jerrold's *Black-Ey'd Susan* (1829), for instance, was popular throughout the period, and still stirs a response today. The more highbrow dramas of the period too often seem stolid and constipated. Browning's failed attempts at verse-drama in Shakespearean mould are like this: *Strafford* (1837), *King Victor and King Charles* (1842), *A Blot on the 'Scutcheon* (1843) are all dreadful.

One reason why the serious theatre suffered during the period had to do with the licensing laws. In effect British theatre was under the strict control and censorship of the Lord Chamberlain (a member of the royal household). Following a 'Licensing Act' of 1737 only Drury Lane Theatre and Covent Garden in London (plus the Haymarket in summer) were permitted to stage serious 'spoken' drama. The 1843 Theatre Regulation Act relaxed this restriction (and in fact by this stage a number of other theatres had obtained royal licence, as well as there being various unlicensed theatres in the capital); but the later act gave the Lord Chamberlain greater censoring powers extending across the whole country. New plays could be performed only with his express permission and official licence. In practice the Lord Chamberlain denied licences to plays he considered seditious, obscene, irregular or in any way liable to breach the peace, and there was no appeal against his decision. This power was only repealed in 1968, and it placed serious constraints on the theatre during the Victorian period.

Some of the traditions of the Victorian stage resulted from these official restraints. During the nineteenth century a number of 'song and supper' clubs had grown up, where patrons dined whilst being entertained by variety of musical and comedy numbers; since these establishments were not producing 'serious theatre' they did not need to be licensed. In the nineteenth century this form of entertainment had grown in popularity: 'melodrama' (a name that means literally 'musical-drama') and 'music hall' (the first purpose-built music hall opened in Lambeth in 1852) enjoyed great success.

This emphasis on comedy and entertainment found expression in a theatre of sensation: Astley's Amphitheatre presented equestrian performances; Sadler's Wells had a large water tank in which naval battles were re-enacted. The technologies of stage craft advanced considerably during the period, but the plays themselves were often mere excuses for spectacular action or special effects. Fans of modern-day Hollywood cinema know, perhaps, whereof I speak.

Another technical change of great importance was the improved forms of lighting available to theatre producers. In the eighteenth century productions had been mostly candlelit; unsatisfactory in terms of glare, heat and the impossibility of focusing or directing candlelight effectively, not to mention the fire hazard. The 1820s saw the introduction of gaslit theatres, and in the 1830s limelight was developed by the actor-manager William Macready (1793–1873) and actor Charles Kean (1790–1833): by burning a stick of lime in a jet of flammable gas the director could direct a single bright beam onto an individual character or feature on the stage. A whole new range of stage effects became possible.

One thing that the nineteenth-century theatrical climate did cultivate was great acting, especially if one considers great acting to be acting larger than life. Shakespeare was a perennial, as were literary adaptations of novels by SCOTT, DICKENS and other current bestsellers. Translations from continental plays were also very popular. Indeed, the career of possibly the most important Victorian playwright, Dion Boucicault (1820–90), enjoyed an early success with an adaptation of a French play, *The Corsican Brothers* (1852). Boucicault is the author, or adapter, of some 200 play titles. Tom Taylor (1817–80), another successful figure on the mid-Victorian stage, explored some social issues in his *The Ticket of Leave Man* (1863), although the play was still recognisably melodramatic. Victorian comedies of manners, such as *Money* (1840) by Edward Bulwer-Lytton (1803–73), or the elegant and controlled plays of Thomas Robertson (1829–71) – such as *Ours* (1866), *Caste* (1867) and *M.P.* (1870) – provide a theatrical experience more in tune with much contemporary taste, and occupy a position in the development of Restoration and eighteenth-century comedies through to the wit of Wilde. Arthur Wing Pinero (1855–1934) began writing farces, but moved on to well-made plays of social comedy, such as the enduring *The Second Mrs Tanqueray* (1893).

Further reading

Theatre in the Victorian Age (1991) by Michael Booth.

Dramatic monologue A mode of poetry distinctively Victorian. A poem is said to be a dramatic monologue if its implied speaker is evidently not the poet – for instance, if he or she is a historical character (the 'dramatic' part), and if other speakers or auditors are only implied in the speaker's words, rather than having lines of their own (the 'monologue' part) – if another speaker is present the poem is, strictly, a duologue, or perhaps even a portion of a play. Both TENNYSON and BROWNING are credited with inventing the form in the 1830s, although critics identify precursors to the form in a number of works (for instance, Thomas Gray's 'The Bard' (1757) or Robert Burns' 'Holy Willie's Prayer' (1799)). Tennyson's dramatic monologues, such as 'Ulysses' and

'Tithonus' (both composed in 1833, and published in 1842 and 1860 respectively) are striking and beautiful, but it is Browning who most brilliantly explored the potential of the form. Most of his best-known shorter poems are dramatic monologues, and collections such as *Dramatic Romances and Lyrics* (1845) and MEN AND WOMEN (1855) are exclusively made up of the form. An early example, 'My Last Duchess' (1842), demonstrates the supple ambiguities the mode opens up. The speaker of this poem is a sixteenth-century Italian duke; his silent interlocutor is an ambassador from another nobleman, with whom the duke is discussing his own future marriage. In the poem the duke shows this person a portrait of his previous wife, the 'Last Duchess' of the title. Boasting of the excellence of the portrait, the duke elaborates the reasons for the special Mona Lisa-esque expression on the duchess's face. The smile, he confides, came to her lips not only when her husband was present, but for all sorts of reasons: not only 'my favor', but 'the dropping of the daylight in the West,/The bough of cherries some officious fool/Broke in the orchard for her, the white mule/She rode with . . .' (ll. 25–9). This offended the haughty duke's ancient pride. 'This grew,' he says. 'I gave commands;/Then all smiles stopped together'. After thus recalling having (presumably) ordered his wife's death, the speaker goes on with startling coolness to point out another work of art, a statue of Neptune, to the ambassador with whom he is negotiating for another marriage. Critics have produced dozens of varying interpretations of this poem, analysing the duke's admissions as evidence of stupidity, of Machiavellian cunning, of the staging of Power, and many other things. Contemporary critics have pointed out how dramatic monologues position the reader between *sympathy* for the speaker (because you have to enter into an empathetic relation with him or her to understand the poem) and *judgement* (so that we do not, for instance, endorse the duke's attitude to murder). It is this ironic possibility, the open-ended nature of dramatic monologues, the way they involve the reader in interpretative exercise, that has given the form such longevity: most twentieth-century poets have written dramatic monologues, to the point perhaps that outside the 'confessional school' (and even, arguably, there too) the dramatic monologue has become the chief mode of the short poem today.

Further reading

The Poetry of Experience (1957; reprinted 1963) by Robert Langbaum.

Dreyfus Affair   A scandal that polarised French political opinion in the 1890s. Alfred Dreyfus (1859–1935), a military officer on the French general staff, was suspected of passing military secrets to the Germans. Convicted by a secret court martial in 1894 he was sent to an appalling prison on Devil's Island. Friends, amongst them the novelist Émile Zola (1840–1902), believed him innocent, and insisted that suspicion had fallen on him only because he was Jewish. Anti-Dreyfusards insisted that the honour of the army was closely connected with the honour of France, and that these two concerns took precedence over everything else. Dreyfus received an amnesty in 1898 after evidence emerged confirming his innocence, but he was not legally exonerated until 1906. The split between Dreyfusards and Anti-Dreyfusards exposed the rift between reactionary ANTI-SEMITES and more liberal reformers, revealing the dominance of the former party through most European countries.

E

Earthly Paradise: a Poem, The (1868–1870), by William Morris   Morris's masterpiece is made up of 25 separate long poems, amounting to 42,681 lines of poetry in all – the longest poem published in the nineteenth century. It was modelled on Geoffrey Chaucer's unfinished *Canterbury Tales* (*c*.1380–1400). As in that medieval classic, some of the tales are in heroic or octosyllabic couplets, some in stanzaic form, and the whole thing concludes with an envoi to Chaucer. But the work is not merely derivative: Morris works through his guiding influence to create a poem with a degree of self-conscious old-fashioned English narrative, in which a northern medievalism is mirrored, poem for poem, with a luminous classical Greek mood. Morris himself played up the nostalgic, escapist element in the work, such that its opening lines encourage us to:

> Forget six counties overhung with smoke,
> Forget the snorting steam and piston stroke,
> Forget the spreading of the hideous town;
> Think rather of the pack-horse on the down,
> And dream of London, small and white and clean,
> The clear Thames bordered by its gardens green.

(Book 1, ll. 1–6)

In fact, this poem is not the work of an 'idle singer of an empty day' (Morris's self-characterisation), but a much more complex, elegiac and melancholic poem about the impossibility of the ideal world of its title.

A prologue called 'The Wanderers' describes how a company of thirteenth-century Norsemen arrive at a 'nameless city . . . white as the changing walls of faerie', a haven of Ancient Greek culture somewhere in the Mediterranean, where the Olympian gods are still worshipped. Before the Elder of the City the wanderers tell of how they left Scandinavia fleeing an outbreak of the plague, hoping to reach the fabled Earthly

Paradise 'across the western sea where none grow old'. Their fruitless search had taken many years and had left them 'old and grey/Before our time'. The Elder of the City invites them to spend the rest of their days on the island.

Twice a month the Norsemen and the Greeks meet at a great banquet, and a representative from each people tells a tale; the tales of the former being based on Norse mythology and those of the latter on Greek. Morris divides the rest of the poem into 12 months, from March to February, introduces each section with a brief lyric section, and relates each tale. These tales are integrated to the time of year, from the cheerfulness of spring to the tragic cast of winter, and then back again to spring narratives:

March. Atalanta's Race; The Man Born to be King
April. The Doom of King Acrisus; The Proud King
May. The Story of Cupid and Psyche; The Writing on the Image
June. The Love of Alcestis; The Lady of the Land
July. The Son of Croesus; The Watching of the Falcon
August. Pygmalion and the Image; Ogier the Dane.
September. The Death of Paris; The Land East of the Sun and West of the Moon
October. Acontius and Cydippe; The Man Who Never Laughed Again
November. The Story of Rhodope; The Lovers of Gudrun
December. The Golden Apples; The Fostering of Aslaug
January. Bellerophon at Argos; The Ring Given To Venus
February. Bellerophon in Lycia (a sequel to January's *Bellerophon at Argos*);
    The Hill of Venus

In an epilogue we are told that the wanderers lived peacefully until their death, and the narrator concludes by saying that 'all these images of love and pain/Wrought as the year did wax, perfect, and wane' are now 'cold':

> And thou, O tale of what these sleepers were,
> Wish one good-night to them thou holdest dear,
> Then die thyself, and let us go our ways,
> And live awhile amid these latter days!

Morris's verse is stately and melodic, its metrical patterning so regular that some critics find it monotonous. But monotony is part of the point, the sort of beautiful stasis that all nostalgia implies, or the harmonic repetition of waves sounding on a shore. What Morris does best is evoke the gorgeous agony of loss, and many of his most effective tales blend a Romantic descriptive power with elegiac content.

October's second tale, 'The Man Who Never Laughed Again', is a case in point. The protagonist, Bharam, has lost all his wealth and is despondent; an old friend, Firuz, comes across him, and invites him back to a spectacular hidden palace, where six other miserable men live. Bharam is offered the chance to oversee this mansion whilst these men pine away and die, on the understanding that when they are all dead he can take the house's treasure and return to the real world wealthy. Firuz also gives him a key, the secret (it seems) behind the misery of the seven. After they have all died Bharam returns to the city with his money, but he cannot quell his curiosity as to the root of the men's unhappiness. Returning to the mansion he unlocks an iron door in the garden and passes into an underworld kingdom; there, beside the sea, he sees a black barge approach and two beautiful women invite him to come with them. They sail over the sea to a green, paradisical land:

> Upon the green slopes Bharam could behold
> The white tents and the spears of many men,
> And on the o'erhanging height a castle old,
> And up the bay a ship o'erlaid with gold,
> With golden sails and fluttering banners bright,
> And silken awnings 'gainst the hot sun dight.

Bharam's eyes are wet 'with happy tears' as he approaches the queen of this fair land and declares his love. He lives two years in that place, after which the queen departs for a hundred days, telling him not to look in a certain room; but in his loneliness he does so, and the punishment for his curiosity robs him of his paradise. He returns to our world as 'The Man Who Ne'er Shall Laugh Again'. The tropes here of a retreat from our world into an old-fashioned paradise, of the inevitability of fate and the unavoidable misery of deprivation are common throughout many of the tales. Overall, 'The Earthly Paradise' suggests a tragic trajectory: we may be tantalised with a glimpse of possible paradise in this world, but in most cases it will be taken away from us, and our lot will be only yearning. In the longest of the tales, November's 'The Lovers of Gudrun', Bodli and Kiartan both love the beautiful Gudrun, and although Bodli wins her hand she feels more for Kiartan. When, after a complex narrative, Bodli kills his friend, his remorse is all-consuming: 'And such a storm of grief on him did fall. . . . That men for shame must turn away their eyes,/Nor seem to see a great man fallen so low'. But, should this give the impression that Morris's poem is in any sense grim or dowdy it should be emphasised that at every point the superb verse fills the whole with a brimming, luminous beauty.

Economic cycles (or 'depressions')   The pre-Keynesian British economy suffered pronounced cyclical highs and lows, and economic depression occurred repeatedly throughout Victoria's reign causing very genuine hardship and human misery. Richard Brown argues that the two chief influences on economic wellbeing were harvests and wars, with agriculture as the 'largest single component':

> Harvests affected the economy as a whole in different ways. Their effect was
> most obvious on purchasing power. Poor harvests pushed the price of food up
> and depressed the purchasing power of most of the population for other

> goods . . . poor harvests were often followed by slumps in manufacturing industries.

(Brown, 1991: 261–2)

Immediately after the end of the Napoleonic Wars the economy dipped into recession through 1819, but by 1821 a recovery was evident and Britain saw a boom through the latter 1820s and early 1830s. Between 1836 and 1842 the economy crashed, with a crisis in industry and investment exacerbated by two years of poor harvest in 1838 and 1839. The first years of the 1840s saw widespread hardship and misery. 'The hungry forties' (as the decade became known) were characterised by high levels of unemployment, and associated starvation and distress. Working class disaffection manifested itself through the popularity of CHARTIST movements, and literature's 'Condition of England' fiction described the consequences of the poverty. Harvests on the mainland of Britain improved early in the decade, although economic recovery took several years longer. In Ireland, however, a blight specific to the potato harvest had devastating consequences; for a population that depended upon the potato as a staple the partial failure of the crop in 1845 and the general failure in 1846 had appalling consequences. Famine was widespread, especially through the winter of 1846/7. A million died of hunger, a million more emigrated, chiefly to the United States – writing such a sentence with its inevitably blasé use of such large numbers seems almost impertinent, riding as it does over almost unimaginable human suffering. It took the Irish economy many decades to recover.

Generally speaking, and despite the expense and mismanagement of the Crimean War, the economy grew rapidly through the 1850s. The next downturn occurred in the 1860s. War – the American Civil War, and a confederate trade embargo – was behind the COTTON PANIC, or 'Cotton Famine', of 1861–64; the English textile industry in the north of the country suffered severe unemployment and reduced hours for those in work. Depression spread to the general economy a few years later, with bad harvests in 1865 and 1866, and a series of high-profile bankruptcies in the powerful London financial houses of Overend and Gurney. But the period from the end of the 1860s to 1873 represented 'one of the most frantic booms of the nineteenth century both in the international and the British economy' (Feuchtwanger, 1985: 112). After the boom, bust: by the mid-1870s the economy had collapsed again. Some economic historians refer to the long stretch of time from 1873 to 1896 as the 'Great Depression'; although others have argued that this oversimplified a volatile period of occasional growth and more pronounced reverses. Certainly the agricultural world saw a succession of poor harvests between 1873 and 1879; international imports prevented the price of food from rising, and caused hardship to many farmers and the workers they employed. Other sectors of the economy fluctuated up and down, but the agricultural sector continued depressed; over the last quarter of the century land values, rents and rural wages had all fallen by about 20 per cent. Thomas HARDY's *Tess of the*

D'Urbervilles (1891) gives some flavour of what it was like to be on the sharp end of this slump.

Further reading

Society and Economy in Modern Britain 1700–1850 (1991) by Richard Brown.

Education   School education in the period varied sharply with different classes. Prior to the 1870 Education Act there was no nationwide or state provision for education. For the wealthy there were a number of elite so-called 'public schools', of which the most ancient were Eton, Harrow, Rugby, Winchester, Westminster, Shrewsbury, Merchant Taylors', St Paul's and Charterhouse. There were also a larger number of so-called 'grammar schools', also fee-charging, and spread throughout the country. The education that boys (not girls) received at these institutions was grounded in the classics (Latin and to a lesser extent Ancient Greek language and literature) and in sport, but the underlying principle was expressed by Herbert Spencer (1820–1903) in 1850 when he declared that 'education has for its object the formation of character' (Spencer, *Social Statics* (1850), Part 4 Chapter 30). At a public school in particular a boy learned modes of gentlemanly behaviour and self-confidence, as well as establishing connections and networks that would serve him well in adult life. As the century proceeded, the educational aspect of public school life came more to the fore, particularly under the influence of Thomas Arnold (1795–1842), whose headmastership of Rugby School from 1828 onwards transformed that establishment into a morally serious and disciplined institution with a greater emphasis on intellectual attainment. With Arnold's example as inspiration many Victorian schools had changed by mid-century, and many new schools were formed. Modern scholar John R. Reed estimates that there were 500 private schools in the later period, of which between 60 and 100 could realistically claim the more 'exalted' public school status.

> The public school served only a tiny proportion of the age group (they had only about 7,500 students in 1865 and 20,000 in 1890), but their graduates dominated admission to Oxbridge, ordination to the clergy, entry into the professions, officerships in the army, posts in politics, and appointments in the imperial and domestic civil services.

> (Reed, 1999: 201)

This was a situation that did not change much throughout the twentieth century in Britain. For those not wealthy enough to afford an education at this level the options were limited. Many working-class children, perhaps as many as two-thirds, received no education at all beyond occasional attendance at a religiously sponsored 'Sunday school', and sometimes not even this; literacy levels were low. A small number of 'charity' schools, sometimes called 'model schools', had been established by PHILANTHROPISTS, and in the countryside education was sometimes to be found in 'dame schools', often run by a single elderly woman who had sole pedagogic responsibility for all her charges. In the city children might attend what was called 'ragged school', at which a very rudimentary education was available for a nominal fee, usually a penny or a few pence. In all these cases the education was what we today would call 'primary', covering little more than basic reading, writing and arithmetic (facetiously known as 'the three Rs'); working-class children were expected to start paid work at the age of ten, or even earlier. DICKENS, who approved of the idea of ragged schools, worried at their manifold insufficiencies, calling them 'a slight and ineffectual palliative of an enormous evil. They want system, power, means, authority, experienced and thoroughly trained teachers' (Dickens, 'Boys to Mend', HOUSEHOLD WORDS (11 September 1852)). One main problem was a lack of teachers; single adults might have responsibility for several hundred pupils, a charge they managed by appointing certain pupils as 'monitors'. In 1846 a 'pupil-teacher' scheme was inaugurated, whereby certain pupils received training and practice in teaching during their own schooldays, eventually acquiring a government certificate of competence, opening the path to a career as a teacher. In Dickens' *Our Mutual Friend* (1864–5), the schoolteacher Bradley Headstone picks out Charley Hexam to be a pupil-teacher.

The educational opportunities for girls were even more limited. Working-class girls might receive ragged school education; middle-class girls would not usually go to secondary school, but might receive personal tuition at home, perhaps from a governess. Activists such as Frances Buss (1827–94) and Dorothea Beale (1831–1906) campaigned for the establishment of girls' private schools, and the eventual passage through Parliament of the Endowed Schools Act (1869) enabled the setting up of many academic high schools for girls in the later decades of the century.

The situation at university level was similar. For working-class men and women, as the ambitious but doomed Jude Fawley discovers in HARDY's JUDE THE OBSCURE, university was simply not an option. At the start of the century, only Oxford and Cambridge Universities provided tertiary educational opportunities in England and Wales, although there were a number of ancient universities in Scotland. The educational bias was towards classics at Oxford and mathematics at Cambridge, although in both places the education provided was fundamentally religious and Anglican: students and fellows were required to accede to the XXXIX ARTICLES, and fellows had to remain unmarried and to take holy orders in the Church of England. In 1828 University College was founded in London to provide a university education to NONCONFORMISTS; this institution joined with King's College in 1836 to create the University of London, and after the 1850s universities were founded in a number of other British cities (for instance, the University of Wales was founded in 1878). As the century progressed, university education became more comprehensive, particularly with the inclusion of SCIENCE on the curriculum. The merits and possibility of female university education was debated throughout the century; TENNYSON's early long poem *The Princess* (1847) concerns the establishment of a women-only university, but only in terms of fairy-tale and ultimate impossibility. Oxford and Cambridge established women's colleges in the 1870s (Sommerville and Lady Margaret Hall at the former, Girton and Newnham at the latter), but their students were not permitted to graduate with a university degree until the twentieth century; indeed, the first woman in the British Empire to graduate with a university degree was a New Zealander, in 1877.

Electoral reform. *See* **Reform Act 1832**, **Reform Act 1867**, **Reform Act 1884–1885**.

Elegy   Elegy is an ancient literary genre, with roots in Classical Greek and Roman literature. English elegy modelled itself closely on these classical roots, with works such as Milton's *Lycidas* (1637) plangently and elegantly expressing the grief felt at the death of a friend. The Romantic period produced some of the most powerful elegies in the language, including Shelley's (1792–1822) beautiful *Adonais* (1821) written on the death of John Keats (1795–1821). One enormous elegy dominates the Victorian literary scene: Tennyson's *In Memoriam* (1851), in one sense the defining poem of the age. Queen Victoria, grieving after the death of Albert, kept a copy of Tennyson's work beside her bed to console her. As elegy the poem works grief and its pain into a complex lyric meditation on religious doubt and certitude. Other elegies from the century are perhaps less complex, but several achieve great beauty. Arnold wrote 'Thyrsis' 'to Commemorate' as the poem's subtitle says, 'the Author's Friend, Arthur Hugh Clough who Died at Florence, 1861'. This pastoral elegy connects Clough with the 'dreaming spires' of Oxford (l. 19), and records Arnold's own depression, 'the heart less bounding at emotion new,/And hope, once crushed, less quick to spring again' (l. 139–40). Swinburne's elegy on the death of the French poet Charles Baudelaire (1821–67), 'Ave Atque Vale' (1878), lacked the personal intimacy of these other Victorians elegies, in that its author had never known its subject, but captures a moving tone nonetheless. Hopkins' 'Wreck of the Deutschland' (written in 1876, although not published until 1918) can also be considered elegy, although the five Franciscan nuns whose deaths it marks were not personally known to Hopkins and are not even named in the work.

Eliot, George (Mary Ann, or Marian, Evans) (1819–1880)   Evans was born in Warwickshire as 'Mary Anne', the daughter of a land agent; which is to say, a family in the upper register of respectable working class. She spent a mostly happy rural childhood, extremely close to her older brother Isaac. At school, she became a convert to Evangelicalism and studied theology in depth; running the family house for her father on her mother's death in 1836. Her friendship with Charles Bray (1811–84), a Coventry manufacturer, weaned her from conventional Evangelicalism and onto a more independent-minded blend of Christianity and free-thinking. Mary Ann, as she now called herself, consequently refused to attend church with her father, which caused friction. In 1844 a publisher approached her to translate Strauss's *Das Leben Jesu*, a detailed study and critique of the Biblical life of Christ by a German scholar. Her translation of this massive work (1500 pages) was completed in 1846 and published without her name on the title page. Her father's death in 1849 left her with a small inheritance of £90 a year. Now calling herself Marian she undertook editorial work on John Chapman's (1821–94) WESTMINSTER REVIEW, writing articles and reviews as well as steering other material through the press. The early 1850s saw an abortive love affair with Herbert Spencer (1820–1903), whom it seems could not see past her undeniably unprepossessing exterior; and 1854 saw the publication of her translation of Feuerbach's *Essence of Christianity* – it was also the year that she formed a love-partnership with George Henry Lewes (1817–78). She had met Lewes in 1851, and the two fell in love (neither of them deterred by the other's spectacular ugliness); but Lewes was already married, and although Eliot always regarded herself as married to Lewes, referring to him as her husband, the union was not legal. Her family and many of their friends shunned them for this unorthodox arrangement, but Eliot found great happiness in the union.

Lewes also encouraged her literary abilities. She wrote a number of shorter sketches, based on her childhood experience of rural life, which were gathered together as *Scenes of Clerical Life* (1858). The public and even the publisher were initially kept ignorant of the true identity and gender of 'George Eliot', the pseudonym she adopted. Encouraged by this success Eliot wrote her first novel, *Adam Bede* (1859), an enormous hit with Victorian readers. Her increasing celebrity destroyed the pretence of anonymity, but she continued writing under her pseudonym. *The Mill on the Floss* (1860) drew on Eliot's own autobiographical experiences, especially in the portrayal of the heroine Maggie Tulliver's close relationship with her brother; in real life Eliot was now estranged from Isaac. *Silas Marner* (1861), a short novel again on a rural theme, was also well received.

Her next work marked a change of direction, away from the nostalgic rural fiction by which she was mostly known. *Romola* is a complex historical novel set in Renaissance Florence; serialised in the *Cornhill Magazine* 1862–3, it earned Eliot the large sum of £10,000, and she and Lewes were able to buy a large house in St John's Wood. *Felix Holt the Radical* (1866) dramatised the contemporary anxieties surrounding the climate that led up to the REFORM ACT OF 1867. Her masterpiece, MIDDLEMARCH, appeared in eight serial instalments 1871–2. This brilliantly controlled and understated novel of ordinary life is her most assured, complex and involving work. Her final novel, *Daniel Deronda* (1874–6), was a similarly complex and ambitious, although less lucidly handled, work; its fascination with Jewishness, sympathetically rendered, did not alienate Eliot's readership and the book was extremely popular. She and Lewes moved to a larger house in the country, near Haslemere, in 1876; but Lewes died there two years later. Deeply grieving, Eliot effectively abandoned her own writing, and devoted her energies to editing her late husband's work. She married in 1880, a friendship-union with a young admirer and disciple, John Cross (1840–1920), a sincere but rather unstable man; pompously, her brother Isaac finally got back in contact with her after this wedding had 'made an honest woman' of her. Eliot was already ill of a kidney complaint, and died only a few months later.

Emigration   The perception that this process only involved the forced transportation of criminals is largely inaccurate. It is true that (between 1788 and 1853) approximately 125,000 male and 25,000 female convicts were shipped to Australia, such that in the 1820s the population of convicted settlers outnumbered free settlers by three to one; but during the 1830s this situation was progressively reversed, helped in part by bounty schemes instituted by the Colonial Office (in 1832 and 1836) that were designed actively to encourage skilled artisans to emigrate. From 1853 to 1860, 273,100 English, Scottish and Welsh emigrants chose to sail to Australia and New Zealand, and although the numbers fell a little in the 1860s (184,400) and 1870s (241,500), the 1880s saw 317,300 emigrants start new lives in Australasia. The Australian government's policy of intervention, in part to offset the great expense of so long a voyage, meant that of the 800,000 emigrants who travelled to the antipodes between 1860 and 1900, some half had received financial assistance to make the trip.

The most popular destinations for emigration were the United States and Canada, with Australasia third and South Africa fourth. Over the period 1853–1920 some four and a third million emigrants moved to the United States (a figure that does not include the very large number of Irish emigrants to the USA during this period); two and a third million people emigrated to Canada, 1.7 million to Australasia, 670,000 to South Africa and a similar number to various other destinations: a total of nearly ten million English, Scottish and Welsh people leaving the country and starting new lives overseas in the second half of the century.

Empire   'The years from 1815 to 1902,' says Andrew Porter, 'were pre-eminently "Britain's Imperial century".' Over the course of the century, Britain vastly increased the size and population of the territory, and the financial value, it owned. Porter distinguishes 'three distinct but over-lapping components' of the nineteenth-century Empire: 'an Empire of white settlement' such as Canada, Australia and South Africa; 'an Empire in India' and 'an Empire of conquests or wartime acquisitions, the "dependent empire"' (Porter, 1999: 4). In the 1840s and the 1850s British Imperial interest was mostly focused on the Indian sub-continent. But in the 1860s British Imperialism waned, with little or no new Imperial acquisition, and by 1870 the impetus towards colonialism 'appeared to be approaching a nadir'. But at the end of the 1870s there was 'a tremendous burst of imperialistic interest and activity, not only in Britain but across Europe' (Hayes, 1963: 216). There seem to have been several reasons for this apparent volte-face. In the case of Africa, which had been dominated by seven European powers for most of the century, the initiation of what is generally known as the 'scramble for Africa' by the 1879 territorial expansion into the Congo of the Belgian King Leopold II (1835–1909) spurred other European powers into similar action: Britain occupied Egypt in 1882, subdued the Sudan in 1885, occupied Uganda and 'British East Africa', and competed with the French for control of West African territories around the Niger river. A European Conference, held at Berlin in 1884, attempted to resolve this European conflict before it spilled over into European war. But the 'scramble' continued. Cecil Rhodes (1853–1902) made a fortune from South African diamonds and, motivated by an ardent Imperialism, supervised an expansion northwards into the African continent, naming the country he created Rhodesia (it is now Zimbabwe). His dream of a British-controlled spine running the whole length of East Africa 'from Cape to Cairo', was interrupted by the German seizure of 'German East Africa', and by his own premature death. By 1914 only Liberia and Abyssinia possessed even notional independence; the whole of the rest of the continent had been seized by European powers. That this 'scramble' for African lands and wealth involved enormous suffering and oppression for the native population must, of course, be kept continually in mind.

Resistance to British Imperialism in Africa came from Zulu tribes under the rule of Cetshwayo (1836–84), who defeated the British at the battle of Isandlwana, was held off with great difficulty at Rorke's Drift, and was ultimately defeated at the battle of Ulundi (all three battles took place in 1879). The Dutch 'boers' also resisted British Imperialism in the costly BOER WARS, but their opposition was eventually overcome. Speaking generally the British enjoyed military superiority in the continent. A similar situation had enabled them to hold on to India despite the INDIAN MUTINY of 1857; when DISRAELI passed the Royal Titles Act in 1876 conferring on VICTORIA the pretentious title 'Empress of India' the sub-continent was firmly in the British grasp. An Imperial control based more on carefully extorted trading rights characterised British interest in China, following the OPIUM WARS of the 1840s and 1850s, a situation cemented by the occupation of Hong Kong and the creation of trading posts under military guard in Borneo and New Guinea (1881–4). By the century's end a large fraction of the globe was under British control.

That this huge Imperial expansion happened without a concerted central push still puzzles historians; prime ministers avowedly hostile to Imperial expansion, such as GLADSTONE, nevertheless presided over a large growth in the Empire. The contemporary historian John Seeley (1834–95) published a series of lectures on this topic, *The Expansion of England* (1883):

> . . . there is something very characteristic in the indifference which we show
> towards this mighty diffusion of our race and the expansion of our state. We

seem, as it were, to have conquered and peopled half the world in a fit of absence of mind.

(Quoted in Boehmer, 1998: 74)

We think today of 'empire' as a bad thing; so, for example, Elleke Boehmer can talk with unembarrassed praise of those nineteenth-century writers who were able to 'slice open' the 'hypocrisies, peeling the sordid reality away from the inflated platitudes of empire', just as she can condemn unambiguously the 'coerciveness and oppression' upon which empire was built (Boehmer, 1998: xxiii). Yet it is a mistake to refer to 'the Empire' or 'Imperialism' as a monolithic quantity, good or bad. The British justified their Empire to themselves by comparisons with the Romans, and discourses of 'civilisation', but their practical approach to the different portions of their domain was determined as much by attitudes to RACE as to economic or cultural categories. Accordingly, the British invested heavily in INDIA, building a railway network, bridges and many other items of infrastructure where the financial return was uncertain; this was possible in part because they considered the 'Indian people' to be, racially, on a level or a little below themselves. At the same time they presided over a brutalisation of African people, and could ransack South Africa of its diamonds and gold without bad conscience, because they considered black Africans 'savages' and racially inferior by several degrees. Apologists for empire tend to concentrate on the former and ignore the latter aspects; but those antipathetic to Britain's Imperial past run the risk of simply reversing this partial sightedness.

Further reading

Empire Writing: an Anthology of Colonial Literature 1870–1918 (1998) edited by Elleke Boehmer; *Empire* (1996) by Dens Judd; *The Oxford History of the British Empire: Volume III, The Nineteenth-Century* (1999) edited by Andrew Porter.

Essays and Reviews (1860)   A collection of essays by seven theologians (six churchmen and one layman) addressing a variety of religious questions from a Broad Church, liberal perspective. The book caused a sensation. The most controversial piece was 'On the Interpretation of Scripture' by Benjamin Jowett (1817–93), master of Balliol and an ordained clergyman in the Church of England, in which he urged people 'to read Scripture like any other book'. Many Anglicans regarded the collection as offensive and even dangerous to religious orthodoxy. Anglican bishops met at Fulham and wrote a public letter condemning the book, and several bishops took matters further by instituting legal proceedings against the writers. One of the authors, Rowland Williams, was convicted of heresy by the Court of Arches (an ecclesiastical court), although the judgement was overturned by the Privy Council in 1864. A protest against the volume was signed by 11,000 clergymen and 137,000 laity, and the Convocation of the Church of England officially condemned the book. Reading the *Essays and Reviews* today, however, it is hard to see why it excited such passion.

Such questioning of scripture as the volume undertakes happens within a respectful, even pious, context, and as S.C. Carpenter puts it, 'four fifths of the actual contents of the book has since been digested into the system of the church' (quoted in Moorman, 1973: 376). But for many Victorians in the 1860s, 'essays-and-reviews' epitomised the corrosion of religious certainty and value. Robert Browning's 'Gold Hair' (1864), for instance, concludes:

> The candid include to surmise of late
> That the Christian faith proves false, I find:
> For our Essays-and-Reviews' debate
> Begins to tell on the public mind.

('Gold Hair', ll. 141–4)

Evans, Marian. *See* **George Eliot**.

Evolution   Although sometimes thought to be DARWIN's original theory, evolution had been a widespread scientific idea since the eighteenth century. French scientist Jean Baptiste de Monet, chevalier de Lamarck (1744–1829), noted the way farmers and horse-breeders encouraged selective changes in their stock over several generations. Lamarck argued that the combination of a shaping environment and an inherent will within each organism to change produced gradual alteration – he believed, for instance, that the height of the edible leaves and the desire of the giraffe to reach up to them stretched out the giraffe's neck, with each giraffe passing on this alteration to its offspring (this theory is now not generally accepted by scientists). Lamarck's colleague Georges-Louis Leclerc, Comte de Buffon (1707–88), also noted the tendency of species to alter over time, a process he called 'degradation', although he could not identify the mechanism for this change. Erasmus Darwin (1731–1802), Charles' grandfather, wrote up his observations on the gradual complexification of life in poetic form, *The Botanic Garden* (1791), although again he could not identify the mechanism involved. Throughout the nineteenth century, various forms of the 'evolution' theory were argued. Robert Chambers's (1802–71) anonymously issued *Vestiges of Creation* (1844) posited an initial creation by God of organisms that later altered and evolved. Some scientists wondered whether selective breeding could have produced the variations in race of the human family, an opinion expressed in (for instance) James Prichard's *The Natural History of Man; comprising Inquiries into the Modifying Influences of Physical and Moral Agencies in different tribes of the Human Family* (1843). In his PRINCIPLES OF GEOLOGY (1830–3) Charles Lyell was mostly concerned with establishing geological evidence for the great antiquity of the Earth; but Chapters 34–51 of the work also summarised a widely held six-point consensus on the subject of evolution:

1st. That there is a capacity in all species to accommodate themselves to a certain extent to a change of external circumstances.

2nd. When the change of situation they can endure is great, it is usually attended by some modifications of the form, colour, size, structure or other particulars; but the mutations thus superinduced are governed by constant laws, and the capability of so varying forms part of the permanent character.

3rd. Some acquired peculiarities of form, structure, and instinct are transmissible to the offspring.

4th. The entire variation from the original type which any given kind of change can produce, may usually be effected in a short period of time, after which no further deviation can be obtained by continuing to alter the circumstances, though ever so gradually – indefinite divergence, either in the way of improvement or deterioration, being prevented, and the least excess beyond the defined limits being fatal to the existence of the individual.

5th. The intermixture of distinct species is guarded against by the aversion of the individuals composing them to sexual union.

6th. From these considerations it appears that species have a real existence in nature, and that each was endowed, at the time of its creation, with the attributes and organization by which it is now distinguished.

(Review of Lyell, *Principles of Geology* (7th edn), *Quarterly Review* 86, 1850: 18–19)

The version of 'evolution' being advanced here is fundamentally determined by the nature of the organism as originally created by God; it is limited and divinely sanctioned. In the 1850s these opinions were still regarded by many scientists as (in the words of the conservative *Quarterly Review*) 'valid in all essential points.'

Darwin's contribution to the debate was to theorise a mechanism – natural selection – by which this process of evolution could occur. According to this model alteration in organisms is a fundamentally random process, with the exacting natural environment rewarding beneficial mutations and eliminating disadvantageous ones, such that those organisms best fitted to their environment survive to pass on their alterations. This notion, which Darwin arrived at simultaneously with Alfred Russell Wallace (even though they worked independently of one another), first emerged in 1858 in a scientific paper joint-authored by Darwin and Wallace called 'On the Tendency of Species to Form Varieties; and on the Perpetuation of Varieties and Species by Natural means of Selection'. Darwin elaborated the theory in two books, *On the Origin of Species, by Means of Natural Selection* (1859) and *The Descent of Man*

(1871). The fuss that surrounded Darwin's publications had less to do with the idea of evolution as such, and more with the fact that his theory dispensed with the need for a supernatural Creator, and with any inherent boundaries on the extent of evolutionary change.

Further reading

Darwin's Plots: Evolutionary Narrative in Darwin, George Eliot and Nineteenth-Century Fiction (1983; pb 1985) by Gillian Beer.

Exhibitions   The Victorians loved to exhibit things. Artworks, archaeological curiosities, examples of technological advancement, and (at a different social scale) waxworks, human deformities and other manifestations of popular culture – all were arranged, displayed and exhibited to paying audiences.

The greatest example of this cultural phenomenon was, of course, the GREAT EXHIBITION OF 1851, which attracted 6,063,986 visitors. The Paris *Exposition Francais* of 1854 was visited by 4,553,464 persons, of whom 40,000 were British (*Chambers's Journal*, 1856: 347). These figures are exceptional; a more usual sense of the number of visitors an exhibition might expect is given by the 1856 *Annual Report of the Department of Science and Art*, which records that museums in different parts of the nation were visited by 330,000 people, 'being 56 per cent. more than in the previous year, the increase chiefly due to the "travelling museum" which attracted great numbers'. But a wide range of exhibitions were mounted in all major Victorian cities, and many smaller towns, all through the period, and all manner of curiosities were displayed to an appreciative, paying public.

For example, in 1835 Sir Henry De la Beche (1796–1855), having conducted the Geological Survey for a number of years, decided to exhibit a collection of geological materials to the public. This display was first housed in Charing Cross, and afterwards at the Museum of Practical Geology in Jermyn Street, Piccadilly. It says a great deal for the passion of the Victorians for all manner of exhibitions that this (to modern sensibilities) enormously dull collection of 'specimens of the various mineral substances used in constructing public works or buildings, employed for useful purposes ... arranged with every reference to instruction' could have been so great a success. But the intellectual curiosity of the age seems to have encompassed all manner of exhibited objects with a salutary curiosity. George Pegler (1825–1914), a Huntingdonshire teacher, visited London in 1850. In his diary, whole entries are given over to the exhibitions he attended: 'August 11. Today I visited the British Museum and confined myself to the inspection of Minerals. I saw Native Mercury in Quartz. Opalized wood from Van Dieman's Land interested me, and Bitumen in large lumps' (Creaton, 2001: 16).

F

Fabian Society   Founded in 1884, the Fabians sought to advance SOCIALIST aims with-out advocating the proletarian revolution insisted upon by MARX and his followers. The name was taken from the Roman 'Fabius' (Quintus Fabius Maximus, a fourth century BCRoman leader who specialised in 'delaying tactics'; the point being that Fabians sought to 'delay' Marxist revolution). Although some key Fabians were from working-class backgrounds (for instance, one of the founders of the movement, Thomas Davidson (1840–1900), who was the illegitimate son of a shepherd), the organisation soon acquired the reputation of a group of intellectuals and wealthy lib-erals. Sidney Webb (1859–1947) and Beatrice Webb (1858–1943), key players, advo-cated a rather elitist, anti-trades union socialism, and other Fabians came from literary and cultured backgrounds, such as George Bernard SHAW and the novelist Walter Besant (1836–1901). The Fabians published a number of tracts, including *Why the Many are Poor* (1884), and Shaw's *A Manifesto* (1884). The movement is still active today.

France   British culture was more intimately connected to French culture in the nine-teenth century than to any other. The century began with Britain at war with Napoleonic France, and after the French defeat at the Battle of Waterloo (1815) the country was ruled by a restored monarchy. Nevertheless the French Revolution of 1789 cast a lengthy shadow across the century, partly as an inspiration to radicals, and partly as dire warning to political conservatives. CARLYLE's epic *History of the French Revolution* (1837) anatomised the causes of the terror in Homeric style, simultane-ously expressing a conservative horror of its excesses whilst slyly valorising the heroic overtones of the uprising. The proximity of this politically volatile nation made it all the more alarming to many in Britain; further, though lesser, French revolutions in 1830 (the so-called 'July Revolution') and 1848 (*see* REVOLUTIONS OF 1848) meant that the rise to power of the authoritarian NAPOLEON III was seen as a positive development by a range of British political opinions. The FRANCO-PRUSSIAN WAR of 1870 humiliated France; Émile Zola (1840–1902) conveys a sense of this in the title of his novel set during the war: *La Débâcle* ('The Disaster', 1892). With the downfall of Napoleon, the 'Third Republic' was declared, the regime that lasted until the Second World War. Its first president was Louis Adolphe Thiers (1797–1877).

Many Victorian writers took frequent holidays in France; DICKENS stayed there often, and set several novels partly in the country, amongst them *Dombey and Son* (1846–8), *Little Dorrit* (1855–7) and *A Tale of Two Cities* (1859). BROWNING lived for long stretches in France, especially in the 1870s after the death of Elizabeth Barrett

Browning, and many of his later long poems are either set in France or else dramatise French topics. The speaker of *Prince Hohensteil-Schwangau* (1871) is a thinly veiled cipher for Napoleon III, attempting to justify his political career; *Fifine at the Fair* (1872), a lengthy, complex and rewarding study of adultery and faithfulness, transplants the iconic figure of Don Juan to a French setting; *Red Cotton Night-Cap Country* (1873) is a SENSATION novel in verse set wholly in France. SWINBURNE was amongst the most frantically enthusiastic Francophiles England has ever produced; a fluent French-speaker, he often visited the country, and proclaimed, loud and long, poet and novelist Victor Hugo (1802–85) the greatest writer in the world.

Franco-Prussian War (1870–1871)   NAPOLEON III declared war against the increasingly powerful German state of Prussia in the belief that other German states, particularly in the south, would join with France to resist Prussian hegemony. Otto von Bismarck (1815–98), the Prussian statesman, welcomed the war for exactly contrary reasons, believing it would precipitate German unification. The more efficient and better-trained German army quickly defeated the French at Metz and Sedan, capturing Napoleon. Paris was besieged through the winter of 1870/1, causing very great hardship; socialist 'communards' in the city seized power. Napoleon, deposed, fled to England and the 'Third Republic' was declared in France. The new President, Louis Adolphe Thiers (1797–1877), surrendered to Germany in January 1871. The terms of the Treaty of Frankfurt gave Alsace-Lorraine to Germany and compelled France to pay indemnities to the victors. On 21 May troops of the Third Republic entered Paris, whose communards had refused to recognise the new administration. In the following week over 20,000 communards were summarily shot.

Fin de siècle   The French phrase, meaning 'end of the century', is usually applied to the cultural production and mood of the 1890s. Often DECADENT and SYMBOLIST in mode, the art produced in this last decade was nonetheless extremely varied: writers as different as SWINBURNE, PATER and WILDE, and artists as unalike as Aubrey Beardsley (1872–98) ROSSETTI, and Edward Burne-Jones (1833–98) are all brought under the umbrella of the term. What these writers had in common was a general rebellion against the high-Victorian belief in the moral function of art, a reaction against REALISM and a stress upon beauty as the sole criterion of aesthetic value (to quote Wilde's famous assertion from the preface to 1891's *The Picture of Dorian Gray*, 'there is no such thing as a moral or an immoral book. Books are well written or badly written'). Indeed, a shorthand definition of the period might be 'studied *anti*-Victorianism'. Isobel Armstrong has persuasively argued that, with the death of the two most dominant figures in Victorian poetry (Browning died in 1889 and Tennyson in 1892) the culture was aware of a change in emphasis: 'the history of the 1890s and fin-de-siècle poetry seems to belong rather to the history of modernism than to that of Victorian poetry' (Armstrong, 1993: 479).

Food   The Victorians loved their food. For the poor, food was a governing concern, marshalling the wherewithal to purchase it was a main object of existence and the food, once bought, was relished accordingly. For the English working class, bread was the staple food, supplemented by dairy products, meat, beer, seafood and other food when possible. For working-class Irish, potatoes were staple. For middle- and upper-class Victorians, food-taking was often a celebratory event: DICKENS, whose novels pay close attention to food and for whom food is always an index of plenty and joy, describes his 'spirit of Christmas present' in digestible terms:

> Heaped up upon the floor, to form a kind of throne, were turkeys, geese, game, poultry, brawn, great joints of meat, sucking-pigs, long wreaths of sausages, mince-pies, plum-puddings, barrels of oysters, red-hot chesnuts, cherry-cheeked apples, juicy oranges, luscious pears, immense twelfth-cakes and seething bowls of punch that made the chamber dim with their delicious steam.

> (Dickens, *Christmas*: 43)

Although the cultural norm was to enjoy food with gusto, there were variations for certain grades of well-bred women. The food-historian Joan Jacobs Brumberg notes that

> . . . in advice books such as the 1875 *Health Fragments; or, Steps toward a True Life* women are cautioned to be careful about what and how much they ate. Authors George and Susan Everett enjoined: 'Coarse, gross, and gluttonous habits of life degrade the physical appearance. You will rarely be disappointed in supposing that a lucid, self-respectful lady is very careful of the food which forms her body' . . . Young women were told directly that 'gross eaters' not only developed thick skin but had prominent blemishes and broken blood vessels on the nose.

> (Brumberg, 1997: 168–9)

There was a degree of anorexia amongst Victorian girls and women; it is likely, for instance, that Elizabeth Barrett BROWNING's physical ailments owed something to this pathology.

In the mid-century there was a certain anxiety about food adulteration. Food supplies, particularly for the poor, were often mixed with various substances to increase the supplier's profits. Tea and coffee was sometimes adulterated by cheaper herbs such as chicory; cheap bread had alum mixed into the dough; milk was sometimes skimmed for cream and then thickened again by mixing in brain matter from slaughtered animals; water was added to butter and meat. After reporting on the Model Prison regime introduced at Pentonville in the 1850s, Henry Mayhew commented tartly that it was

... strange evidence of the 'civilisation' of our time, that a person must – in these days of 'lie-tea' and chicory-mocha, and alumed bread, and brain-thickened milk, and watered butter – really go to prison to live upon unadulterated food.

(Mayhew, *Great World of London*, 1856: 100)

In 'The Poor Man at Market', *Chambers's Journal* (14 June 1856: 373) complained that the poor were compelled to buy sugar mixed with sand and salt, and that their bread was adulterated by 'potatoes, bone-ashes, clay ... Indian corn, rice, gypsum, Plaster of Paris' or 'chalk'.

G

Gaskell, Elizabeth Cleghorn (1810–1865)   Born Elizabeth Stevenson, the daughter of a Unitarian minister and later an official in the Treasury, she was brought up largely by her aunt in Knutsford, Cheshire. In 1832 she married William Gaskell (1805–84), also a Unitarian minister, who worked in nearby Manchester. The couple produced four daughters and a son who died young, a sorrow from which Gaskell sought relief in writing a novel. The result was the powerful, hard-hitting representation of Manchester working-class suffering, *Mary Barton* (1848), an early masterpiece of INDUSTRIAL FICTION. DICKENS admired the novel, and approached Gaskell to contribute to HOUSEHOLD WORDS, telling her 'there is no living English writer whose aid I would desire to enlist in preference to the authoress of *Mary Barton* (a book that most profoundly affected and impressed me)' (quoted in Schlicke, 1999: 254). Gaskell went on to become one of Dickens' most prolific contributors, publishing nearly 30 short stories and essays with him. Some of these were collected as *Cranford* (1853), a series of interconnected sketches of domestic life in the charming village of the title (modelled on Knutsford). Other short stories were collected in several volumes, the best being *Cousin Phillis and Other Stories* (1864).

Ruth, a daring novel in which the title character gives birth outside marriage, was published the same year that the collected *Cranford* emerged. *North and South* (1855) was another industrial novel, although Gaskell's treatment of the problems of employers and dissatisfied workers was much less inflammatory in this later book. In this same year Gaskell's friend Charlotte BRONTË died. The family asked Gaskell to write a biography, to lay to rest some of the rumours that were already circulating. Her *Life of Charlotte Brontë* appeared in 1857; a fine Victorian biography it was well received in many quarters and proved popular. That Gaskell was paid the large sum of £800 by her publishers demonstrates her increasing level of commercial success. Some of the Brontë family, however, objected to certain parts of the work, which they regarded as libellous. Gaskell was compelled to publish a partial retraction in *The Times*. *Sylvia's Lovers* (1863), a HISTORICAL NOVEL set during the Napoleonic Wars, was purchased by Smith, Elder for £1000: its vigorous plotline, containing press-gangs, betrayal, battle-scenes and two men competing for one woman, is entertaining, although in many senses it is her least controlled novel. Her last novel was *Wives and Daughters* (1865–6), which was bought for SERIALISATION by the *Cornhill Magazine* for £1600. Gaskell's husband had recently retired, and she used the money to buy a handsome house in Hampshire in which they could both live; but she died, of heart disease, shortly after moving in, and before she was able to complete *Wives and Daughters*.

Gentleman The Victorian notion of the gentleman is a little difficult to pin down. It relates to, but is not exclusively described by, a man of good breeding (which is to say, of respectable or longstanding family) who acts in well-mannered way. The notion that it is through *manners* – which is to say, a code of behaviour – that gentility is chiefly defined has wide currency today, and can lend the concept as a whole a pedantic and arcane flavour. This is unfair. It is true that some Victorian 'rules' for gentlemanly behaviour can seem arbitrary: the idea that a gentleman must eat the fish dish with a piece of bread rather than with cutlery, or Lord Curzon's (1859–1925) opinion that 'gentlemen do not take soup at luncheon', or Baron Fisher's (1841–1920) insistence that a gentleman should 'never contradict, never explain, never apologise' are of this class (Partington, 1992: 229, 283). For Victorians, though, a gentleman was a gentleman by virtue of something much less strictly defined, by his *being* as well as his manner.

A Victorian gentleman is determined by his duties to others, rather than his rights or pride in himself. 'It is almost a definition of a gentleman,' opined John Henry NEWMAN in *The Idea of a University* (1852) 'to say that he is one who never inflicts pain.' In TROLLOPE's novel *Rachel Ray* (1863) the hero Luke Rowan hopes to marry the poor but pretty Rachel, but is opposed by her fanatically devout widowed mother (who thinks every young man 'a wicked wild beast') and by the repulsive evangelical clergyman Mr Prong. Trollope describes this latter character as 'not a gentleman', a phrase expressive of an eloquent range of meanings to an 1860s readership. Reticence is also an important characteristic of the true gentleman: 'the only infallible rule we know is,' says Robert Surtees (1805–64) at the beginning of his novel *Ask Mamma* (1858), 'that the man who is always talking about being a gentleman never is one'. This reticence can easily become mannered politeness of speech and behaviour, which makes it very hard for the non-initiate to read one's actual feelings, as when Byron nicely describes his hero Don Juan as a man 'with such true breeding of a gentleman,/You never could divine his real thought' (*Don Juan*, Canto 4, ll. 41–2)

Not everybody in the nineteenth century was enamoured of this particular idea. 'Men are very generally spoiled,' wrote American Henry David Thoreau (1817–62) in his *Journal* for 1851, 'by being so civil and well-disposed. You can have no profitable conversation with them, they are so conciliatory, determined to agree with you.' Nor was the concept entirely regarded in an idealist sense. 'I am afraid,' said an anonymous writer in *Chambers's Journal*, 'that this term "gentleman" is mostly applied by the lower classes to those of their superiors who are most lavish and extravagant.' He goes on to say that in society a gentleman 'who was otherwise unexceptionable, and possessed of all the virtues' would be

> deprived of that honourable name if he were seen eating fish by help of a
> knife, and not, at hazard of choking himself, with an unpleasant piece of bread
> ... A man of high title may do, however, pretty much as he likes. He certainly

may commit an incredible amount of vicious actions without losing this designation; and, on the other hand, a man of humble fortunes, however worthy, scarcely ever has it bestowed upon him even by the wisest.

('What is a Gentleman?' *Chambers's Journal*, 21 June 1856: 399)

Ghost stories   DICKENS was very attached to the ghost story. His *A Christmas Carol* (1843), in which the miserly Scrooge is persuaded to change his ways by three ghostly apparitions, is perhaps one of the most famous ghost stories in literature; but there are several other powerful short stories dealing with ghosts, including 'To Be Read at Dusk' (1852) and the chilling 'The Signalman' (1866). The uniquely powerful if sometimes adolescent tales of American writer Edgar Allan Poe (1809–49) often dealt with the psychological torment of being haunted and life after death, as in 'The Tell-Tale Heart' (1843) and 'The Facts of the Case of M. Waldemar' (1845). Some of the most effective ghost stories of the period were by LE FANU, who began publishing his distinctive supernatural tales in the *Dublin University Magazine* in the 1840s: 'Uncle Silas' (1864) and 'Green Tea' (1872), a tale of horrific possession, are especially chilling. The revival in GOTHIC towards the end of the century saw a revival in ghostly 'tales of horror', including work by STEVENSON, WILDE and Henry James (1843–1916), whose *The Turn of the Screw* (1898) is a superb if involuted ghost story.

Gladstone, William Ewart (1809–1898)   Gladstone was born in Liverpool, his Scottish father a merchant who owned plantations in the West Indies. He attended Eton and Christ Church, Oxford, married the aristocratic Catherine Glynne (1812–1900) in 1839 and began a political career as a TORY MP (his first seat was the rotten borough Newark, only partially reformed in the REFORM ACT OF 1832; he took his seat in Parliament at the beginning of 1833). A deeply principled, religious young man – to the point, indeed, of priggishness – his first political instincts were shaped by his sense of responsibility to the Church. But despite an attachment to the past, his political beliefs were to lead him to the WHIGS, and he was to die the most influential LIBERAL politician of the century.

He served under the Tory Robert PEEL on the Board of Trade, and was offered a post in the Colonial Office, but after Peel's downfall (and after being elected MP for Oxford in 1847), Gladstone found himself increasingly siding with PALMERSTON's Whigs. 'Political differences no longer lie between parties,' he inaccurately wrote in 1855, 'but within parties. The most Conservative Liberal and the most Liberal Conservative ... are near one another' (Shannon, 1999: 309). Gladstone became Chancellor of the Exchequer under Palmerston in 1859. According to historian Colin Matthew,

the Palmerston–Gladstone government of 1859–65 – stormy though the relationship between the two men often was – successfully drew together many aspects of mid-Victorian social and political life. Its MPs were mostly

Anglicans, but its attracted also Roman Catholics, Nonconformists, Jews and secularists. In class terms, it retained the great Whig landowners, it represented the industrial and commercial middle classes, and it was supported by most of those artisans who had the vote.

(Matthew, 2000: 113)

Gladstone served under Lord John Russell (1792–1878) after Palmerston's death, and then worked with Lord Derby (1826–93) to produce the Reform Act of 1867; but Derby was defeated by Disraeli's Conservative Party in the election of 1868, and when the Liberals regained power later that year Gladstone was Prime Minister. He deliberately pushed through major legislation, partly from principle and partly as a means of pulling his party together: 1869 saw the disestablishment of the Irish Church, and 1870 an Irish Land Act. An Elementary Education Act was passed for England and Wales in 1870, and a similar act for Scotland in 1872. Religious tests were abolished at Oxford and Cambridge (1871), and the electoral secret ballot was enacted in 1872; 1874, however, saw the Tory's win the general election, and Disraeli become Prime Minister for a second time. He remained premier until 1880; but the elderly, though still hale, Gladstone harried him effectively over foreign and colonial affairs. In 1879–80, in the run-up to another general election, Gladstone campaigned from hustings to hustings in southern Scotland: the fiery speechmaking and seemingly exhaustless energy of this 'Midlothian Campaign' helped the Liberals to electoral victory in 1880.

Gladstone's second government (1880–5) saw the enactment of the Reform Act of 1884, but became increasingly overshadowed by the Irish Question. Gladstone himself had changed his mind over Ireland, coming to the opinion that Irish Home Rule was the best option for the country. This question split the Liberals, and the Tories, under Robert Cecil, Third Marquis of Salisbury (1830–1903), formed a minority government for a while. But in 1886 Gladstone's Liberals were returned to power. This third administration was dominated by the Irish Question; on hearing of his victory in 1886 Gladstone's first words were 'my mission is to pacify Ireland' (Partington, 1992: 307). He introduced a Home Rule Bill in 1886, but its failure led to Salisbury forming a second Conservative government that year. At the election of 1892 Salisbury lost power, and Gladstone formed his fourth government. In 1893 his Second Home Rule Bill passed the Commons, but was defeated by the Lords. Gladstone resigned in 1894, Lord Rosebery (1847–1929) succeeding as Liberal leader, and in 1895 the Liberal government was defeated.

In addition to his political life, Gladstone was a passionate student of Homer, publishing several books of Homeric scholarship, including *Studies on Homer and the Homeric Age* (1858), *Juventus Mundi* ('The Youth of the World', 1869) and *Homeric Synchronism* (1876), a detailed and slightly mad work that attempted to reconcile

Homeric paganism and Christian revelation. This Homeric bias gave his perspective on foreign affairs a distinct pro-Graeco, anti-Turkish bias (because Homer's Greeks had fought against the Trojans, in modern-day Turkey); his outrage at atrocities committed by Turks, amongst other things, found impassioned rhetorical expression in his tracts *Bulgarian Horrors and the Question of the East* (1876), and *Aggression on Egypt and Freedom in the East* (1884). His meticulously kept *Diaries* (subsequently published in 14 volumes, 1968–94) give a sense of how conscientiously he followed literature, as well as giving fascinating though prurient glimpses into his psychological make-up. A highly sexed individual, he repressed his erotic urges with the help of self-flagellation, and transferred his libido into earnest personal campaigns against prostitution, in which he would visit London prostitutes in person at night and urge them to give up their sinful ways.

Further reading

Gladstone 1: Peel's Inheritor 1809–1865 (1999) and Gladstone 2: Heroic Minister 1865–1898 (1999) by Richard Shannon.

Goblin Market (1862), by Christina Rossetti   This extraordinary fairy-tale poem was written for children, but has found many enthusiastic adult admirers. It's rattling two- or three-stress lines and exuberant rhymes carry the 567-line poem rapidly along, but afterwards it leaves potent resonances in the mind. Lizzie and Laura, two sisters, live together happily in their cottage; but their idyll is punctured by the sinister-comical goblin men, who come bearing fruit for sale, 'Morning and evening/Maids heard the goblins cry:/"Come buy our orchard fruits,/Come buy, come buy"' (ll. 1–4). Sensible Lizzie knows better than to succumb to this temptation, and reminds her sister of the fate of 'Jeanie', who took the fruit and afterwards 'pined and pined away', but Laura sneaks away and meets the goblins. Purchasing the fruit with 'a precious golden lock' of her hair, she devours the fruit:

> She never tasted such before,
> How should it cloy with length of use?
> She sucked and sucked and sucked the more
> Fruits which that unknown orchard bore;
> She sucked until her lips were sore.

> (ll. 133–7)

Afterwards, of course, Laura pines away, and her sister goes out to confront the bestial goblins:

> Laughed every goblin
> When they spied her peeping:
> Came towards her hobbling,

> Flying, running, leaping,
>
> . . .
>
> Cat-like and rat-like
>
> Ratel- and wombat-like,
>
> Snail paced in a hurry,
>
> Parrot-voiced and whistler,
>
> Helter skelter, hurry scurry
>
> (ll. 329–44)

Lizzie pays for the fruit, but refuses to eat it; the goblins assault her, squeezing the fruit all over her, after which Lizzie returns home to offer herself to her sister, 'hug me, kiss me, suck my juices . . . eat me, drink me' (ll. 468–71). Laura tasting the fruit a second time is cured of its effects, and the two sisters live happily ever after. Expertly suited for children (in whose universe eating and drinking is a very important activity), adults find many secondary meanings in the work, from sexual allegory and proto-feminist solidarity, to religiously symbolic account of the Eucharist.

Gothic   The first great vogue for Gothic occurred in the late eighteenth and early nineteenth century, when works such as *The Castle of Otranto* (1764) by Horace Walpole (1717–97), *The Mysteries of Udolpho* (1794) by Ann Radcliffe (1764–1823) and *Frankenstein* (1818) by Mary Shelley (1797–1851) enjoyed great success. The components of a Gothic novel included innocent heroines caught up in evil goings-on, dark and night-time set-pieces, remote castles, hidden secrets, blood, murder and sexual threat, supernatural elements such as ghosts or monsters. Critics usually argue that Gothic as a coherent genre was exhausted by the 1820s: Jane Austen (1775–1817) parodied the melodramatic excesses of this sort of writing in her *Northanger Abbey* (1818). Yet there are persistent Gothic elements present throughout Victorian literary culture, not only in such genres as PENNY DREADFULS or SENSATION fiction, but in mainstream and DOMESTIC fiction as well. Emily BRONTË's *WUTHERING HEIGHTS* (1847) is a case in point; the novel is balanced between the domestic conventionality of Thrushcross Grange and the Gothic excess of Heathcliff and the Heights. Charlotte BRONTË's *JANE EYRE* (1847), similarly, employs many of the conventions of Gothic (the remote country house, Thornfield Hall, that appears to be haunted by a destructive spirit, the moody, secretive Gothic hero Rochester). Chris Baldrick traces this thread of Gothic (he argues that *Jane Eyre*'s Bertha Mason, and Miss Havisham from DICKENS' *Great Expectations* (1861) 'are unmistakably and unforgettably Gothic figures'), through the 'Sensation' fiction of the 1860s, 'appearing once again towards the close of the century in more overtly Gothic works by STEVENSON, WILDE and Bram Stoker (1847–1912)' (Baldrick, 1992: xviii). Certainly, Stevenson's *The Strange Case of Dr Jekyll and Mr Hyde* (1886), Wilde's *Picture of Dorian Gray* (1890) and Stoker's vampire masterpiece *Dracula* (1897) are all thoroughly Gothic.

Great Exhibition (1851)   Hyde Park in central London was the site for this International Exhibition; an enormous glasshouse, 'the Crystal Palace', dominated the 26-acre site, and provided a home for some 14,000 international exhibitors, displaying commodities, curiosities and various things. The main point of the exhibition was to underline the dominant position of Britain in terms of world trade, and it marked a high point of mid-Victorian national self-confidence. Well over six million visitors attended the exhibition between 1 May and 15 October 1851, when the site was dismantled and the Crystal Palace moved to south-east London, near Croydon. Over half a million pounds was taken in receipts, and much of the profit was put towards building the Victoria & Albert Museum.

Grotesque   Walter Bagehot (1826–77), published an analysis of the world of Victorian poetry as 'Wordsworth, Tennyson and Browning; or, "Pure, Ornate and Grotesque Art" in English Poetry' in the *National Review* (1864: 27–67). This influential essay characterised Wordsworth's plain verse as the best, because the 'purest', classical poetic style, ranking Tennyson's poetry next on the grounds that it sometimes achieved Wordsworthian purity but also strayed into 'ornate' Romantic embellishment; and ranked Browning as the least, because his poetry was wholly given over to a 'grotesque' medieval idiom. Bagehot's negative assessment of 'grotesque' art ('struggling with difficulties', 'encumbered with incongruities', displaying 'the distorted and imperfect image') has not been endorsed by more recent critics, who see this 'grotesque' style as the most characteristically Victorian: embodied not only in Browning's poetry, but in Dickens' prose, in the distinctively architectural stylings of St Pancras Station, The Palace of Westminster or Royal Holloway, University of London. Isobel Armstrong, for instance, has praised Browning's grotesque 'as a technique for exposing complexity' (Armstrong, 1993: 287), capturing the messy diversity of actual lived experience instead of subordinating it to a simplified ideal.

H

Hansard   Luke Hansard (1752–1828) began publishing his *Journal of the House of Commons*, known as *Hansard*, in 1774. The intention was to record all the speeches made by MPs in the Commons, to produce in other words a journal of Parliamentary record. In the early Victorian period there were several rival publications that did the same thing; Dickens worked as a shorthand reporter for *The Mirror of Parliament*, a weekly journal founded by John Henry Barrow (1796–1858) that ran from 1828 to

1841. Indeed, many MPs preferred the *Mirror of Parliament*: it employed its own reporters to record parliamentary speeches, and was therefore more accurate than *Hansard*, which copied accounts of speeches from newspapers and did not employ its own shorthand reporters until 1878. Nevertheless, it was *Hansard* that survived. It is still the journal of record for Parliamentary proceedings, now published by HM Stationery Office.

Hardie, James Keir (1856–1915)   The son of a poor Scottish farm servant, Keir Hardie grew up with first-hand knowledge of working-class poverty. He worked as a miner and became an active TRADES UNIONIST serving as a miners' union leader. He was elected to Parliament in 1892 as an Independent Labour Candidate, and it is as a key player in the creation of the Independent Labour Party in 1893 (later the Labour Party) that he is mostly remembered.

Hardy, Thomas (1840–1928)   Hardy was born in Dorset, and attended school in Dorchester. His family, although not poor, had seen better days, and at 16 Hardy was articled to John Hicks, a local architect who specialised in church restoration. After six years of training he moved to London, where he worked for the architect Arthur Blomfield, returning to Dorchester in 1867, working again for Hicks. He had a torrid affair with a cousin, Tryphena Sparks, that ended in 1870 when she moved to London to attend a teacher training college. He finished his first novel, *The Poor Man and the Lady*, in 1868, and although it was turned down by publishers (it has since been lost) he was sufficiently encouraged by the kindliness of the rejection letters to try again with the SENSATION novel *Desperate Remedies*, which was published in 1871. He was only moderately successful at the beginning of this new career; *Under the Greenwood Tree* (1872) and *A Pair of Blue Eyes* (1873) sold modestly. But he established a public reputation with *Far from the Madding Crowd* (1874), a powerful work saved from sensationalism by the thoroughly grounded and evocative sense of place, an unsentimental vision of actual country living in Dorset.

Meanwhile Hardy had met Emma Gifford whilst working to restore a church in Cornwall, in 1870. They married in 1874, the same year that Hardy finally gave up architecture to concentrate on writing. *The Hand of Ethelberta* (1876) was a less successful novel, but *The Return of the Native* (1878) remains a masterpiece. For this novel Hardy returned to the West Country, refashioning the actual counties of Devon and Cornwall as 'Wessex'. By renaming all the real-life towns and features with his own names Hardy created a fantasy land, but one that is at all times closely rooted in the actual existence of nineteenth-century rural England. The somewhat melodramatic plot of *The Return of the Native* is less important than the extraordinary sense of place that Hardy evokes, most especially in the beautiful, starkly haunting descriptions of 'Egdon Heath' that dominate the narrative.

Hardy was now becoming nationally famous, and was a well-known figure on the London literary scene. His only HISTORICAL novel, *The Trumpet-Major* (1880), was set during the Napoleonic Wars. *Two on a Tower* (1882) is a more pessimistic work, flavoured by Hardy's own atheistic, somewhat gloom-laden and morbid outlook – a frame of mind that caused tension in his marriage. He moved back to Dorchester in 1885, and set his next novel in the town (which he renamed 'Casterbridge'). *The Mayor of Casterbridge* (1886) is one of Hardy's most Shakespearean studies of character and destiny, whose protagonist, a labourer, sells his wife and child when drunk; unencumbered and sober he rises to become mayor of his town, but the past returns to unsettle his prosperity. The gloom of the novel's conclusion (the last words of Chapter 45 of the novel are 'to teach that happiness was but the occasional episode in a general drama of pain') is saved from mere grumpiness by the humane eloquence of Hardy's characterisation.

The Woodlanders (1887) was a less grim work, but Hardy was unhappy with the conformist pressure his fame was putting on him to be morally 'improving'. *Tess of the D'Urbervilles* (1891) was designed to upset middle-brow readers. The heroine of this novel suffers much, is raped by the aristocratic Alec, gives birth to a baby that dies, loses the chance of happiness with another man and lives for a while, miserably, as the kept woman of her rapist. Finally Tess kills her oppressor Alec and is hanged. '"Justice" was done,' Hardy's narrator concludes ironically in the novel's final sentence, 'and the President of the Immortals (in Aeschylean phrase) had ended his sport with Tess.' But the novel is less Aeschylean, despite its tragic cast, and more Modern in its fascination with the arbitrariness of our fates. 'A novel is an impression,' Hardy argued in the Preface to *Tess*, 'not an argument.' But the book was taken as an argument by many nevertheless, and an endorsement of immorality. *The Well-Beloved* (1892), in which a sculptor pursues three generations of women because of their resemblance to an ideal in his heart, was similarly criticised for lack of moral uplift. But the greatest hostility was unleashed at the publication of JUDE THE OBSCURE (1896). So extreme was the backlash at this story of adultery, child-suicide and crushed hopes that Hardy gave up writing fiction altogether. His marriage, childless, was breaking down, and Hardy devoted himself to writing poetry; first an epic verse-drama of the Napoleonic Wars, *The Dynasts* (1904–8), and then to a large number of very beautiful lyric poems. His poetic career belongs, properly, to the twentieth century.

Historical novel It is important to distinguish between two different sorts of novel that might be termed 'historical'. Most mainstream Victorian fiction was not set contemporaneously, but in the recent past, usually 20 or 30 years before the date of composition: DICKENS' *Great Expectations* (1860–1), for instance, was set in the 1810s and 1820s, and ELIOT's *MIDDLEMARCH* (1871–2) was set in the 1820s. These, for the Victorians, were not really historical novels, a genre they associated above all with SCOTT: exciting romances set at some eventful and colourful period in history, in which ordinary people become involved in extraordinary events. Scott himself set most of his historical 'Waverley' novels either in seventeenth- or eighteenth-century Scotland, or in the Middle Ages. His enormous commercial and aesthetic success inspired many imitators, and this Scott-like form of writing was the mainstay of the mid-Victorian 'historical' novel. Harrison Ainsworth (1805–82) built his reputation largely upon historical fiction, some of them NEWGATE novels of celebrated eighteenth-century criminals (1834's *Rookwood* or 1839's *Jack Sheppard*), but more often novels dramatising and celebrating English location and spirit in various historical periods: *The Tower of London* (1840) was an Elizabethan adventure in which Elizabeth herself clashes with Mary, Queen of Scots, over a love-object; *Old Saint Pauls* (1841) and *Windsor Castle* (1843) followed this topographical theme with stories set in and around the London of the Great Fire (1666) and Henry VIII respectively. Increasingly 'Tory' as he aged, many of Ainsworth's titles took Jacobite themes, with various self-explanatory titles: *Saint James's, or the Court of Queen Anne* (1844), *The Spanish Match: or Charles Stuart at Madrid* (1865) and *The Good Old Times: the Story of the Manchester Rebels of the Fatal '45* (1873). Edward Bulwer-Lytton (1803–73) was another novelist drawn to the historical mode: *Devereux* (1829) and *Paul Clifford* (1830) were set in the eighteenth century. *The Last Days of Pompeii* (1834) created a taste for 'late Roman' fiction that was to inform, amongst many others, PATER's *Marius the Epicurian* (1885) and *Ben-Hur: a Tale of the Christ* (1880) by American Lew Wallace (1827–1905). Bulwer-Lytton also enjoyed success with a novel of medieval Italy, *Rienzi* (1835). Later in his career Bulwer-Lytton was drawn to English history: *The Last of the Barons* (1843) and *Harold* (1848) anatomised the origins of 'the English' in a patriotic, heartfelt way.

Most Victorian novelists wrote at least one historical novel, although usually not more than one or two. DICKENS' *Barnaby Rudge* (1841) is a Scott-like tale of the 1780 Gordon Riots; his *Tale of Two Cities* (1859) is a more sophisticated novel set during the French Revolution. TROLLOPE's only historical novel, *La Vendée* (1850), is also set during this period, although it is a weak work. George Eliot's one historical work, *Romola* (1862–3), is set during the Italian Renaissance, and Elizabeth GASKELL's sole excursion in the genre, *Sylvia's Lovers* (1863), is a Napoleonic love story. A sub-genre of the mode was a type of novel that dramatised contemporary religious debates: KINGSLEY's *Hypatia* (1853) is set in fifth-century Alexandria, but is in fact an anti-Catholic work; NEWMAN's *Callista* (1856), set in third-century Tunisia, is a pro-Catholic tale of persecution and martyrdom. Nicholas Wiseman (1802–65), the first Catholic Archbishop of Westminster and later a cardinal, wrote another pro-Catholic historical novel, *Fabiola: a Tale of the Catacombs* (1854), which was very successful with readers of all denominations. Later in the century, STEVENSON's Jacobite romances *Kidnapped* (1886) and *The Master of Ballantrae* (1889) reached Scott-like levels of writerly skill and popularity.

History of England (1849–1855) by Thomas Macaulay   The short title of this masterpiece of nineteenth-century historiography is rather misleading; Macaulay's intention was to trace English history not from its first origins to the present day, but from the so-called 'Glorious Revolution' of 1688 to the nineteenth century (the full title is *History of England from the Accession of James II*). He later amended his finish-date to 1714, but by his death he had only reached 1697. In fact, after a first chapter ranging across English history, almost all of the work detailed the crisis of 1688, in which James II's son, also called James, heir to the throne, was excluded from power because of his Catholicism, and the Protestant German George I became king. Macaulay hoped to demonstrate that the careful groundwork laid by statesmen in 1688 had rendered the sort of bloody and destructive revolutions that were common on the continent (for instance, the REVOLUTIONS OF 1848) unnecessary and unlikely in Britain. Though scholarly and detailed, the work is nevertheless partisan; Macaulay's own 'Whig' leanings, and his belief that history was a tale of progress are evident throughout.

The work, though detailed and long, remains a superbly readable narrative of social and political history. Volumes 1 and 2, published in 1849, were enormously successful. Longman, the publishers, advanced Macaulay the enormous sum of £20,000 for the third and fourth volumes when they were published in 1855, and made the money back easily. Henry Crabb Robinson (1775–1867) reported reading the first two volumes, declaring the work 'quite as interesting as a novel', but also stressed the ideological nature of the undertaking. By detailing the political clash that had given birth to the two political parties (the Jacobite Tories and the Georgian Whigs), which still ruled Victorian politics, Macaulay was commenting upon the political scene of his own day. Robinson commented with approval that 'the disgust he excites towards James and the Tory principles must have a salutary effect on the public mind. It will shame the High Church and Tory party' (Robinson, 1938: 687).

Homer   Homer's two great epics, the *Iliad* (concerning the war at Troy) and the *Odyssey* (detailing the long journey home and many adventures of Odysseus, after the end of the war) were composed probably in the seventh century BC. Long recognised as central masterpieces of world culture, they have dominated literature for nearly three millennia. The Victorian public school system was rooted in CLASSICAL literature, and trained its pupils up in the business of TRANSLATION. It is not surprising, therefore, that the issue of how best to translate into English the greatest poet of the classical tradition was one of the most vigorously discussed throughout the century. The English version of the *Iliad* and *Odyssey* that had the highest reputation was Alexander Pope's (1688–1744) elegant but over-polished rendering in heroic couplets (1715–26). But many Victorians worried away at the necessity of producing a proper modern translation of Homer. In 1862 the *Westminster Review* described this topic 'one of really national importance' ('On Translating Homer', *Westminster Review* 77, 1862: 151);

and 12 years later the *London Quarterly* reiterated the point: 'the subject of Homeric translation is one of national importance to a highly civilised country such as our own' ('Homer's *Iliad* in Translation', *London Quarterly Review* 43, 1874: 375).

Matthew ARNOLD's first significant intervention into the arena of prose criticism was a response to a translation of Homer he regarded as inadequate; his 'On Translating Homer' and 'On Translating Homer: Last Words', whilst hilariously insulting to Newman, provide also a rationale for Homeric poetry that had a wide influence outside the narrow field of translation studies.

Home Rule   There were various attempts by Irish political radicals to separate their country from the Union of Great Britain, and to establish Home Rule for an independent Ireland (*see* IRISH QUESTION). The 'Irish Republican Brotherhood' was founded in 1858 by James Stephens (1825–1901) after the failure of the 1848 Irish rebellion against Britain; the organisation was nicknamed the 'Fenians'. Hostile to the activities of more conventional Irish politicians, the Brotherhood pressed for immediate succession, but a rising in 1867 was quickly suppressed by the British, and many Fenians executed (they were known as the 'Manchester Martyrs'). Greater pressure was brought to bear by the creation of an effective Home Government Organisation in 1870, founded by Isaac Butt (1813–79). This movement became the Home Rule League in 1873, and enjoyed considerable electoral success in Irish seats in subsequent Parliamentary elections, giving the movement a Westminster base. In the later 1870s and 1880s, as Ireland recovered from the famine of the 1840s, talented politicians such as Michael Davitt (1846–1906) and Charles Stewart Parnell (1846–91) were able to compel GLADSTONE to adopt Home Rule as a LIBERAL Party policy by 1886, and to introduce a Home Rule Bill in Parliament (which was rejected). A less extreme Second Home Rule Bill was defeated by the Lords in 1893. Parnell's adulterous private life led to a moralistic split in the Home Rule Party of the 1890s, which divided between Parnellites and anti-Parnellites.

Homosexuality   The *Oxford English Dictionary* cites the first use of the term 'homosexual' in English as 1892; earlier in the century the category of 'sodomite' had been employed to describe male sexual relations with men. The move, conceptually, from 'sodomite' (a word that describes a particular act) to 'homosexual', 'Uranian' or 'invert' (all words describing a sort of person, and all terms used in the 1890s) is a move from an instrumental to an essential sense of the concept. Two theories in particular became popular towards the end of the century; one that saw homosexuality as a hermaphroditic state, in which a female 'soul' was trapped in a male body, the other that saw homosexuality as 'inversion', a self-oriented sexual anomaly. This latter view was influentially argued by physician and sexologist Havelock Ellis (1859–1939), who together with the homosexual scholar John Addington Symonds (1840–93) published *Sexual Inversion* in 1897. Despite a number of advocates of the liberalisation of sexual legislation, in many ways conditions were harder for those convicted of homosexual acts at the end of the century than they had been earlier. Although the death penalty for sodomy had been lifted in 1861, after decades of non-use, the legal vacuum that ensued revealed a pervasive social anxiety rather than opening up possibilities for homosexual activity. In an influential argument, the contemporary French theorist Michel Foucault (1926–84) put forward an article published in 1870 by the German physician Carl Westphal as the point when the new category of 'homosexual' was created out of the wreckage of the category of 'sodomite':

> We must not forget that the psychological, psychiatric, medical category of homosexuality was constituted from the moment it was characterised – Westphal's famous article of 1870 on 'contrary sexual relations' can stand as its date of birth – less by a type of sexual relations than by a certain quality of sexual sensibility, a certain way of inverting the masculine and feminine in oneself.

(Foucault, 1976 (trans. 1990): 43)

In 1871 two London men were arrested and tried for conspiracy to commit sodomitic acts; their widely reported trial exposed the lack of legal precision on the subject. In 1885 the Labouchere Amendment to the Criminal Law Amendment Act of 1885 was passed, penalising male homosexual acts with up to two years' hard labour, although female homosexuality was not identified, or punished, in law.

This legal identification of homosexuality as 'a problem' created the cultural category of the 'homosexual scandal', of which there were numerous high-profile examples in the later years of the century. One example is the Cleveland Street affair of 1889, which involved members of the royal family; various aristocratic 'society' figures were in the habit of visiting an establishment in Cleveland Street, London, in order to pay for sex with London telegraph boys. A warrant was eventually issued for the arrest of Lord Arthur Somerset, a son of the Duke of Beaufort, who fled the country to avoid prosecution. Prince Albert Edward, later Duke of Clarence (1864–92) – Victoria's grandson, the eldest son of the Prince of Wales – was also implicated, but no criminal charges ensued.

There was also a close connection between homosexuality and the 'decadent' writers associated with the FIN DE SIÈCLE movement. The trial of Oscar Wilde was only the most famous of these.

Hopkins, Gerard Manley (1844–1889) Born in Essex to a middle-class High Church Anglican family, Hopkins grew up with a passion for literature. Educationally precocious, he went to Highgate School and Balliol, Oxford, where he became friends with the poet Robert Bridges (1844–1930) and wrote some poems. At university he fell under the influence of the OXFORD MOVEMENT and he followed his inspiration John Henry NEWMAN in converting to Catholicism, joining the Church in 1866. Two years later he began training to become a Jesuit priest. He studied at several Jesuit colleges, and then worked as a priest between 1877 and 1884 in London, Oxford, Liverpool and Glasgow; in general these industrial parishes wore out and depressed the fey, aesthetic Hopkins. In 1884 he became Professor of Greek at the new Catholic University of Dublin (later University College, Dublin).

Hopkins wrote poetry all through this period, encouraged by his friend Bridges but often discouraged by his Jesuit superiors (who considered poetry, and especially Hopkins' strangely intense, experimental poetry, an inappropriate occupation for a priest). Indeed, Hopkins' career as a priest began with his burning all his earlier poems, an act of renunciation somewhat undermined by the knowledge that Bridges had copies. Much of his subsequent verse was written in moods of spiritual anguish or doubt. Sonnets such as 1885's 'Carrion Comfort' (which begins 'Not, I'll not, carrion comfort, Despair, not feast on thee'), 'No worse, there is none' (1885), or most famously the long poem *The Wreck of the Deutschland* (1876) confront doubt and despair. This latter poem, a lengthy and densely complex meditation on the death of five Franciscan nuns in a shipwreck, is sometimes seen as Hopkins' masterpiece. He sent it to the Jesuit journal *The Month*, but it refused to publish it, finding it too difficult. Indeed, almost none of Hopkins' poems were published in his lifetime; not until long after his death, when Bridges edited a collected *Poems* in 1918, did his work see the light. Accordingly his poetry had a greater influence on Modernist poetics than on Victorian. He died, aged 44, a victim of the typhus bacillus, having made no impression on the poetic world of his day.

Formally, Hopkins was drawn to constraint: he liked particularly the SONNET form, favoured complex rhyme schemes and prosodic patterns, and overlaid traditional structure with alliterative and rhythmic designs of his own. Yet the impression created by his poetry is not particularly formalist, and certainly not restrained or stultified. An example of a typically Hopkinsian effect is given by the first four and a half lines of his sonnet about a falcon hovering in the teeth of a strong wind, taken as a type of Christ, 'The Windhover: to Christ our Lord':

> I caught this morning morning's minion, king-
>   dom of daylight's dauphin, dapple-dawn-drawn Falcon, in his riding
> Of the rolling level underneath him steady air, and striding
> High there, how he rung upon the rein of a wimpling wing
> In his ecstasy!

This exuberant, onward-striding, musically assonantial and alliterative verse seems to many beautiful, vigorous, vivid and affecting. His own theories of 'sprung rhythm' are less coherent than they first appear (he wrote a prose account of his own poetry, probably in 1876, that Bridges printed as the Preface to the 1918 edition of *Poems*), and perhaps do little else than allow the poet to spool and stress the line as he wishes, rather than sticking to classical metrical patterns. Hopkins' own stress marks, sometimes added to the poems to guide the reader, can be distracting, and his distinctive voice slides easily into an over-adjectival self-parody ('Duns Scotus's Oxford', 1879, describes the city as 'branchy between towers;/Cuckoo-echoing, bell-swarmèd, lark-charmèd,/rook-racked, river-rounded'). His self-agonising homosexuality, necessarily repressed in the Jesuit environment in which he lived, makes remarkably few appearances in his poetry, although his diaries record his frequent sense of physical self-disgust and disgust at others, as well as his guilty attraction to men (as Valentine Cunningham puts it, 'he was guiltily attracted to certain sorts of male, young and old, especially lower-class ones and foreigners, navvies, labourers, soldiers, buglers, Norwegians' (Cunningham, 2000: 854)). But at its best Hopkins moulds a new idiom in which to express the same intensity that PATER (one of Hopkins' tutors at Oxford) praised in his writing.

Household Words   *Household Words* was a weekly magazine of topical journalism, essays, short fictions and poetry, which was first published 27 March 1850 under Dickens' general editorship, and which ran under that title until 1859. Thereafter the title changed to *All The Year Round*, and publication continued weekly until Dickens' death (and beyond, under Charles Dickens' Jr's editorship, until the 1890s). The journal was in many respects central to Dickens' writing life in his last two decades of existence. In *Household Words* he serialised *Hard Times* (1854) as well as *A Child's History of England* (1851), *The Lazy Tour of Two Idle Apprentices* (1857) and a variety of Christmas stories, as well as writing a large body of shorter journalist pieces. The list of names of other contributors to this magazine includes: Elizabeth Barrett BROWNING, Edward Bulwer-Lytton (1803–73), Wilkie COLLINS, Elizabeth GASKELL, Sheridan LE FANU, Harriet Martineau (1802–76), George Meredith (1828–1909), Coventry Patmore (1823–96), Charles Reade (1814–84) and many others.

Hymns   The British nineteenth century was a golden age of hymn writing. Songs of praise had long been (and remain) a central feature of worship in the Church of England, and many of the most celebrated and enduring Anglican hymns were composed during Victoria's reign. The metrical versions of Biblical psalms collected in the *Book of Common Prayer* (1662) were still widely sung in churches, and hymns of great beauty, plainness and metrical skill were composed by Isaac Watts (1674–1748) and Charles Wesley (1707–88). But the nineteenth century produced a greater range of mood and effect, and a greater number of hymns that are great poetry, despite some critical claims to the contrary (Albert Shaw, for instance, who declares that century saw 'a great outpouring of religious verse on both sides of the Atlantic. The bulk of it was weak and unsatisfactory' (Shaw, 1974: 358)). A central text in this respect is *Hymns Ancient and Modern* (first edition, 1861) by Henry Williams Baker (1821–77), a collection of several hundred hymns still used in Anglican churches today. For this volume Baker composed a number of fine hymns himself and translated many more from the original Latin – John Mason Neale (1818–66) had recently produced a scholarly edition of Latin hymns, *Hymni Ecclesiae* (1851). It is the emotional scope of Victorian hymns, rather than their devotional qualities per se, that sets them apart. It is true that the happiness and positivity of Cecil Frances Alexander's 'All Things Bright and Beautiful' (1848) can seem banal to modern ears:

> All things bright and beautiful,
> All creatures great and small,
> All things wise and wonderful,
> The Lord God made them all.

But her 'There is a green hill far away' (1848) achieves a bright-lit serenity and beauty that raises it above the ordinary:

> There is a green hill far away,
> Without a city wall,
> Where the dear Lord was crucified
> That died to save us all.

At another emotional pole, Christina Rossetti's 'Mid-winter' (1875) approaches serenity through the bleakness and vacancy of the nativity landscape:

> In the bleak mid-winter
> Frosty wind made moan,
> Earth stood as hard as iron,
> Water like a stone;
> Snow had fallen, snow on snow,
> Snow on snow,
> In the bleak mid-winter,
> Long ago.

Many Victorian hymns strike a note of worship through exaggerated abasement that can seem sycophantic. John Whitter's (1807–92) pleading 'Dear Lord and Father of mankind,/Forgive our foolish ways!' (1872) seems perhaps a little watery. A hymn such as 'Immortal, invisible, God only wise' (1867) by the Scottish clergyman Walter Chalmers Smith (1824–1908) moves with a stately slowness that comes dangerously close to dreariness, an impression strengthened by the polysyllabically 'unhasting' rhythmic steadiness:

> Immortal, invisible, God only wise,
> In light inaccessible hid from our eyes,
> Most blessed, most glorious, the Ancient of Days,
> Almighty, victorious, thy great name we praise.
> Unresting, unhasting, and silent as light,
> Nor wanting, nor wasting, thou rulest in might.

But many hymns are free of this worm's-eye frame of mind, and indeed explore emotional registers that are far from the conventional notion of Victorian piety. Rohcard Luttledale (1833–90) was a clergyman whose hymn 'Come down, O Love divine' articulates an eroticism that would seem outré in a Victorian secular poem:

> Come down, O Love divine,
> Seek thou this soul of mine,
> And visit it with thine own ardour glowing;
> O Comforter, draw near,
> Within my heart appear,
> And kindle it, thy holy flame bestowing.

Hymn singing was a feature of almost all denominations of Victorian Christian practice.

I

Illustrated London News   The famous illustrated weekly newspaper was founded by Herbert Ingram (1811–60), a Nottingham bookseller and printer. Ingram noticed that sales of conventional newspapers increased on the occasions they included woodcut illustrations, and he founded his own paper to capitalise on this demand. The first issue (14 May 1842) was 16 pages, with 32 engravings, and was priced at a relatively expensive 6d. This edition sold 26,000 copies and the circulation quickly rose to 60,000 by the end of the year. In 1848, when the paper covered the course of the revolution in Paris, sales increased again to top 80,000 copies. In 1851 the paper managed to publish Paxton's designs for the GREAT EXHIBITION before Prince ALBERT had even approved them: sales rose to 130,000 a week. During the CRIMEAN WAR (1853–56) the paper sent six war artists to the front and engravings were also published of Roger Fenton's photographs. The first colour supplement appeared in the Christmas edition of 1856. By the end of the decade circulation figures approached 200,000. The political affiliation of the paper was broadly Liberal (Ingram was elected Liberal MP for Boston in 1856), although a strongly patriotic, royalist and Imperial bias is present throughout.

The success of the paper reached a peak in 1863 when the issue reporting the marriage of the Prince of Wales sold 310,000 copies. Its success prompted a number of imitators, including the *Penny Illustrated Paper* (founded 1861), the *Graphic* (1869) and the *Pictorial World* (1874); as well as *L'Illustration* (1843) in France and *Leslie's*

Illustrated Paper (1855) in America. Photographs occasionally appeared in the paper in the 1860s, although it wasn't until 1887 that the half-tone process (by which a photo is translated into a series of dots) made this an easy or widespread process. Eventually, competition from rival titles squeezed the *Illustrated London News* from its position of dominance, although it survived well into the twentieth century.

Imperialism, see **Empire.**

Importance of Being Earnest: a Trivial Comedy for Serious People **(1895), by Oscar Wilde**   Wilde's charming drawing-room comedy of manners is raised from the level of the ordinary by the high degree of extraordinary and dazzling witty epigrams. In a way, this polished and economical wit is more important in the play than its half-tongue-in-cheek plot. Two young London gentlemen, Jack Worthing and Algernon (or 'Algy') Moncrieff hope to marry two well-born young women, Gwendolen Fairfax (Algy's cousin) and Cecily Cardew (Jack's ward). Both men have invented fictitious characters; Jack goes by the name 'Ernest' when in town, and when visiting his ward in the country talks of the London Ernest as a wicked brother. Algy, similarly, has created a character called 'Bunbury', a sickly individual who lives in the country and who can function as an excuse whenever he wishes to escape social obligations in London. Through a complex plotline, including a series of comical confusions of identity, it transpires that Jack was abandoned in a handbag in Victoria railway station when a baby, and that although raised as Jack his name was in truth Ernest. Gwendolen, one of whose fixed ideas is that she can only marry a man called Ernest, is satisfied. 'Jack' and Algy are revealed to be brothers, and all ends happily.

Of the many witty lines in the play, many are voiced by the forbidding old matriarch, Lady Bracknell (Algy's aunt): on Jack's orphan status, she observes 'to lose one parent, Mr Worthing, may be regarded as a misfortune; to lose both looks like carelessness'. 'All women,' we are told, 'become like their mothers. That is their tragedy. No man does. That's his.'

India   The conquest of India was the largest single annexation of territory in British history. Beginning in the 1740s, through the commercial ambitions of the East India Company backed up with military force, a variety of Indian states fell to British control. Hindsight can give an illusory sense of inevitability about the subsequent domination of the whole sub-continent, but exactly how Britain came by its most significant Imperial possession is still something of a puzzle to historians. British forces in India never amounted to more than 250,000 men at any one time; that these troops, much more susceptible to illness than the native population and not markedly better armed or better trained, over-ran the 50 millions of the sub-continent probably had more to do with luck than is generally acknowledged. Whatever the reasons for it, 'between 1791 and 1849 British forces had successively defeated the three most powerful and resilient Mughal successor states: Mysore, the Maratha polity and the Punjab' (James, 1997: 120). British military action was especially intense during the 1840s, with the first Afghan War subduing the north-west, occupying and then retreating from Afghanistan (1838–2), and engaging in the fiercely fought battles in the Punjab of the Second Sikh War (1848–9). Initially, native rulers continued in power under the British, but Governor General Lord Dalhousie chipped away at this with his much-resented 'Doctrine of Lapse'. By Indian tradition, childless rulers had adopted heirs, but Dalhousie refused to recognise these adoptees, and states in which the succession had lapsed were absorbed by the East India Company. British control was far from sure throughout the early 1850s, and the INDIAN MUTINY of 1857, although relatively swiftly suppressed, changed British attitudes to governing the sub-continent. With the Government of India Act (1858) control was moved from the East India Company – still nominally a private trading concern – to the British government, the military and civil services were thoroughly reformed, and the Doctrine of Lapse was abandoned.

After the mutiny, India saw a 30-year period of economic expansion, mirrored by an increase in population and urban development. Universities were established at Calcutta, Bombay and Madras in 1857, and a comprehensive transportation and communication network was built up over many years. In 1876 VICTORIA was proclaimed Empress of India; the sub-continent was viewed, in Disraeli's phrase, as 'the jewel in the crown' of British Imperial rule. Further liberalisation occurred in the 1880s, particularly with Sir Courtney Ilbert's Bill (1883) enabling Indian magistrates and judges to try those Europeans charged with criminal offences who fell under their jurisdiction. The intention was to challenge the hitherto existing sense that (in the words of the liberal Viceroy Lord Rippon) 'in all ways ... the interests of the Natives of India were to be sacrificed to those of England', and to recognise 'the legitimate aspirations' of Indians (quoted in Moore, 1999: 433). Widespread 'white' British opposition to such measures, however, persuaded the more politicised Indians of the need for an organisation of their own to further their own interests. The Indian National Congress was founded in 1885.

Despite the increasing affluence of some portions of India, most of the sub-continent continued in dreadful poverty. Newer Indian radicals blamed this rural backwardness on Britain's Imperial rule: for instance, Dadabhai Naoroji's *Poverty and Un-British Rule in India* (London, 1901) advanced the 'drain' theory, that Britain siphoned off India's wealth to pay for the high cost of the army and civil administration. According to Robin Moore, 'modern scholarship has, while acknowledging the existence of 'the drain', been sceptical of its significance, believing it too small to explain the persistence of poverty' (Moore, 1999: 444). What is undeniable is that India in the nineteenth century did not become significantly industrialised: by 1900 nearly three-quarters of adult males worked in agriculture, and only 10 per cent of the population lived in cities.

Pre-Mutiny, India had a low profile in British culture. The most notable exception to this was Captain Meadows Taylor's (1808–76) novel *Confessions of a Thug* (1839), in which Ameer Ali, a devotee of the secretive and murderous 'thugee' cult, relates his shocking adventures. The popularity of the novel introduced the word 'thug' into the English language, but it represents an example of early Victorian 'orientalising': characterising eastern culture as exotic, sensual and violent. Even with the widespread interest provoked by the Mutiny, India continued to appear in this caricature form in English fiction: three Hindu thugs haunt the background of Wilkie COLLINS' *The Moonstone* (1868), attempting to retrieve the cursed Indian gemstone of the book's title; and Neville Landless, a character in DICKENS' *Edwin Drood* (1870), reveals his Indian racial heritage via dark skin and a tendency to fly into passionate rages. Not until Rudyard Kipling (1865–1936) did a British writer of genius take up India as theme and subject, and treat it with anything approaching sensitivity. Kipling had been born in Bombay, and grew up steeped in Indian life until returning to a boarding school in Britain at the age of six. In 1882 he returned to India, working on the *Lahore Civil and Military Gazette* as a journalist, and writing many novels, stories and poems. Although he settled in England in 1899, India appeared in his writing throughout his career, beginning with *Plain Tales from the Hills* (1888) and the stories of Indian-set military life *Soldiers Three* (1888). *Kim* (1901) is his most celebrated, and most Indian, novel: in the title character, an English boy who grows up running wild in Indian bazaars and so suntanned as to be mistaken for a native, Kipling found a correlative for the point of contact between West and East.

Further reading

Raj: the Making and Unmaking of British India (1997) by James Lawrence; 'India 1818–1860: the Two Faces of Colonisation' by D.D. Washbrook and 'Imperial India 1858–1914' by Robin J. Moore in *The Oxford History of the British Empire: Volume III, The Nineteenth-Century* (1999) edited by Andrew Porter.

Indian Mutiny (1857)   No more generally accepted name for this event has gained general currency, although calling this uprising a 'mutiny' necessarily aligns us with the cultural bias of the British 'overlords' rather than the native Indian population. In the nineteenth century it was sometimes known as the 'Sepoy Rebellion', sepoys being the locally recruited Indian troops that augmented the British army.

The British had annexed the whole of INDIA by the end of the 1840s, but the conquest was far from sure, especially in the more recently occupied states of the north. The trigger for the mutiny was a rumour that passed through the Sepoys in several northern states concerning cartridges. The army had been equipped with the Enfield rifle, which was loaded by tearing open a paper cartridge of gunpowder, tipping it down the barrel and ramming a bullet home after it. In the hurry of battle soldiers often used their teeth to rip this cartridge, and the rumour (which had some basis in truth) was that the cartridge paper was greased with pig and cow fat. The cow is a sacred animal for Hindus, and Muslims regard pig products as unclean; such troops refused to handle the cartridges, and were punished under military law, sometimes very harshly. The actual mutiny began in Meerut, in northern India, in June 1857 with an attempt by sepoys to free their imprisoned fellows. The revolt moved swiftly up and down the Ganges valley, although it never spread beyond the north of the country.

Fighting was fierce, and the British responded with much brutality; a common form of execution, for instance, was to tie mutineers to the mouths of cannons and blow them to pieces. This was reported in detail and with enthusiasm in the British press; the ILLUSTRATED LONDON NEWS published a rather grisly illustration of this form of execution at Peshawur (3 October 1857), subtitling it 'blowing from the guns'. Earlier in the year the same paper had insisted that 'our house in India is on fire . . . To lose that house would be to lose power, prestige and character – to descend in the rank of nations . . . the fire must be extinguished at any cost' ('The Mutiny in India', 4 July 1857).

The mutineers finally surrendered on 20 June 1858. As a direct consequence of the mutiny, the British ended direct rule of the sub-continent by the East India Company, bringing it officially into the British Empire to be governed by a Viceroy from Britain. The uprising also marked the end of the (by this time much reduced) Mughal Empire; the deposed Emperor Bahadur Shah (1775–1862) was exiled to Burma.

Industrial novels   Fictional reactions to the increasing process of the 'Industrial Revolution' form an important strand of the novel. The first industrial novels tended to express 'liberal' concern at the particular misery of specific individual industrial workers rather than trying to encompass or anatomise 'industrialisation' itself. Harriet Martineau's (1802–76) 'A Manchester Strike' (1835) – often cited as the first industrial tale – deals in sentimental but heartfelt style with the miseries of a factory worker's life; although Martineau herself was an aggressive champion of the rights of factory owners too, and published *The Factory Controversy: a Warning Against Meddling Legislation* (1855). Frances Trollope's (1780–1863) *Michael Armstrong: the Factory Boy* (1839) and Charlotte Tonna's (1790–1846) *Helen Fleetwood* (1841) highlighted the abuse of child-workers, and contributed to the climate of opinion leading up to the passing of the FACTORY ACTS. A more sophisticated and more systemic analysis is brought to bear by DISRAELI in *SYBIL* (1845), although the emphasis on this novel is less strictly industrial and more broadly 'condition of England' (*see* SOCIAL PROBLEM novels). Charles KINGSLEY's *Alton Locke* (1850) focuses its wide-ranging critique of contemporary malaise on the figure of its CHARTIST hero, rather than on a factory worker. Elizabeth GASKELL's *Mary Barton* (1848) is perhaps the most famous industrial novel of the period, a brilliant portrayal of working suffering and the breakdown of communication between factory owners and their employees. Gaskell's later *North and South* (1855) is a much less inflammatory work, with a stronger emphasis on the difficulties of the employers; a shift of ideological content that is generally reflected in industrial fiction in the 1850s. DICKENS' *Hard Times* (1854) portrays the factory worker's lot as grim, but also goes out of its way to ridicule TRADES UNIONISM in the malignly absurd figure of the firebrand Slackbridge.

Although the predominantly middle-class authors of industrial fiction in the 1840s and 1850s approached the subject with a genuine concern for the manifest miseries of industrial workers, many of them – including Gaskell and Dickens – watched revolution sweep through Europe in 1848 with alarm, and retreated from more radical positions in their writing. In the opinion of some critics this effective backsliding vitiated the industrial novel as a force for positive social good; Raymond Williams, famously, considered the genre 'more a symptom of the confusion of industrial society than an understanding of it' (Williams, 1958: 97)

Further reading

The Industrial Reformation of English Fiction 1832–1867 (1985) by Catherine Gallagher.

Industrial Revolution   It was not the invention of steam TECHNOLOGY as such, but rather its perfection by such individuals as James Watt (1736–1819) and George Stephenson (1781–48) that propelled Britain, and afterwards the western world as a whole into the industrial expansion and technological change known as the 'Industrial Revolution'. The famous phrase was coined by Victorian historian Arnold Toynbee (1852–83) who gave a series of 'Lectures on the Industrial Revolution in Britain' in 1884, by which time the effects of rapid expansive industrialisation were unmistakable. Steam-powered machines had changed manufacturing practices, made it possible (by pumping to clear mines of water) to mine deeper and more profitably, and changed the nature of transport (see TRANSPORTATION: RAILWAYS). By the 1840s steam engines were cheap enough to become cost-effective devices in many factories. Productivity rose, and with it wages and standards of living, although this improvement was patchy, with some areas benefiting much more than others.

Our image of the Industrial Revolution tends to be one of urban misery, squalor and soul-destroying factory work, as represented in INDUSTRIAL NOVELS such as DICKENS' *Hard Times* (1854). But Norman Gash has persuasively argued that

> for all its harshness and crudities the industrial revolution was the savior of British society in the conditions which prevailed between 1815 and 1865. It enabled the mass of the working classes to improve their standard of living, eat more and better food, have better houses and clothes ... and organise themselves for further social and political advancement.

(Gash, 1983: 3)

Inheritance   Wills embody the Victorian legal belief in the sanctity of individual contract. Under the law any person over the age of 21 (excepting felons, unless pardoned, those insane, or those deaf and dumb) was legally entitled to leave their property to whom they pleased. Suicides were legally permitted to bequeath personal effects, but their property was forfeited to the crown. All wills had to be written, signed by the testator, and three witnesses (soldiers and sailors on active service were permitted to leave their estates by word of mouth). Codicils – supplements to the will altering one or more of its terms – could be added provided they were signed and witnessed. Under Victorian law it was not allowed to leave any or all of your estate to charity, excepting the British Museum, Oxford and Cambridge Universities, Eton, Winchester or Westminster Schools, or 'to the augmentation of Queen Anne's bounty' (a pseudo-charitable fund for the maintenance of poor clergymen). Legal disputes on matters of inheritance were dealt with by the court of Chancery until 1875 (see LAW).

Isabella Beeton, writing in 1861, declared that 'the last proof of affection which we can give to those left behind, is to leave their worldly affairs in such a state as to excite neither jealousy, nor anger, nor heartrendings of any kind, at least for the immediate future' (quoted in Beeton (ed. Humble), 2000: 569). However, it was precisely the possible 'heartrendings' of inheritance that attracted the attention of writers. As several critics have noticed, wills and inheritance in Victorian fiction tend to be productive of distress, tension and upset; the dead hand of the past lying heavy on the living present.

The legal complexities of inheritance form plot devices for many novels of the period; ELIOT's *Felix Holt* (1866) is structured around an immensely complicated inheritance plot to do with the ownership of a valuable estate; in MIDDLEMARCH Casaubon attempts to manipulate his wife Dorothea after his death by making her inheritance of his wealth dependent on her not marrying a particular man; Dorothea rejects the inheritance and marries the man. TROLLOPE was also drawn to 'inheritance' as a plot McGuffin: in *Orley Farm* (1862) the farm of the title is left in a will to a child, and most of the novel concerns attempts by other possible heirs to prove their right to the property; *The Belton Estate* (1866) similarly traces a valuable inheritances through various heirs; *Ralph the Heir* (1871) concerns the attempt by one character to will his property to his bastard son, Ralph; the tension in *Is He Popenjoy?* (1878) depends upon the question of whether or not Popenjoy is the legitimate heir to the Marquis of Brotherton's wealth. But the greatest 'inheritance' novel of the Victorian period is almost certainly DICKENS' *Our Mutual Friend* (1864–5): the Harmon fortune, embodied in the valuable but disgusting 'dust-heap' piles of rubbish that lour over the novel, cannot be claimed by the intended heir, who is presumed dead. Various characters circle round the next in line to the money, the simple former servant Boffin, and the dangers and corruption of relying on inherited wealth become a general satire on society as a whole.

In Memoriam A.H.H. (1850), (Alfred, Lord) Tennyson

In Memoriam A.H.H. **(1850), (Alfred, Lord) Tennyson** The occasion for Tennyson's great elegy was the death of his closest friend, Arthur Hallam, of a brain aneurysm in Vienna in September 1833. News reached England on the 28th of that month, and Tennyson was 'prostrated' with grief. He began writing various poems to articulate his sorrow in October 1833, and continued doing so throughout the 1830s and 1840s. Some of these poems adopted blank-verse or dramatic-monologue forms ('Tithonus', 'Ulysses'), but many were lyrics written in formally distinctive four-line stanzas. Tennyson continued charting the shifting terrain of his bereavement over the course of the next 17 years, with the working title of *Elegies*. Whether, or at how early a stage, Tennyson decided that he was writing one long poem rather than a collection of small ones is unclear. The work was finally published in 1850, appearing anonymously, perhaps because the painfully intimate nature of much of the poetry made Tennyson disinclined to reveal himself to a public that had (up to that point) been rather hostile to his verse.

In Memoriam is an arrangement of 133 lyrics (131 numbered sections plus a prologue and an epilogue), some as short as three stanzas long, some as long as 33, all with the same rhyme scheme: abba. The whole thing charts what the first stanza of the first lyric calls the 'stepping-stones' of continuing experience, the movement of the mind and spirit out of the blackest depression occasioned by the death of a loved one and towards a state of acceptance and healing. Tennyson himself talked about the 'structure' of the poem as tripartite, and cited Dante:

> it was meant to be a kind of *Divina Commedia*, ending with happiness. The sections were written at many different places, and as the phases of our intercourse came to my memory and suggested them. I did not write them with any view to weaving them into a whole, or with any view of publication, until I found that I had written so many.

> (Tennyson, 1897, Vol. 1: 304–5)

Very few critics have seen *In Memoriam* as a satisfyingly unified poem. Christopher Ricks is of the opinion that it 'evades the proper responsibilities of the long poem', that its mode of operation is 'weaving, not growing or building' (Ricks, 1989: 152). We need not take this judgement as pejorative: this formal fragmentation effectively embodies the theme and content of the work as a whole.

The poem evidences a repeated worrying at questions of religious faith and doubt, particularly in the light of contemporary scientific discoveries. Among the most famous lines in Tennyson is the pitiful description of man as deluded in his belief in God; as a creature

> Who trusted God was love indeed
> And love Creation's final law –
> Tho' Nature, red in tooth and claw
> With ravine, shrieked against his creed –

> (Lyric 56)

This statement is ultimately contradicted by the poem's conclusion, which tries hard to inject actual belief into the statement that 'it is better to have loved and lost/Than never to have loved at all' (Lyric 27). But the overall mood of the poem is far bleaker than any positive conclusion, and it is this mood that tends to stay with the reader. Similarly, the pious invocation of God at beginning and end are undercut by the sensuality with which the poet recalls the dead love object, his 'dearest' who 'can be clasped no more' (Lyric 7) and whose loss has left him 'widowed' (Lyric 9).

Irish Question   The island of Ireland is presently divided between, in the south, an independent republic called Eire, and in the north, 'Northern Ireland', which is part of the United Kingdom. This partition was a twentieth-century attempt to solve 'the Irish question', a phrase used by British politicians to describe the disaffection of the general Irish population for several hundred years. Throughout the nineteenth century the whole of Ireland was part of the United Kingdom; as such the official religion was Protestant Anglicanism, despite the fact that most of the population were Catholic. Much of the land was owned by Protestants resident in mainland Britain, who derived rents from the estates without troubling themselves to visit. The life of the indigenous population, largely Catholic tenant rural workers, was frequently hard: the staple crop, potatoes, suffered a series of devastating blights in the 1840s. Starvation was widespread, with attendant political agitation and intermittent violence. 'Thus you have,' said a young Benjamin Disraeli near the beginning of Victoria's reign, 'a starving population, an absentee aristocracy, and an alien Church, and in addition the weakest executive in the world. That is the Irish Question' (speech quoted in *Hansard*, 16 February 1844). Solution was complicated by the fact that, whilst many Irish Catholics had little desire to be part of the United Kingdom, a sizeable population of Irish Protestants in northern Ireland (Ulster) and in Dublin were vehemently opposed to Home Rule.

Several Irishmen campaigned vigorously for the dissolution of the Union with Britain and independence of Ireland, most prominently Daniel O'Connell (1775–1847), who was known as 'the Liberator'. Political agitation was less in the 1850s and 1860s, partly because the famine had forced so many Irish men and women abroad that the population was severely denuded, and partly because Irish agriculture enjoyed a revival during these years. But the famine focused Irish animadversion very powerfully on the English; although technically part of the United Kingdom, in effect Ireland was just another colony. The Irish Republican Brotherhood, known as the 'Fenians', was founded in 1858, and pledged itself to direct action. In 1867 a Fenian bomb in Clerkenwell, London, killed or wounded over 100 people, forcing the 'Irish Question' back onto the political agenda.

On receiving the news that he was to form his first cabinet in 1868, Gladstone noted: 'my mission is to pacify Ireland' (*Diary*, 31 December 1868); although pacification is clearly a different thing from liberation. But Gladstone's view on Ireland was to undergo an important shift. Isaac Butt (1813–79), who founded the Home Government Organisation in 1870, pressing for Home Rule; and Irish MPs Michael

Davitt (1846–1906) and Charles Stewart Parnell (1846–91) were able to put pressure on the Liberal administration. Gladstone came round to the view that Home Rule would be the best course, and put an Irish Home Rule Bill before Parliament in 1886. It was rejected, as was a less extreme Second Home Rule Bill in 1893. Parnell's adulterous private life led to a moralistic split in the Home Rule Party of the 1890s, which divided between Parnellites and anti-Parnellites. Gladstone, moral to the point of priggishness, denounced Parnell, turning him from an ally into a dangerous opponent. Home Rule was another two decades away.

Italy   Before 1861 'Italy' referred to the Italian peninsula, and its many separate independent states; as Austrian statesman Metternich (1773–1859) put it in an 1847 conversation with PALMERSTON, 'Italy is a geographical expression' (Partington, 1992: 459). That changed in 1861 when the General Giuseppe Garibaldi (1807–82) led an army of 'red shirted' soldiers in a war of unification. British enthusiasm for this project was widespread, and the 'garibaldi', a red shirt in imitation of this military uniform, became popular in the 1860s (the biscuit of the same name, with currants in it, was not baked until the 1890s). Victor Emmanuel II (1820–78), previously King of Sardinia-Piedmont, became King of United Italy in 1861. The Italian politician Giuseppe Mazzini (1805–72) visited England several times to help cultivate support for Italian unity, and he inspired devotion in some. The minor poet Harriet E. Hamilton King (1840–?1920), for instance, published a lengthy poem called *The Disciples* (1873) – the title refers to Mazzini's followers, and Mazzini himself is referred to as 'he, the Seer, the Master and the Saint'.

Robert and Elizabeth Barrett BROWNING eloped together to Italy in 1846, and lived in Florence in a house called Casa Guidi for many years. Many of their poems concern Italy, and the climate of political turmoil that led to Italian unity in 1861. Elizabeth Barrett wrote directly about this topic – for instance, in *Casa Guidi Windows: a Poem in Two Parts* (1851), detailing the aftermath of the REVOLUTIONS OF 1848 in Florence and other Italian states, and looking forward to an Italy unified and free of foreign domination. The explicitly political *Poems Before Congress* (1860) ploughed a similar furrow. Her husband was similarly enamoured of Italy: in 'De Gustibus' (1855) he declared 'Italy, my Italy! . . . Open my heart and you will see/Graved inside of it, Italy' (ll. 39–44). But he expressed his Italophilia in a less stridently political manner. Many of the poems in MEN AND WOMEN concern Italian locations, or give voice to famous historical Italians; and Browning's masterpiece *THE RING AND THE BOOK* recreates in extraordinary detail a seventeenth-century Italy.

J

Jack the Ripper   Gruesome nickname for an otherwise unidentified serial killer who murdered a number of prostitutes in the Whitechapel region of east London in the autumn of 1888. Mary Ann Nichols, Annie Chapman, Catherine Eddowes, Elizabeth Stride and Mary Kelly were all working-class London women, killed with a knife; some of them were then mutilated. The culprit was never caught, but the crimes have possessed a great fascination for many, then and since; 'Ripperologists' have proposed a number of possible names as the identity of this figure, including (most plausibly) the working-class George Chapman (1865–1903), who was later apprehended and executed for poisoning his wife. Sir William Gull (1816–90), Victoria's personal physician, and the painter Walter Sickert (1860–1942) have also been put forward as the murderer, although less convincingly.

Further reading

The Complete History of Jack the Ripper (2002) by Philip Sugden.

***Jane Eyre* (1847), Charlotte Brontë**   Published as by 'Currer Bell' (Brontë's pseudonym) in 1847, *Jane Eyre* is a *Bildungsroman*, which is to say a novel in which the central character grows and develops across the course of the story.

Jane, a penniless orphan, begins the novel in the family of her aunt, Mrs Reed; neglected and bullied by turns, she breaks out passionately and is punished by being sent to Lowood Institution, a severely puritanical school. There the routine is leavened by the kindness of one superintendent, Miss Temple, and by Jane's friendship with a fellow orphan Helen Burns. Helen dies of tuberculosis in Jane's arms, and Jane endures her time at school until she herself becomes a teacher. After Miss Temple's marriage Jane goes to work as a governess at Thornfield Hall in the Yorkshire countryside. She is expected to tutor Adèle, the young daughter of the master of the House, Mr Rochester. Rochester, though a grim and forbidding man has a sardonic wit and becomes fascinated with the plain, poor figure of Jane. After various vicissitudes they fall in love; but on the eve of the wedding Rochester's secret is revealed: he is already married, and his wife Bertha, a violent madwoman, has been confined to the attic of Thornfield Hall. Jane runs away, nearly dies of starvation on the moors, and is eventually taken in and cared for by the Reverend St John Rivers and his sisters. Jane inherits a little money, and nearly marries the earnest but dull Rivers to become a missionary's wife; but she hears what seems to be a telepathic appeal from Rochester, and returns to Thornfield Hall. She finds that it has been burned to the ground by Mad Bertha (who died in the fire she had started), and that Rochester is now blind and humbled. The last chapter of Jane's narrative begins with the famous line, 'Reader, I married him.'

Jerrold, Douglas (1803–1857)   Jerrold's eventful life saw him join the Navy at the age of ten (an experience he drew on for some of his later dramatic writing); he became disillusioned with the way the officers treated the men, and left after a few years to become apprenticed to a printer. He worked for several years as a compositor on the *Sunday Monitor*, eventually rising to become the newspaper's drama critic, as well as writing his own plays. The son of an actor-manager, Jerrold's interest in the theatre was life-long. He caused a splash with his vigorous, superb melodrama *Black-Ey'd Susan, or All In The Downs* (1829), a colourful piece set in the Royal Navy of the day. He wrote a large number of often successful plays in the same popular idiom, including *Fifteen Years of a Drunken's Life* (1828), *The Mutiny of the Nore* (1830) and *The Prisoner of Ludgate* (1831).

In 1831 Jerrold started a short-lived journal *Punch in London*. Ten years later he joined with Mark Lemon (1809–70), Henry Mayhew (1812–87), and the illustrator John Leech (1817–64) to form the satirical-political magazine Punch. Jerrold and Mayhew shared concerns about political and social reform, and used the magazine to critique the status quo and the Tory establishment, lending *Punch* a reputation as a radical journal throughout the 1840s. By the 1850s, however, Jerrold became disillusioned with that he saw as an increasingly Tory flavour to the magazine, and a diminution of the political content in favour of broader comic effect. A good friend of Charles Dickens, Jerrold worked as a sub-editor of the *Daily News* during Dickens' brief editorship. He also set up a number of journalistic vehicles of his own, including *The Illuminated Magazine* (1843–44; an illustrated periodical in the style of, and published by the publisher of, the Illustrated London News), *Jerrold's Shilling Magazine* (1845–8) and *Lloyd's Weekly Newspaper* (1852–7). He died unexpectedly in 1857, and Dickens organised a number of benefits for his widow and children.

Jingoism   This term for excessively nationalistic, bigoted or chauvinistic patriotism derives from a comic song by G.W. Hunt (1825–77). In 1878 Disraeli was considering sending a fleet to intervene in the Russo–Turkish War; the popular music hall song was cheered by those who supported the policy, especially the verse:

> We don't want to fight, but By Jingo if we do,
> We've got the ships, we've got the men, we've got the money too.
> We've fought the Bear before, and while we're Britons true,
> The Russians shall not have Constantinople.

More considered Victorian opinion deplored 'jingoism' as a form of bullying, and although the phrase is still used as a shorthand for excessive patriotic enthusiasm it does not very accurately reflect mainstream Victorian opinion.

Journalism   At the beginning of the Victorian period, journalism was a relatively restrained profession, and newspaper and magazine articles were usually published anonymously. However, newspaper and journal culture in Britain began changing rapidly and drastically in the 1860s. Advertising duties for newspapers were abolished in 1837, stamp tax (which had usually added a penny to newspaper prices) in 1855, and paper duty in 1861. The abandonment of these so-called 'taxes on knowledge' led to a boom in journalistic media: many new newspapers were founded, amongst them the *Liverpool Daily Post*, the *Manchester Guardian* (nowadays the *Guardian*, and based in London) and the *Daily Telegraph*. A huge number of increasingly specialised journals appeared as well, perhaps as many as 25,000 separate titles were published in the Victorian period, most in the latter half. A list of only a few of these titles gives a sense of the range: *The Sussex Agricultural Press*; *The Edinburgh Medical and Surgical Journal*; *Ironworkers Journal*; *Baptist Magazine*; *Primitive Methodist Magazine*; *British Quarterly Review*, *Northern Star* (a Chartist journal); *Suffragette*; *Art Journal*; *Nature*; *The Englishwoman's Domestic Magazine*; *The Queen*; *Boys' Own Paper*; *Girl's Own Paper* (Matthew, 2000: 200). The leading Whig magazine was the *Westminster Review*, the leading Tory journal the *Quarterly Review*, and the dominant newspaper remained *The Times*. By the 1870s and 1880s a 'New Journalism' was beginning to dominate reporting in Britain, sometimes called 'yellow journalism' (after an issue of the *New York World* in 1895 that printed a cartoon figure in a yellow dress on its front page as a gimmick to attract readers with colour). Unashamedly populist, this form of journalism stressed 'human interest', gossip, sports, celebrity and a punchy narrative structure to stories that replaced the discursive, prolix, associative elegance of older journalism. Headlines and sub-headings were given greater prominence, stories tended to be shorter, and a sensationalist tone became more common. In America Joseph Pulitzer (1847–1911) led the way in this new journalism; in 1885 in Britain, William Stead (1849–1912) created a sensation for the *Pall Mall Gazette* with his article 'Maiden Tribute to Modern Babylon', which exposed the prevalence of child prostitution. Perhaps the man most responsible for the revolution in popular journalism in Britain was Lord Northcliffe, whose *Answers* (founded 1888), and especially his ha'penny *Daily Mail* (1896) and *Daily Mirror* (1903) were the first manifestations of genuinely mass press. By the end of the century the 'fourth estate', as the press became known, had assumed the position of dominance it maintained throughout the twentieth century.

Jude the Obscure (1894), by Thomas Hardy

This prodigiously gloomy masterpiece was so savagely received by critics (the *Pall Mall Gazette* called it 'dirt, drivel and damnation') that it dissuaded Hardy from writing any more fiction; he totally abandoned the form that had served him so well for so long, and concentrated on writing poetry.

Jude, an orphan in a small Wessex village called Maygreen, is inspired to better himself. By day he works as an apprentice stonemason, and by night studies, hoping to go to Christminster University (as Hardy fictionalises Oxford). His plans are destroyed by Arabella Dorn, who traps him into marriage by pretending to be pregnant. The marriage is miserable, and Jude takes to drink, until Arabella leaves him suddenly. Jude goes to Christminster to work as a mason, and meets his beautiful cousin Sue Brideshead, a free-thinking NEW WOMAN. After various vicissitudes, in which Sue marries Jude's old schoolteacher, she and Jude decide they cannot live without one another. They live together, without marrying, in a new village where they are not known, and have two children; their family is enlarged by a strange little boy, nicknamed 'Old Father Time', sent to Jude by Arabella. The family move to Christminster again, where Sue is insulted by the mistress of their boarding house. The unusually gloomy and sensitive boy Old Father Time hangs himself and his two younger siblings, leaving a note that reads: 'done because we are too menny'. Sue then miscarries, and renounces her atheism in the belief that God is punishing her; she returns to her husband. Jude returns to Arabella, but drinks himself to death.

Kingsley, Charles (1819–1875) Kingsley was born in Devon, the son of a curate, and despite a period of doubt at university it was his religious faith that most thoroughly defined him as a man. His popular novels and many poems treat their varied themes from religious points of view, and it is as the leading advocate of MUSCULAR CHRISTIANITY and CHRISTIAN SOCIALISM that he is remembered. He apparently wrote poems and sermons at the age of four, and according to his wife 'his delight was to make a little pulpit in his nursery, from which, after putting on his pinafore as a surplice, he would preach to an imaginary congregation' (Kingsley, 1883: 3). Indeed, his religious devotion is only saved from priggishness by the enormous vigour and energy with which he followed through his convictions.

He attended King's College, London, and Magdalene College, Cambridge, graduating with a first-class degree in 1842 and becoming a curate at Eversley, Hampshire, in the same year. He was to live in Hampshire for the rest of his life. In 1844 he married Fanny Grenfell, and became vicar of Eversley. Four children followed in quick succession, and in 1848 Kingsley published his first major work, *The Saint's Tragedy*, a verse-drama. This won him the admiration of Frederick Maurice (1805–72) who was to become a lifelong friend and supporter. Prompted by Maurice, Kingsley accepted a Professorship at Queen's College, London.

It was also in 1848 that Kingsley became involved in the CHARTIST agitations, writing pamphlets under the pseudonym 'Parson Lot', which declared support for the aims of 'moral force Chartism'. His first novel, *Yeast*, was serialised in *Fraser's Magazine* in 1848, and published in book form in 1851. The story, in which a young country gentleman, Lancelot Smith, becomes politicised by witnessing the suffering of the rural poor and by reading Carlyle, was met with hostility by many readers of *Fraser's* (a journal subtitled 'For Town and Country', and much patronised by the English squirearchy). The controversy, and Kingsley's own heavy workload, led to a nervous breakdown in 1849, which perhaps explains the gap between serial and book publication. Over the winter of 1849/50 Kingsley worked at *Alton Locke, Tailor and Poet: an Autobiography* (1850), a more explicitly SOCIAL PROBLEM NOVEL. The protagonist is a working-class Londoner who toils in a sweatshop making 'cheap clothes and nasty'. He is introduced to Chartism, survives various hardships, manages to educate himself, and becomes a famous working-class poet. Caught up in a Chartist riot Locke is sent to prison, and after his release falls ill. Nursed by the heroine Eleanor, he moves from Chartist belief to Christian Socialism. The novel ends with Locke and Eleanor emigrating to America, although Locke dies on the voyage. Through 1850 and 1851 various establishment figures, and journals such as the *Quarterly Review* and *Edinburgh Review* denounced Kingsley as a dangerous radical, and Christian Socialism as akin to Communism; one sermon Kingsley preached in London on 'the Message of the Church to Labouring Men' was so inflammatory that the Bishop of London forbade him from preaching in the city again (although this interdiction was later lifted).

After 1851, however, Kingsley's radicalism became increasingly muted. He wrote a much tamer historical novel, *Hypatia* (1853), a colourful and sometimes violent novel set in Alexandria in the fifth century, and after spending time in Torquay wrote a book of popular biology about the marine life he observed there, *Glaucus, or the Wonders of the Shore* (1855). Another historical novel, *Westward Ho!* (1855), follows its violent, passionate young hero Amyas Leigh through various sixteenth-century maritime adventures, including bloodily rendered battle scenes with Spaniards, hazard at sea, treks through jungle, and fighting the Spanish Armada in 1588 with Sir Francis Drake. *Two Years Ago* (1857) is set, as its title suggests, in 1855, and is largely concerned with the impact of a cholera epidemic on a Cornish village. Kingsley used the novel to advance his very sensible ideas on the need for proper sanitation. Works for children included a retelling of Greek myth for young readers, *The Heroes* (1856), and the much-loved modern fairy tale, *The Water Babies* (1863).

By the 1860s Kingsley was, as far as the Establishment was concerned, no longer the radical to be shunned, but a respectable figure to be embraced. He was appointed one of the Queen's chaplains in 1859, and became Professor of History at Cambridge in 1860. The religious beliefs of his younger days had led him to campaign energetically for social and sanitary reform; in later life his lifelong anti-Catholicism came to the fore. In *Macmillan's Magazine* for January 1864 he insisted that 'truth, for its own sake, had never been a virtue with the Roman clergy'. This remark, which Kingsley connected to one of John Henry NEWMAN's sermons, led to an (on his side) ill-tempered public quarrel with Newman over this question of Catholicism and 'truth', one result of which was Newman's elegant self-defensive autobiography *Apologia Pro Vita Sua* (1864). Kingsley's health started to fail in the 1860s. *Hereward the Wake* (1865), another violently masculine-heroic historical novel, was to be his last. He travelled to the West Indies with his daughter in 1869, and travelled over the Atlantic again in 1874, this time to America. His health gave out whilst there, and he returned to England to die at Eversley in January 1875.

Kingsley's writings often strike modern-day readers as too didactic and too explicitly religious, although the sheer range of his achievement is impressive in its own right: a list of the literary forms he mastered would include novels, poems, plays, historical studies, children's literature. What links the various aspects of his achievement is less religion, and more a particular concept of manliness. A London lawyer, hearing Kingsley lecture in 1851, wrote to him revealingly:

> no other man in England could have done what he did. I say *man*
> emphatically, because if I were to seek a word to express my opinion of it, I
> would say it was the *manliest* thing I had ever heard. Such a right, bold, honest
> way . . .

> (Kingsley, 1883: 115)

Most of his novels and much of his poetry celebrate an exaggerated form of masculine virility and hardiness, even unto ultraviolence. A poem such as 'Ode to the North-East Wind' (1858), for instance, makes the unspoken connection between manliness, race, physical strength and endurance, and God that is also the cornerstone of 'Muscular Christianity':

> 'Tis the hard grey weather
> Breeds hard English men.
> . . .
> Come; and strong within us
> Stir the Vikings' blood;
> Bracing brain and sinew;
> Blow, thou wind of God!

Kitchener, Horatio Herbert (1850–1916)   Soldier of Irish birth who rose to senior positions in the army rapidly: he was appointed commander of the British army in Egypt in 1892, and played a decisive military role in defeating the 'Mahdi' (Muhammad 'Ahmad Ibn 'Abadallah (1844–85), the popular Islamic leader who led an uprising against colonial rule in the Sudan in 1881). After the re-conquest of the Sudan, Kitchener was made Governor-General of the country in 1889. He played a significant military role in the Boer War as Commander-in-Chief of British forces from 1900, and was later Secretary of State for War in 1914 at the beginning of the First World War.

L

Laissez-faire   The dominant economic doctrine of the nineteenth century, a belief (the French means 'allow [people] to do') that government should not interfere in the workings of business, trade or manufacture by way of taxation or legislation, but should rather allow businessmen and traders to do as they please. It is often opposed to 'interventionist' or 'statist' philosophies, such as were theorised by Karl Marx and others. According to its advocates laissez-faire produces the greatest wealth for society as a whole and encourages self-reliance; for its opponents it enriches the rich whilst allowing more general poverty, injustice and oppression to carry on unchecked.

As Boyd Hilton has argued, the dominance of laissez-faire economics throughout the Victorian period was linked to religious belief, resulting often in 'evangelical economics' based on the belief that 'God runs the world on laissez-faire lines, in the sense that he does not meddle with his own mechanism, and so man should not meddle either' (Hilton, 1977: 17). The issue was productive of tremendous vehemence. Lord Londonderry gave a speech to Parliament in 1850 deploring a bill to establish a safety inspectorate for mines that could ensure mine owners' compliance with safety measures – something that seems to us, as David Newsome points out, 'a very moderate' piece of legislation. Londonderry, however, called it 'the most mischievous and unjust measure that could possibly be imagined', allowing outsiders to pry into 'the interior concerns of [the pit-owner's] work, all his wealth, all his property' (quoted in Newsome, 1997: 59–60).

Opponents of laissez-faire saw it as an abdication of moral responsibility. Henry Spencer (*Studies in Sociology* 14, 1873: 352) called laissez-faire 'almost wicked in its indifference'; although the use of the word 'almost' here is extremely revealing of Victorian liberal havering on the issue. Serious opponents of laissez-faire economics appeared only on the most radical left; even Utilitarianism, which otherwise proposed a number of government and legislative interventions into the economy, believed in laissez-faire principles. Nor was nineteenth-century laissez-faire a simple non-interventionist philosophy: many of its proponents were in favour of measures such as the Corn Laws.

Laureateship   'Poet Laureate' is the title given by the ruling monarch to a poet who becomes thereby an officer of the royal household. Originally the holder of the post was expected to write court odes and celebratory poems on royal occasions, although latterly the position has become instead predominantly a marker of poetic reputation.

At Victoria's accession Robert Southey (1774–1843) was Poet Laureate, a position he had been granted in 1813, although by 1837 his mental powers were waning and he did no significant work in his last seven years. On his death in 1843 the elderly William Wordsworth (1770–1850) was made Laureate. Like Southey, Wordsworth's greatest achievements were all behind him by this stage in his life, and he wrote little poetry during his time in the post. On his death public interest was high regarding his successor. The *Athenaeum* (1 June 1850: 585) proposed that a female Poet Laureate was most appropriate to a female monarch, and insisted that 'no living poet of either sex ... can prefer a higher claim than Mrs. Elizabeth Barrett BROWNING'. Barrett Browning herself thought Leigh Hunt the most deserving choice. In the event Samuel Rogers (1763–1855) was asked, but declined on grounds of age, and in November 1850 Alfred TENNYSON accepted the post. Tennyson took his duties as laureate seriously, writing a number of stately (in several senses) 'official' odes, including his 'Ode on the Death of the Duke of Wellington' (1852) and 'Ode on the Jubilee of Queen Victoria' (1887) with its optimistic appraisal of Victorian achievements:

> Fifty years of ever-broadening Commerce!
> Fifty years of ever-brightening Science!
> Fifty years of ever-widening Empire!

> (ll. 52–4)

On Tennyson's death in 1892 Algernon SWINBURNE was canvassed by some as the natural successor (Queen Victoria is supposed to have remarked 'I have heard that Swinburne is the best poet in my kingdom'), but his professed republicanism, and the – in the opinion of many – indecent nature of much of his poetry effectively disqualified him. In the event, the minor poet Alfred Austin (1835–1913) was appointed Laureate in 1896, to widespread derision. When, shortly after the appointment, he published an ode in *The Times* celebrating the Jameson Raid – a shabby and unsuccessful Imperial adventure in South Africa that led to the BOER WAR – critics mocked that the appointment had been made by the Tory administration for ideological rather than poetic reasons. Austin was broadly ridiculed, and indeed, the office of the Laureateship no longer held the glamour it once had. The *Literary Digest* (8 February 1896) quoted William Dean Howells: 'the notion of any great man seriously performing [the Laureate's] duties is inextinguishably comic; and the selection of a man who is not great and never can be great had the highest propriety and fitness imaginable'.

Law and legal institutions   Law in England and Wales is based chiefly on the principle of precedent, which is to say on a body of 'case law', specific judgments made in specific cases collected over time and which are supposed to guide judges in adjudicating current cases. Such precedent is augmented on occasion by specific legislation from Parliament. There was (and, shamefully, is) no written Constitution in the British Isles, and no American-style Bill of Rights codifying the law and enshrining underlying principles, although several influential Victorian legal theorists campaigned for just such a 'codification'. In particular, Jeremy Bentham (1748–1832) advocated an English version of the French Code Napoléon to establish a 'science of legislation', and his followers pursued the cause through the century. James Fitzjames Stephen (1829–94) was probably the most distinguished jurist of the period; he spent three years, from 1869 to 1872, codifying Indian Law, and pressed for similar reforms in Britain, writing such books as *A General View of the Criminal Law of England* (1863) and *Liberty, Equality, Fraternity* (1873). But despite a number of important reforms of the legal establishment, this key change was not brought about. Such reform as occurred over the period (and Simon Petch argues that 'substantive legal reform was more extensive in the Victorian period than at any time in English history since . . . the English Civil War' (Petch, 1999: 164)) was practical rather than fundamental: the extension of the POLICE, an increase in welfare provision via education, health and local government, the shift towards greater parliamentary democracy in the three REFORM ACTS of 1832, 1867 and 1884, together with the legalisation of trades unions in 1871 – all this contributed to a change in the legal basis of the nation, secularising and socialising it. One benchmark year was 1861, in which capital punishment 'was effectively limited to the crimes of murder and treason' (Petch, 1999: 165), and which also saw the *ESSAYS AND REVIEWS* case. In this latter case, some of the authors concerned were prosecuted for heresy; the eventual decision by the Privy Council in favour of these writers undermined the power of ecclesiastic courts.

At VICTORIA's accession there existed, for historical reasons, three common law courts (Queen's Bench, Exchequer and Common Pleas) and another court that dealt with 'equity', known as the Court of Chancery. 'Equity' was a system of law that existed side by side with common law (precedent) and statute law (legislation passed by Parliament), and could on occasion supersede it. It, and its court of Chancery, had particularly to do with questions of trust and inheritance, but its practice was extremely complex and dilatory, so much so that in the nineteenth century Chancery became a byword for ruinous delay and expense. One notorious case was that of Jennings (an alternate spelling of the name sometimes used was 'Jennens'), a dispute over the rights to some property that began at the beginning of the century and dragged on until 1878. The costs of the case were so high (£140,000) that they consumed all the property involved. Charles DICKENS used the Jennings case as the basis for the case of Jarndyce versus Jarndyce at the core of his novel *Bleak House* (1852–3), a masterly satire on the legal profession generally, in which a great number of individuals are snared by the Chancery proceedings to their financial and psychological ruin, and in which lawyers are portrayed as financially avid and fundamentally alienated from the population they purport to represent. Dickens' portrait was of its time: in 1851 *The Times* attacked the abuses of Chancery in particular ('a name of terror, a devouring gulf ... a suit in the court is endless, bottomless, and insatiable') and the legal establishment in general: 'we believe that the time is rapidly approaching when the public will and must triumph over the inertia of an antiquated jurisprudence and the obstacles raised by personal or professional interest' (quoted in Sanders, 1994: 846–7). Reform followed, beginning with the Chancery Procedure Acts of 1852. Eventually, with the Judicature Acts of 1873 and 1875, Equity was merged with common law, and the common law courts and Chancery were replaced by a single High Court, with three divisions.

Professionally the legal system was two-tier. The upper tier was 'the bar'; barristers were entitled to plead in court, and it was from the rank of barristers that judges were chosen, a situation that remains the case today. Being a barrister was an archetypal 'gentlemanly' profession; typically, barristers had been to public school and Oxford or Cambridge, although they would not have studied law at university, the subject not appearing on the syllabus (the University of London established a Law School in 1826, but it did not flourish). After university, an aspiring barrister would spend five years as apprentice at one of the Inns of Court in London, after which they would be 'called to the bar' and allowed to practise law. Whilst expensive, this path to the bar provided only a nugatory legal education. Some barristers nevertheless went on to make a great deal of money: in the 1880s Charles Russell charged £500 to accept a brief and £100 a day for as long as the case lasted. But income was not guaranteed, and in general a barrister needed private means, at least whilst establishing a reputation for himself. This fact tended to reserve the profession to the moneyed classes.

The lower tier was that of solicitors and attorneys-at-law (the latter category was abolished in the reforms of 1875). Excluded from the monopoly of the bar, solicitors had their own monopoly on conveyancing (preparing legal documents required for the buying and selling of property), and dealt with all manner of legal documentation, contracts and wills and the like. They might be gentlemen, like the trusted Dedlock family solicitor Tulkinghorn in *Bleak House*, or Mortimer Lightwood in *Our Mutual Friend* (1864–5), but more generally they were middle-middle or even lower-middle class, and would generally have been expected to use the tradesman's rather than the main entrance to a house. Although barristers were socially superior to solicitors, they were professionally dependent upon them, for barristers were employed by solicitors on behalf of their clients, rather than directly by the clients themselves.

However class-bound Victorian legal institutions appear to us, many Victorians themselves saw the law as (to quote the *Quarterly Review*) an elastic band, uniting the aristocracy with the classes below it . . . the humblest tradesman, who can give his son a good education and enter him at an Inn of Court, may hope to see him rise to fame and opulence at the Bar, become a Judge and even Lord Chancellor.

('The English Bar and the Inns of Court', *Quarterly Review* 275, January 1875: 139–40)

In practice such social mobility was severely limited, and most barristers and solicitors were upper middle class or aristocratic, often the younger sons who could not expect an inheritance; but Scawthorne, a character in George Gissing's (1857–1903) novel *The Nether World* (1889), rises from the lower-class 'nether world' of the book's title to the 'upper world' of social respectability by becoming a solicitor.

Victorian literature manifested a deep interest in the law, and in two aspects of legal practice in particular. On the one hand, the ins and outs of INHERITANCE law provide the plot mechanism for countless Victorian novels. Books like Dickens' *Bleak House, Great Expectations* (1861) and *Our Mutual Friend* are unusual in depicting lawyers solely as rapacious, morally compromised or idle. More usually, as in Antony TROLLOPE's *Cousin Henry* (1879) and *Orley Farm* (1862), or George ELIOT's *Felix Holt* (1866), the law emerges in a positive light: missing or contested wills are balanced against concepts of natural justice, and the legal establishment is purely facilitatory. In addition, many Victorian writers became fascinated with the essential legal notion of 'testimony'. Particular texts are structured as various characters presenting 'evidence' to a higher authority, or to the reader. Wilkie COLLINS was struck, whilst attending a court hearing in 1856, by the narrative possibilities of court testimony, and his most successful novel *The Woman in White* (1860) is divided between a number of first-person narrators who all tell their side of the tale. The greatest example of this form of fundamentally 'legal' text is Robert BROWNING's epic poem THE RING AND THE BOOK (1868-9), based on an actual case-at-law, and structured around the testimony before court of several individuals. Although Browning's text satirises the pedantry and quibbling of the two actual lawyers (Book 8, 'Dominis Hyacinthus de Archangelia', and Book 9, 'Juris Doctor Johannes-Baptista Bottinius') the conception of the work as a whole depends upon a fundamentally legal ideological structure, with the Pope as the ultimate legal authority ensuring that wickedness is punished and right rewarded.

Further reading

An Introduction to English Legal History (1990) by J.H. Baker; 'Legal' by Simon Petch in A Companion to Victorian Literature and Culture (1999) edited by Herbert Tucker.

Lear, Edward (1812–1888)   Born to a large London family, Lear's first employment resulted from his considerable talents as an artist and illustrator. In 1831, aged only 19, he was hired by London Zoo to draw the birds, in particular the parrots and budgerigars (he published a gorgeous volume of these pictures, *The Family of the Psittacidae* in 1832). This led to other work, drawing *The Knowsley Menagerie* (1832–6), the varied collection of wildlife owned by the Earl of Derby at his house Knowsley. In 1836 Lear left Britain to travel widely in Europe, the Middle East and India, painting a large number of landscapes and other works. In 1846, back in Britain, he gave Queen Victoria drawing lessons, and published his most famous work, *A Book of Nonsense* (1846), a masterpiece of children's literature. The hilarious and suggestive limericks collected here were a great popular hit, and the volume went through dozens of editions through the rest of the century. Lear published several other collections of nonsense verse, including *Nonsense Songs, Stories, Botany and Alphabets* (1871), *More Nonsense* (1871) and *Laughable Lyrics: A Fourth Book of Nonsense Poems, Songs, Botany, Music, Etc* (1876). These later collections contained such nonsense-Romantic and atmospheric poems as 'The Dong with a Luminous Nose', 'The Owl and the Pussy-cat' and 'The Jumblies'. As with the best children's poetry there is a violent and subversive undercurrent to the apparently ludicrous little poems, as with the old woman from Stroud with her excessive reaction to being hemmed in by people:

> There was an old person of Stroud,
> Who was horribly jammed in a crowd;
> Some she slew with a kick, some she scrunched with a stick,
> That impulsive old person of Stroud.

> (Lear, *More Nonsense*, 1871)

This infectious vigour of action and idiom ('jammed', 'scrunched') captures the enthusiasm of childhood. Similarly, there is genuine threat behind the landscape of 'The Dong with a Luminous Nose' ('When awful darkness and silence reign/Over the great Gromboolian plain'), whose chorus alludes to Macbethian witchcraft and monstrosity behind a playful front:

> Far and few, far and few
> Are the lands where the Jumblies live;
> Their heads are green and their hands are blue,
> And they went to sea in a sieve

Lear continued his art, producing attractive illustrated volumes such as *Journals of a Landscape Painter in Albania and Illyria* (1851), but his life had its share of miseries; homosexual in an age hostile to such predilections, he worried about his physical appearance, especially his tubby body and bulbous nose (a fact that has led some biographers to see a mournful personal significance in the miserable Dong of his poem). He died in San Remo in 1888.

Le Fanu, Sheridan (1814–1873) Born into an Irish Protestant family, Le Fanu (the name is pronounced 'lef-anew') worked as a journalist, newspaper editor and writer. His first GOTHIC-influenced tales were published in the *Dublin University Magazine* in the 1840s – a journal he later acquired and ran. He serialised a number of best-selling novels in the 1860s and 1870s, amongst them *Uncle Silas* (1864), *The Tenants of Malory* (1867), *The Rose and the Key* (1871) and several others, all of which featured dark secrets, brooding atmospheres and blood. He is best remembered today for a number of superbly chilling short stories, amongst them 'Carmilla' (a vampire tale) and 'Green Tea' (a story of possession), both published in *All in the Dark* (1866). He died of bronchitis in 1873.

Letters and postal service At the beginning of the century, letters were carried by various organisations and individuals, and usually paid for on arrival. In 1840 the Penny Post began, by which a penny stamp could be purchased and affixed to letters to pay for postage in advance, and the Post Office (later Royal Mail) established its monopoly. In 1870 a ha'penny postcard service was introduced, and parcel post was reformed and rationalised in 1883. Anthony TROLLOPE, a Post Office employee from 1834 to 1867 (as well as being a novelist), introduced public pillar boxes, into which mail could be posted, in the 1850s. 'In 1840, 46,237 letters were delivered daily in the UK; in 1890 it was 4,673,900' (Matthew, 2000: 87). In 1861 an Act of Parliament created a Post Office Savings Bank, which started the process by which postmasters and postmistresses became increasingly agents of the state in village and town life.

Lewes, George Henry (1817–1878) Best known as 'Mr George ELIOT', Lewes, though not a writer of his partner's genius, had a wide range of interests and achievements. Born into a London theatrical family, his schooling was intermittent, and his education largely self-taught. He gave up medicine, in which he was training himself, because of an inability to endure others' suffering and in 1838–9 travelled to Germany where he learnt the language and acquainted himself with German literature, philosophy and culture (he published a well-regarded life of Goethe in 1855). He married Agnew Jervis (1822–1902) in 1841, and supported himself by writing journalism, in 1850 setting up a radical weekly newspaper, *The Leader*, with his friend Thornton Hunt (1810–73). He did not seem to object when Agnes and Hunt formed a liaison, even when his wife bore his friend four children, but when he met and fell in love with George Eliot in 1852 he could not divorce her, having condoned her adultery. After 1854 Lewes and Eliot lived together as if married, causing no small scandal in the narrow world of London letters and society. Lewes' own attempts at fiction (the Goethe-inspired novel *Ranthorpe* (1847) in particular) are not successful, but as a synthesiser and communicator of continental PHILOSOPHY Lewes was important: his *Comte's Philosophy of the Sciences* (1853) introduced to Britain the positivist thought of August Comte (1798–1857), which influenced Eliot amongst others; and his *Biographical History of Philosophy* (1845–6) covered a great deal of ground. His own attempt at psychological philosophy, the multi-volume

Problems of Life and Mind (1873–9) was left unfinished at his death, and was completed by Eliot. His friend Trollope wrote an obituary praising Lewes' contributions to philosophy, criticism and biography, and adding 'there was never a man so pleasant as he with whom to sit and talk vague literary gossip over a cup of coffee and a cigar' (quoted in Ashton, 1991: 283).

Further reading

G.H. Lewes: An Unconventional Victorian (1991) by Rosemary Ashton.

Liberal   The transition from the old Whig Party – which had existed, more or less loosely, since the seventeenth century – to the Liberal Party occurred roughly halfway through the century. The old Whig Party traced its lineage back to the so-called 'Glorious Revolution' of 1688, in which the Protestant trading establishment succeeded in blocking the aristocratic, Catholic-leaning 'Tory' choice for monarch. Largely out of power from the later eighteenth century until the 1830s, the 'Whigs' returned by seizing the political initiative over the REFORM ACT OF 1832. By doing so they aligned themselves with new political ideas (which stemmed from the climate of the major eighteenth-century revolutions, although much modified) that stressed the importance of individual liberty, economic, social and religious, and with the expansion of the franchise (although the old Whigs had never been particularly democratic). The classic statement of 'liberal' values was John Stuart MILL's ON LIBERTY (1859). It followed from these principles that Liberals tended to support the abolition of the CORN LAWS (which is to say, supported liberty of trade), to support widening the franchise, and later in the century to support Irish HOME RULE (liberty for whole peoples). But party ideologies were not fixed and absolute in this period, and the Liberals included a spectrum of opinion. GLADSTONE, for instance – the most prominent and influential Liberal politician of the second half of the century – began his political career as a PEELite TORY and throughout his life was drawn to the idea of tradition. John Bright (1811–89), on the other hand, and despite serving in Gladstone's governments for many years, was much more radical and forward-looking, insisting in 1861 that 'Towns and great populations' would be a match for the 'traditions of the last century' (quoted in Shannon, Vol. 2, 1999: 7).

The emergence of SOCIALISM in the later decades of the century put new pressures on the Liberal Party, effectively moving it from a LAISSEZ-FAIRE ideological position to a more 'welfare', interventionist one, guaranteeing a basic standard of living and education. Leslie Stephen (1832–1904), writing in the last year of the century, noted

> . . . the singular change which has come over British opinion . . . The people who still call themselves liberal have disavowed all the doctrines which used to be call liberal in my youth. Cobden and Bright and J.S. Mill and all the old idols have been deposed.
>
> (Maitland, 1906: 451)

The much more socially engaged and centralist Liberal Party of Lloyd George (1863–1945) was already, by the late 1890s, established.

London   The feature of London most noted by Victorians was its enormous and increasing size. Already the largest city in the world by the eighteenth century it grew steadily throughout the nineteenth; in particular it drew huge immigrant populations, from elsewhere in Britain and around the world – in the 1850s, it has been estimated that 40 per cent of all Londoners were not born in the city. The French visitor Hippolyte Taine (1828–93) observed the city in 1862:

> Three million five hundred thousand inhabitants: it adds up to twelve cities
> the size of Marseilles, ten as big as Lyons, two the size of Paris, in a single mass
> ...Enormous, enormous – that is the word that recurs all the time.

(Quoted in Newsome, 1997: 22)

The 1841 census recorded the population of urban London to be 1,870,727; by 1851 this had risen to 2,363,341 in the urban area, with perhaps another 2,500,000 in the surrounding suburban areas. The census of 1871 recorded an urban population of 3,261,396 and a 'Greater London' population of 3,840,595.

London had always been a city divided sharply between the rich and poor, with certain districts (especially the west, the south-west and the north) affluent, and others (especially the East End, but also portions of the south-east) deprived. The well-to-do lived in such pleasant districts as Mayfair, St James, 'Belgravia', Chelsea, Knightsbridge (developed as a fashionable area in the 1860s) – and, as the city expanded later in the century, Brompton, Clapham, Putney, Hampstead and Highgate. People of good breeding but less money lived, as does Harold Skimpole in DICKENS' *Bleak House* (1852–3) in Somer's Town, or in Wandsworth, Fulham or similar places. The poor lived in the east of the city, especially Whitechapel and Bermondsey, near the docks. OLIVER TWIST in 1837 and *Our Mutual Friend* (1864–5) both portray a London divided between fashionable wealth and subsistence-level poverty. This contrast between (in the words of Asa Briggs) 'the two worlds of London, one dark and mysterious, the other dazzling and ostentatious, were of increased public interest' in the latter half of the century, 'just because late-Victorian London was being thought of more and more as a world city', the hub of a vast empire (Briggs, 1968: 317). The JACK THE RIPPER murders in the 1880s happened in deprived Whitechapel, and emphasised the contrast between the two Londons. Recruiting soldiers for the BOER WAR from London's East End revealed how prevalent malnutrition and disease were amongst the working-class population. On the other hand, a series of lavish architectural developments transformed the Embankment, Whitehall and the west of the city.

Further reading

The London Encyclopedia ((1983) 1993) by Ben Weinreb and Christopher Hibbert.

Lyric   As a broad category of poetry 'lyric' refers to poems that are neither dramatic nor narrative. Lyric poems are often short, intense descriptive or meditative verses, sometimes expressing an emotional rather than intellectual content, usually reliant on rhyme and musical poetic forms (originally 'lyric' poetry was written to be accompanied by music, a feature still registered in today's 'song lyrics'). Victorian poetry is often thought of as being predominantly dramatic (especially in the DRAMATIC MONO-LOGUE) with a strong narrative component; and yet some of the most enduring achievements of Victorian poetry were in the lyric mode. ARNOLD is a case in point: he struggled to produce the sorts of poetry he though most valid, as with EPIC fragments such as *Sohrab and Rustum* (1853) or with experiments in classical dramatic form such as the tiresome *Merope* (1858). But it is his lyric poems that have lasted best, capturing the perhaps listless but nonetheless beautiful bleakness that 'official' Arnold repudiated:

> Who order'd, that their longing's fire
> Should be as soon as kindled, cool'd?
> Who renders vain their deep desire?
> A God, a God their severance rul'd!
> And bade betwixt their shores to be
> The unplumb'd, salt, estranging sea.

('To Marguerite: Continued', 1853: ll. 19–24)

Similarly, Browning styled himself a 'dramatic' poet, but his lyric skills informed all aspects of his writing. Sometimes he wrote straightforward lyrics of great skill and affective power ('Home Thoughts from Abroad' (1845); 'Memorabilia' (1855); 'Never the Time and Place' (1883)); more usually he combined lyric form with dramatic approach. A short poem such as 'Meeting at Night' (1845), quoted in full below, reads like a lyric in its vivid brevity, and yet it includes a narrative (although an oblique one) and enacts a mode of psychological insight:

> The grey sea and the long black land;
> And the yellow half-moon large and low;
> And the startled little waves that leap
> In fiery ringlets from their sleep,
> As I gain the cove with pushing prow,
> And quench its speed in the slushy sand.
>
> Then a mile of warm, sea-scented beach;
> Three fields to cross till a farm appears;
> A tap at the pane, the quick sharp scratch
> And blue spurt of a lighted match,
> And a voice less loud thro' its joys and fears,
> Than the two hearts beating each to each!

We can read this poem as the story of a secret liaison; but we can also read it as a pure lyric, its imagery carefully paralleled from the first stanza to the second (sea/beach, moon/farm, phosphorescent waves/lighted match, boat meets beach/lover meets lover) and its effect intensely inward and affectively precise. In fact the poem requires to be read as both at once, dramatic-lyric. Browning called several of his collections after this hybrid form: *Dramatic Lyrics* (1842), *Dramatic Romances and Lyrics* (1845). As Isobel Armstrong says, the lyric

> *internalises* its status as commentary and conceals its textuality and ideology. The drama *externalises* these things . . . Later Browning discovered how to create the lyric as drama and to make the subjective lyric become the opposite of itself . . . the dramatic monologue is literally the two things at once, lyric and drama concurrently.

(Armstrong, 1993: 126)

One of Browning's most astonishing achievements is in managing this hybrid. Tennyson's genius, arguably, was wholly lyrical. He also attempted this cross-pollination, but the results were heavily biased towards lyric intensity, to the point of obscuring the narrative and dramatic elements. This is true of Maud (1855), which reads as a collocation of beautiful lyric moments but is confusing and inchoate on the level of narrative; and it is true of In Memoriam (1850) that the individual lyrics function more brilliantly by themselves than as part of a larger structure. Christina Rossetti's many beautiful, though mournful, lyrics show how close a Victorian handling of the form could come to a hymnal aesthetic.

Macaulay, Thomas Babington (1800–1859)   Although he practised as a barrister and served as Member of Parliament, it was as an essayist, reviewer and historian that Macaulay gained his greatest reputation. A Whig MP 1830–4 he was closely involved in the Reform Act of 1832, and in 1834 he took a position on the Supreme Council of India (at an annual salary of £10,000), moving to the sub-continent and playing an active role in its development, reforming the criminal code and also establishing English rather than Indian culture as the basis for Indian education. He returned to England in 1838 a wealthy man, and re-entered Parliament in 1839, serving as Secretary at War 1839–41 and Paymaster General under Lord John Russell. But by the

1840s he was much better known as a writer. Many of the essays and reviews he published throughout the 1820s and 1830s were later collected in *Essays Contributed to the Edinburgh Review, Critical and Historical* (1843), and established, amongst other things, the so-called 'Whig' conception of history – to quote Macaulay himself 'the history of England is emphatically the history of progress' ('Sir James Mackintosh'). In 1842 he published *The Lays of Ancient Rome*, poems on heroic Roman topics in rollicking ballad form that proved immensely popular, initially with the general public and later with several generations of public school pupils, although they are nowadays rather out of favour. He had been working on his large-scale History of England since 1838; the first two volumes of this work were published in 1849 to tremendous acclaim and huge sales; Volumes 3 and 4, appearing in 1855, did even better. Having lost his Parliamentary seat in 1847 he was elected again in 1852, and PALMERSTON made him First Baron Macaulay of Rothley in 1857. But his health, never good, was failing, and he died in 1859 without having either completed his *History of England* or built a career for himself in the House of Lords.

Macpherson, James. See **Ossian**.

Madness   J.C. Pritchard's *Treatise on Insanity* (1835) inaugurated a Victorian discourse of madness as a moral rather than intellectual defect, a 'morbid perversion of the feelings, affections, and active powers' that might very well exist in an individual with 'an apparently unimpaired state of the intellectual faculties' (Pritchard, quoted in Faas, 1988: 45). The treatment of insanity was therefore tinged throughout the period with moral considerations. Women were more likely to be adjudged mad than men; the pseudo-medical category of 'hysteria' – a word derived from the Greek for womb – suggests that emotional instability and insanity were intrinsically more female than male. The 'madness' of Bertha Mason Rochester in Charlotte BRONTË's JANE EYRE, for instance, has been taken by some feminist critics as a disproportionate reaction to a sexuality that, whilst inappropriate according to Victorian ideology, would not be thought of as pathological today.

Legally, the concept of 'insanity' was shaped by judicial discussion following the case of Daniel M'Naghten (1814–1865) who in 1843 attempted to assassinate the Prime Minister Sir Robert PEEL, and succeeded in killing his private secretary. Tried for murder, it emerged that M'Naghten suffered from delusions of persecution and was eventually found not guilty on grounds of insanity. The so-called 'M'Naghten rules' that were formulated after this case established that a plea of insanity could be successful only if the court was convinced that the accused was so defective in mind 'as not to know the nature and quality of the act he was doing, or, if he did know it, that he did not know he was doing what was wrong' (Chief Justice Tindal, quoted in Petch, 1999: 159).

There was in the earlier period of VICTORIA's reign a vogue for a 'literature of madness', in which perception, filtered through extreme or insane consciousness, can be used to create interesting poetic effects in the early Victorian period. Many early DRA-MATIC MONOLOGUES by BROWNING are spoken by mad characters: the pathologically possessive narrator of 'My Last Duchess' (1842) has murdered his wife; 'Johannes Agricola in Meditation' (1842) suffers an extreme religious mania; the speaker of 'Porphyria's Lover' (1842) is so insane we cannot be sure whether his tale of killing his girlfriend is actual or a sort of hallucination, and the monk in 'Soliloquy of the Spanish Cloister' (1842) is insanely irritated by a mild-mannered colleague. Later in Browning's career, however, the SPASMODIC excesses of this sort of poetry become less common in his poetry (an exception is the splendidly baroque insanity of 'Childe Roland to the Dark Tower Came' (1855). TENNYSON, similarly, wrote of religious mania ('Saint Simeon Stylites', 1842), sexual insanity ('Lucretius', 1868), and subtitled one of his major poems *MAUD: or the Madness* (1855). He was particularly proud of the 'mad scene' in *Maud*, in which the narrator is in an asylum and believes himself buried in a shallow grave. All of these works tend to portray madness as an anomalous, monomaniacal state; Dickens' mad characters, like Miss Flyte in *Bleak House* (1852–3) or Miss Havisham in *Great Expectations* (1860–1), tend to have been driven insane by a single aspect of existence that has overwhelmed all others (the legal troubles that have embroiled Miss Flyte in her case, the marriage-day jilt in Miss Havisham's). For a more inclusive model of insanity we must turn to nonsense literature, and especially the world of Lewis CARROLL's *ALICE'S ADVENTURES IN WONDERLAND* (1865) in which madness is normative. Alice's timid remark that she doesn't want 'to go among mad people' is dismissed by the Cheshire Cat:

> 'Oh you can't help that,' said the Cat: 'we're all mad here. I'm mad. You're mad.'
> 'How do you know I'm mad?' said Alice.
> 'You must be,' said the Cat, 'or you wouldn't have come here.'
>
> (Carroll, *Alice in Wonderland*: 57)

Mariana by Sir John Everett Millais (1851)   MILLAIS' famous image of neglected and frustrated womanhood was first exhibited at the Royal Academy in 1851; it was accompanied by a quotation from TENNYSON's poem 'Mariana': 'She only said, "My life is dreary,/He cometh not," she said./She said "I am aweary, aweary,/I would that I were dead!"'. The image of Mariana, the character from Shakespeare's *Measure for Measure*, cloistered in her moated grange and pining for her lost lover Angelo has been taken by most critics as expressing the weariness, solitude and frustration of many Victorian women's lives. The 1851 census revealed that for every 100 women over the age of 20, 57 were married, 12 were widows and 30 were spinsters; contemporary estimates spoke of 1,248,000 women in England and Wales left 'unnaturally single' on account of a population imbalance between male and female (Vicinus, 1973: 57). Millais paints his Mariana as a thirtysomething spinster, stretching at a window in a manner that displays her full figure with an oblique but palpable eroticism. Her gaze meets the eyes of the stained-glass archangel in the window; as George Macbeth observes 'the meeting of his [the archangel's] eyes, not with those of the virgin in the window, but with the hotter, more lustful eyes of the girl in the room, pronounce the preliminary sexual arousal of a secular annunciation' (quoted in Pearce, 1991: 67). The lushness of Mariana's velvet gown and the plush padded stool on which she has been sitting suggest her warm-bloodedness, and are deliberately contrasted with the thinness and coldness of the linen on which she works, and of the stained-glass and stone window frames.

Marriage   In the 'official' ideology, Victorian society marriage was expected to last for life, and was the only licit arena for sexual activity. Until the Divorce Act of 1857, the only ways to end a marriage were by proving non-consummation (in which case the marriage was annulled), or by passing an individual act through Parliament legally divorcing one's partner. In practice, of course, many people separated permanently from their spouses and formed new relationships; George Henry Lewes and George Eliot, for instance, lived together despite the fact that Lewes was married to somebody else.

Within marriage the gender roles were not equally defined; marriage was not a partnership of equals, but a hierarchy in which the husband was dominant and the wife expected to be submissive. Often challenged (for instance, by Mill's *On The Subjection of Women*, 1869) it was nonetheless the case that most Victorians took this circumstance for granted. It was, for example, enshrined in law. A woman's property became her husband's on marriage, and remained so after separation. Caroline Norton (1808–77) separated from her abusive husband and found not only her access to her own children blocked, but that her estranged spouse still had legal rights over her earnings. Her vigorous campaigning led to the Infants Custody Act of 1839, which guaranteed her right of access, but she continued her campaign, publishing an open letter to the Queen in 1855. The Divorce Act of 1857 allowed secular divorce, and established a Court of Divorce and Matrimonial Causes, although the legislation still enshrined gender bias (a woman had to prove legally adultery *and* desertion, cruelty or bigamy; a man had only to prove a single instance of adultery). Not until a series of the Married Women's Property Acts of 1870 and 1882, however, were women entitled to keep their own separate property (capital, possessions and earnings). A further two acts, the Child Custody Act (1873) and the Guardianship of Children Act (1886), clarified and rationalised the care of children in case of divorce.

Marx, Karl (1818–1883)   Born to a prosperous Prussian family, Marx studied philosophy, law and history at the University of Berlin, where he became influenced by the philosophy of Hegel (1770–1831). Politically radicalised in early life, he worked as a newspaper editor, pioneered SOCIALIST causes and was involved in the REVOLUTIONS OF

1848. That year he moved to London, partly to escape the anti-revolutionary reaction on the continent. Working in collaboration with his friend and patron Friedrich Engels (1820–95) he published the *Communist Manifesto* in London in 1848 in German; an English translation appeared in 1850. This immensely influential pamphlet laid out the distinctively Marxian socialist philosophy: that social justice and equality was to be achieved by a revolution of the industrial proletariat, after which a communistic society would be created. For all the urgent, rousing rhetoric of the work ('the proletarians have nothing to lose but their chains. They have a world to win. WORKING MEN OF ALL COUNTRIES, UNITE!' (Marx, *Communist Manifesto*: 123)), Marx nevertheless regarded this impending revolution as a historical inevitability.

In London, Marx concerned himself with researching and writing a series of important analyses of Victorian society and class, spending long sessions in the Reading Room of the British Library. He published *Contribution to a Critique of Political Economy* (1859), in which he argues that 'it is not the consciousness of men that determines their being, but, on the contrary, their social being that determines their consciousness' (Marx, *Contribution*: 146). The first volume of his monumental study *Das Kapital* ('Capital') appeared in 1867, but despite their huge importance in later years Marx managed only a small audience for these writings. Some of his most important works were not even published until several decades after their composition; for instance, the penetrating *Theses on Feuerbach* (written 1845, published 1888). The *Economic and Philosophical Manuscripts* and *Grundrisse* of the 1840s and 1850s respectively were not published until the middle of the twentieth century. Nevertheless, as socialism became an increasingly important political phenomenon in the 1860s and 1870s, Marx reached more and more people. He was involved in the First International Working Men's Association (1864–76), an attempt to coordinate working-class action across national borders, and continued writing until his death.

***Maud: a Monodrama* (1855), by (Alfred, Lord) Tennyson** Tennyson's alternate title, 'The Madness', accurately sums up the topic of this elaborate, ornately constructed and often very beautiful dramatic monologue. Its germ was a brief lyric written after the death of Tennyson's close friend Arthur Hallam in 1833; but the story Tennyson wove around this kernel was quite removed from his own life. The narrative is only ever obliquely alluded to, and is therefore sometimes difficult to follow; the chief interest of the work is its precise delineation of a morbid consciousness descending into insanity.

In the first part, the narrator's father has committed bloody suicide ('O father! ... was it well? – /Mangled, and flattened, and crushed, and dinted into the ground?') after having been ruined in financial speculation. The unnamed speaker rails against the corruption and misery of his age. We then learn 'of the singular beauty of Maud', the daughter of a local landowner. The narrator and Maud were betrothed as children, and although no passion has grown up between them during their childhood it seems to blossom now.

> She came to the village church,
> And sat by a pillar alone;
> An angel watching an urn
> Wept over her, carved in stone;
> And once, but once, she lifted her eyes,
> And suddenly, sweetly, strangely blushed
> To find they were met by my own.

The romance continues, but seems doomed when the narrator learns that Maud's hot-headed and rather tyrannical brother (they nickname him 'the Sultan') disapproves of the match, and wishes to see her married to a young lord. The section ends with the famous lyric beginning 'Come into the garden, Maud', which tells of the narrator waiting for his beloved to come to him in the garden at dawn, after an all-night ball at her house.

In the second part the tone changes dramatically. It transpires that Maud was followed to her garden rendezvous by her brother and the 'babe-faced lord'; a quarrel breaks out, and the brother strikes the narrator 'over the face . . . struck for himself an evil stroke'. The two fight a duel, and Maud's brother is killed (as he dies he whispers 'the fault was mine . . . fly!'). The narrator escapes to the north French coast, where he learns that Maud has died of grief that her lover has killed her brother. On receiving this news the narrator himself loses all touch with sanity. Section 5, the 'Mad Scene' (which Tennyson claimed to have written in 20 minutes), is apparently set in a French asylum, although the narrator believes himself to have died and been buried in a shallow grave:

> Only a yard beneath the street
> And the hoofs of the horses beat, beat,
> The hoofs of the horses beat
> Beat into my scalp and my brain.

The section ends with his pitiful request 'to bury me, bury me/Deeper, ever so little deeper'. The brief (50-line) third part acts as a sort of coda to the poem. In it, the narrator claims to have regained his sanity, although he adds that a vision of the dead Maud appeared to him in the night sky, and instructed him to join the army for the coming war in the CRIMEA. He himself sees this as a positive conclusion to his saga: 'It is better to fight for the good than to rail at the ill . . . I embrace the purpose of God and the doom assigned'. Critics have seen the conclusion as either reprehensible jingoism, or (more frequently) as a finely balanced Tennysonian irony.

Medicine and health   Early nineteenth-century theories of the body talked in terms of 'organs' and 'tissue'; but in 1839 the German scientist Theodor Schwann (1810–82) advanced the now-accepted theory that bodies are not composed of 'tissues' but of cells. By the 1870s this theory had become orthodoxy. Important advances in surgical technology included both a better understanding of importance of hygiene, and new techniques of anaesthesia. The best the early-century surgeon could do by way of effecting analgesia was alcohol; the introduction of ether as a general anaesthetic (1846), soon followed by the invention of chloroform (1847), revolutionised surgery, rendering it not only more pleasant for the patient but much more survivable. Joseph Lister (1827–1912) was educated at a Quaker school and afterwards at University College, graduating in medicine. Appalled at the high incidence of gangrene and sepsis in the hospitals of his time, he developed the germicidal use of carbolic acid, and stressed the importance of surgeons washing thoroughly. In 1867 he announced to the British Medical Association meeting that his wards at the Glasgow Royal Infirmary had remained clear of sepsis for nine months. The widespread adoption of these antiseptic practices cut surgical infection and death markedly as the century progressed.

Disease was better and better understood as the century progressed. In 1882 German doctor Robert Koch (1843–1910) identified the tuberculosis bacillus as the infectious agent in the disease that had previously been known as 'consumption'; in the following year he identified the rabies bacillus.

Medievalism   RUSKIN defined the historical stretch indicated by the term in his *Lectures on Architecture and Painting* (1854, iv: 194): 'you have, then, the three periods: Classicism, extending to the fall of the Roman Empire; Medievalism, extending from that fall to the close of the 15th century; and Modernism'. The nineteenth century saw a pronounced revival of interest in these middle ages. In part, this was a mere fascination with chivalry, colour and romance; DISRAELI's YOUNG ENGLAND movement yearned for a medieval age that was mostly idealised fantasy, and there was the much-ridiculed Eglintoun Tournament of 1839. Archibald Montgomerie, the Thirteenth Earl of Eglintoun (1812–61) held this quasi-medieval tournament on his Ayrshire estate, in which guests dressed in armour and medieval dress. However, constant rain brought bathetic nineteenth-century reality to the gathering: the fields turned to mud and the knights in armour carried umbrellas.

Yet there were more considered appeals to medieval values. CARLYLE's PAST AND PRESENT (1843) valorised the social harmony and unity of the Middle Ages, contrasting this with the fragmented cash-governed miseries of contemporary life. The PRE-RAPHAELITE movement advocated a return to pre-Renaissance aesthetic ideals of colour, clarity and representation, although this was not the same thing as advocating the *moral* superiority of medieval times. The revival in interest in ARTHURIAN topics was coloured by this climate, such that King Arthur was almost wholly conceptualised as a monarch with medieval courtly trappings, rather than the Dark Age reality. At the end of the century, medievalism was, if anything, a stronger cultural force than it had been earlier; it informed the romantic socialism of William MORRIS, and SWINBURNE's poetry.

Melodrama   Originally 'melo-drama' was distinguished from 'drama' by the inclusion of music, either a musical accompaniment or interspersed songs (*melos* being the Greek for 'music'); such form became popular after the theatrical licensing laws were tightened in the eighteenth century. Following the 1737 Licensing Act, conventional drama required a licence from the Lord Chamberlain and could be played in only a limited number of theatres, but 'music entertainment' was not restricted in this manner. By the nineteenth century, however, the form had mutated to mean less 'musical drama' (although music was often included) and more a form of romantic and sensational play, in which characters typical of virtue and vice clashed in thrilling manner; the writing was often self-consciously artificial and high-flown, the acting deliberately mannered and exaggerated. Although denigrated for many years as a 'lesser' form of drama, critics have recently praised the method of melodrama as aesthetically legitimate. For critic and director Peter Brooks, melodrama is a deliberately invoked mode of excess, whose mannerist binarisms and externalised formalism gave writers such as DICKENS, Balzac (1799–1850) and Henry James (1843–1916) new freedoms to embody their vision (Brooks, 1995). In the words of Matthew Buckley,

> almost negligent critical dismissal of melodrama, a commonplace of literary scholarship of the last two centuries, has been replaced in recent decades by a strong consensus that this most dominant and ubiquitous form of nineteenth-century drama played a significant role in shaping, articulating, and contesting changes in social and political relations, as well as in reshaping popular consciousness on the individual level.

> (Buckley, 2002: 423)

Thomas Holcroft's (1745–1809) *Tale of Mystery* (first staged 1802) is sometimes credited with being the first British melodrama, although the term was coined in France. *Black Ey'd Susan* (1829), by Douglas Jerrold (1803–57) exhibits all the strengths of the form; an exciting, tense tale in which the virtuous hero seems doomed to an unjust death at the hands of inexorable naval justice, but is reprieved at the last moment; it ran for 400 performances at its first staging, and was often restaged. In the spectacular *The Corsican Brothers* (1852) one brother is killed and the other promises revenge; plot twists, ghosts and tension characterise the piece.

Further reading

The Melodramatic Imagination: Balzac, James, Melodrama and the Mode of Excess (rev. edn, 1995) by Peter Brooks.

Men and Women (1855), by Robert Browning   Browning's collection of 50 DRA-
MATIC MONOLOGUES (with a fifty-first poem in his own voice and addressed to his wife,
Elizabeth Barrett BROWNING, dedicating the volume to her) appeared in two volumes in
1855. He had been working on the poems since moving to Italy after his marriage in
1846, and many of them reflect this context. Browning's newly stimulated interest in
Italian art resulted in a number of the most famous short poems of the Victorian age
('Fra Lippo Lippi', 'Andrea del Sarto', 'Pictor Ignotus'); similarly, his passion for key-
board music is articulated in 'A Toccata of Galuppi's' and 'Master Hughes of Saxe-
Gotha'. His continuing interrogation of religious questions (from a position of
personal religious faith) finds expression in the subtle sophistries of 'Bishop
Blougram's Apology', an ambiguous critique of Roman Catholicism in Britain, as well
as 'An Epistle . . . of Karshish' (in which a contemporary doctor reports on the 'case' of
Lazarus being raised from the dead), or 'Cleon' (in which a first-century Greek poet
ironically dismisses Christ as 'a mere barbarian Jew'). The warmth of Browning's love
for his wife is captured in some of the most beautiful love poems in English: 'Love
among the Ruins', 'A Woman's Last Word', 'By the Fire-Side' and 'Any Wife to Any
Husband', and for some readers it is the moving nature of this sort of work that is the
greatest strength of the collection. Browning seems to have had high hopes for the
volume, but was disappointed by the largely negative reviews ('it is really high time,'
opined the *Saturday Review*, one among many, 'that this sort of thing should, if possible, be stopped'; quoted in Jack and Inglesfield, 1995: 49). During the twentieth century the extraordinary technical virtuosity and the energy of the collection has seen it
come to be regarded as one of Browning's greatest achievements.

   One of the things that reviewers objected to was what they saw as a GROTESQUE aesthetic of the collection; a penchant for bizarre or disgusting subject matter that was
fantastically embellished, distorted or diseased, and a style that lacked the classical
simplicity of Milton or Wordsworth. The Gothic extravagance of a poem such as
'Childe Roland to the Dark Tower Came' – in which a medieval knight-apprentice
travels through a nightmare landscape on a nameless quest – epitomises this. The
sheer vibrant ugliness of the imagery in this poem directly challenges conventional
Victorian aesthetics:

> No! penury, inertness and grimace,
> In some strange sort, were the land's portion . . .
> As for the grass, it grew as scant as hair
> In leprosy; thin dry blades pricked the mud
> Which underneath looked kneaded up with blood.

> ('Childe Roland', ll. 61–75)

Crossing a river the narrator fears 'to set my foot upon a dead man's cheek,/Each step',
and kills a rat declaring 'it may have been a water-rat I speared,/But, ugh!, it sounded

like a baby's shriek' (ll. 121–6). The dark intensity of this sort of writing has found many modern admirers (present-day horror writer Stephen King, for instance, has admitted being obsessed with this poem). Critics have, moreover, seen Browning's 'grotesqueness' as something more aesthetically profound. Isobel Armstrong argues for the strengths of this idiom, and says that 'because the Grotesque is not a unifying mode, *Men and Women* is a fragmented and composite work, RUSKIN's "broken mirror, with strange distortions and discrepancies"' (Armstrong, 1993: 291).

Indeed, it is the very variety of these diverse points of view that is the primary strength of *Men and Women*. The speakers are drawn from all historical periods and all classes: Arab doctors, Ancient Greek tyrants, Renaissance painters, contemporary Victorian gentlemen and gentlewomen, poets and musicians, Biblical figures and criminals, madmen and grammatical scholars. More than this, the poems themselves register the vigorous diversity of existence (both the beautiful *and* the ugly) as a primary good: as Fra Lippo Lippi, a prototype of the Browning-style creative artist, observes:

> However, you're my man, you've seen the world
> – The beauty and the wonder and the power,
> The shapes of things, the colours, lights and shades,
> Changes and surprises . . .
> . . . What's it all about?
> To be passed over, despised? or dwelt upon,
> Wondered at? oh, this last of course! – you say.
> . . . .
> . . . This world's no blot for us,
> Nor blank; it means intensely, and means good.
>
> ('Fra Lippo Lippi', ll. 282–314)

It is this that makes the work so extremely Victorian. Critic J.B. Bullen says 'the words which Browning put into the mouth' of Lippi 'as George ELIOT realized when she reviewed *Men and Women*, are not so much the sentiments of a Renaissance painter as a mid-Victorian' (quoted in Jack and Inglesfield, 1995: 49). Armstrong's insight, that 'the central project of *Men and Women* is the investigation of cultural fictions and the form in which they are constructed' (Armstrong, 1993: 290), indicates the ways this collection continues to function as a rich resource for the student of the cultural fictions that underlay Victorian society.

Mesmerism   Named after the Austrian physician Franz Anton Mesmer (1734–1815), 'mesmerism' was an early form of the phenomenon we now call 'hypnotism'. Though often ridiculed, quite properly, it nevertheless enjoyed great popularity in certain circles throughout the nineteenth century. DICKENS came to believe that he himself possessed mesmeric powers, and practised on his family and friends, attempting to cure a

Swiss acquaintance, Madame Emile de la Rue, of various neurasthenic symptoms by mesmerising her. Mesmerism often appears in Dickens' fiction, usually associated with evil or dangerous characters: Quilp from *The Old Curiosity Shop* (1840–1) and Jasper from *Edwin Drood* (1870) seem to have this power over others. The greatest focus of interest in the phenomenon was in the 1840s, when a number of books appeared, including Chauncey Hare Townsend's *Facts in Mesmerism* (1840), John Elliotson's *Surgical Operations without Pain in the Mesmeric State* (1843) and Harriet Martineau's *Letters on Mesmerism* (1845) (see Otis, 2002: 391–422). Frances Trollope (1780–1863), TENNYSON and Edward Fitzgerald (1809–83) both believed in mesmerism. BROWNING was sceptical, but used the concept for an exquisite image in one of his poems: 'When the mesmerizer Snow/With his hand's first sweep/Put the earth to sleep' ('A Lover's Quarrel', 1855, ll. 72–4). The mystery at the core of Wilkie COLLINS' detective novel *The Moonstone* (1868) is explained in mesmeric terms.

Middlemarch (1871–1872), by George Eliot

Seen by many as ELIOT's masterpiece, *Middlemarch* details life in the fictional Midlands town of the title during the 1820s. It contains two main plot strands, interwoven. The story that Eliot initially intended to tell concerned the beautiful, idealistic young heroine Dorothea Brooke. Rejecting the attentions of Sir James Chettam (who contents himself with marrying Dorothea's sister Celia instead), Dorothea persuades herself that she has fallen in love with an elderly scholar, the dry Edward Casaubon, a man who has devoted decades of his life to writing a densely conceived and incomplete study of comparative myth called 'The Key to All Mythologies'. Dorothea believes that by marrying Casaubon she will be sacrificing herself to a greater good, and the marriage happens; but on honeymoon in Rome she comes to the realisation that she has made a mistake, and that she cannot love her inward, pedantic husband. Coming to know the young, handsome Will Ladislaw, a distant cousin of Casaubon's, emphasises what she has missed. Meanwhile, Eliot worked in a second narrative strand, a tale she had intended for a separate novel. This is the story of a young Doctor Lydgate, who has come to Middlemarch with dreams of one day making important discoveries in medical science. He also marries unwisely, and his life with the beautiful but shallow and selfish Rosamund Vincy is unhappy. The plot of the work becomes increasingly complex towards the end, with minor characters becoming engaged in political dreams, in blackmail and murder. Casaubon, increasingly ill, becomes jealous of the intimacy between Dorothea and Will. He eventually dies of heart disease leaving his young wife a wealthy widow, but a codicil to his will disinherits her if she were to marry Will. Dorothea and Will do eventually marry, and leave Middlemarch for London, where he begins a political career, and she contents herself with a mundane though virtuous life. Lydgate also leaves Middlemarch, taking his wife to a fashionable watering place and becoming a society doctor, although abandoning his youthful dreams.

Such a summary perhaps makes *Middlemarch* sound like a downbeat, or even grim, novel; but despite its sober conclusion it is very far from being a depressing read. The texture of Eliot's writing is extremely, and beautifully, sympathetic to the ordinary lives she is describing. Dorothea's awakening to the realities of life and love is extremely moving, and the recreation of life in a small English town 50 years before (for which she undertook enormous and detailed research) is well-nigh perfect. Indeed, so expert is her representation of the quotidian that it is almost a pity that the conventions of the Victorian novel intrude to the extent they do in the later books; with an inheritance plot, a blackmail plot and a scapegrace plot making, as it were, too much noise. 'If we had,' says her narrator, 'a keen vision of all ordinary human life, it would be like hearing the grass grow and the squirrel's heart beat, and we should die of that roar that lies on the other side of silence' (*Middlemarch*, Book 2, Chapter 20). Eliot's genius in this novel is to capture a sense of the aesthetic and moral power of this sort of ordinariness.

Mill, John Stuart (1806–1873) Mill's early years were extraordinarily regimented; drilled in intensive educational routines by his father James Mill (1773–1836) he was studying Ancient Greek at the age of three, Latin at eight, he had read six Platonic dialogues by ten and had studied mathematical logic before he was a teenager. By 1823 he was employed as a clerk in the India House. Mill's later *Autobiography* (1873) expresses a certain mournful regret for his lack of childhood ('I never was a boy, never played at cricket; it is better to let nature have her own way') although there is no doubt that it set him up for his life as a widely learned and brilliant intellectual thinker.

His first philosophical work was in the tradition established by Jeremy Bentham (1748–1832), who had inspired James and John Stuart Mill both. It was the younger Mill who coined the term UTILITARIAN to describes Bentham's philosophy, and in 1825 he edited Bentham's *Treatise Upon Evidence* for publication. In 1826, however, he found himself suffering a crisis, in reaction to the extreme rationality of his upbringing and the limitations of Bentham's approach to human existence. He found, reading the poetry of Wordsworth (1770–1850) and Coleridge (1772–1834) 'a greatly increased interest in the common feelings and common destiny of human beings'. Although his systematic works of philosophic logic, *System of Logic* (1843) and *Principles of Political Economy* (1848) can be thought of as Utilitarian, Mill was moving beyond a strictly Utilitarian perspective. His later account of the movement, *Utilitarianism* (1861), diverged from Bentham in many respects.

This revival in Mill's emotional life coincided with his meeting, in 1831, Harriet Taylor (1807–58), with whom he fell profoundly in love and who helped shape his philosophical development. Throughout the 1830s and 1840s to the death of her husband in 1851 the two of them were intimate, marrying as soon as it was possible. Largely influenced by Taylor, Mill moved beyond 'Benthamism' and became interested in social equality and women's rights. His landmark book, *On Liberty* (1859), and a two-volume collection of *Dissertations and Discussions* (1859) were influential interventions in this field, although it was his powerfully argued proto-feminist polemic *On the Subjection of Women* (1869) that is, perhaps, his most heartfelt work. The East India Company was abolished in 1858, a consequence of the INDIAN MUTINY, and Mill retired with a pension; but he continued working, publishing many works, including *Thoughts on Parliamentary Reform* (1859), *Representative Government* (1861) and his important philosophical work *Examination of Sir William Hamilton's Philosophy* (1865). He served as MP for Westminster 1865–8, attempting during that time to pass an amendment to the REFORM ACT OF 1867, which would have granted women the vote (the amendment was defeated).

Further reading

Mill (OUP 1985), by William Thomas.

Millais, Sir John Everett (1829–1896)   Millais' astonishing technical skills as a painter were evident when he was a child. He was not yet 20 when he became associated with the PRE-RAPHAELITE BROTHERHOOD, exhibiting the Keats-based canvas *Lorenzo and Isabella* in 1849. *Christ in the House of his Parents* (1849–50) treats the subject with an unprecedented, although luminous, realism: the carpentry studio is painted with minute detail, and instead of idealising Christ, Joseph and Mary, Millais renders them as ordinary and even unprepossessing human beings. DICKENS hated the picture, and attacked it, in *HOUSEHOLD WORDS*, as merely ugly (Dickens thought that the painting, instead of being uplifting and spiritual, embodied 'the lowest depths of what is mean, odious, repulsive and revolting', and that Christ Himself is painted as 'a hideous, wry-necked, blubbering, red-headed boy' ('New Lamps for Old', *Household Words* 15 June 1850)). Nevertheless, this painting does represent one of the early acmes of Pre-Raphaelite sensibility. *Ophelia* (1851–2) is a much more conventionally 'beautiful' painting, the exquisitely rendered details of river naturalism and the other-worldly expression of the water-borne model given a disturbing inflection by the madness and impending death revealed by the Shakespearean context. *MARIANA* (1851) similarly articulates a sense of the miseries of female entrapment. *Autumn Leaves* (1856) is a more conventional, though still lovely, image of girls burning old leaves at dusk.

Championed by RUSKIN, Millais painted his portrait amongst Scottish scenery in 1853, accompanying Ruskin and his wife Effie on their Scottish holiday to do so. Millais fell in love with Effie and later the two ran away together; Effie obtained an annulment on grounds of Ruskin's impotence and married Millais in 1855. Despite the whiff of scandal associated with this circumstance, Millais' general reputation increased enormously during the 1860s and 1870s, to (according to some critics) the detriment of his art. He was knighted, and later (1896) became President of the Royal Academy of Arts; but his paintings became more conventionalised, more sentimental (and more marketable to middle-class Victorians as a result). A number of slushy animal portraits, or the empty and rather ponderous playfulness of *Bubbles* (1886; later used as an advertisement for Pears soap) seem a diminution of his talent.

Missionaries   A very great many individuals travelled from Britain into the world at large to proselytise their Christian Protestant faith. This 'spiritual imperialism' was closely interconnected with the material imperialism of trade and conquest that expanded the British Empire over the nineteenth century, although there were also frictions between the two. According to Andrew Porter, 'religious dynamics proved unpredictable and often at odds with Imperial needs. In the white settlement colonies, a religious establishment at first seemed desirable.' However, high-profile indigenous religious disaffection, such as sparked the INDIAN MUTINY in 1857, 'forced politicians and officials to conclude that only a policy of religious neutrality would serve their purpose' (Porter, 1999: 222)

The first missionary organisations were established by Evangelical organisations: the Baptist Missionary Society (founded 1792), the London Missionary Society (founded 1795) and the Wesleyan Methodist Missionary Society (1818). An Anglican organisation, the Church Missionary Society (founded 1799) was also influential. Most of the missionaries recruited by these societies were from working-class backgrounds. Not until the latter portion of the century, after the high-profile missionary deaths of David Livingstone (1813–73) in Africa and Bishop Patteson (1827–71) in Melanesia, did the social status of missionaries improve.

South America was seen as already Catholic, and North America was a net exporter of missionaries; the emphasis, therefore, was on sending missionaries to Africa, to Asia and especially East Asia, and to the Pacific islands. Mission work to China became possible after the ANGLO-CHINESE WARS of the early 1840s; a surge in missionary activity in the mid-1840s, and another in the late 1850s followed. From the 1870s onward an increasing number of university graduates and individuals from the middle and upper classes became missionaries. According to Brian Stanley, 'the global Protestant missionary force had grown by the turn of the century to over 18,000. The bulk (70% by 1910) of this force was made up of lay persons' (Stanley, 1994: 388). A shift away from purely religious missions to medical and humanitarian missions (with a religious bias) became evident.

Money: currency   The basic unit of currency in the nineteenth century was the *pound*, written as a '£' prefix or as an 'l' suffix (i.e. '£100' or '100l.') – both being versions of the letter 'L' from the Latin 'libra', an equivalent weight. The name points to its origin as a weight-measure of silver, although by 1800 the monetary 'pound' was worth considerably less than its equivalent weight in the metal. Each pound was divided into 20 *shillings*, and each shilling into 12 *pennies* (or *pence*), such that there were 240 pennies in a pound. Sums in pence were written with the suffix 'd' (from the Latin *denarius* or *denarii*, an equivalent Roman coin): 'shillings' was abbreviated to 's'.

Ten shillings and sixpence would accordingly be written '10*s*. 6*d*.' This was the more polite monetary notation. Tradesmen and some others might also write sums with a forward-slash: thus two shillings could be written '2/-', and the 10s. 6d. Mad Hatter's hat in the illustrations to CARROLL's *ALICE IN WONDERLAND* carries a card marked 'In This Style 10/6'.

There were two coins minted that divided the penny: a *half-penny* (pronounced and often written 'ha'penny') and a *farthing*, or quarter-penny. Farthings and ha'pennies were small copper coins. The old-style penny was a large copper coin. After 1860 these three denominations were minted from bronze instead of more expensive copper. The threepenny piece (or 'thruppeny bit') was a small silver coin (the nickel-brass dodecagonal thruppeny bit was a twentieth-century innovation). Fourpenny pieces or 'groats' were also in circulation, although were less usual. The sixpence (or 'tanner') was a small silver coin, and the shilling (or 'one bob') a larger silver coin. Threepennies, sixpences and shillings were later minted from cupro-nickel rather than silver. A *crown* was a large silver coin with the value of five shillings. The *half-sovereign* was a gold coin worth ten shillings, or half a pound. The *sovereign* was a large gold coin worth one pound. A *guinea*, also a gold coin, was worth one pound and one shilling (21s. or 252d.). The last guineas were coined in 1813, and were supposedly superseded by the 20/- sovereign, a denomination first minted in 1817; although guineas were in circulation throughout the century and remained the ordinary unit for professional fees or for membership of an upper-class society or organisation. Prices for works of art, racehorses and some property were also often quoted in guineas.

Most ordinary Victorian monetary transactions utilised coins, but for larger sums paper money was used. One-pound and five-pound notes were issued by several banks, but early in the nineteenth century paper money had not yet acquired the normative status it has today, and was closer to its origin as a promissory document or authorisation on behalf of an individual or bank. Accordingly bank notes for a wide variety of sums were issued during the period. In 1833 Bank of England notes were declared legal tender, which meant that traders were obliged to accept them as money. The Bank Act of 1844 decreed the Bank of England to be the only legitimate bank of issue, and although bank notes from other banks remained in circulation they were gradually superseded by Bank of England notes.

This system seems, perhaps, rather complex and even arcane to many modern readers, but was accepted by a population habituated via school duodecimal arithmetical tables to multiply and divide lots of 12. One of the political campaigns of Plantagenet Palliser, in TROLLOPE's *Palliser* novels (1864–80), is for a decimalisation of the monetary system, a cause that makes him seem faintly ridiculous in the eyes of his contemporaries. On the other hand, Dickens' Pip from *Great Expectations* (1861) lives in fear of his Uncle Pumblechook who sets him random spot-tests in the awkward mathematical process of converting sums into pounds, shillings and pence ('First . . .

forty-three pence?', Chapter 9). In 1971 this monetary system was finally superseded by a decimalised pound made up of 100 pennies (guineas, crowns, shillings, groats, threepences and farthings all being abolished), which in due course will be superseded again by a pan-European currency, the 'Euro' made up of 100 cents.

Money: monetary value   British currency has devalued very considerably since the nineteenth century, and the contemporary pound no longer has the purchasing power of the Victorian pound. Having said that, it is not easy to translate Victorian monetary value into contemporary terms. A straightforward factoring will not do, because many items have become relatively cheaper (in the case of some – for instance, tea and sugar – very much cheaper), and other things have become relatively more expensive (the poorest of Dickens' characters in *Oliver Twist* are portrayed eating oysters, for instance). As a rule of thumb it gives some sense of the purchasing power of money in the nineteenth century to multiply the numbers by between 100 and 200. A penny then had something like the purchasing value of between 50p and £1 today, and an annual income of £400 would be worth about £50,000 today. Another factor to be considered is that there was a much more pronounced gap between the rich and the poor then than is the case today. At one end of the scale, the Speenhamland System of poor relief (superseded by the POOR LAW of 1834) calculated the cost of supporting, feeding and clothing a child to be 18 pence a week, or under £4 a year. At the other end, the Whig politician Lord Durham in 1821 could pronounce '£40,000 a year a moderate income – such a one as a man *might jog on with*' (Partington, 1992: 407).

E.P. Thompson and Eileen Yeo list weekly costs of certain basic commodities over a number of years, basing their calculations on the budget for a poor family of two adults and three children. They assume a weekly consumption of five quartern (4lb) loaves, 5lb of meat, 1lb of sugar, 1lb of butter, 3oz. of tea, about half a pound of candles and a similar weight of soap, and seven pints of beer. This diet, they note, is derived from a Victorian source, S.R. Bosanquet's *The Rights of the Poor and Christian Almsgiving Vindicated* (1841), and the prices adjusted for different years with reference to various other contemporary publications (Thompson and Yeo, 1971: 585)

	1825	1831	1841	1851
Bread	3/6	3/9	3s. 6½d.	2/6
Butter	7½d.	10d.	9d.	10d.
Sugar	6d.	7d.	7d.	4d.
Tea	11½d.	9d.	11d.	1/-
Meat	2/1	2/6	2/1	2/1
Candles/Soap	10½d.	8d.	6½d.	6d.
Beer	7d.	7d.	1/2	1/2
TOTAL:	9s. 1½d.	9/8	9/7	8/5

The above table does not include certain other expenditures, most notably rent.

London rents fluctuated over this period, and accommodation for the poor deteriorated in quality after many slum landlords raised rents after the introduction of income tax in 1843; Thompson and Yeo (1971) suggest weekly rents varying between 2/6 and 4/- for family accommodation (which could be a suite of rooms, or in certain circumstances two rooms or even a single room). Other items not shown include milk (which sold for 1d. a pint in 1850) and coal. Coffee was about half the price of tea per oz. over this period, which led to many poorer families switching from tea to coffee. Bread, meat and cheese were English working-class staples; Irish labourers working in London would be more likely to consume potatoes and fish, the prices of which varied with supply.

Overall, then, a plausible subsistence wage for a Londoner with a family to support during this time might be something between 12/- and 14/- a week, or between £31 and £36 per annum. A single individual could live on rather less than this. Many salaries, moreover, included perquisites; household servants, for instance, might earn as little as 50/- a year, although food, board and sometimes clothes were included in the salary. A head butler or senior housekeeper in a prosperous family might earn £60–80 a year. When DICKENS began work in 1827 as a junior clerk in the legal office of Ellis and Blackmore he was paid 10/6 a week (£27 6s. a year); this was later increased to 15/- weekly. In 1846, having become the country's most famous writer, he agreed to become the editor of a national newspaper, the *Daily News*, for a salary of £2000 per annum – although this sum was about twice what other newspaper editors were earning. At the end of his career he earned more than £10,000 for each of his novels. Dickens' first family house was a five-storey terraced house in Doughty Street, central London. He rented this very attractive property in 1837 for £80 a year. In 1856 he bought the only house he was to own outright: Gad's Hill in Kent, a very sizeable house set in 26 acres of ground, which cost him £1700. He spent nearly £1000 on improvements. Were it sold in today's market it would surely fetch one and a half million pounds.

Another literary middle-class couple, Thomas and Jane CARLYLE, lived in a much smaller house in Chelsea on £300 a year through the 1830s and 1840s; although they had no children. They broke down their expenses to: £75 on food, £35 on rent, £25 for Jane's clothes, £12–16 for a live-in maid, and £25 for rates and taxes. For a single individual, £250 was a prosperous salary; in the 1850s, *Chambers's Journal* (25 March 1856: 176) declared that 'a man with a gentlemanly employment in a public office, and a snug salary of L.250 a year, has no reason to be dissatisfied.'

In 1858 *The Times* wondered in print whether it was practicable for a gentleman to marry on £300, although the expectation here was that the sum would have to support children as well as a wife. At the top end, a senior banker or industrialist might earn £10,000 or £20,000. More affluent members of the aristocracy subsisted on much more than this; for instance, the annual income of the Duke of Devonshire in the 1860s was around £200,000.

Monodrama   Strictly, a drama for one performer, this term was often used in Victorian literary culture to refer to works written to be read (not performed) in which the action or character was narrated by a single individual. The more usual modern term is 'monologue'. The most famous example of monodrama is Tennyson's *Maud* (1855), although the work of other poets was sometimes described in these terms. For instance, the *Eclectic Review* (26, 1849: 211) declared of Browning's writing that 'the entire sum of his poetry may be said to be dramatic, though much of it is simple monodrama'. The most useful way of thinking about monodrama is as an elongated form of the DRAMATIC MONOLOGUE, with the PSCHOANALYTIC insights and emphasis of that mode.

Morris, William (1834–1896)   Morris was a man of staggering versatility and productive energy: a poet, designer, craftsman and fantasist of genius, and his paintings and engravings are of high quality. He worked in almost all fields of artistic endeavour excepting only music and sculpture, and he excelled in most. Born of well-to-do bourgeois parents, Morris was educated at Marlborough School and Exeter College, Oxford. He was articled to an Oxford architect, and worked with his new friends Rossetti and Edward Burne-Jones (1833–98) on some frescoes in the Oxford Union. He wrote short poems and essays throughout the 1850s, many of which appeared in the *Oxford and Cambridge Magazine*, which he helped found in 1856. His first collection of poetry, *The Defence of Guenevere and Other Poems*, appeared in 1858, and won him an immediate reputation, although few sales. Its powerful lyrics and brief narratives balanced finely between beauty and violence, and were all rendered with a Keatsian precision of visual image.

In 1859 Morris married the beautiful Pre-Raphaelite model, Jane Burden. They moved to the famous Red House (in Bexley), which had been designed for Morris by his friend Philip Webb (1831–1915). Unable to find suitable furniture for their new home, Morris began designing and creating his own pieces. This led to the creation of a firm – Morris, Marshall, Faulkener and Co. – to produce high-quality fittings that were beautiful and functional: furniture, textiles, wallpaper and stained glass. But his marriage to Jane, although it produced two children, was not happy. She began a long-term affair with Rossetti, a circumstance of which Morris was almost certainly aware.

A large and often, frankly, fat man, Morris was hugely kind-hearted, gentle and civilised; but he was also prone to mania. Stories from university have him flying into apoplectic rages, banging his head so hard against the walls of his room as to leave a large dent in the plaster, biting through the wood of his window-ledge. In less extreme form, this mania manifested itself as a titanic enthusiasm, and a remarkable capacity for sustained creative work. At the same time as putting tremendous amounts of energy into his firm, Morris was, throughout the 1860s and 1870s, writing good verse at a rate exhausting to contemplate. Some days he managed to turn out 1000 lines of poetry; 600- and 700-line days were not uncommon (as his biographer Fiona

MacCarthy points out, most serious writers are content with 1000 *words* of *prose*). He liked to compose on railway journeys, where the motion of travel soothed him into a sort of writing trance. If the poetry were poor, or padded out, we might understand this prolixity; but, despite what some critics assert, the poetry is never less than adequate to the tasks of the poem and is more often than not striking, beautiful, perfectly cadenced and timed. He fashioned a sweeping, onward-moving poetic voice ideally suited to the sweep of epic narrative, forging a distinctive style that was (to quote SWINBURNE) 'so broad and sad and simple'. He moved the firm to Bloomsbury in central London in 1865.

Through the 1860s Morris was working on a large-scale collection of long poems, a sort of modern-day *Canterbury Tales*, called THE EARTHLY PARADISE, which Morris hoped to publish with 500 of his own woodcuts (this plan was eventually abandoned). In 1867 he published *The Life and Death of Jason*, a long poem originally intended for *The Earthly Paradise* that had grown too long for inclusion. The work was a great success. The publication of *The Earthly Paradise* followed, the 25 connected works emerging in four volumes between late 1868 and early 1870.

With Rossetti, whom by now had been Jane's lover for some years, Morris took a joint tenancy of Kelmscott House, Hammersmith, in 1871. This was later to be the site of Morris's own, famous printing press. In 1872 he travelled to Iceland for the first time; this and subsequent visits aroused Morris's passion for the sagas and legends of Icelandic literature. With the help of Eirikir Magnusson he worked at translating some of these (including *Grettis Saga* and *Laxdaela Saga*), also publishing translations of the *Aeneid* (1875), the *Odyssey* (1887) and *Beowulf* (1897). This work also informed his creative writing. His epic treatment of the Volsung saga, *Sigurd the Volsung* (the same material Wagner treated in *Der Ring des Nibelungen* – opera that Morris rightly disliked) appeared in 1876. Morris regarded this work as his masterpiece, a judgement with which few critics have concurred. But although the archaisms that pepper Morris's poetry can strike a modern reader as ugly, and although we are generally not as familiar with the legends behind the poetry as would be good for the aesthetic effect of the whole, *Sigurd* is indeed a powerful and muscular work. It is a saga in the genuine sense, an epic of war and love located in convincingly realised landscapes of huge scale, and with the freshness of the created myth of (say) Tolkien.

The lukewarm reception of *Sigurd* disappointed Morris; he wrote no more of his own long poems, and apart from two further collections of short poetry, *Chants for Socialists* (1884–5) and *Poems by the Way* (1891) he wrote no more verse, turning instead to prose. From the late 1870s onwards Morris became more and more involved in the burgeoning SOCIALIST movement. His membership of the newly formed Social Democratic Federation in 1883 saw him arguing passionately and effectively for a utopian socialist vision that saw necessary connections between a more just society, the dignity of work and a less hideous world (in his essay, 'Why I Became A Socialist' (1894), Morris wrote: 'apart from the desire to produce beautiful things, the leading passion of my life has been and is hatred of modern civilisation ... this sordid, aimless, ugly confusion'). He headed the breakaway Socialist League in 1884, and his later novels often carry socialist morals, and many of the tricks (including the fondness for archaism) of the poems re-emerge in strange, symbolist prose rhapsodies that prefigure twentieth-century Fantasy writing: *The House of the Wolfings* (1889), *The Roots of the Mountains* (1890), *News from Nowhere* (1891), *The Wood Beyond the World* (1894) and *The Sundering Flood* (1898) all have their admirers today. Morris's work in printing and binding with his Kelmscott Press, mostly from this period, is also famous. Morris's literary achievements, too large perhaps to fit easily into critical categories, have been sadly neglected since his death, although his designs and artisan beliefs have enjoyed continuous admirers and cachet.

Muscular Christianity   A form of religious practice, and an ideal of Christian living, most closely associated with the work of Charles KINGSLEY. The label was often regarded as faintly derogatory, and Kingsley himself objected to it, but it nicely captures the strenuous physicality with which Kingsley's followers attempted at once to divert what they considered potentially dangerous corporeal impulses into more acceptable outlets (in everyday life, but also in sport: boxing, rowing, walking and the like). The *Edinburgh Review* for January 1858 epitomised it in the following terms:

> The principal characteristics of [Kingsley's] work are his deep sense of the
> sacredness of all the ordinary relations and the common duties of life, and the
> vigour with which he contends ... for the great importance and value of
> animal spirits, physical strength, and a hearty enjoyment of all the pursuits
> and accomplishments which are connected with them.
>
> (*Edinburgh Review* 107, 1858: 190)

It stands in opposition to the more ethereally spiritual reputation of higher church or Anglo-Catholic beliefs.

Music   Victorian Britain is often seen as possessing only a second-hand glory in terms of music. Great nineteenth-century composers visited and lived in the country, and the larger cities possessed thriving musical communities of both professional and amateur performers and admirers; but few home-grown composers or musicians achieved lasting fame. Most of the great continental names came to Britain during the Victorian period, attracted by the wealth and enthusiasm of potential audiences: Wagner first visited London in 1839, and returned often; the German composer Felix Mendelssohn (1809–47) spent his last few years in England; French composer Hector Berlioz (1803–69) was a frequent visitor, after the success of a Drury Lane concert of his music in 1848; the Russian Peter Tchaikovsky (1840–93) visited in 1861; Czech composer Antonin Dvořák (1841–1904) premiered his seventh symphony in London in 1885, and Norwegian Edvard Grieg (1843–1907) debuted in the city three years later to enormous acclaim. The German composer Richard Strauss (1864–1949), and Russian pianist and composer Sergei Vasilyevich Rachmaninov (1873–1943) both visited London in the 1890s. Several musical colleges were founded, including the Kensington Royal College of Organists (in 1864), the Trinity College music conservatoire in London (1875) and the Royal College of Music (1883). Concerts and other performances drew large, often passionate crowds. The inaugural Promenade Concert, conducted by Henry Wood (1869–1944) in London, August 1895, was the first of a continuing and lively tradition that indicates the intensity of musical appreciation in Britain. VICTORIA herself was an amateur pianist, and received the composer Richard Wagner (1813–83). Robert BROWNING was also an enthusiastic musical amateur: several of his most successful DRAMATIC MONOLOGUES take music as their theme (particularly 'A Toccata of Galuppi' (1855) and 'Abt Vogler' (1864)). His late work 'Parleying with Charles Avison' (1889) prints two pages of musical notation towards the end.

Not until the very end of the century, with Edward Elgar's (1857–1934) *Enigma Variations* performed in St James's Hall, in London, in 1899, did a home-grown classical music tradition actively reassert itself. Twentieth-century British composers such as Elgar, Frederick Delius (1862–1934) and Ralph Vaughan-Williams (1872–1958) developed their art partly in reaction to the more grandiose continental high-Romantic music of Wagner, Berlioz, Verdi and Puccini. Contemporaries wondered at this apparent void of musical compositional talent in the United Kingdom. Ralph Waldo Emerson (1803–82) opined that 'England has no music' (*English Traits*, 1856), and philosopher Friedrich Nietzsche (1844–1900) pondered whether the English had a defect in their national soul, a lack of rhythm or sense of musical movement, to explain the barrenness of their culture in this regard.

Yet such an attitude, though so widespread as to be almost ubiquitous amongst critics, is profoundly wrong-headed. British musical culture of the nineteenth century was not absent; it was, rather, enormously vigorous, although it expressed itself in popular rather than 'high classical' idioms. Where serious opera, though popular in Britain, was almost always of foreign provenance, the composition and production of operetta – the more usual English phrases were 'light opera' or 'comic opera' – was unparalleled. The witty librettos of William Schwenck Gilbert (1836–1911), matched with the sparkling music of Arthur Sullivan (1842–1900), produced some of the century's most enduring music, the 'Savoy Operas' produced by the D'Oyly Carte company from 1875 through to the 1980s. Works such as *HMS Pinafore* (1878), *The Pirates of Penzance* (1879), *Iolanthe* (1882) and *The Mikado* (1885) were enormously successful: *Pinafore* ran for 700 performances, the *Mikado* for 672. Only a snobbish disinclination to pay comic music the same degree of critical attention as 'serious' compositions obscures the excellence of this art. A vibrant tradition of musical comedy accompanied Gilbert and Sullivan's success.

In addition to such middle-class entertainments, there were other broader-based popular musical styles. MUSIC HALL and burlesque shows were always popular and, in the words of Peter Gammond, the nineteenth century was 'the point at which commercial popular music found its own identity in Britain' (Gammond, 1991: 463). Pleasure gardens, such as London's Vauxhall, drew an increasingly lowbrow clientele, and the music performed there became more song-based. As the music gardens waned in popularity, and the indoor music hall mixed bill of entertainment drew the crowd instead, popular songs achieved an even greater cultural currency. Dickens' novels, and his earlier writings especially, are absolutely suffused with quotation and allusion to popular song lyrics, in the unstated expectation that readers would not only recognise the specific allusion, but the mood and reputation of the particular songs. Versions of older folk songs such as 'Greensleeves' and 'All Around My Hat' remained popular; but newly composed songs with deictic working-class tone – for instance, sung in cockney or other regional dialects, or making reference to working-class experience – acquired a particular popularity. Many such compositions were anonymous, but Harry Clifton (1832–72) was one composer whose name has survived. His 'motto' songs, such as 'Paddle Your Own Canoe', 'There's Nothing Succeeds like Success' and 'Work, boys, work, and be contented' were popular; and his 'Polly Perkins of Paddington Green' (c.1863) captures the droll, rather sharp tone of many music hall songs. The final stanza goes:

> In six months she married, this hard-hearted girl,
> But it was not a 'Wicount' and it was not a 'Nearl';
> It was not a 'Baronite' but a shade or two wus' –
> 'Twas a bow-legg'd Conductor of a twopenny bus.

> (Quoted in Gammond, 1991: 411)

This romantic-cynical, witty tradition of popular songwriting had a great, and largely unacknowledged, influence on the shape of popular songwriting through the second half of the twentieth century; different from the blues and jazz influences, but in its way as vital.

Music hall   The essence of music hall is variety; a theatrical establishment, generally catering for lower-brow or working-class audiences, and which would put on a bill of a medley of different modes of entertainment: comic songs, sentimental songs, short comic skits and burlesques, recitals of poetry, snatches from Shakespeare and other dramatists, and various other sorts of sketch and short performance. Often a compere would introduce each act, and struggle half-comically to keep order amongst the boisterous, interacting audience. The most important aspects of music hall culture were its creation of certain 'star' names, and its husbandry of the developing tradition of popular songwriting.

The music hall tradition evolved out of the popular entertainments associated with coffee houses and public bars. So-called 'song and supper rooms', such as 'Evans's Music and Supper Rooms' in Covent Garden, were popular in the 1830s and 1840s. Specific music halls began appearing in the late 1840s; the Mogul in Holborn opened a burlesque saloon in 1847; the 'Grand Harmonic Hall' opened in Southwark in 1848 and the 'Canterbury Hall' in Lambeth in 1851. By 1868 there were approximately 200 music halls operating in London alone, with several hundred more in the rest of the country. Popular sentimental songs such as Tom Costello's 'My Nellie's Blue Eyes' (*c*.1886) became parodied, in this case by Charles Coburn's 'Two Lovely Black Eyes' (obtained 'only for telling a chap 'e was wrong'). Coburn's 'The Man Who Broke the Bank at Monte Carlo' is a song still recognised by most people today.

Napoleon III (1808–1873)   Born Charles Louis Napoleon Bonaparte, nephew of the famous Napoleon. His cousin, who had been styled 'Napoleon II' despite never ruling France, died in 1832 and after this Charles presented himself as the Bonapartist pretender to the throne of France. He was regarded by most as a joke, and his political aspirations came to nothing until the REVOLUTIONS OF 1848. Adopted by French monarchists as an anti-radical candidate, he stood for President and won by a landslide: helped by the talismanic 'Napoleon' name he obtained 70 per cent of votes cast. In 1851 he staged a coup and declared himself emperor for life, a move endorsed by a popular plebiscite in 1852. Thereafter he ruled France with an autocratic severity that modulated, as the years passed, to a more liberal and eventually quasi-democratic approach. The debacle of the FRANCO-PRUSSIAN WAR of 1870 gave his enemies the leverage they needed to oust him; he fled to England where he spent the rest of his life. MARX's *Eighteenth Brumaire of Louis Napoleon* (1848) remains a classic analysis of Napoleon III's rise to power: of the relationship between Napoleon III and his illustrious uncle Napoleon I Marx memorably observed that 'all great events and personalities in world history reappear in one fashion or another . . . the first time as tragedy, the second as farce' (Marx, 1848: 123). Robert BROWNING was also aware of the farcical aspects of Napoleon III's career; the speaker in his lengthy DRAMATIC MONOLOGUE *Prince Hohensteil-Schwangau, Saviour of Society* (1871) is a transparent cipher for Napoleon, recently fallen from power and contemplating his successes and failures.

Newgate novels   Newgate was one of the more celebrated of London's prisons (it was pulled down in 1902); and 'the Newgate novel' was a sub-genre of fiction that dealt with picaresque tales of low life and often criminal adventure that had their vogue from the early 1830s through to the beginning of the 1840s. Harrison Ainsworth (1805–82), Edward Bulwer-Lytton (1803–73) and Charles DICKENS were the authors most closely associated with the school. The enormous popularity of these novels stirred up enormous controversy. John Sutherland summarises the situation most economically: 'very simply, Newgate novels dealt with criminals recorded in the *Newgate Calendar*. Simply, again, to write fiction about criminals was misapprehended as condoning (or even advocating) criminal behaviour' (Sutherland, 1988: 462). Bulwer-Lytton's *Paul Clifford* (1830) followed the career of a gentlemanly highwayman; its inclusion of criminal slang, or 'thieves' cant' as it was known, gave spice to the story and became an important component in subsequent 'Newgate' novels. Bulwer followed the success of this novel with another controversial work, *Eugene Aram* (1832), in which a scholar-murderer's crimes are apparently condoned on account of the criminal's genius and superiority to his victims. Ainsworth's *Rookwood* (1834) featured a heroic Dick Turpin, and *Jack Sheppard* (1839) centred on the career of an eighteenth-century thief and cracksman. Despite the fact that Jack eventually gets his comeuppance, hanged theatrically at Tyburn in a riotous public execution, Ainsworth was nevertheless accused of corrupting morals by presenting a villain as an attractive character (a murderer called Courvoisier apprehended in 1840 claimed to have been inspired to his crimes by reading *Jack Sheppard*). The representation of pickpockets, prostitutes and housebreakers in Dickens' OLIVER TWIST (1837–9) seems highly moral by comparison. THACKERAY's *Catherine* (1839–40), detailing the murderous career of its heroine Catherine Hayes, functions as a brilliant pastiche of the genre.

Further reading

The Newgate Novel 1830–1847: Bulwer, Ainsworth, Dickens and Thackeray (1963) by Keith Hollingsworth.

Newman, John Henry (1801–1890)   After an education at Trinity College, Oxford, Newman became a fellow of Oriel, where he became friendly with Edward Pusey (1800–82) and John Keble (1792–1866). In early life he wrote a number of devotional poems, 109 of which appeared, anonymously, in the collection *Lyra Apostolica* (1836). One of these poems 'Lead Kindly Light' (also known as 'Faith', and 'The Pillar of Cloud') became one of the century's most popular HYMNS:

> Lead, Kindly Light, amid the encircling gloom,
> Lead Thou me on!
> The night is dark, and I am far from home –
> Lead Thou me on!

(ll. 1–4)

Newman became vicar of St Mary's Church, Oxford, where his sermons attracted a great deal of attention, and by 1833 he had abandoned the Evangelical leaning of his youth in favour of a more High Church belief. He was one of the founding figures of the OXFORD MOVEMENT, writing his various *Tracts for the Times* (from 1833 onwards). These pamphlets interrogated various aspects of Christian doctrine, but not until 1841, with the publication of *Tract XC* (in which Newman argued that the XXXIX ARTICLES were in fact compatible with Roman Catholicism), did Newman incur official censure. He withdrew from Oxford and lived a monk-like life for a while, resigning his curacy at St Mary's in 1843. His conversion to Catholicism, in 1845, shocked many, amongst his fellow 'Tractarians' as well as the general public. After visiting Rome he was ordained as a Catholic priest in 1846, and returned to England with Papal instruction to set up the Oratory in Birmingham, a form of Catholic church.

The re-establishment of a Catholic presence in Britain in the 1850s, with a Catholic archbishop, priests and churches, caused much friction with some hostile Protestants who complained of 'Papal aggression', and Newman acted as a weather-vane for a great deal of this criticism. His autobiographical novel *Loss and Gain* (1848) attempts to explain his own conversion. In 1851 Newman was appointed the first Rector of the newly founded Catholic University in Dublin, Ireland (later University College, Dublin), a post he held until 1858. His belief in the importance of university education found expression in a series of lectures, later published as a book, *The Idea of a University* (1852). Later, after a series of personal attacks from vigorously Protestant Charles KINGSLEY, who labelled him an inconsistent and untruthful man, Newman issued his autobiography, *Apologia pro Vita Sua* ('Justification for his life') in 1864. This work explains the change that came over Newman's beliefs prior to his conversion, tracing the more important (as Newman saw it) continuities. The chapter 'History of My Religious Opinions from 1833 to 1839' asserted that

> from the age of fifteen, dogma has been the fundamental principle of my
> religion: I know no other religion; I cannot enter into the idea of any other
> sort of religion; religion, as mere sentiment, is to me a dream and a mockery.

He published *The Dream of Gerontius* in 1865, a long devotional poem dramatising the death of an elderly man and the passage of his soul to heaven. One of Newman's most enduring achievements, it was set to music by Edward Elgar (1857–1934) in 1900. In 1879 Newman was made a Cardinal.

New woman   The 'new woman' was a cultural invention of the 1890s, reflecting the sense that female roles and identity was changing. Debates around the proper dress for women, the proper role of female education, the sorts of jobs and careers that women ought to occupy, whether women should have the vote, and questions of sexuality, contraception and venereal disease – all found outlets in the media and literature of the age. In particular there were a great many novels written that became known as 'new woman' fiction, dramatising this perceived 'new' model of womanhood. That the vogue for this sort of cultural discussion happened in the 1890s should not detract us from the fact that proto-feminist thinkers had been rehearsing these questions for a hundred years.

The Woman Who Did (1895) by Grant Allen (1848–99) was perhaps the most notorious and widely read 'new woman' novel; its well-bred heroine Hermina Barton refuses to marry Alan Merrick, the man she loves, instead forming a non-hypocritical 'rational' relationship with him. She gives birth to a daughter, but Merrick dies, and Barton determines to raise her daughter in the teeth of bourgeois outrage at her 'bastardy'. The novel ends ironically with the daughter growing up mean-spirited and conventional, and Barton killing herself – 'Hermina Barton's stainless soul had ceased to exist for ever' concludes the narrator. HARDY's novels contain several 'new women', most famously Sue Brideshead in JUDE THE OBSCURE. *A Superfluous Woman* (1894) by Emma Frances Brooke (1859–1926) was also a scandalous success; a kind of proto-*Lady Chatterley's Lover*, its aristocratic heroine Jessamine Halliday offers herself to a handsome Scottish peasant to bear sturdy children with him, but his sense of honour does not permit it. Instead she returns to London, marries the degenerate Lord Heriot, and dies giving birth to his cretinous children; unspoken in the narrative but unavoidably implied is that she dies of syphilis contracted from her husband. 'Iota' (the pen name of Kathleen Mannington Caffyn, 1855–1926) wrote less extreme 'new woman' fiction, including *A Yellow Aster* (1894) in which the heroine, though thoroughly modern in many respects, remained largely within the confines of contemporary morality. George Egerton (pen name of Mary Bright, 1859–1945) published an influential collection of short fiction under the musically themed title *Keynotes* (1893) in which modern women were represented in vignettes as they coped with depression, alcoholism and sex-related issues.

Responses to 'new woman' fiction were polarised between enthusiastic endorsement of the redefinition of 'proper womanliness' on the one hand, and outraged hostility at the impurity and malign influence of such writing on the other. In the words of Kate Flint,

> the controversy induced by the emergence of the 'New Woman' fiction in the 1890s bears a close similarity to the wave of anxiety expressed about the SENSATION novel some thirty years earlier: should girls be allowed to read such fiction? What would be its effects upon them?

> (Flint, 1993: 294)

By the later 1890s reviewers were proclaiming that the 'new woman' mode was now passé; but in a broader sense it fed into the currents of the renewed feminist impulse that led to such breakthroughs as votes for women in 1918.

Nobility, The. *See* **Peerage**.

Nonconformity　A 'Nonconformist' is a Protestant who does not belong to the official British Protestant Church, the Church of England (also known as the Anglican Church). Originally the term denoted those Anglicans who had been expelled from the Church for refusing to accede to the Act of Conformity of 1662 (the dispute centred on the legitimacy of certain church ceremonies). By the nineteenth century the term was interchangeable with 'dissenter', and referred to a member of one of the following non-Anglican Protestant groups: UNITARIANS and Presbyterians, Baptists (also known as Anabaptists), Methodists, Quakers and various others. Roughly speaking, Nonconformists believed in the authority of scripture over the authority of the church; at the other end of this notional scale were Anglo-Catholics (and, indeed, Catholics) who believed in the authority of the church over that of scripture. ELIOT's *Felix Holt* (1866) dramatises a hilarious public debate between a committed Nonconformist preacher called Lyon and a timid Anglican; her *Adam Bede* (1859) portrays the strong, principled female Methodist preacher Dinah Morris, pointing up the fact that several Nonconformist sects permitted women to preach, when the Church of England resolutely did not.

Northcliffe, first Viscount (1865–1922)　Born Alfred Harmsworth in Dublin, Lord Northcliffe became one of the first press magnates. Largely autodidact he worked as a freelance journalist, founding *Answers* in 1888, a gossipy populist news-and-entertainment sheet modelled on the successful *Tit-Bits*. In 1894 he purchased the *London Evening News* and turned it into a hugely popular news-sheet. He founded the ha'penny *Daily Mail* in 1896, and the first tabloid newspaper, the *Daily Mirror*, in 1903. (*See* JOURNALISM.)

Novel　The novel is the quintessential nineteenth-century form of art. Fictional prose narratives, often of considerable length, allowed Victorian writers to portray both the inner delineations of individual consciousness and the broader diversity and richness of society.

To trace the development of the novel across the century is to see a variety of distinct novelist sub-genres in the earlier decades (the NEWGATE novel, the SILVER-FORK novel, GOTHIC writing) coalesce in to a hybridised mainstream, pulled along in part by the slipstream of Charles DICKENS' extraordinary success. This mainstream form of the novel was dominant in the 1840s, 1850s and 1860s, with mutations such as DOMESTIC fiction, SENSATION fiction and INDUSTRIAL fiction still embodying its central concerns, specifically a fictive attempt to position and/or locate a representative individual in his or her social context, along the two key poles of romantic love and identity. As far as the first of these two categories go, most Victorian novelists would have agreed with Trollope's assertion that 'very much of a novelist's work must appertain to the intercourse between young men and young women. It is admitted that a novel can hardly be made interesting or successful without love' (Trollope, (1875–6) 1999: 138). But

153

the best Victorian novels do more than merely relate boy-meets-girl narratives; they uncover the epistemological and ontological problematics of social existence in the period. William Makepeace THACKERAY, who was often taken by his contemporaries as one of the two most important novelists (the other being Dickens) structures all his novels along the vector of Romance, using these conventions to explore the hypocrisies and awkwardnesses of fitting in to Victorian society. For Elizabeth GASKELL this love plot was a more comfortable thing; for Charlotte and Emily BRONTË more passionate and all-consuming, but in every case it is played out in a creative tension with social requirements. We might say, to summarise the situation, that almost all mainstream Victorian novels explore civilisation and its discontents.

Later in the century George ELIOT, George Meredith (1828–1909), George Gissing (1857–1903), Thomas HARDY and the English-resident American Henry James (1843–1916) redefined the novel, without ever detaching it wholly or even largely from this mid-Victorian norm. REALISM, and a variety of experiments in form, tone and register made the novel more complex but not radically new.

Further reading

The Victorian Novel (1990) by Alan Horsman; The True Story of the Novel (1996) by Margaret Anne Doody; An Autobiography ((1875–6) 1999) by Anthony Trollope.

Oliver Twist (1837–1839), Charles Dickens   Dickens' second novel was published in instalments between February 1837 and April 1839, and was an immediate and enduring success. Its image of the starving workhouse boy Oliver asking for more gruel from the astonished Mr Bumble with his 'please, sir, I want some more' is perhaps Dickens' single most iconic moment.

The earlier stages of the novel are more picaresque than the later, more densely plotted chapters. Oliver is born in the workhouse, his unmarried mother dying in childbirth. He grows up precariously, first on a baby-farm, and then in the workhouse proper. His 'impudence' in asking for more gruel prompts the outraged Poor Law authorities to apprentice him out to an undertaker, Mr Sowerberry. Here he is miserable, and after fighting with a Charity Boy he runs away to London. In the city he falls in unwittingly with a gang of pickpockets, run by the sinister old Jewish man Fagin. The scenes elaborating the criminal underworld are especially vivid: Oliver meets the irrepressible 'Artful Dodger' Jack Hawkins, the prostitute Nancy and her boyfriend, the violent Bill Sikes. Oliver accompanies the boys on a pickpocketing excursion, and is apprehended, but saved from the depredations of the brutish judicial system by the patronage of kindly old Mr Brownlow, a wealthy Londoner. Oliver's circumstances seem to have improved, but he is kidnapped by Nancy and Sikes, and returned to Fagin's den. Sikes insists that Oliver accompanies him on a housebreaking expedition, during which Oliver is shot and Sikes escapes. The inhabitants of the house, including the beautiful Rose Maylie, believe Oliver's protestations of innocence, and they take him under their wing.

About halfway through the novel there is a palpable thickening of the narrative, as if Dickens belatedly decided to make up for the more episodic earlier sections with an excess of plotting. A shadowy criminal, Monks, is introduced as Fagin's partner; he turns out to be Oliver's half-brother, eager to swindle Oliver out of his legitimate inheritance. Myriad characters interact and the plot complexifies. The virtuous Rose and Mr Brownlow attempt to rescue Nancy from her life of prostitution, but she considers herself beyond help. Fagin informs Bill Sikes that Nancy has spoken with these respectable figures, and he, raging, batters her to death. Sikes then flees in a guilty terror, and is chased through Jacob's Island, an especially run-down and seedy portion of east London south of the river. In a melodramatic touch, Sikes tries to escape the angry crowd over the rooftops, is startled by a vision of Nancy's eyes, and falls to his death, accidentally hanging himself on his own rope. Fagin is arrested and hanged, although it is not clear for what crime (the impression is that he is executed for being, non-specifically, a 'villain' and a Jew, neither of which, it has to be said, were capital offences in Victorian Britain). One of the book's most powerful chapters is the penultimate, in which Dickens imagines the terrified, faintly phantasmagoric perspective of Fagin in the condemned cell, 'The Jew's Last Night Alive'. In a final chapter we learn that Oliver lives happily ever after.

Oliver Twist is, as a novel, often crude, and reductively schematic, but its crudity and schematism are both gloriously, colourfully, grippingly and evocatively handled. The energy of Dickens' youthful imagination lifts the book into the realm of myth. It is as powerful a read today as ever, even though the specific applicability of its satire on the Poor Laws and judicial abuses has lost point. Paul Schlicke argues that 'it is appropriate to think of *Oliver Twist* as the first Victorian novel', not only because Victoria herself acceded to the throne before Chapter 9 (of 53) had appeared in print, but also because it is the first novel to place a child at its centre and to develop 'in a contemporary context Wordsworth's idea of childhood as a special state' (Schlicke, 1999: 439), thereby initiating a fertile Victorian tradition of writing of childhood and childish protagonists. It is a book that touches both on the bourgeois romance of the perfect, affluent family life and on the more dynamic underworld of urban CRIME and deprivation, the two most vigorous Victorian novelistic idioms.

Further reading

The Adventures of Oliver Twist (1837–39; edited by Steven Connor 1994) by Charles Dickens.

On Liberty (1859), John Stuart Mill   Mill's concisely eloquent assertion of English liberal values remains a classic work of ethical philosophy, its arguments still compelling and its relevance still acute. 'Liberty,' Mill common-sensically says, 'consists in doing what one likes.' This liberty can legitimately be curtailed for only one reason: 'the liberty of the individual must be thus far limited: he must not make himself a nuisance to other people' (Mill (1859) 1991: 62). This is the theme that reoccurs throughout Mill's book:

> The only purpose for which power can be rightfully exercised over any member of a civilized community, against his will, is to prevent harm to others. His own good, either physical or moral, is not a sufficient warrant.
>
> (Mill (1859) 1991: 14)

'If all mankind minus one,' Mill strikingly asserts, 'were of one opinion, and only one person were of the contrary opinion, mankind would be no more justified in silencing that one person, than he, if he had the power, would be justified in silencing mankind' (Mill (1859) 1991: 21).

One of the effects of Mill's book was to make this position *socially* as well as intellectually respectable. There is little in his definition of liberty that is not in the declarations of the rights of man associated with the American and French Revolutions, or in the writings of Voltaire (1694–1778) or Tom Paine (1737–1809). But for many middle-class and aristocratic Victorians this Paineite 'liberty' was taken to be equivalent to 'licence', and therefore 'anarchy', a code-word for radicalism and rebellion. Mill powerfully argues that individual liberty is not only a personal but a social good, because it tends to free individual creative and dynamic talents that in turn benefit the state as a whole. 'A State which dwarfs its men, in order that they may be more docile instruments in its hands even for beneficial purposes – will find that with small men no great thing can really be accomplished' (Mill (1859) 1991: 128).

Further reading

On Liberty and Other Essays (1859; edited by John Gray 1991) by John Stuart Mill.

Opera. *See* **Music**.

Opium Wars (1839–1841, 1856–1860)   Collectively these conflicts are often called the 'Anglo-Chinese Wars', with the first known as the 'Opium War' and the second the 'Arrow War'. From the end of the eighteenth century, British traders had traded Indian-grown opium through the port of Canton to make great profits from the growing market for the drug amongst the Chinese. Indeed, Britain's shipments of opium to China were deliberately, we might say cynically, encouraged to counter an imbalance of trade between the two countries: British demand for porcelain, silk and tea was not matched by Chinese demand for any British goods. With large quantities of this highly addictive drug being shipped into China, the taste for it spread through all classes of society. By the 1830s some 3.75 million pounds (weight) of opium passed through Canton every year.

In 1839 the Chinese authorities sent Lin Tse-Hsu (1785–1850), one of the country's most distinguished diplomats, to Canton specifically to suppress this trade. Lin confiscated and destroyed all the opium in the city and confined the community of British traders to their warehouses, where they were besieged for several weeks. The British population at Hong Kong was also forced out. Britain sent an expeditionary force to China to extract reparations and reinstate the trade. The naval operations along the Chinese coast that ensued, including shelling and blockading, forced the Chinese Emperor to sign the treaty of Nanking in 1842. This 'unequal treaty' (so called because China relinquished much and gained nothing) ceded Hong Kong to British rule in perpetuity, forced the Chinese to open five 'treaty ports', and gave British traders the right to trade with whom they chose. These treaty ports became, effectively, foreign enclaves in Chinese soil, with British traders granted 'extraterritoriality', the right to be subject to their native laws rather than Chinese jurisdiction. Reparations for the destroyed opium were also paid by China.

By the 1850s these concession were seen by the British as inadequate, and they pressed the Chinese for further 'treaty ports' to be opened, and for British diplomats to be granted direct access to the Emperor. In 1857 the Chinese impounded a Hong Kong ship called the *Arrow* that flew the British flag, charging the crew with piracy. Britain, joined by France, used this as a pretext to launch military action. Anglo-French attacks along the Chinese coast led to the negotiations for the Treaty of Tientsin (1858), which granted the British ten further treaty ports, gave Christian missionaries the right to travel anywhere in the country, ensured the right of diplomatic access to the Chinese Imperial court, officially legalised the opium trade and imposed substantial reparations. When Chinese courts refused to ratify this treaty, British and French troops invaded, capturing Peking in 1860. The Convention of Peking that followed reaffirmed the terms of the treaty.

***Origin of Species* (1859), by Charles Darwin**   Darwin had been working on his ideas of EVOLUTION by natural selection since the 1830s, and was in no hurry by the 1850s to publish. But another English naturalist, Alfred Russel Wallace (1823–1913), working entirely independently, had arrived at a similar hypothesis. In the summer of 1858 Wallace sent Darwin a paper entitled 'On the tendency of varieties to depart indefinitely from the original type'. Although Darwin and Wallace then published a joint paper on evolution in the *Journal of the Proceedings of the Linneaus Society* in 1858, Darwin became reluctant to press ahead with the publication of his own work for fear that Wallace would consider it an un-GENTLEMANLY attempt to pre-empt him. Darwin's friends had to apply considerable pressure to persuade Darwin to write anything at all. The composition was 'often interrupted by ill health ... It cost me 13 months and ten days hard labour' he later wrote in his autobiography. *On the Origin of Species by Means of Natural Selection, or the Preservation of Favoured Races in the Struggle for Life* appeared in November 1859.

The first edition of Darwin's book was divided into 14 chapters. The first seven of these introduce and discuss the theory of natural selection, with two chapters on the tendency of variation in domestic and wild animals, one chapter on what Darwin called the 'Struggle for Existence', a chapter on 'Natural Selection' itself, one on 'Laws of Variation', and one considering various 'Difficulties on Theory'. Chapter 7 considers 'Instinct', and argues that natural selection tends towards 'accumulating slight modifications of instinct' as for physical features. The remaining chapters address the topic from a slightly different angle, considering the relative merits of 'evolution' as opposed to 'divine creation' as an account of the myriad separate species in the world. Darwin discusses the geological record, as well as the morphological and embryological affinities of various organisms. Throughout Darwin's prose is clear, largely jargon-free and makes for a pleasurable reading experience, unlike most contemporary scientific writing. The bulk of the book is an elegant and judicious selection of many specific examples of anatomy and behaviour from the animal world. Darwin himself denied that he possessed any great intellectual capacity ('my power to follow a long and purely abstract train of thought is very limited; and therefore I could never have succeeded with metaphysics or mathematics' (quoted in Ridley, 1994: 22)); but in *Origin* this becomes a strength. The accumulation of practical example, the refusal to jump to conclusions, the many instances of experiment bolster the argument beyond the point of reasonable disagreement.

With hindsight it is easy to describe *On the Origin of Species* as the most revolutionary and important work of science of the century. The initial storm created by its publication was augmented from an unrelated direction with the publication, a few months after Darwin's book, of the Essays and Reviews collection that seemed also to be challenging religious orthodoxy. Perhaps the most famous contemporary reaction to the book was the debate that took place during a meeting of the British Association for the Advancement of Science in Oxford, 30 June 1860. Bishop Samuel Wilberforce (1805–73), known to his enemies as 'soapy Sam', spoke against evolution; and the theory was defended by Thomas Huxley (1825–95), known as 'Darwin's bulldog' for his energetic support of his friend's ideas. Wilberforce asked Huxley sarcastically whether it was 'through his grandfather or his grandmother that he claimed descent from a monkey?' Huxley's dignified reply bears quoting in full:

> I asserted – and I repeat – that a man has no reason to be ashamed of having an ape for his grandfather. If there were an ancestor whom I should feel shame in recalling it would rather be a *man* – a man of restless and versatile intellect – who, not content with an equivocal success in his own sphere of activity, plunges into scientific questions with which he has no real acquaintance, only

to obscure them by an aimless rhetoric, and distract the attention of his hearers from the real point at issue by eloquent digressions and skilled appeals to religious prejudice.

(Quoted in Partington, 1992: 358)

In some parts of the world the storm created by Darwin's undemonstrative, compelling and brilliant book is still raging.

Further reading

On The Origin of Species (1859; edited by J.W. Burrow 1985) by Charles Darwin.

Ossian   The Scottish poet James Macpherson (1736–96) claimed to have discovered and translated the works of this mythical Celtic poet, a shadowy figure dating from early Scottish history. Various fragments of Ossianic poetry were published in the later eighteenth century, including Macpherson's prose translations of two epic poems, *Fingal* (1762) and *Temora* (1763). This work was greeted with enormous excitement in Scotland (where 'Ossian' was claimed as a poet on a par with Homer, evidence of the rich cultural history of the nation) and around Europe. There were, nevertheless, sceptics who doubted the authenticity of these poems. Macpherson was challenged to produce the originals, and was forced to fabricate them: after his death a committee declared 'Ossian' to be a forgery, constructed from elements of traditional Gaelic poetry intermixed with Macpherson's own writing. Despite the scandal of their forgery, Ossian's poems remained very popular throughout the nineteenth century; the writing is vivid and powerful in a distinctively melancholic, 'celtic' manner. In 1866 Matthew Arnold praised Macpherson's 'Ossian' works as a masterpiece of Celtic literature, despite their author's dishonest claims for them. Arnold especially admired the 'vein of piercing regret and sadness' in the works, adding 'choose any of the better passages of Macpherson's *Ossian* and you can see even at this time of day what an apparition of newness and power such a strain must have been to the eighteenth century'.

Owen, Robert (1771–1858)   Born in Wales, the son of a shopkeeper, Owen became by adulthood a self-made wealthy cotton magnate, owning several spinning mills in Manchester. He is remembered today as a socialist and philanthropist, the model of an enlightened employer, after he bought the New Lanark mills in Scotland and built a model village for his workers. This community was established on principles of cooperation, and provided the workers with housing and education for their children together with other benefits, whilst Owen made sure that conditions in his mill were humane. His example played an important part in bringing about the passage of the Factory Act of 1819, legislation that moved towards a climate of safeguarding workers' health. Owen moved to America in the 1820s and established a second model community – called New Harmony in Indiana – for workers. He published two important early socialist works: *A New View of Society* (1813) and *The Revolution in Mind and Practice of the Human Race* (1849).

Although he remains an important figure in the development of British socialism and workers' rights, Owen himself was in many regards far from a socialist; he was deeply paternalistic towards his workers, he expressed hostility to democracy and he was opposed to CHARTISM. But his secularism, his commitment to worker cooperation and trades unions, and his profound belief in the material and social determination of human consciousness proved influential. Followers, known as 'Owenites', organised a number of projects aimed at ameliorating the conditions of workers. In 1835 an Owenite organisation, the 'Association of All Classes and All Nations', or 'AACAN', began raising money and buying land at Queenswood in Hampshire to establish a workers' community. As many as 50 local branches of the AACAN were in existence in the early 1840s, holding meetings (both cultural and political) in 'halls of science' and advocating cradle-to-grave care for members. But the Queenswood community did not prosper and by 1845 the AACAN had been dissolved.

Further reading

Citizens and Saints: Politics and Anti-Politics in Early British Socialism (2002) by Gregory Claeys.

Oxford English Dictionary, The (1857–1928) The (to this day) standard and authoritative dictionary of the English language began life in 1857 as a paper presented to the PHILOLOGICAL SOCIETY entitled 'On some Deficiencies in our English Dictionaries' by Richard Trench (1807–86), the Dean of Westminster. A 'Proposal for the Publication of a New English Dictionary by the Philological Society' was issued by the Society in 1859, inaugurating the work on a wholly new dictionary on the following principle: 'in the treatment of individual words the historical principle will be uniformly followed'. This 'historical principle' was the tenet that definitions of words should be extensively illustrated by a chronologically wide-ranging set of quotations showing the word in use. The initial editors of the new dictionary were Herbert Coleridge (1830–61), and after him Frederick Furnivall (1825–1910) but the exacting requirements of the historical principle meant that 20 years passed during which time nothing happened but exemplary quotations and other preliminary material were gathered. The name with which the *Dictionary* is most associated is James Murray (1837–1915), who took over the editorship in 1878 and who effectively devoted the rest of his life to the work. Resisting pressure to speed up the work, and managing a complex task and a huge team with great skill, Murray brought out the first volume of the dictionary (*A–Ant*) in 1884. The title page read 'A New English Dictionary on Historical Principles', and it was under this title that all subsequent volumes were issued (not until a reprint of the whole dictionary in 1933 was the work officially named *The Oxford English Dictionary*). The work proceeded slowly, with intermittently issued 352-page instalments being issued for sale at the price of 12/6 each (later, shorter and more frequent instalments were issued). The whole of 'B' had been published by 1888, and at the close of the century the project had reached 'G'. At Murray's death in 1915 the dictionary had reached 'T'. Editorial duties were assumed by Charles Talbut Onions (1873–1965) and the final volume of the whole was published in 1928. A complete revision and second edition of the *Dictionary* was issued in 1989.

The *OED*, as the work is commonly abbreviated, remains one of the most astonishing and useful monuments of Victorian scholarship. Its period provenance renders it especially useful to a scholar of the nineteenth century; many of the illustrative quotations are drawn from nineteenth-century works, and the first edition captures a flavour of the range and biases of Victorian cultural and literary assumptions.

Oxford Movement   A religious movement inaugurated and largely perpetuated by academic clergy at the University of Oxford, beginning in 1833. The movement was also known by a number of alternative names: 'Tractarianism' after the 90 tracts issued by its proponents; 'Anglo-Catholicism' because of its High-Church quasi-Catholic affiliations; and (derogatively) 'Puseyism' after Edward Pusey (1800–82), one of its founding figures. James Anthony Froude (1818–94), writing in 1883, called it 'The Oxford Counter-Reformation', because its effect was to undo the Protestant Reformation and return to an earlier model of the Catholic faith.

Oxford was traditionally more TORY, traditional and 'High Church' (which is to say, more wedded to ritual and tradition in the actual practice of church worship) than the largely Whiggish, Evangelical Cambridge. In 1833 a number of high-profile clergymen began to protest against what they saw as the secularisation of the official religion of the land, 'Anglican' or 'Church of England' Christianity. Edward Pusey, John Keble (1792–1866) and John Henry Newman (1801–90) argued that the Church of England was becoming increasingly subservient to the temporal powers, a situation known technically as 'Erastianism'. They announced themselves especially alarmed at the result of the general election of 1833 (which is to say, the first post-1832 Reform Act Parliament) and in particular at the government's plans to reform the Church. The Oxford Movement as such is said to date from July 1833, when Keble preached his famous 'National Apostasy' sermon at Oxford deploring the government's interference in the affairs of the Church. Following this the group began publishing a series of 'tracts', polemics and discussion papers issued under the general title of *Tracts for the Times*. These papers, of which 90 appeared in all between 1833 and 1841, developed a series of arguments for the deep historical roots of the Church, for a revival in neglected spirituality, revival in the authority of bishops and the need for absolute faith. Newman is the dominant figure in the authorship of the tracts, and many of them depended upon his scholarship and eloquence.

These publications had an enormous impact. Newman's attempts to demonstrate that the Church of England was actually 'the Catholic Church in England' alienated some and inspired others. His last tract, *Tract 90* (1841), argued that the XXXIX ARTICLES had been designed by the Church of England to meet a particular, strategic need, and that in fact they could be interpreted in a way that was compatible with Roman Catholic doctrine. The public debate over this tract, and Newman's own soul-searching, which is eloquently described in his autobiography *Apologia Pro Vita Sua* (1864) ('Apology *or* Justification for His Life'), led him to convert to Roman Catholicism in 1845. Many were profoundly shocked by this move, however obvious it seems in hindsight; it was widely regarded as a sort of betrayal. None of the other Tractarians took so extreme a step, but nonetheless the defection of their most powerful figure effectively ended the Oxford Movement. Theological conflict ceased 'as if', in Mark Pattison's phrase, 'by the wand of a magician'. 'If a man had gone to sleep in 1846,' Pattison (1813–84) wrote of this change in his *Memoirs* (1885), 'and had woke up again in 1850, he would have found himself in a totally new world' (quoted in Newsome, 1997: 49–50).

The significance of the Oxford Movement goes beyond the specific concerns of religious ritual; it is one of the earlier Victorian manifestations of intense religious questioning that is linked to the prevailing Victorian issue of RELIGIOUS DOUBT. According to Robin Gilmour, by the 1840s 'what was at issue was no longer the validity of Anglican orders, but for an increasing number of thinking people the validity of Christianity itself' (Gilmour, 1993: 86).

P

Palmerston (1784–1865)   Henry John Temple, the third Viscount Palmerston, entered politics out of a sense that it was a duty of his position. He served as First Lord of the Admiralty from 1807 to 1809, and then spent many years as Secretary at War (1809–28). He later crossed to the WHIG Party, but remained a small-c conservative throughout his life, and had little sense of party loyalty – this was not an unusual feature of early nineteenth-century MPs. His independence of manner alienated some of his colleagues, but he cultivated the newspaper-reading public with skill, and served as Home Secretary from 1852–5 and Prime Minister from 1855 to 1858. His accession to power was helped, in part, by a popular disenchantment with the way Lord John Russell's (1792–1878) Whig government was handling the CRIMEAN WAR. His political philosophy was quietist in the domestic arena, and cannily ambitious on the world stage. 'The function of government,' Palmerston said, 'is to calm, rather than to excite agitation' (quoted in Partington, 1992: 505); but despite his Imperial reservations he presided over a number of expansions of the Empire, including the annexation of the Oudh and the 'Arrow War' with China, both 1856 (*see* INDIA, OPIUM WARS). His philosophy of empire disguised an expansionist agendum beneath the rhetoric of making Britain respected and safe throughout the world:

> As the Roman, in the days of old, held himself free from indignity, when he could say Civis Romanus sum [i.e. 'I am a citizen of Rome']; so also a British subject, in whatever land he may be, shall feel confident that the watchful eye and the strong arm of England will protect him against injustice and wrong.
>
> (*Hansard*, 25 June 1850)

The INDIAN MUTINY in 1857 created a political climate hostile enough to unseat Palmerston, but he served a second term as Prime Minister from 1859–65. He died in office, his last words being 'Die, my dear Doctor? That's the last thing I shall do!'

Parody and imitation   Victorian literature, and especially poetry, supported a vigorous and creative culture of parody and imitation. Comic magazines, such as PUNCH, filled many of their pages with parodies of the literary worthies of the day; THACKERAY started his literary career as a parodist and writer of comic skits, and his parodies of contemporary fiction – for example, *Mr Punch's Prize Novelists* (1847) – were very popular. Thackeray's novel *Catherine* (1839) began life as a parody of the vogue for NEWGATE novels, but grew in the telling into something rather more significant. William Aytoun (1813–65) wrote a lengthy parody of the dominant trends in the poetry of his day, *Firmilian, or the Student of Badajoz: a Spasmodic Tragedy* (1854): the success of this cod verse-drama encouraged Aytoun to expand it from excerpts in a review of an imaginary work in *Blackwood's Magazine* in 1851 to a complete poem in 1854. As with the best parody, this goes beyond merely mocking the poetry that it stigmatised as SPASMODIC, and went further, creating a distinctive, comic masterpiece, an example of social commentary that we might, with today's critical vocabulary, label 'Pythonesque'. SWINBURNE was another poet who possessed parodic skills that equalled or surpassed his skills as a conventional poet; his versions of seven of his contemporaries in the *Heptalogia, or the Seven Against Sense* (1880) are amongst the sharpest parodies of the age. TENNYSON's fuzzily religious 'The Higher Pantheism' (1869) asserts:

> The sun, the moon, the stars, the sea, the hills and the plains –
> Are not these, O Soul, the Vision of Him who reigns?
>
> Is not the Vision He? tho' He be not that which He seems?
> Dreams are true while they last, and do we not live in dreams?
>
> . . .
>
> And the ear of man cannot hear, and the eye of man cannot see;
> But if we could see and hear, this Vision – were it not He?
>
> (ll. 1–18)

The first and last stanzas of Swinburne's Parody, 'The Higher Pantheism in a Nutshell', skewer this perfectly:

> One, who is not, we see: but one, whom we see not, is:
> Surely this is not that: but that is assuredly this.
> . . .
> God, whom we see not, is: and God, who is not, we see:
> Fiddle, we know, is diddle: and diddle, we take it, is dee.

Past and Present (1843), by Thomas Carlyle   Carlyle's critique of contemporary society was shaped as a study in contrasts. A central section of the volume, Book II, portrays the social harmony and happiness of an idealised medieval England, centred on a description of the life of a monk, Abbot Samson (based on the historical Jocelin de Brakelond, *fl.* 1200). Book III contrasts this society, based on genuine human rights and responsibilities, with a present day governed only by money, or 'Mammon': 'O, it is frightful when a whole Nation … has "forgotten God"; has remembered only Mammon, and what Mammon leads to!' (Carlyle, *Past and Present*: 195). Books I and IV act as shorter prologue and epilogue to this central contrast. If the past is idealised in Carlyle's book, the present is subject to some of his most penetrating and, often, intemperate criticism. As David Newsome observes, the present is chiefly charac- terised by its villains, which are 'paraded in the fullness of their iniquities in Past and Present: Benthamites, Mammon-lovers of the business world, idle aristocrats, mealy mouthed politicians, all given fanciful names like Sir Jabez Windbag and Plugson of Undershot' (Newsome, 1997: 164).

Pastoral literature   Though most Victorians were drawn to a pastoral ideal, the great achievement of Victorian literary culture was the creation of a distinctive urban aesthetic. The tradition of 'pastoral' literature had valorised and lovingly described the life of the countryside, either in idealised form (as in the classical pastoral of Theocritus and Virgil), or else as a reflection of the actual hardships of rural life, such as are found in the poetry of William Wordsworth (1770–1850) – although Wordsworth also stresses the transcendent spiritual beauty of rural living. Some Victorian poets continued Wordsworth's theme: Arnold's pastoral elegy 'The Scholar Gipsy' (1853) contains some very beautiful renderings of the countryside around Oxford, and Swinburne wrote excellent pastoral verse, particularly in his later career (for instance, the volume *A Channel Passage and Other Poems*, 1899). But in general, and despite the importance of Wordsworth to Victorian culture, 'pastoral' literature faded as a vigorous literary mode over the century. Dickens' representations of the countryside in his fiction are flat and conventional; but his representations of the city are extraordinary, powerful, multifarious and unique. Browning is capable of lovely observations of nature, but his imagination is more characteristically embodied in the nightmare landscape of 'Childe Roland to the Dark Town Came' (1855). Christina Rossetti's landscapes are mournful and redolent of death; James Thomson (1843–82) wrote his greatest poem as a response to London, not the countryside: *The City of Dreadful Night* (1874).

Pater, Walter (1839–1894)   Although he only published a relatively small quantity of prose in his life, Pater's influence as a critic and thinker has been enormous. In particular he is thought of as capturing precisely the mood and aesthetic of the FIN DE SIÈCLE. He was born in east London; his father, a doctor, died when Walter was only four and his mother moved the family to Canterbury, where he enrolled in the King's School at the age of 13 (his mother died when he was 15). In 1858 Pater went up to Oxford to read classics at Queen's College, the environment that was most to shape his life. Although he only graduated with a second-class degree in 1862, and although he was unable to follow his vocation to become an Anglican clergyman (he was reported by a friend to the Bishop of London in somewhat mysterious circumstances; presumably for unorthodoxy) he nevertheless continued living in Oxford in the early 1860s, supporting himself by occasional journalism. In 1865 he was awarded one of the first non-clerical Fellowships at Brasenose. In addition to collegiate duties, Pater began writing for the *Westminster Review* in 1862, and for the *Fortnightly Review* in 1869, covering a range of topics. He was during this time formulating his aesthetic theories, heavily under the influence of Ruskin. His essays on painters and painting were collected as *Studies in the History of the Renaissance* (1873). Included in this influential volume were Pater's response to the painting of the *Mona Lisa* ('she is older than the rocks among which she sits; like the vampire she has been dead many times, and learned the secrets of the grave') and his belief that 'all art constantly aspires to the condition of music'. The 'conclusion' to the volume praised aesthetic intensity:

> A counted number of pulses is given to us only of a variegated and dramatic
> life. How may we see in them all that is to be seen in them by the finest senses?
> How can we pass most swiftly from point to point, and be present always at
> the focus where the greatest number of vital forces unite in their purest
> energy? To burn always with this hard, gemlike flame, to maintain this ecstasy,
> is success in life.

This conclusion was a revised version of a review of William Morris's poems, and was omitted from subsequent editions of the book on account of the dubious moral tone it embodied. Pater's own homosexuality, repressed though it was, caused him trouble; his friendships with a number of men who became notorious one way or another prevented his election to a Proctorship at Brasenose. Most of his friends were particularly of the Pre-Raphaelite, aestheticist and fin-de-siècle cast, and included Swinburne, the academic and critic Oscar Browning (1837–1923), poet Arthur Symons (1865–1945) and novelist George Moore (1852–1933). Pater's own novel *Marius the Epicurian*

(1885) was set in the later years of the Roman Empire, and subordinated plot and character to discussions of religious and secular philosophy and the question of 'the beautiful'. He planned two thematic sequels to this work, but a second novel, *Gaston de Latour*, remained unfinished at his death.

In 1886 Pater moved to Kensington to live with his sisters (still retaining his Fellowship at Brasenose); he published *Appreciations: with an Essay on Style* in 1889, and a more scholarly study, *Plato and Platonism*, in 1893. This latter work reconciled him somewhat to Oxford, and he moved back to the city in the year of its publication; but he died in 1894 of fever and pleurisy.

Peel, Robert (1788–1850)   Born in Lancashire the son of a cotton manufacturer, Peel went on to become one of the most influential Tory politicians of the first half of the nineteenth century. He served in a variety of cabinet posts, including Irish Secretary and Home Secretary, eventually becoming Prime Minister, first 1834–5, and then again more significantly from 1841–6. In a sense this second term saw a new kind of Toryism, more akin to today's Conservatism: based not on social tradition and hierarchy so much as on economic growth and the logic of the market. Though a Tory, Peel was moderniser, and as Prime Minister he oversaw what Colin Matthew describes as an 'experiment in fiscal modernisation' of great significance for the Victorian period. This involved the reintroduction of Income Tax in 1842 (unprecedented in peacetime), the reduction of various protective trade tariffs, the Bank Act of 1844 and attempts to repeal the Corn Laws. As Matthew points out, all this 'dismayed those in his party (such as the romantic Young England group) who believed that conservatism should be a bastion against modernization' (Matthew, 2000: 111). Moreover, one of Peel's most lasting achievements was the modernisation of the criminal code, and especially of the police. He created the Metropolitan Police in 1829, the first police force of its kind in Britain. The close association between these policemen and their sponsor is reflected in their two common nicknames, 'bobbies' and 'peelers', derived from the two parts of his name, the former term still in common usage today. This intervention in the question of policing was the culmination of a concerted attempt by Peel, when Home Secretary, to reform the system of law in Britain. He told the House of Commons in 1827:

> I may be a Tory. I may be an illiberal – but ... Tory as I am, I have the satisfaction of knowing that there is not a single law connected with my name which has not had as its object some mitigation of the severity of the criminal law; some prevention of abuse in the exercise of it; or some security for its impartial administration.

> (Partington, 1992: 511)

Peerage   A 'peer' is a nobleman or noblewoman whose title is either inherited through his or her family or awarded by the monarch; somebody notionally 'above' the ordinary populace. This division of the British population into superior 'lords' and inferior 'commoners' goes back to Anglo-Saxon times, remaining today as a vestigial hangover from feudal society. Peers are entitled to sit in the House of Lords (one of the two HOUSES OF PARLIAMENT, the other being the House of Commons), and throughout the nineteenth century the Lords had an equal place in legislature, although in the twentieth century their role was made subservient to the elected chamber. A peer is not necessarily guaranteed a wealthy lifestyle – although of course many peers were (and are today) rich – but in nineteenth-century culture deference to people with titles was automatic, deep-felt and genuine. A 'peer of the realm' enjoyed tremendous status. A peer need not be a GENTLEMAN, or more precisely need not act in a gentlemanly manner, nor need a gentleman be a peer, but a titled man nonetheless represented for much nineteenth-century culture the epitome of proper authority, good breeding and status.

Lords feature in a great many works of art and literature of the period: especially SILVER-FORK novels, but in many other genres as well. Those interested in the barren complexities inherent in the codes of nobility should consult Debrett's *Peerage* – still published today as depressing testimony to the continuing fascination this institutionalised inequality holds on the British imagination. For those attempting to unpick the complications of the relative position of peers as they appear in many of the novels of the time (a knowledge taken for granted by their authors) the following list ranks them from the top down.

1. Monarch: *King* or *Queen*, addressed as 'your highness'. Below this rank are the immediate family of the monarch, *Prince* or *Princess*.
2. Peers: all of the following may be referred to by specific title (e.g. Baron Tennyson, Marquess of Queensberry); the ranks of Earl, Viscount and Baron may also be instanced generally (e.g. 'Lord Tennyson' or 'Lord Lytton'). It would be incorrect to refer to a Duke or a Marquess as 'Lord so-and-so'. An Earl, Viscount or Baron carries the title Lord before his surname; so, Alfred, Lord Tennyson, not Lord Alfred Tennyson (this latter would imply he was the son of a Duke or Marquess).
- *Duke* or *Duchess*, addressed as 'your grace', ranking immediately below Prince. A Duke of the royal family (known as a Royal Duke) takes precedence over other Dukes. The sons of Dukes are given the courtesy title 'Lord', placed before the given name instead of before the surname, as is the proper styling for an actual lord. Thus the third son of the Duke of Beaufort was Lord Arthur Somerset.
- *Marquess* or *Marchioness*, addressed as 'your grace', ranking below a Duke but above an Earl. Together with 'Count', 'Marquess' is used less specifically to refer to all ranks of foreign nobility. When a Duke is also a Marquess, the latter title is given as a courtesy title to his eldest son: so, for example, the Duke of Devonshire's eldest son is known as 'The Marquess of Hartington' until his father's death, when he inherits the Dukedom. All the sons of Marquesses are given the courtesy title 'Lord', placed

before the given name instead of before the surname: thus the famous son of the Marquess of Queensberry was Lord Alfred Douglas (1870–1945; see WILDE)

- *Earl*, addressed as 'my lord'. An Earl's wife is 'Lady so-and-so' and is addressed as 'my lady'. When a Duke or a Marquess has an earldom as a second title, it is given as a courtesy title to his eldest son.
- *Viscount* or *Viscountess*, addressed as 'my lord' or 'my lady'.
- *Baron* or *Baroness*, addressed as 'my lord' or 'my lady'. This is the lowest rank of nobility entitled to a seat in the House of Lords.
- *Baronet*. The lowest rank of hereditary nobility; a baronet is addressed as 'sir', and although not permitted to sit in the House of Lords he takes precedence over all other Knights of the Realm excepting only Knights of the Garter. Edward Bulwer-Lytton (1803–73) was a hereditary baronet; his son Edward was awarded an earldom and became Lord Lytton (1831–91). The wife of a baronet is 'Lady so-and-so'.

3. *Knights* are also addressed as 'sir', the title coming before the first name. Below Knights, technically, are *Esquires*, a title applied to various individuals including the younger sons of peers, the elder sons of Knights, some royal officers, officers of state and some commoners. In practice, many middle-class men appended the title 'esquire' to their names, a touch regarded (when not strictly proper) as comically pompous, as in 'Henry Pooter Esq.'.

Penny dreadfuls   Populist and melodramatic newspaper or magazine titles, sometimes reporting news with an emphasis upon 'tabloid' excesses of violence and extremes, sometimes publishing crude and colourful fiction. John Hotten's *Dictionary of Modern Slang, Cant and Vulgar Words* (1874) defines the term as: 'those penny publications which depend more upon sensationalism than upon merit, artistic or literary, for success'. Penny dreadfuls were sometimes known as 'bloods'; some scholars distinguish between 'bloods' as published in the first half of the century, and 'penny dreadfuls' in the second.

A precursor to the penny dreadfuls was *The Terrific Register*, which flourished in 1824 and 1825. The *Register* declared on its cover that it was 'Published Weekly, Price 2d., Each Number Embellished with a spirited Engraving': the illustration to the first number was a graphic depiction of the Frenchman Damiens being publicly disembowelled for attempting the assassination of Louis XV of France. Other stories covered in that first edition were: 'the Jew's Leap – The Marine Spectre – An Account of a Family who were all afflicted with the Loss of the Limbs – Universal Pestilence – Punishment of the Knout in Russia – Immolation of Human Beings' and so on. The *Newgate Calender*, which had been running intermittently since the 1770s, continued to be popular through the early nineteenth century with its account of Newgate criminals and their depravities. Journals such as the penny *Weekly Magazine* (late 1840s) were a little more upmarket, although they carried many bloody and savage true stories. The public appetite for gore and sensation was as avid in the nineteenth century as it is today. A *Punch* cartoon from the period shows a semi-ragged youngster in a newsagent: 'now, my man,' says the news vendor, 'what is it?', to which the boy replies 'I vonts a nillustrated newspaper with a norrid murder and a likeness in it' (reproduced in Neuberg, 1977: 192).

Penny dreadful fiction was a vigorous and significant undercurrent to the mainstream of the novel during the period. George Reynolds (1814–79) issued a gargantuan encyclopaedic novel between 1841 and 1856 under the catch-all title *Mysteries of London*. Each weekly penny instalment sold between 30,000 and 40,000 copies. A contemporary, John Parker, described the work as containing

> all the disgusting facts which have from time to time, during the last fifty years, been brought to light and exposed in the public journals as reports from police courts, criminal trials, and cases of seduction and adultery . . . artfully and cleverly dressed up and aided by the depraved pencil of an artist skilled in depicting the sensual and the horrible.

> (John Parker, *Meliora: or Better Times to Come, Second Series* 1853)

Thomas Rymer's sub-Gothic *Varney the Vampire, or the Feast of Blood* (1846–7), subtitled 'A Romance of Exciting Interest', was more fantastic although less well written. Malcolm Errym's *Ada the Betrayed; or, the Murder at the Old Smithy* was issued in 56 penny instalments during the same period. Thomas Prest's 92-part *The String of Pearls, or, the Barber of Fleet Street* (1850-52) was the first to fictionalise Sweeney Todd's psychopathic career. Many penny dreadfuls related the blood-soaked and dashing adventures of highwaymen, most notably the well-named Edward Viles (1842–91), whose *Black Bess; or, the Knight of the Road* was serialised in a mammoth 254 parts between 1867 and 1869. Nor did this enormous novel satiate its readership, for Viles composed and published a sequel, *The Black Highwayman, being the Second Series of Black Bess* (1869–70) in 86 parts.

The nature of this sort of popular publishing changed as the century went on. The 1850s saw the reduction or abolition of a number of so-called 'taxes upon knowledge' (Stamp Duty, paper and advertising taxes). Accordingly, periodical publication became much more cost-effective: 115 separate magazine and newspapers were established in 1859 alone, many of them penny titles. The 1870 Education Act substantially increased levels of literacy, and was symptomatic of a wider Establishment philosophy that the masses needed an 'improving' cultural context. Titles such as *Family Circle* (established 1877, and specialising in 'entertaining and elevating tales and fiction'), *Crystal Stories* (est. 1880, specialising in temperance stories), *Catholic Fireside* (est. 1878) and *Home Words* (est. 1870) all sold for a penny, and none of them was 'dreadful' except in an aesthetic-evaluative sense. By the end of the century the 'penny dreadful' had become both more respectable and more juvenile; its 'thrilling tales' increasingly the province of 'boy's own' youth magazines and (later) crime and science fiction pulps. By the end of the century 'American influence had increased. The exploits of Buffalo Bill (William Cody) had given impetus to the publication of Western cowboy literature' (Smith, 2002: 2)

Further reading

A Feast of Blood: Bloods and Penny Dreadfuls (2002) by Helen R. Smith.

Philanthropy   As the New Poor Laws made official state-sanctioned welfare harder to come by, the Victorian poor came to rely increasingly on private philanthropy. There was a good deal of this during the nineteenth century, although much of it was attached to highly judgmental ideologies that distinguished the 'deserving' poor from the 'undeserving', and insisted that all charity be conditional upon strict religious observance. There had been a tradition of private individuals dispensing charity for hundreds of years in Britain. Dickens' early novels often include such philanthropic individuals, amongst whom might be included Mr Pickwick, Mr Brownlow from *Oliver Twist* and the Cheeryble brothers from *Nicholas Nickleby* (1838–9).

The most distinctive nineteenth-century development in philanthropy, however, was the great increase in philanthropic organisations. In the eighteenth century a number of these charities had been set up, with fund-raising apparatus and a particular rationale for the distribution of money. By 1840, however, the number of these organisations had mushroomed: a public survey identified 28,880 separate charities (it was later claimed that some 4000 charities had been omitted from the list) with a total income of £1,200,000; although half of these institutions had an annual income of £5 or less, and only 1 per cent were large enough to clear more than £500 a year. The state of affairs was hopelessly tangled; maladministration and corruption were widespread, and in many cases the intentions of the founders were no longer appropriate to the changed culture in which the organisation operated. Reform of this state of affairs was a long-drawn-out process. The Charity Commissioners were established by Act of Parliament in 1853, and began a process of rationalisation (this is the climate behind the events of Anthony Trollope's novel *The Warden* (1855), in which proposals to reform the charitable Hiram's Hospital shake up the comfortable life of the warden of the institution). Reforms notwithstanding, philanthropic organisations continued to multiply as the century went on. According to E.P. Hennock, 'by the mid-1880s the income of the London charities alone exceeded the public revenues of Sweden' (quoted in Belchem and Price, 1994: 469)

Further reading

'Philanthropy' by E.P. Hennock in *The Penguin Dictionary of Nineteenth-Century History* (1994) edited by John Belchem and Richard Price.

Philological Society   Founded in 1842 by Connop Thirlwall (1797–1875), Arthur Penrhyn Stanley (1815–81) and Thomas Arnold (1795–1842) to further and promote the study of language. Meetings were held regularly and papers on various linguistic topics read. Amongst the most famous of the society's members were Richard Trench, Dean of Westminster (1807–86), Frederick Furnviall (1825–1910) and James Murray (1837–1915). These three, under the aegis of the society, were instrumental in establishing the project that led to the creation of *The Oxford English Dictionary*.

Philosophy British thinkers made significant contributions to philosophy in the seventeenth and eighteenth centuries, amongst them John Locke (1632–1704) and David Hume (1711–76). The 'empiricist' school of Locke placed philosophical emphasis on the experience of the world that the mind derived through the five senses. A rival school (in effect) was established by a number of German philosophers later in the century, associated particularly with the extremely influential work of Immanuel Kant (1724–1804).

The main achievements of British philosophy in the nineteenth century followed in the empiricist tradition. The Utilitarianism associated with Jeremy Bentham (1748–1832) and continued by his disciple John Stuart Mill (perhaps the greatest British philosopher of the period) is an example of this. We might also include the thought of Charles Darwin in this category of essentially empirical philosophical theorising. German Idealism, such as the post-Kantians Johann Schiller (1759–1805) and Friedrich Schelling (1775–1854), or the distinctive 'will'-based philosophy of Arthur Schopenhauer (1788–1860), had little impact upon British intellectual traditions until the 1870s, when Oxford academics T.H. Green (1836–82) and F.H. Bradley (1846–1924) began teaching it. A different stream of nineteenth-century philosophical thought sees the influence of the individual systematising philosophy of Georg Hegel (1770–1831) filtered through the materialist sociology of Marx into late century socialist thought and practice.

Photography Although pinhole boxes and *camerae obscurae* have been known since the Renaissance, the first method for fixing the image derived thereby was not invented until 1827, when Frenchman Joseph Nièpce (1765–1833) exposed a pewter sheet covered in bitumen of Judea. This first surviving photograph (of the courtyard from Nièpce's attic) required an eight-hour exposure and is faint but recognisable. Nièpce's partner, Louis Daguerre (1787–1851), developed a more effective technique, in which copper plate was covered in a film of light-reactive silver iodide, producing a negative image; the first daguerreotype was displayed to the public in 1839, and the technique continued to be used until the 1850s. Close behind him came Englishman William Henry Fox Talbot (1800–77), whose Calotype (sometimes also called 'Talbotype') technique used silver nitrate-soaked paper rather than copper. Fox Talbot patented his technique in 1841. Calotypes could be treated as photographic negatives, and a number of 'positive' images could be copied from them; accordingly Talbot has the best claim to have invented photography as we understand the term.

Various advances followed quickly. Englishman Frederick Scott Archer (1813–57) introduced a wet collodion method in 1851 that produced glass negatives, a technique producing much sharper photographs in a much shorter time. This method was sometimes called 'albumen printing' because the photographs were printed onto paper treated with egg whites. It quickly established itself as the most popular method of photography, and lasted through to the 1890s. Despite the cumbersome nature of the equipment necessary, portable darkrooms were carried to the Crimean War (1854–6) and the American Civil War (1861–5). The fact that wet collodion photography was not a patent technique aided its very rapid spread through the world.

A mid-Victorian photograph required exposures of between one and two minutes in good light, constraints that largely dictated the images that have come down to us. Landscapes and townscapes were widely photographed, but pedestrians and horses mostly moved too fast to be captured. The bulk of Victorian photos are portraits, either of individuals, couples or families. Many of these appear to modern eyes to possess a stiff, slightly awkward charm: the long exposure times destroyed spontaneity and often required the sitter to be fitted into a (hidden) neck brace to encourage the necessary motionlessness. More recent studies see this mannered, stiff-armed and glazed-faced posing as having its own valid aesthetic. It is certainly extraordinary redolent of the period. Cheaper than conventional oil-paint portraiture, and advertised as more 'realistic', it is that form of portrait art tied most closely to the rise of the middle classes, the same classes that embraced it enthusiastically as their own.

From the 1850s to the end of the century saw a continuing craze for photographic *cartes de visite*. Queen Victoria effectively endorsed this practice by issuing 14 different *cartes* of the royal family, including seven of herself and Albert, in August 1860. The images were taken by the American photographer J.E. Mayall, and 'hundreds of thousands of Mayall's *cartes* were quickly sold', leading directly to a market where 'three or four hundred million *cartes* were sold annually in England' in the early 1860s (Helmut and Alison Gernsheim, quoted in Homans, 1998: 48). These millions of slightly puzzled-looking, startled or complacent faces are the most characteristic visual icons of the Victorian age.

It was in the 1860s that photography became a culturally central Victorian phenomenon: the number of professional photographers in London was only 51 in 1851, but had grown to 2534 by 1861 (Green-Lewis, 1981: 52). The first colour photographs were made by the scientist James Clarke Maxwell (1831–1879) in 1861, although the vast majority of images continued to be taken in black and white until the century's end. In 1895 American George Eastman (1854–1932) invented a form of gelatin-coated film that functioned much more efficiently than the albumen-based coatings. He also designed the familiar 'roll' of film, and invented the mass-market box camera that he named the Kodak (a word that Eastman intended as a world-friendly brand name with no specific meaning). By 1900, with the invention of the $1 'Box Brownie', snapshot photography became the norm.

The great critical study of Victorian photography has yet to be written, and many libraries – including the British Library – have enormous uncatalogued collections of photographic images. Some critics have stressed the Victorians' sense of the photograph as the epitome of verisimilitude, 'a superior grasp of reality, a realism more real than the thing itself' (Green-Lewis, 1981: 30). More fertile, from a critical point of view, is the way that photography altered the Victorians' own apprehension of sight. As Lindsay Smith puts it,

> the invention and popularisation of a myriad of optical instruments widely exposed the intricacies of the sense of sight during the Victorian period. Most crucially, the invention of the camera and the public announcement of the photographic process of daguerreotypy in Paris in 1839 signaled an unprecedented disturbance in a range of cultural investments in the visual.

(Smith, 1995: 3)

Amongst the celebrated photographic portraitists of the period was writer Lewis CARROLL; more technically skilled was Julia CAMERON, who photographed a number of famous figures from the day. Cameron also contributed photographic illustrations to TENNYSON's *The Idylls of the King*, with artist's models standing in as Merlin, Vivien and the like. In 1860–1, another photographer, Henry Peach Robinson (1830–1901), produced an elaborate photographic representation of Tennyson's 'The Lady of Shallot' floating down the river. It is something of a puzzle that criticism has to date largely ignored the aesthetic and textual consequences of what Martin Jay has called 'the most extraordinary technical innovation in vision during the nineteenth-century, indeed perhaps in all human history' (Jay, 1993: 124).

Further reading

Framing the Victorians: Photography and the Culture of Realism (1981) by Jennifer Green-Lewis; Victorian Photography, Painting and Poetry: the Enigma of Visibility in Ruskin, Morris and the Pre-Raphaelites (1995) by Lindsay Smith.

Poet Laureate. See **Laureateship**.

Poland Partition in 1772, 1793 and 1795 had destroyed Poland as a geographical entity, subsuming it into Russia, Prussia and Austria, a situation persistently resisted by the Polish people throughout the century. But apart from a notional Polish state (the small Cracovian republic, and even this was annexed by Austria in 1846) the country remained partitioned until the twentieth century. Several home-led insurrections were oppressed by the occupying powers, and a population of emigrée nationalist Poles lived in various European countries, canvassing support from Liberals. The November Insurrection of 1830 was followed by the forced emigration of a number of eminent Poles, many of them to London; the same thing happened after the failure of the Polish REVOLUTION OF 1848. Their distinctive appearance – large cloaks, hats, prodigious whiskers, gloomy demeanour – provided writers with a readily identifiable archetype. In the 1830s young TENNYSON affected the Polish style himself. In THACKERAY's *The Newcomes* (1853–5), set mostly in the 1830s, Colonel Newcome returns from India with splendid whiskers and old-fashioned clothes, and is taken to be a Polish exile: 'Polish chieftans were at this time so common in London that nobody . . . took any interest in them' (Thackeray, *The Newcomes*: 89). A further Polish rising, the January Insurrection of 1863, was crushed, despite a heroic struggle, in April 1864. The Russians and Prussians then attempted to extirpate all Polish spirit with harshly repressive rule, although without success.

Police   Since the early eighteenth century France had had a *lieutenant general de police* for Paris and a national force of mounted police called the *maréchausée* (who were known as *gendarmes* after 1791). British society, on the other hand, resisted the creation of a centralised police force, seeing such a body as a threat to individual liberty. The duties we now associate with the police were undertaken by a series of often unpaid parish officers: justices of the peace, parish constables, beadles, bailiffs and watchmen. More serious disturbances, such as riots, were handled by the military.

Dissatisfaction with this hotchpotch system grew, however, throughout the eighteenth century. The Middlesex Justice Act (1792) created a number of police officers, constables and magistrates for metropolitan Middlesex and Surrey (which is to say, the north and south banks of the Thames in the London area). Patrick Colquhoun (1745–1820) was appointed as one of the first magistrates under this new legislation, and his *Treatise on the Police of the Metropolis* (1795), arguing for a properly constituted London force, went through many editions in the early years of the century. A proper police force for the capital was finally created by Robert PEEL's legislation passed through Parliament in 1829. By 1830 his new London Metropolitan Police force was some 3200 men strong. The close associations between these policemen and their sponsor is reflected in their two common nicknames, 'bobbies' and 'peelers', derived from the two parts of his name, the former term still in relatively common usage today.

The spread of such police forces through the country happened only slowly. The City of London created its own force, distinct from the Metropolitan Police, in 1839, and some cities and counties did likewise in the late 1830s, although others were dissuaded by the cost, and the perceived overlap with the existing parish officers (a role that was not discontinued). By 1841 fewer than half the English and Welsh counties had established professional police forces. Government legislation was eventually passed in 1856 mandating the creation of such forces throughout the land.

This move, which strikes us today as inevitable, was fiercely rejected by many at the time as continental-style quasi-tyranny. Handbills were distributed in Manchester, opposed to the creation of what was called 'Bourbon Police'; and the MP for Walsall voted against the 1856 legislation on the grounds that 'the system of centralization [of the police] ... however it might suit the Governments of the Continent, was repugnant to the feelings and habits of Englishmen' (quoted in Newsome, 1997: 97). But others supported the move. DICKENS' earlier novels tended to portray the old-fashioned system of justices, bailiffs and watchmen as incompetent or corrupt, and he welcomed the orderliness of the new uniformed officers. London policemen as they appear in *Bleak House* (1852–3) are efficient and imperturbable embodiments of the law, handling the crime scene of Nemo's murder, or asking Jo the crossings-sweeper to 'move on'. The constable who takes down Lightwood and Wrayburn's details at the beginning of *Our Mutual Friend* (1864–5) is similarly characterised by an unrufflable and orderly prosecution of his duty. By the century's end, with the British more used to, and comfortable with, the idea of the police they begin to appear in literature as bungling plods, as in CONAN DOYLE's Sherlock Holmes stories (from 1887), or as lugubrious sentimentalists as in Gilbert and Sullivan's *The Pirates of Penzance* (1879), who complain that 'when constabulary duty's to be done, to be done,/A policeman's lot is not a happy one.'

Poor Laws   Poor relief of one sort or another has been provided in Britain since Elizabethan times. When nineteenth-century historians or critics talk of the 'Poor Laws', they are generally referring to the so-called 'New Poor Law', which is to say the 'Poor Law (Amendment) Act' of 1834. But a complex of earlier legislation and tradition (sometimes known as the 'Old Poor Law'), together with a number of private schemes – mutual help, such as Friendly Societies, and charitable or PHILANTHROPIC relief – were in widespread operation before this time.

England was divided up into approximately 15,000 parishes, each centred on a church (technically, this situation still applies to contemporary Britain). Under the Poor Law Act of 1601 financial help for the sick, the aged and the unemployed was deemed to be a parish responsibility: an (unpaid) parish overseer was expected to provide relief to the needy in his parish, levying a poor rate from wealthier parishioners to this end. This rate was unpopular amongst those expected to pay it, and the system came under increasing pressure in the later eighteenth and nineteenth centuries as more and more people left their parishes to find work – for instance, moving to the cities; their new parishes were under no legal obligation to provide them with poor relief. The so-called 'Speenhamland System' added to the pressure. Following a scheme formulated by a number of Berkshire magistrates in 1795, poor relief was offered not only to the infirm and impotent, but also to able-bodied men in work whose wages were deemed to be too low for them to support their families. The scheme, widely followed in the country, lead to a general increase in the poor rate. The year 1815 saw the demobilisation of the army that had fought the Napoleonic Wars. This together with continued population growth meant that unemployment and attendant poverty became a greater and greater problem through the 1820s and 1830s.

By 1832 opposition to the levels of the poor rate from the prosperous had reached levels whereby a Royal Commission on the Poor Laws was set up to look into the matter. The Commission deliberated for two years, and the Poor Law (Amendment) Act became law in 1834.

The new law had the stated aim not so much of relieving poverty, as discouraging people from applying for poor relief in the first place. The Speenhamland principle of giving relief in aid of wages was discontinued; able-bodied applicants for relief would now join all other paupers in the workhouse. 'Workhouses' – parish-maintained houses for the unemployed – had existed under the Old Poor Law, but under the New Poor Law the 'workhouse test' was instituted. This test required that the standard of living inside the workhouse be lower than that of the lowest-paid labourer outside the workhouse. The idea here was to discourage applicants on the grounds that they would be better off finding work in the outside world, even at the merest remuneration, than they would be entering the workhouse. In the words of one of the Commissioners, the aim was 'to let the labourer find that the parish is the hardest taskmaster and the worst paymaster he can find, and thus induce him to make his application to the parish his last and not his first resort' (quoted in Connor, 1994: 418). In practice this meant that workhouses were officially ghastly: near-starvation levels of food provision, separation from family members, segregation by sex, miserable regimentation. Paupers were set monotonous tasks, such as picking oakum or crushing animal bones to produce fertiliser. Inmates in the Andover workhouse in 1845–6 engaged in this latter work were so hungry that they fought amongst themselves to eat the scraps of meat and marrow still adhering to the bones.

Legislators considered themselves to be rationalising and bringing up to date an unsystematic and ineffective process of poor relief. But opposition to the system started almost as soon as it was introduced. Dickens' powerful portrait of Oliver's workhouse sufferings in the early chapters of OLIVER TWIST (1837–9) still resonates. A decade after the law was introduced Punch mocked it with heavy-handed sarcasm: 'what a beneficent presence is this same Poor-Law, that it takes to its bosom babes and suckings – and lavishes upon callow infancy the tenderness, the love, the gushing kindness of maternal instincts' (Punch, 'The "Milk" of Poor-Law "Kindness"', 3, 1843: 46). Reform of the reforms was slow in coming, however, and when it did happen it tended to be weighted towards the administration of the system rather than the paupers the system supposedly served. Many parishes, for instance, objected to the expense of constructing and maintaining workhouses. In 1852 parishes were permitted to provide outdoor relief – which is to say, they were not obliged to place all applicants for relief into the workhouse – although they were still required to apply a deterrent labour test, so that relief could only be provided at a level below the standard of living enjoyed by the poorest-paid worker. The Union Changeability Act of 1865 changed the way poor relief was funded. The New Poor Law had required parishes to be grouped together into 'unions' of about 20 parishes. The Union Changeability Act shifted the financial burden from individual parishes to the union, which simplified funding and went some way towards addressing the problem of paupers who migrated between parishes.

Nevertheless the principle inherent in the New Poor Law was, in anything, more deeply enshrined in welfare thinking in the later years of the century. Despite its severity and its rationale of efficiency, the system of poor relief required increasing national expenditure: in 1852 the whole system cost £4.9 million a year (5s. 5d. per head of population); by 1872 this had risen to £8 million (nearly 7s. a head). Further legislation increased the deterrent component of relief – for instance, by removing the right to vote of those who applied for poor relief (in 1885 this was overturned, but only for those who claimed poor relief on grounds of illness or infirmity). By the end of the century this social philosophy was beginning to be challenged, and the climate was shifting towards the one that enabled the great twentieth-century triumphs of welfare legislation.

Poverty   The great masterpiece of Victorian 'poverty' literature is *London Labour and the London Poor*, by Henry Mayhew (1812–87). Mayhew began chronicling the lives and ill-rewarded occupations of the capital's poor in a column published in the *Morning Chronicle* in 1849; in 1851–2 a two-volume collection of these writings was published, and in 1861–2 a four-volume version was issued. This latter is a monumental achievement: 2000 close-printed and double-columned pages covering every possible incarnation of the London poor. The work consists mostly of testaments from the men and women themselves, with Mayhew limiting himself to occasional judgement and more frequent financial explanation. The subsistence nature of much London labour is spelled out with frequent assessments of exactly how many pennies a (for instance) costermonger uses to buy his or her stock, and how many pennies profit a day he or she may expect in good conditions.

One insight to be derived from Mayhew's work is the perception of poverty as a relative thing. From the upper- or middle-class perspective, a worker earning less than a hundred pounds a year would be described as poor (see MONEY: MONETARY VALUES). He describes costermongers surviving on pennies a day, who nevertheless look down on those who have even less. '"Poverty is as much despised among us costers," says one of these, "as among other people. People that's badly off among us are called 'cursed'"' (Mayhew (1849–62) 1985: 52). DICKENS provided eloquent and powerful fictional expression to the situation of the Victorian poor in his novels.

Further reading

The Idea of Poverty: England in the Early Industrial Age (1984) by Gertrude Himmelfarb.

Pre-Raphaelite Brotherhood   A small group of like-minded although diverse artists, including John MILLAIS, Dante Gabriel ROSSETTI, William Holman Hunt

(1827–1910), together with a number of affiliated poets and critics such as Algernon Swinburne and William Michael Rossetti (1829–1919). The name of this grouping was decided on in 1848, as a way of signalling the group's preference for the earlier aesthetic practice of fourteenth-century Italian art, rather than the treatment of Raphael (1483–1520) as the greatest of all painters by many mainstream nineteenth-century artists. The painters of the group exhibited work at a Royal Academy exhibition in 1849 with the letters 'P.R.B.' appended to their work. The following year more 'PRB' works, and particularly Millais' painting of 'Christ in the House of his Parents' (a realistically rendered carpenter's shop, with the parts accurately capturing the look of the real, rather ugly, people used as models for Christ, Joseph and Mary, rather that idealised versions of beauty) created a small storm of protest. Dickens objected forcefully to the painting, and by extension to the school, in an article entitled 'Old Lamps for New Ones' (*Household Words*, 15 June 1850), describing the Christ as a 'hideous, wry-necked, blubbering, red-headed boy, in a bed gown' and facetiously likening 'Pre-Raphaelite' art to 'Pre-Newtonian' physics.

Typically, Pre-Raphaelite paintings exhibit a fidelity to nature – artists would, for instance, obtain actual sheep if they wanted to paint sheep, rather than being content with the fuzzily conventionalised painterly representation of 'sheep' – a liking for bright colours, clarity of line and shade, vividness of composition, and a high degree of detail. Subjects of paintings were often historical, and mostly medieval, and many Pre-Raphaelite artists chose to illustrate scenes from favoured literature: authors such as John Keats (1795–1821) – for instance, Hunt's *The Flight of Madeline and Porphyro during the Drunkenness attending on the Revelry* (1848) illustrating 'The Eve of St Agnes' and Millais' 'Isabella' (1848–9); Shakespeare – Millais' beautiful *Ophelia* (1852); Rossetti's many illustrations of scenes from Dante; and images taken from Tennyson's poetry, including Millais' extraordinary Mariana (1851), or Hunt's tempestuous *The Lady of Shalott* (1886–90).

Of the three key Pre-Raphaelite painters, Millais was moving away from the tenets of the school as early as the mid-1850s, and Rossetti was always too individual an artist usefully to be described by a catch-all term, but the deeply religious Holman Hunt remained 'an impenitent Pre-Raphaelite' until his death in 1910 (Maas, 1988: 128). Other artists, such as Ford Madox Brown (1821–93) and Thomas Woolner (1825–92), were also true to the vision of the movement.

Further reading

The Pre-Raphaelite Imagination: 1848–1900 (1968) by John Dixon Hunt; *Victorian Painting* (1988) by Jeremy Maas.

Principles of Geology (1830–1833), by Charles Lyell Lyell (1797–1875) published his three-volume study of geological forms over three years. He argued for the great antiquity of the earth, as opposed to the religiously sanctioned view that everything had been created at once by God in the year 4004 BC. Geologists, he suggested, had previously 'misinterpreted the signs of a succession of events, so as to conclude that centuries were implied where the characters imported thousands of years, and thousands of years where the language of nature signified millions' (quoted in Otis, 2002: 250). The work is bolstered with a wealth of scientific evidence from all parts of the globe. Its publication provided the conceptual background of millions of years against which EVOLUTION could be theorised; DARWIN was greatly influenced by Lyell's work. TENNYSON also read the book, and recorded the depressed sense of RELIGIOUS DOUBT that it occasioned in him in several poems, most famously *In Memoriam* (1851) lyrics 55–7.

Psychoanalysis and psychology   Strictly speaking psychoanalysis is a twentieth-century development of the ideas of Sigmund Freud (1856–1939). Psychology, the science of mental processes underlying this analysis, whilst also owing much to Freud, was developed over the course of the nineteenth century. The word itself was not much used before the 1890s; William James (1842–1910) begins his study *Principles of Psychology* (1890) with a sentence explaining what the subject involved: 'Psychology is the Science of Mental Life, both of its phenomena and of their conditions' (quoted in Otis, 2002: 373). Previous models of consciousness had been rooted in spiritual-religious notions of 'soul', although empirical PHILOSOPHY had theorised a materialist mind built up from sense data.

Ekbert Faas has convincingly argued that literary experiments in representing subjectivity, particularly the tendency of the DRAMATIC MONOLOGUE to represent mad and extreme states of mind, fed into the climate that led to Freud and the acceptance of psychology as a science. According to Faas,

> never before in English literature had a specific genre been as intensively
> defined, circumscribed, praised and denounced as the dramatic monologue
> during the later Victorian era. In short, there emerged not only a new school of
> psychological poetry, but also a tribe of critics (including diverse alienists)
> who jealousy watched over all of that school's activities.

(Faas, 1988: 16)

Further reading

Retreat into the Mind: Victorian Poetry and the Rise of Psychiatry (1988) by Ekbert Faas.

Punch   *Charivari* was a Parisian comic magazine of the late 1830s. Inspired by its success, Henry Mayhew (1812–87), Mark Lemon (1809–70) and Joseph Stirling Coyne (1803–68) decided to found a British equivalent, and established themselves as joint-editors. The first issue of *Punch, or the London Charivari* appeared on 17 July 1841. Issues contained comic illustrations, stand-alone cartoons, humorous prose, verse,

PARODY and the like. It was very successful, and the list of contributors eventually included Douglas Jerrold (1803–57), THACKERAY, and superb illustrators including John Leech (1817–64), who was chief illustrator until his death, and John Tenniel (1820–1914) who worked on the magazine from 1850 and became chief illustrator in 1864. Shirley Brooks (1816–74) became editor for a few years in 1870; Tom Taylor (1817–80) was editor from 1874 until 1880, and Francis Burnand (1836–1917) from 1880 to 1906.

Quarterly Review   Founded in 1806 this journal was intended as a TORY rival to the influential WHIG *Edinburgh Review*. Its tone was appropriate to its aristocratic self-belief; very much *de haut en bas*. During the Romantic period it became famous for the swingeing and destructive reviews of authors of whom it disapproved – the review of John Keats' (1795–1821) *Endymion* (1818) was so savage it was widely believed to have hastened the poet's death. In its first years the *Quarterly* presumably felt its aggressive approached justified by the spread of revolutionary and Jacobinical ideas. In 1825 the editorship was taken by John Lockwood (1794–1854), and a more considered tone became the norm. By the century's end the *Quarterly* was one of the most serious and considered Establishment journals.

Issues of the journal consisted of lengthy anonymous review articles that considered one or a group of related books, although the articles themselves often departed from the business of reviewing to pontificate on the subject in hand more generally. Each issue would be a substantial volume of approximately 300 close-printed pages, containing between 10 and 12 reviews. A sample issue (chosen at random) is No. 172, from March 1850. The first review deals, in 40 pages, with five separate Italian-language studies of the life and work of Giacomo Leopardi; the second reviews von Ranke's *Memoirs of the House of Brandenburg and History of Prussia*; the third considers Queens College, London (an offshoot of the Governesses' Benevolent Institution) by way of reviewing five books on the college and on governesses generally; the fourth reviews George Grote's *History of Greece*; the fifth reviews Urquhart's *Pillars of Hercules*; the sixth is a review of *Facts in Figures, a Quarterly Digest of Statistics, abstracted chiefly from Official Returns*; the seventh a review of *Diary of a Dutiful Son*; the eighth of two histories of London; the ninth of a collection of the speeches of the Earl of Roden appertaining to the IRISH QUESTION; the tenth reviews William Baxter's *Impressions of Central and Southern Europe* together with four other travel books, and the final review of seven books, most in French, on the topic of revolution. This list gives some sense of the serious, weighty tenor of the whole.

R

Race As a term designating 'a line of descent' or a general term ('the human race') 'race' had been in usage since the sixteenth century; but the modern connotations of the word as a sub-category of *Homo sapiens* is a nineteenth-century invention. Arthur de Gobineau's (1816–82) *Essai sur l'inégalité des races humaines* (1853–5) invented the category of the 'Aryan' race, and promulgated doctrines of the racial superiority of the 'nordic' and the dangers of interbreeding between races that have cast a spectacularly long and baleful shadow through the twentieth century. The impact of DARWIN's theories, via the doctrine of 'Social Darwinism', shaped belief in race into a pseudo-science. One branch of this, inevitably RACIST, was 'eugenics' (a word coined in 1883) in which 'ideas of both class and racial superiority were widely propagated . . . in its gross forms, this doctrine of inherent racial superiority interacted with ideas of political domination and especially IMPERIALISM' (Williams, 1983: 249). Race in this sense is sometimes invoked to praise the 'virtues' of the Anglo-Saxon peoples: 'courage . . . was a heritage of the whole German race' (John Green, *The Conquest of England*, 1883: 54). European scientists such as the German Blumenbach and the Frenchman Alfred Moquin-Tandon (1804–63) divided the races of the world into five: '1st, the Caucasian; 2nd, the Mongolian; 3rd, the Ethiopian; 4th, the American; 5th, the Malay'.

Further reading

'Racial' by Raymond Williams in *Keywords* (1983).

Racism Through the 1860s the notion of race as, broadly, a common cultural and historical inheritance was being replaced in many quarters by the notion of race as a determinist and essential biological category. A necessary consequence of this ideological shift was a tendency towards a more explicitly and pseudo-scientific racism. There were many humane and tolerant individuals in the Victorian period, some of whom tenaciously fought the legal and cultural biases against people from non-British ethnic origins. That said, it is impossible to deny the often casual and brutal racism of most of the figures associated with British Victorian culture. It was a ubiquitous assumption, first, that there existed such a category as RACE and, second, that some races (the 'white' 'Anglo-Saxon' races) were superior to the other races of the world. This unpleasant fact must be taken as a sort of cultural background noise. Those people who opposed racism are the more commendable in that they were compelled to work against a stupefying cultural inertia on the issue.

The most simplistic, and most brutal, racism was directed against blacks. TENNYSON's 'Locksley Hall, Sixty Years After' (1886) opines that 'ev'n the black Australian dying hopes he shall return, a white' (l. 70). At a dinner party in 1865 Tennyson argued with

GLADSTONE over the 'Governor Eyre controversy' (plantation workers in Jamaica had rebelled, and Eyre, the colony's governor, had put down the rising with extreme force, torturing and executing many). In response to Gladstone's indignation at this inhumanity, Tennyson asserted that 'we are too tender to savages; we are more tender to a black man than to ourselves. Niggers are tigers, niggers are tigers' (Tennyson, 1897: 513). In similar mode is Anthony TROLLOPE's astonishingly offhand opinion, expressed in his memoir *Australia* (1873), that genocide was desirable with regard to Australian aborigines:

> it is their fate to be abolished; and they are already vanishing. . . . Of the Australian black man we may certainly say that he has to go. That he should perish without unnecessary suffering should be the aim of all who are concerned in the matter.
>
> (Boehmer, 1998: 31–2)

ANTI-SEMITISM was also widespread, although there were more members of the cultural mainstream prepared to oppose it. Many shared Carlyle's assumptions that Jews were dishonourable money-grubbers, 'millionaire Hebrews, Rothschild money-changers, Demosthenic DISRAELIS . . . weep, Britain, if these . . . are among the honourable you now have!' (Carlyle, *Reminiscences*: 207). But George ELIOT could portray Jews sympathetically in *The Spanish Gypsy* (1868) and *Daniel Deronda* (1874–6). She wrote to Harriet Beecher Stowe:

> Not only towards the Jews, but towards all oriental peoples with whom we English come into contact, a spirit of arrogance and contemptuous dictatorialness is observable which has become a national disgrace to us.
>
> (Quoted in Haight, 1985: 476)

One of the most infamous anti-Semitic caricatures of the period is Fagin in DICKENS' *OLIVER TWIST*, where (to quote Bill Sikes' vehement expression) 'the infernal, rich, plundering, thundering old Jew' is a mean-spirited villain, hanged at the end apparently for no reason other than the fact that he is Jewish. Dickens, however, had a change of heart, effected in part by a friendship with Eliza Davis. Davis, the wife of a Jewish banker, convinced Dickens that he had done 'a very great wrong' to Jews; he subsequently portrayed a number of 'good' Jews in *Our Mutual Friend* (1864–5), and he revised *Oliver Twist* in 1867, eliminating or altering most of the offhand references to Fagin as 'the Jew'.

The Irish were also the subject of racial stereotype and caricature. Henry Mayhew (1812–87) talked with disgust of 'the low foreheads and long bulging upper lips' of Irish men, although he had praise for 'the pretty faces' of Irish girls: 'their black hair, smoothed with grease, and shining almost as if "japanned", and their large grey eyes with the thick dark fringe of lash, seemed out of place among the hard features of their companions' (Mayhew (1849–62) 1985: 58)

MACAULAY could claim in 1849 that 'in no country has the enmity of race been carried further than in England'. If anything, racialism was stronger at the end of the Victorian period than at the beginning; in 1901 the distinguished English scientist Karl Pearson lectured on 'Darwinism and Statecraft' to the effect that Darwin's teachings endorsed the survival of the higher races and the destruction of what he called 'kaffirs, Negroes, Red Indians', on the grounds that the fittest survive, and that good stock must not cohabit with bad.

Readership and literacy Levels of public literacy increased massively throughout the nineteenth century, a growth that involved two chief aspects; first, a great increase in levels of general literacy and, second, a shift in taste towards reading fiction rather than works of theology and natural philosophy. It is not easy, however, to calculate levels of literacy precisely. Gertrude Himmelfarb argues that literacy figures for the nineteenth century 'are notoriously difficult to come by, not only because the sources are inadequate but because the definition and measurement of literacy are debatable. Is schooling an appropriate index of literacy, or reading and writing, or reading alone, or signing the marriage register?' (Himmelfarb, 1984: 413). The situation is complicated by the fact that many who could not read nevertheless followed literary developments: fiction was often read aloud in the home, or in public venues such as coffee-rooms and public houses, providing the illiterate with access to the printed word.

Perhaps 400,000 to 500,000 middle-class Victorians were in the habit of reading regularly, and perhaps 30,000 amongst the upper classes; there is an inevitable degree of estimation about such figures. With regard to the working classes, E.P. Thompson's *The Making of the English Working Class* points out, over the first half of the century 'as the effect of the Sunday schools and day schools increasingly became felt . . . so the number of the illiterate fell'. This continued throughout the century with the increasing drive to promote working-class education (for instance, through the RAGGED SCHOOLS). By the time of the Education Act of 1870 the reading public had grown by (estimates vary) between 10 and 20 times. Himmelfarb suggests that in the mid-Victorian period between two-thirds and three-quarters of the population (which, in 1851, was 18 million) had some reading ability; although not all of these would have had the necessary sophistication and predisposition to read fiction regularly (Himmelfarb, 1984: 411–12). In other words, the 'reading public' in the 1840s can be thought of as a core of perhaps half a million sophisticated and relatively affluent readers, with a body of several million less skilled readers, a figures that grew steadily throughout the 1860s and 1870s, although the real explosion in literacy was not to come until after the establishment of compulsory EDUCATION in 1871.

Realism Though sometimes used sloppily to mean 'books with a mimetic relationship to actual lived experience' (often to contradistinguish texts from fantastic or science-fictional work), in fact 'realism' is a precise literary-critical term, referring to a specific late-century school of novel writing that began in France. The French writer Champfleury (1821–89) published a manifesto for fiction entitled *Le Réalisme* in 1857, in which he argued for greater 'sincerity' in place of the 'liberty' he argued was at the heart of Romantic literature. Champfleury's influential argument called for accurate documentation of actual lived experience and fictive attempts to analyse society truthfully by focusing on the everyday lives of ordinary people; to be achieved by novels that presented a great deal of factual detail to the reader, and that avoided poeticism, exaggeration or idealisation. The prolific French novelists Honoré de Balzac (1799–1850) and Émile Zola (1840–1902) are the pre-eminent 'realist' novelists of the age. There had been a widespread commitment to 'real life' in the Victorian novel (as with CHARLOTTE BRONTË's promise at the opening of her novel *Shirley* (1849) that 'something real, cool and solid lies before you; something unromantic as Monday morning'), but it is not until the end of the century that schematic French-style Realism filters into English letters, and even here it tends to lack the encyclopaedic sweep of the great realist *romans-fleuves*. Novelists like George Moore (1852–1933), George Gissing (1857–1903) and Arnold Bennet (1867–1831) were writing as much in reaction to the imaginative grotesque of DICKENS as in imitation of Balzac or Zola.

A great deal of critical time and energy has been spent analysing Realism as a literary movement, and in anatomising the various splinter-group formations of similar aesthetic principles (such as 'Naturalism', 'Social Realism', 'Psychological Realism' and others), but critic Margaret Anne Doody is surely correct when she identifies the form as a minor branch of the nineteenth-century novel, over-represented in critical studies at the expense of a broader novelistic tradition of Romance, fantastic, imaginative and inventive writing:

> The cult of Realism affected critical practice and literary history far more than it did the creative practice of novel-writing. Undeniably there are many wonderful realistic novels – among them such 'masterpieces' as *Père Goriot*, *Madame Bovary*, *War and Peace* and *Middlemarch*. But the *novelists* of the nineteenth-century (as distinct from the critics) were in touch with the entire tradition of fiction, and their deeper roots tapped into the great stream, even if it was running underground.
>
> (Doody, 1996: 296)

Reform Act (1832)   The first of the three great Reform Acts, the other two following in 1867 and 1884, was concerned with broadening the electoral franchise (which is to say making more inclusive the legal definition of the 'voter' who elected members of Parliament to the House of Commons) as well as tidying up a number of aspects of electoral practice. Over centuries the balance of parliamentary constituencies had become seriously unrepresentative: only a tiny proportion of adult men were entitled to vote: 366,000 (one in eight men) in England, and 4500 (one in 125 men) in Scotland. Moreover, many once-populous constituencies had become so denuded of population – or in the case of some, had vanished altogether (Dunwich, for instance, which had fallen into the sea) – that 'election' was a sham and these so-called 'pocket' or 'rotten' boroughs were in the gift of a small group or even a single landowner. On the other hand, many of the newer large conurbations that were growing up as the Industrial Revolution gathered pace were not represented in Parliament at all. Manchester's population was 182,000 and Birmingham's 146,000, yet neither town had MPs. Following years of agitation, including riots of farm labourers and industrial unrest, the WHIG Lord John Russell (1792–1878) introduced a bill into the House of Commons that removed representation from many rotten boroughs, gave representation to new towns, and revised the legal relationship between property requirement and the right to vote. This raised the number entitled to vote to 586,000 in England, although the vote was still limited to adult males who owned fairly significant real estate – only those whose property could raise an annual rent of £10 or more a year in the towns and 40/- (£2) in the country. Russell's bill was fiercely debated, and passed the House of Commons with a majority of just one at 3 am on 22 March 1832; but it was rejected by the House of Lords. The resultant crisis meant that a general election was called, effectively a referendum on this one issue. Lord Grey's Whig government was returned with an increased majority and again passed the Reform Bill through the Commons; after five days of debate the Lords rejected it again, by 41 votes. Grey put through the Bill a third time, and called on the King to create enough new peers (he estimated that 50 would be enough) to ensure that it passed the Lords. Faced with this threat the Lords acquiesced to the Bill rather than allow itself to be over-run with new appointees. The Act became law.

Lawrence Poston thinks the Act 'may well have saved England from revolution, and it certainly moved the country peacefully and without Continental-style convulsions towards democracy' (Poston, 1999: 7). But post-1832 politics were still fiercely restrictive: the increasing working classes were not franchised, some rotten boroughs remained, and although the new industrial towns had been given token representation, seats were still proportionately heavily weighted towards the rural south. As Richard Altick points out, the chief effect of the Act was 'a long-overdue adjustment of the balance of power between the TORIES and the Whigs. The Tories' possession of some two hundred "safe" seats had virtually guaranteed their permanent control of Parliament.' The Reform Act 'divided the representation somewhat more equitably between the two parties, both of which remained essentially aristocratic in composition and interest' (Altick, 1973: 88).

Reform Act (1867)   The second great piece of electoral legislation in the nineteenth century, following the REFORM ACT OF 1832, and much more thoroughly establishing the principles of democratic electoral process, something brought to greater fruition in the third REFORM ACT OF 1889. Dissatisfaction with the limitations of the 1832 Act bubbled through the 1840s and 1850s, and in 1864 Liberal politician John Bright (1811–69) founded a 'National Reform League' to press for more wide-reaching changes. GLADSTONE, Chancellor in Lord John Russell's (1792–1878) government, introduced a Reform Bill in 1866, but it was defeated in the Commons. At the ensuing election the Conservative Lord Derby (1826–93) became Prime Minister, and Benjamin DISRAELI seized the initiative by proposing a more wide-ranging Reform Bill in 1867.

The staunchness, and in some cases the ferocity, of opposition to the Bill should remind us that 'democracy' was a heavily contested term in Victorian England. Even by the 1860s 'full democracy' (as we understand and presently practise it) was a cause supported only by political radicals. Many Victorians equated 'democracy' with violent mob rule. CARLYLE, in his *Reminiscences*, defines the word as 'the gradual uprise, and rule in all things, of roaring, million-headed, unreflecting, darkly suffering, darkly sinning "Demos" [Greek for 'the People'] come to call its old superiors to account, at its maddest of tribunals' (Carlyle, *Reminiscences* (1881) 1997: 382). For Carlyle and like-minded TORIES, 'democracy' was equivalent to the bloody Terror of Revolutionary France, or liable to lead to a like situation. Carlyle's own response to the 1867 Reform Act was a famously titled essay, published in *Macmillan's Magazine* for August 1867, 'Shooting Niagra – and After?' Carlyle was certain that the widespread popular enthusiasm for reform (demonstrations in its favour in London, Manchester, Leeds, Glasgow and Edinburgh drew crowds of up to 10,000) would carry the country to disaster, by 'the calling in of new supplies of blockheadism, gullibility, bribeability, amenability to beer and balderdash'. Needless to say, history proved Carlyle's fears unfounded, but contemporary anxiety was focused by the Hyde Park Riots of 23 July 1866, when a demonstration, turned away from the park by the police, tore down the railing. This riot is cited by Matthew ARNOLD in *CULTURE AND ANARCHY* (1867) as an example of the 'anarchy' threatening Britain.

The Bill, passed in 1867, extended the franchise beyond owners of property worth £10 a year in rental (the 1832 stipulation) to include almost all male urban dwellers who owned or rented property, provided only that they paid rates (a form of local tax) and had residency of at least a year. Nearly a million men were added to the electoral rolls, and the map of parliamentary constituencies was redrawn to give more proportionate representation to the newer industrial towns than had been the case in the 1832 act. Nonetheless, modern commentators have been unimpressed with the actual 'democratisation' inherent in the bill:

> . . . the admission to the constitution of urban male householders who paid
> their own rates was very deliberately designed to maintain that ancient
> tradition of a limited polity of independent freemen, and to exclude those

deemed incapable of political and economic independence (women, lunatics, agricultural labourers, and the 'residuum' of the casual poor).

(Jose Harris, quoted in Hughes, 1999: 36)

One concrete consequence of this Reform Act, however, was a general understanding that EDUCATION needed to be put on a sounder footing, 'to ensure', in David Newsome's words, 'that the future masters of the nation's destiny should at least be able to read and write' (Newsome, 1997: 235). The Forster Education Act, passed in 1870 and mandating schooling for all children five to 12 years old, is a piece of legislation 'inseparable from the Second Reform Bill' (Hughes, 1999: 36).

Further reading

1867: Disraeli, Gladstone and Revolution: the Passing of the Second Reform Bill (1967) by Maurice Cowling.

Reform Act (1884–1885)   The third of the three great Reform Acts (after 1832 and 1867) of the century, passed by GLADSTONE's Liberal administration. It was made up of two pieces of legislation. First, the Representation of the People Act was passed in November 1884, and extended the franchise from the urban to rural working populations. Together with the 1867 Act, it increased the electorate to almost two million men in England and Wales and over a quarter of a million in Scotland. A related Redistribution Act was passed in March 1885 disenfranchising certain boroughs and enfranchising others; London, for instance, returned 22 members of parliament before this Act, and 62 after it. In 1831 5 per cent of the adult population was entitled to vote; in 1833 the figure was 7 per cent, in 1867 16 per cent and in 1885 it rose to 29 per cent.

These two Acts of 1884 and 1885 are usually seen as the culmination of a gradual widening of political representation and democratisation of Victorian society throughout the century, a process that averted the more violent popular uprisings and revolutions seen in the rest of continental Europe. But the Third Reform Bill did not enfranchise women. A women's amendment to the Bill was considered, having received enough pledges, but Gladstone himself set his face against it and the Bill passed without it. Women were not to get the vote until 1917, and it was not until 1918 that the franchise was extended to the adult population as a whole.

Religious certitude   So much critical attention has, traditionally, been given to various Victorian cultural expressions of RELIGIOUS DOUBT that it is easy to get the impression the age was chiefly characterised over anxiety proceeding from 'the disappearance of God'. But by any criteria we may use to measure it the large majority of Victorians were utterly certain of their religious convictions. Their disputative spiritual energies were channelled not into fundamental debates of faith and doubt, but into doctrinal disputes, especially (for mainstream Anglican Victorian society) the question as to the degree of ritual that should be allowed in the practice of worship, a dispute that shaded from low church/High Church debates into Anglo-Catholic anxieties (*see* OXFORD MOVEMENT, CATHOLIC EMANCIPATION). But although these were (for those involved) very real worries, they did not touch upon the fundamental questions of religious belief – belief in God, in a personal afterlife, and so on. 'It is not now known,' pronounced CARLYLE sternly, by way of countering the 'brutal living Atheism and damnable putrescent Cant' he saw threatening the Victorian world –

> it is not now known, what never needed proof or statement before, that Religion is not a doubt; that it is a certainty . . . That none or all of the many things we are in doubt about, and need to have demonstrated and rendered probable, can by any alchymy be made a 'Religion' for us; but are and must continue a baleful, quiet or unquiet, Hypocrisy for us.

> (Carlyle, *Life of John Sterling*, 1851, Vol. 1: 86)

As George Kitson Clark puts it:

> probably in no other century, except the seventeenth and perhaps the twelfth, did the claims of religion occupy so large a part in the nation's life, or did men speaking in the name of religion contrive to exercise so much power.

> (Kitson Clark, 1962: 20)

Religious doubt   The various challenges to RELIGIOUS CERTITUDE in the nineteenth century can be usefully considered as having two main aspects. The first, more significant in the early decades of the century, had to do with the waning of power of the established Anglican Church and a sense of fragmentation of the practices of religious observance. The second, more significant towards the end of the century, was a broader sense of fundamental doubt about whether there exists any God at all. In other words, Victorian religious doubt was a continuum from those who doubted specific aspects of the dogma or practice of the established Church without doubting the fundamental existence of God, Christ and the human soul, to outright atheists who agreed with Nietzsche's famous 1882 assertion 'Gott ist tot' – 'God is dead' (*Der fröhliche Wissenschaft* ('The Gay Science') Vol. 3, Section 116). Nietzsche's celebrated aphorism, of course, is more than a statement of personal atheism, and it does not claim that everybody has abandoned their religious faith; it refers to the nineteenth-century waning of certainty, the chipping-away at absolute values and beliefs by science and philosophy – refers, in other words, to a new climate of thought.

There were various disturbances to the established power of the Church of England from the 1820s through into the 1850s: CATHOLIC EMANCIPATION in 1829 was followed by the REFORM ACT OF 1832, which was as significant for the symbolic shift it represented as for the specific political changes it embodied; in Arthur Cockshut's phrase it represented 'the end of the Anglican monopoly of power, influence and access to higher education' (Cockshut, 1993: 25). The Oxford Movement and the Catholic Revival in the 1830s and the 1840s were matched by a resurgence in Nonconformist and Evangelical Protestantism. George Eliot's novel *Felix Holt* (1866) dramatises a debate about church establishment (which is to say, as to whether the Church should maintain its official links with the state) between a Nonconformist minister called Mr Lyon and an Anglican; but the Anglican, unused to being challenged in his cosy and traditional views, is too cowardly to face Lyon. Here, as in other Eliot novels, Nonconformism is represented as an attractive element; Dinah Morris in *Adam Bede* (1859) is a vigorous female preacher in the Methodist tradition, at a time when the role of women in the Anglican Church was severely restricted. Other representations of Nonconformists in the period were not so flattering; despite the fact that both Dickens and Browning were 'broad church' Anglicans with a tendency towards Unitarianism, they manifested a typically narrow-church Anglican snobbery in their portraits of, respectively, the vulgar Nonconformist preacher Mr Chadband in *Bleak House* (1852–3), and the dirty, unappealing Nonconformist chapel visited by the speaker in *Christmas Eve and Easter Day* (1850).

The Essays and Reviews crisis of 1859 shook many people's complacencies about religious belief. But a more shattering challenge to conventional religious belief occurred in 1859 with the publication of Charles Darwin's Origin of Species, with its detailed scientific evidence for the long-term evolution of life. Scientists such as Charles Lyell had speculated before that the geological record implied far too long a timescale to be accommodated within the framework laid down in the Bible, and the notion that breeding over generations produces variations in livestock was also known. What made Darwin's intervention so shattering was both the range and detail of the scientific evidence he provided, and the receptiveness of the climate of the day. The Higher Criticism had laid the foundations upon which later scientific advances built. George Eliot's translation of Strauss's *Das Leben Jesu* ('The Life of Christ', 1846) brought this massive critique of New Testament literalism to the awareness of the British public. Her later translation of Feuerbach's *Essence of Christianity* (1854) added to the pressure. By the end of the 1850s many people doubted the literal interpretation of the Bible. Arthur Clough, who had experienced pangs of doubt earlier in his life, responded to Strauss's criticisms in his poem 'Epi-Strauss-ium' (1847): 'lost, invisible and gone,/Are, say you, Matthew, Mark and Luke and holy John?/Lost, is it? Lost, to be recovered never?' (ll. 9–11).

Auguste Comte's (1798–1857) Positivist philosophy argued that human society moved from a vulgar theological stage, through a scientific stage, into the final 'positivist' stage in which everything would be logically and properly governed. Some of his followers saw this final stage as a materialist atheist one, although for others it was perfectly consistent with deist beliefs. George Henry Lewes, a prominent British Comtean, said in 1878:

When Science has finally mastered the principles of moral relations as it has mastered the principles of physical relations, all Knowledge will be incorporated in a homogenous doctrine rivalling that of the old theologies in its comprehensiveness, and surpassing it in the authority of its credentials. 'Christian Ethics' will then no longer mean Ethics founded on the principles of Christian Theology, but on the principles expressing the social relations and duties of man in Christianised society. Then, and not till then, will the conflict between Theology and Science finally cease.

(Quoted in Ashton, 1991: 275)

Outright atheism provoked despair in some. James Thomson (1834–82) wrote a miserable poem on the emptiness of the modern urban experience called *The City of Dreadful Night* (1874), in which he asks

> Who is most wretched in this dolorous place?
> I think myself; yet I would rather be
> My miserable self than He, than He
> Who formed such creatures to His own disgrace
> As if a Being, God or Fiend, could reign,
> At once so wicked, foolish, and insane,
> As to produce men when He might refrain

(Section VIII)

Swinburne wrote sometimes in this bitter mode, as when he railed against 'the Supreme Evil, God' in *Atalanta in Calydon* (1865) – the devout Christina Rossetti was so shocked to read that line that she crossed it out in her edition. More characteristic of Swinburne's atheism was a pagan delight in the possibilities of life out from under the rule of the 'pale Galilean' ('the world has grown grey from Thy breath' he said in 'Hymn to Proserpine', 1866). Swinburne's colourful and erotic classicism was informed by this pagan aesthetic; in more considered mode he advanced a humanist secularism. 'But God, if a God there be, is the substance of men which is man,' he wrote in his 'Hymn to Man' (1871): 'Glory to Man in the highest! for Man is the master of things.'

Philosophically, too few thinkers continued Marx's wonderful, ultra-materialist critique of the Church ('religion' he famously asserted in 1843, 'is the opium of the people'). More typical was Thomas Huxley's (1825–95) response to Darwin's work; unable to accede to conventional religion and yet unwilling to embrace atheism, Huxley coined the term 'agnostic' to refer to those who adopted a sceptical perspective on the existence or non-existence of the deity. For others the great danger in the corrosion of religious faith was not spiritual but practical. The English lawyer Fitzjames Stephen (1829–94) wrote in his *Liberty, Equality and Fraternity* (1873):

Whether Christianity is true or false, and whether European morality is good or bad, European morality is in fact founded upon religion, and the destruction of the one must of necessity involve the reconstruction of the other. Many persons in these days wish to retain the morality which they like, after getting rid of the religion which they disbelieve. Whether they are right or wrong in disturbing the foundation, they are inconsistent in wishing to save the superstructure.

In a way, Nietzsche's most penetrating argument on this topic was not so much his denial of the existence of God as the scorn he heaped on precisely those Christian ethics of which Stephen thought so highly; for Nietzsche, Christianity preaches a 'Sklaven-Moral', a 'slave-morality' that debases and vulgarises the human potential for greatness by submerging it in the common herd.

But the most poignant examples of the literature of the sense of declining faith were written by believers; those who were most aware, and most feared, the corrosion of the religious faith into which they had been born. The speaker of Matthew Arnold's 'Dover Beach' (probably written 1851; published 1867) gives voice to the most celebrated of these statements when listening to the tide going out at Dover and reflects that

> The sea of faith
> Was once, too, at the full, and round earth's shore
> Lay like the folds of a bright girdle furl'd;
> But now I only hear
> Its melancholy, long withdrawing roar,
> Retreating to the breath
> Of the night-wind, down the vast edges drear
> And naked shingles of the world.

(ll. 21–8)

Further reading

'Faith and Doubt in the Victorian Age' by A.O.J. Cockshut in *The Penguin History of Literature, Vol 6: the Victorians* (1993) edited by Arthur Pollard; *Gains and Losses: Novels of Faith and Doubt in Victorian England* (1977) by R. Wolf.

Ring and the Book, The (1868–1869), by Robert Browning   In a street market in Florence, June 1860, Browning came across a collection of legal papers relating to the trial of a Roman nobleman in 1698 for the murder of his wife and in-laws. In 1864 Browning began working on an ambitious attempt to turn this factual material into a blank-verse epic poem. It was eventually published in four monthly instalments between November 1868 and February 1869.

Each of the 12 books of this epic construction is a dramatic monologue in which a different speaker gives his or her perspective on the events at the heart. The first book, entitled 'The Ring and the Book', is spoken by somebody very like Browning, who summarises the situation: embittered minor aristocrat Guido Franceschini married Pompilia, the daughter of an elderly Roman couple, in the mistaken belief that she was wealthy. Guido took Pompilia away from Rome to Arezzo and mistreated her, his anger increasing when Pompilia's parents announced that she was in fact a prostitute's child they had adopted. Pompilia was befriended by an idealistic young priest, Caponsacchi, and moved by her plight this young man helped her run away from her husband. Pompilia returned to Rome, Guido – enraged in his belief that his wife and the priest Caponsacchi have become lovers – in pursuit. He tried to gain satisfaction in the courts, and frustrated there stabbed Pompilia and both her parents to death. Arrested, Guido claimed the rights of a husband to defend his honour against the stigma of becoming a cuckold; convicted of murder, he appealed his conviction to the highest legal authority of the day, the Pope, Innocent XII. Innocent, however, upheld the conviction, and Guido was beheaded on 2 February 1698.

The remainder of the epic is divided between different speakers. Book 2, 'Half-Rome', and Book 3, 'The Other Half-Rome', are spoken by representative Roman men, the former sympathetic to Guido's case, the latter moved by Pompilia's fate. The speaker of Book 4, 'Tertium Quid' (Latin for 'third something'), equivocates between the two positions. In Book 5, 'Count Guido Franceschini', Guido addresses the court, with a mixture of sycophancy and self-pity, characterising his wife as a scheming and deceiving adulteress. Book 6, 'Giuseppe Caponsacchi', sees the accused priest telling his side of the story to the court, admitting his love for Pompilia but insisting that this love was pure, and that he helped her escape for no carnal reason. In Book 7, 'Pompilia', she speaks from her deathbed (she survived four days after the stabbing), declares her innocence and that she was never the priest's lover. Book 8, 'Dominis Hyacinthus de Archangelia', and Book 9, 'Juris Doctor Johannes-Baptista Bottinius', are spoken by the two lawyers in the case, and are both colossal examples of legal quibbling and pedantry, both effectively beside the point. Book 10, 'The Pope', takes place after the court has condemned Guido to death; its speaker, Pope Innocent, considers his appeal, meditating on questions of authority, God, truth and justice, before deciding that Guido cannot be pardoned. Book 11, 'Guido', contains Guido's second monologue, delivered from the condemned cell. His conciliatory mask slips and he speaks savagely of his hatred for the 'timid chalky ghost' his wife had been. As the monologue ends, and the steps of the executioner are heard outside the door, Guido breaks down and begs for his life. In the final book – Book 12, 'The Book and the Ring' – Browning concludes his artistic 'ring' in his own voice, relating events in Rome in the aftermath of the trial.

The experience of reading *The Ring and the Book* involves tackling Browning's often ornate and sometimes obscure style, the densely layered historicised reference to the word of seventeenth-century Rome and, perhaps above all, the enormous length of the whole. At 21,116 lines long this is a massive text by any standards, more so in that it was (as Browning's friend CARLYLE pointed out) 'all spun out of a story but a few lines long', that 'only wanted forgetting'. Contemporary reception of the poem was almost universally positive; reviewers praised the 'Shakesperian' variety and colour, the vividness and depth of the recreation of seventeenth-century Italian milieu; Robert Buchanan (1841–1903) called it 'the supremest poetical achievement of our time', involving 'a wealth of nature and a perfection of spiritual insight which we have been accustomed to find in the pages of Shakespeare, and in those pages only' (*Athenaeum*, 20 March 1860). Modern criticism has been less interested in the 'character' and 'incident', and more in the quasi-deconstructivist relativism of telling the same story over and over from different perspectives. This in turn reflects on Browning's relativistic practice of DRA-MATIC MONOLOGUE. The main thrust of present criticism sees the work as a profound hermeneutic enquiry. David Shaw has written of the subtle deconstructivist ironies of Browning's language in this work: 'Browning writes simultaneously against and on behalf of interpretive precision'; although he also reminds us of the differences between accounts of the work and the work itself –

> most paraphrases of *The Ring and the Book* distance us from what actually happens as we read. They translate the discomforts and anxieties into safer, less demanding fictions. To return to the poem is to stretch oneself out on the rack of a tough, obscure poem.
>
> (Shaw, 1989: 94)

This, of course, speaks of an age, distinctively Victorian, in which work and length were not off-putting to a readership intensely interested in poetry.

Romance   Sometimes used as a shorthand term for 'non-realist novels', romance is freighted with the implication of medieval and Renaissance verse- and prose-tale traditions. Traditional romances are usually stylised, conventionalised adventure-narratives (for instance, involving chivalric knights on quests, in search of true love, fighting dragons, and so on) in which some of the conventions of ordinary life are superseded by – for instance – magic. The vogue for DOMESTIC fiction that dominated the eighteenth century involved an official denigration of 'romance' conventions in favour of a bourgeois 'verisimilitude'; such that romances (which continued to be written, and indeed to outnumber 'novels') were seen as vulgar, common, mere entertainment, disposable, and so on. Although many critics reduplicate this bias – both in terms of looking at fiction in the eighteenth and nineteenth centuries, and in modern-day writing, where the inheritors of the Romance tradition are in SCIENCE FICTION.

Rossetti, Christina (1830–1894)   Sister to Dante Gabriel, Christina was educated at home, and spent most of her life in the domestic sphere, attending her sick mother and doing voluntary work associated with the church. She was a devout Anglican throughout her life, and rejected several marriage proposals ostensibly on grounds of religious incompatibility (as, for example, the Pre-Raphaelite painter James Collinson (1825–81), who converted to Roman Catholicism and so ended his chance of marrying Christina). Indeed her life is at first glance characterised by its lack of incident. Arguably the Victorian virtues of meekness, submission and self-restraint that she worked hard to embody in her life tend to emerge in much of her poetry as frustration, impotence and depression. Critics sometimes divide her poetic output into two sorts of verse. First, she wrote a great number of lyric poems, often devotional in character and of great beauty (she wrote the words to the hymn 'In the Bleak Midwinter'), sometimes more personal and expressive of individual sadness and desolation. Second, and more famously, she wrote children's verse, of which GOBLIN MARKET (written 1859) and the shorter verses in the collection called *SingSong* (1871) are perhaps the most famous. In fact this twofold division ignores a wide spread of her poetry, including much powerful love poetry and a fine variety of sonnets.

She wrote poetry from an early age, and used her brother's connections with the Pre-Raphaelite Brotherhood to publish some of her poems in the 'PRB' journal, *The Germ*, in 1850. Other poems were printed in *Macmillan's Magazine* and *Once A Week*. Her first volume of poetry, *Goblin Market and other poems*, was printed by Macmillan in 1862; other volumes followed slowly, including *The Prince's Progress and other poems* (1866) and *A Pageant and other poems* (1881). She rejected two suitors and never married. Her health was not good during her adult years, and her eventual death of cancer was the culmination of much suffering. Death is a prominent theme in her poetry, but if her lyrics can sometimes be morbid her longer poetry rarely is, and her facility with the cadences of spoken English, the inventiveness and fecundity of her poetic imagination (always controlled by a rigorous aesthetic that balances play with austerity), are perhaps her most distinguishing features.

Her disenchantment finds voice in many poems. 'This life,' she asserts in 'Later Life: a Double Sonnet of Sonnets' (1881), 'is full of numbness and of balk,/... Of promise unfulfilled, of everything/That is puffed vanity and empty talk'. But her greatest disenchantment was with herself, not with the world. 'What Would I Give?' (1866) asks the rhetorical question:

> What would I give for a heart of flesh to warm me through,
> Instead of this heart of stone ice-cold whatever I do;
> Hard and cold and small, of all hearts the worst of all.

The 'what would I give?' here perhaps implies a yearning for this warmth, but taken in the context of her other writing we may be justified in taking the question at face value. She was prepared to give very little by way of compromise with the ordinary consolations of life. She writes frequently of her own death: in the bleakly beautiful 'Song', for instance, she avoids self-pity with a remarkable elegiac detachment:

> When I am dead my dearest,
> Sing no sad songs for me;
> Plant thou no roses at my head,
> Nor shady cypress tree:
> Be the grass green above me
> With showers and dewdrops wet;
> And if thou wilt, remember,
> And if thou wilt, forget.

The children's poetry makes a vivid contrast with this bleached tone; it is full of colour, rhythm, energy and invention, *Goblin Market* above all.

Rossetti, Dante Gabriel (1828–1882)   Brother to Christina, Dante Gabriel makes a marked contrast with his self-effacing sibling. Christened 'Dante' (actually Gabriel Charles Dante Rossetti) by his *Divina Commedia*-obsessed father, Rossetti grew up in London immersed in literature. He left school at 14 to study art at Sass's Drawing Academy, and entered the Royal Academy School in 1844, where he became friendly with Holman Hunt (1827–1910) and John Everett Millais. In 1848 these three, together with several others, founded the Pre-Raphaelite Brotherhood. His first important oil painting, *The Girlhood of Mary Virgin*, was exhibited in 1849. Although known primarily through the 1850s for his painting, he was also writing poetry. The short-lived 'PRB' journal, *The Germ*, carried his poem 'The Blessed Damozel' in 1850, and he published other poems in *The Oxford and Cambridge Magazine* in the 1850s. He met William Morris in 1856 and formed a lasting friendship.

In 1860 he married Lizzie Siddall, a working-class woman who had served as model for several images. A child was still-born, and Rossetti's inveterate philandering depressed her. Her death of a laudanum overdose was probably suicide, and a guilt- and grief-stricken Rossetti placed the only manuscript copy of his poems in her coffin. He lived in 16 Cheyne Walk, Chelsea, sharing the house for a while with Swinburne and George Meredith (1828–1909), and formed a relationship with another working-class model, Fanny Cornforth. He sketched her for *Found* (1854), which would, if finished, have been a painting of a prostitute. His poem 'Jenny' (written 1850s, published 1870) is of the same topic; 'laughing, languid Jenny/Fond of a kiss and fond of a guinea' (ll. 1–2) is praised as 'a cipher of man's changeless sum/Of lust, past, present, and to come' (ll. 278–9).

In 1869 a series of sonnets published in the *Fortnightly Review* won great praise, and partly at the urging of his publisher he exhumed his wife's body to get at the manu-script poems buried there. *Poems* (1870) received excellent reviews (some of them by Rossetti's friends). 'Jenny' appeared in print, along with 'Troy Town', 'Sister Helen' and many of the sonnets that would later become his long sequence *The House of Life*. At the end of the 1860s, Rossetti had begun an affair with his friend Morris's wife, Jane. This continued, possibly with William's connivance, as Rossetti and Morris took out a joint lease on Kelmscott Manor. Rossetti used Jane as a model for his sensuous, heavily beautiful *Proserpine* (1873), and wrote more sonnets for his *House of Life*. In 1871 Robert Buchanan (1841–1901) attacked Rossetti in an article published in *The Fortnightly Review* entitled 'The Fleshly School of Poetry', accusing the poet of sensuality and impurity. Such terms do, in fact, describe Rossetti's art and poetry, although posterity has not seen them as necessarily pejorative descriptors.

Buchanan's attack worsened Rossetti's increasing paranoia and his mental health suffered a collapse in 1872 when he was committed to an asylum. He spent the early 1870s with Morris in Kelmscott but the tension now made life difficult between the two men. Increasingly dependent on chloral and alcohol, Rossetti continued to paint and to write. He published *Poems* (1881) and *Ballads and Sonnets* (1881), the latter containing the now-complete *House of Life* sequence of sonnets. His health worsened, and he died in 1882.

Rossetti's poetry is too highly flavoured and impressionistic for some tastes, but draws an increasingly sophisticated critical audience. His sonnet, written to accompany his friend Edward Burne Jones' painting *The Wine of Circe* (1869) gives a flavour of his typical theme and treatment:

> Dusk-haired and gold-robed o'er the golden wine
> She stoops, wherein, distilled of death and shame,
> Sink the black drops; while, lit with fragrant flame,
> Round her spread board the golden sunflowers shine.

His sensual fascinations are almost always accompanied by a debilitating sense of guilt. 'When vain desire at last and vain regret,' says one of the *House of Life* sonnets, 'Go hand in hand to death, and all is vain,/What shall assuage the unforgotten pain?' ('The One Hope'). 'Silent noon' from the same collection begins with a painterly vividness ('Deep in the sun-searched growths the dragon-fly/Hangs like a blue thread loosened from the sky:'), but then loses precision in a windier idiom ('Oh! clasp we to our hearts, for deathless dower,/This close-companioned inarticulate hour'). John Dixon Hunt argues that 'this seems to be Rossetti's special device – a blurring of initial precision by the addition of some emotional colouring. . . . He seeks . . . an escape from a world which always harasses the sensual apprehension of fugitive images' (Hunt, 1968: 98)

Ruskin, John (1819–1900) The only child of a well-to-do Surrey family, Ruskin grew up with a love for Romantic literature and landscape painting. He studied at Christ Church, Oxford, but was more autodidactic than educated. He particularly relished family travels through Britain and the continent, establishing a taste for French and Alpine landscape in particular. His first essay was published in 1834 in the *Magazine of Natural History*, and he contributed to many ANNUALS, such as *Friendship's Offering*, from 1835 to 1846. He also studied drawing, and assembled a large collection of contemporary art. His first major impact on the world of Victorian culture came with the publication of *Modern Painters*. The first volume of this massive illustrated work was published in 1843, with four more in subsequent years (Vol. 2 in 1846, Vols 3 and 4 in 1856, Vol. 5 in 1860). The full title of this beautifully written and perceptive analysis of contemporary art gives a sense of its argument: *Modern Painters: Their Superiority in the Art of Landscape Painting to all the Ancient Masters proved by Examples of the True, the Beautiful, and the Intellectual, from the Works of Modern Artists, especially from those of J.M.W. Turner Esq. RA*. The book insists repeatedly and eloquently upon the necessity of close attention to the actual contours of the world, rather than the superimposition of idealised preconceptions. In fact, the later volumes of this work contradict this title, and sensitively praise old masters, which Ruskin studied in detail on visits to Italy through the 1840s.

In 1847 Ruskin married Euphemia Chalmers Gray (1828–97), but he proved unable to consummate the marriage, possibly because he was disgusted to discover the, to him, unexpected presence of pubic hair on his wife's body. Despite non-consummation, the couple lived together. Ruskin published two classic studies of architecture based in part on his study of Italian buildings: *Seven Lamps of Architecture* (1849) and THE STONES OF VENICE (1851–3). This latter work is perhaps Ruskin's masterpiece and has been probably his most influential volume. In 1854 Euphemia divorced her husband and later married John MILLAIS, who had painted Ruskin's portrait. Ruskin himself endorsed the aesthetic project of the PRE-RAPHAELITES, for instance in his pamphlet *Pre-Raphaelitism* (1851). 'I wish them all heartily good speed, believing,' he wrote, '. . . they may, as they gain experience, lay in our England the foundations of a school of art nobler than the world has seen for three hundred years' (quoted in Hilton Vol. 1, 1985–2000: 155).

The later portion of Ruskin's life was very productive in terms of writing; *Unto The Last*, a thrilling and inspiring critique of 'political economy' appeared in book form in 1862. *Munera Pulveris* (1863) continued this analysis. *Sesames and Lilies* (1865) treats of the respective roles of men and women. Ruskin began issuing an influential and wide-ranging series of pamphlets monthly under the title *Fors Clavigera, Letters to the Workmen and Labourers of Great Britain* in 1871; publication continued until 1878, and thereafter instalments appeared intermittently between 1880 and 1884.

But Ruskin's later private life was characterised by emotional instability, unhappiness and eventual breakdown. In 1858 he met a girl called Rose La Touche (1849–76): she was only nine years old, but Ruskin quickly fell in love with her. In 1866 he proposed marriage, but she prevaricated. Her own health, both physical and mental, was precarious. She finally rejected Ruskin's proposal in 1872, and died insane in 1875. Ruskin later suffered a series of mental breakdowns of his own. In 1877 he accused the painter James Whistler (1834–1903) of defrauding the public with inferior art. Whistler sued, and Ruskin lost the ensuing court case, although the damages awarded – one farthing – were token. But in 1878 he hallucinated that he had finally married the (now dead) Rose, and experienced a prolonged episode of delirium. He recovered to write *The Bible of Amiens*, a study of religious history and reception (it was published between 1880 and 1885), but he relapsed again. Under increasing mental strain, he began his autobiography, *Praeterita*, working on it from time to time between 1885 and 1889, but he did not complete it and after 1889 he wrote nothing more.

Ruskin's reputation nowadays is, perhaps, maintained at second hand rather than at first, and yet for several generations he was a direct and life-changing figure. Clive Wilmer gives some sense of his impact in the later nineteenth and early twentieth centuries:

> *Unto this Last*, said Gandhi, 'captured me and made me transform my life'. For the young William MORRIS, 'The books of John Ruskin were . . . a sort of revelation . . .' In his introduction to *The Bible of Amiens*, Proust declared of Ruskin: 'he will teach me, for is not he, too, in some degree the Truth?' 'He was one of those rare men,' wrote Tolstoy, 'who think with their hearts, and so he thought and said not only what he himself had seen and felt, but what everyone will think and say in the future'.
>
> (Wilmer, 1985: 36; ellipses in original)

Further reading

John Ruskin (1985–2000) by Tim Hilton.

S

Science Eighteenth-century English science was dominated by the Royal Society, an organisation established in 1662 to further scientific knowledge. Although other scientific societies were convened in many provincial towns, it was the London Royal Society that shaped the scientific scene throughout the eighteenth and into the nineteenth centuries. But its culture of gentleman-amateur scientists was not admired by all. Swift (1667–1745), for instance, satirises the pettifogging wrong-headedness, and the malign social consequences of the resulting delays and errors in scientific understanding, in Gulliver's voyage to Laputa (*Gulliver's Travels*, 1726). According to some, the situation had not improved by the nineteenth century. Charles Babbage

(1791–1871), himself a key figure in the development of the computer, published a book on the state of affairs: *Reflections on the Decline of Science in England and some of its Causes* (1830). Babbage attacked the Royal Society, and contrasted the lack of recognition scientists received in Britain with the state of affairs in her European competitors France and Prussia, 'where science was properly taught in the universities and where scientists could even become Ministers of State' (Rose and Rose, 1969: 23). He advocated a campaign 'for the election of the President of the Royal Society to be on merit instead of social status', but got nowhere, and went on to found a rival organisation, the British Association for the Advancement of Science. The situation was better in Scotland, where science was integrated into the educational curriculum; so, for instance, 75 per cent of medical graduates practising in England in 1875 had studied at Scottish universities. Doctors in Victorian fiction are more often than not Scottish, a feature that reflects the preponderance of Scottish doctors in Victorian life.

The climate of which Babbage was a part, and to which he contributed, did begin to change the culture of nineteenth-century science, but only slowly. The government established a number of scientific agencies, such as the Geological Survey of 1835 and the Laboratory of the Government Chemist in 1842. A parliamentary committee was formed in 1849 to look after the interests of science. The GREAT EXHIBITION of 1851 showcased the possibilities for technological advancement, and the aristocratic chemist Lyon Playfair (1818–98) used the exhibition as a platform from which to deliver well-received lectures on the necessity for a national science policy, and calling for the foundation of a British technical university. Parliament voted £150,000 to be added to the profit of £186,000 from the exhibition, the money being used to buy sites in South Kensington and establish three royal technical schools. These schools were later (1907) incorporated as Imperial College of Science and Technology, now part of the University of London. Between, roughly, 1840 and 1870 'the Victorian scientific world was essentially transformed into a modern professional community' with the emergence of a 'new scientific elite' (Lightman, 1997: 101).

Nonetheless, Britain lagged behind Europe in many scientific areas. Individually brilliant scientists produced a series of major scientific advances: for instance Charles Lyell's laying the groundwork for modern geology in *PRINCIPLES OF GEOLOGY* (1830–3), or Charles DARWIN's epochal work on evolution, *On the ORIGIN OF SPECIES by means of Natural Selection* (1859). But Britain lacked the more general culture of science, and more particularly lacked the industrial capacity to take advantage of scientific advance. An example is the dye industry that developed from the invention of blue-purple aniline dye. William Perkin (1838–1907) discovered the first of these coal-derived synthetic dyes in 1856 at the Royal College of Chemistry, and they were to go on to revolutionise commercial dyeing, replacing the older vegetable-based dyes. Perkin and his father set up a factory to produce the dye, but industrialists in Germany established four such factories, and quickly came to dominate the scene. By 1879 Germany was producing £2 million worth of coal-tar products to Britain's £450,000;

a reflection of the more thorough-going scientific and technical climate in Germany, from an eagerness to invest in new technological process to the simple matter of having enough chemists to work in the factories. The German chemical industry, in fact, was the world leader up to the First World War (indeed, Britain armed its troops for this conflict in part by importing from Germany dyes for uniforms, magnetos for transport, tungsten for steel and glass for range-finders; in 1915 Britain was still paying royalties to the German Krupp company for the fuses of the shells it was using to shell German positions).

Further reading

Victorian Science in Context (1997) edited by Bernard Lightman; *Literature and Science in the Nineteenth Century* (2002) edited by Laura Otis.

Science fiction   According to Brian Aldiss's influential theory, the genre that we now think of as science fiction, or 'SF', was inaugurated by Mary Shelley (1797–1851) with her GOTHIC romance *Frankenstein* (1818). There had been, it is true, many fantastic and supernatural adventures in literature before the nineteenth century; voyages to the moon date from the first century AD, and works such as *Gulliver's Travels* (1726) by Jonathan Swift (1667–1745) and Voltaire's (1694–1778) *Micromégas* (1740) ranged widely and fantastically over the cosmos. But it was in the nineteenth century that this imaginative literary mode was married with a scientific-technological idiom that grew out of the INDUSTRIAL REVOLUTION. To quote Peter Nicholls, 'sf proper requires a consciousness of the scientific outlook . . . a cognitive, scientific way of viewing the world did not emerge until the 17th century, and did not percolate into society at large until the 18th (partly) and the 19th (to a large extent)' (Clute and Nicholls, 1993: 567–8).

Tales set in the future were produced throughout the century, often designed to make a specific ideological point. Robert Folkestone Williams' *Eureka, a Prophesy of the Future* (1837), Hermann Lang's *The Air Battle* (1859) and Henry O'Neill's *2000 Years Hence* (1868) all extrapolate Victorian concerns into a notional future. General Sir George Chesney (1830–95) published the brief story *The Battle of Dorking* in 1871 as a deliberate warning to what he saw as the military laxness of his nation. In this story of the near-future Germany successfully invades Britain. The success of this tale inspired a great vogue for militaristic 'near future' stories; I.F. Clarke has collected 16 of these in his *The Tale of the Next Great War 1871–1914* (Liverpool University Press 1995). Chesney published one other SF tale, *The Lesters* (1893), in which the hero discovers a treasure and uses it to build a model English city called Lestertia. Edward Bulwer Lytton's (1803–73) *The Coming Race* (1871) represents a different sort of science fiction; the protagonist, a mining engineer, stumbles upon an advanced subterranean race of aliens called the 'Vril-ya' who live a technologically enhanced utopian existence. Although the hero escapes back to our world, the novel ends with the warning that these beings will eventually invade our upper world. Samuel Butler

(1835–1902) wrote a satirical utopian novel *Erewhon* (1871; the sequel *Erewhon Revisited* appeared in 1901). The prolific novelist Walter Besant (1836–1901) published an SF fantasy, *The Revolt of Man* (1882), set in a future Britain in which women have seized power and relegated men to the position of chattels. TROLLOPE likewise dabbled with SF in his late novel *The Fixed Period* (1882), a proto-*Logan's Run* style novel in which future citizens are gathered at age 65 to be prepared for death at 67. The French writer Jules Verne (1828–1905) published a wide variety of thrillers, but amongst them were the subterranean adventure *Voyage au centre de la terre* ('Journey to the Centre of the Earth', 1864) and the technology-fiction of *Vingt mille lieues sous les mers* ('20,000 leagues under the seas', 1869).

Although SF tales were published all through the nineteenth century, it was not until the 1890s that the genre achieved a degree of cultural saturation. This owed something to the genius of H.G. WELLS, and his enduring and brilliant series of SF novellas: *The Time Machine* (1895), *The Island of Doctor Moreau* (1896), *The Invisible Man* (1897), *The WAR OF THE WORLDS* (1898) and *The First Men in the Moon* (1901). But Wells had many rivals, including George Griffiths (1857–1906), author of *From Pole to Pole: an Account of a Journey through the Axis of the Earth* (?1893) and *Stories of Other Worlds* (1900) in which the Earl of Redgrave and his bride take a honeymoon trip through the solar system; and Grant Allen (1848–1899) whose 'Thames Valley Catastrophe' (1897) dramatised a London-based disaster.

Scott, Walter (1771–1832)   The novelist Walter Scott enjoyed phenomenal success in his lifetime with his series of HISTORICAL 'Waverley' novels. These colourful if, to modern sensibilities, prolix ROMANCES in large measure created the readership expectations and therefore the parameters of the Victorian NOVEL. All the significant Victorian novelists were greatly influenced by Scott, even if that influence manifested itself in contrary ways. By this I mean that though the major names often wrote in direct imitation of Scott – as is the case with DICKENS' first historical novel *Barnaby Rudge* (1841), or ELIOT's *Romola* (1862–3) these works are not characteristic of the authors' genius. Scott, in other words, was an influence that needed to be overcome.

Scott continued a great favourite with readers throughout the century, a fact evidenced by the large number of collected editions of the Waverley novels. Many readers would be in a continual process of reading Scott; the poet William Edmondstoune Aytoun (1813–65), for instance, later claimed that from the age at which he learned to read not a single year went by when he did not re-read the entire works of Scott.

***Self-Help* (1859), by Samuel Smiles**   Smiles (1812–1904), the son of a shopkeeper, pursued a variety of careers, including periods as secretary to a railway company, a surgeon and a newspaper editor. His 1859 book on the virtue and positive results of self-reliance was his greatest popular success; translated into many languages and selling hundreds of thousands of copies, it became in practical terms a bible to a whole generation of aspirant Victorians. *Self-Help* stresses the vital importance of industry, thrift and self-improvement, encapsulating precisely that ethos of Victorian bourgeois individualism that appealed to the Reaganite-Thatcherite political movements of the late twentieth century, and which many others find narrow and repellent.

The bulk of Smiles' book is a series of biographical case studies of individuals who helped themselves to success through work, discipline and perseverance, illustrative of Smiles' fundamental tenet that 'the spirit of self-help is the root of all genuine growth of the individual'. Chief amongst these examples are: Michael Faraday, who reached the front rank of Victorian scientists despite being born a blacksmith's son; Lord Brougham, who was still active and successful in his eighty-second year, his secret being 'that he never left a minute unemployed'; and Bulwer Lytton (1803–73), whose first publications were complete failures, but who through 'pluck and perseverance' forged a notable literary career for himself. Politically Smiles advances an anti-government, LAISSEZ-FAIRE philosophy:

> the function of government is negative and restrictive; being resolvable principally into protection – protection of life, liberty and property . . . there is no power of law that can make the idle man industrious, the thriftless provident, or the drunken sober; though every individual can be each and all of these if he will, by the exercise of his own free powers of action and self-denial.

Smiles published other books exploring this same ideological vein, including *Character* (1871), *Thrift* (1875) and *Duty* (1880). The enormous success of *Self-Help* provoked a vogue for self-help titles through the 1860s and 1870s, including William Anderson's *Self Made Men* (2nd edn, 1865) and the anonymously authored *Small Beginnings, or the Way to Get On* (1859).

Sensation   John Sutherland defines 'sensation fiction' as 'a distinct but essentially minor sub-genre of the British novel that flourished in the 1860s' (Sutherland, 1988: 562). A group of best-selling novels traded on a blend of domestic convention and melodramatic excess to excite their readership: Wilkie COLLINS' *The Woman in White* (1860), *East Lynne* (1861) by Mrs Henry Wood (1814–87) and *Lady Audley's Secret* (1862) by Mary Elizabeth Braddon (1835–1915) are perhaps the three most prominent among many sensation novels: gripping thrillers constructed around the revelation of buried secrets that undermine preconceptions about family life and female docility. DICKENS' later novels also exhibit the attributes of sensation writing. These books can be thought of as 'sensational' in three overlapping senses of the word: first, they are often written in such a way as to emphasise the sensational experience, extreme mental states, the consequences of guilt, incarceration and death on characters' consciousness to evoke 'sensation' reactions in the reader – as Queenie Leavis later put it, 'the sensation novelists make a brute assault on the feelings and nerves' (Leavis, 1939: 154); second, they frequently respond to a particular journalistic sensation (Sutherland mentions two *causes celebres* from the early 1860s, 'the forcible incarceration of the sane in lunatic asylums' and 'bigamy'); and, third, they created a 'sensation' in the public arena, extreme reactions of excitement or of condemnation depending on the attitude of the reader. As a genre, 'sensation' blends seamlessly with late-century DETEC-TIVE fiction, as well as late-Gothic and horror writing.

Sentimentality   Critics of the Victorian novel sometimes accuse it of being 'sentimental' or 'too sentimental', by which is meant that it was prone to a sort of emotional incontinence, a saccharine propensity to associate emotion in literature with tears. The *locus classicus* for this denigrating sense of the period is the death of little Nell in DICKENS' *Old Curiosity Shop* (1840–1). Most contemporaries were genuinely moved by the death of this young, beautiful and innocent character; latterly, though, some readers have found it manipulative and conventional, Oscar Wilde famously quipping that 'one must have a heart of stone to read the death of Nell without laughing' (quoted in Schlicke, 1999: 436). Today the cultural virtues are irony, cynicism and the ability 'not to be taken in', and 'sentimentality' is out of fashion. Yet for the Victorians, 'sentiment' or 'sensibility' (the words are interchangeable) were the cornerstone of an appealingly humane moral code. A school of Scottish Enlightenment philosophers including Francis Hutcheson (1694–1746), Adam Smith (1723–90) and Hugh Blair (1718–1800) theorised 'sentiment' or 'fellow feeling' (the ability to empathise with what another is feeling) as a positive ethical virtue; and a school of sentimental literature developed that included works such as *A Sentimental Journey* (1768) by Laurence Sterne (1713–68) and *A Man of Feeling* (1771) by Henry Mackenzie (1745–1831). Whilst the dangers of relying exclusively on 'sentiment' are explored in Jane Austen's (1775–1817) *Sense and Sensibility* (1811), the novel at no point denies the importance of sentimental empathy. The early Victorian vogue for novels that would make them laugh and cry with their characters reflected a belief that it is good for our feelings to exercise them in this way, and the converse belief that a wholly unsentimental life might result in the withering away of this ability to feel. When a character like Little Nell, or GASKELL's Ruth dies, it is 'sentimental' rather than tragic because the effect is to harness the reader's emotional response in the cause of affective health rather than creating a cathartic purging of the emotion as a 'bad' quality. Dickens' novels are all sentimental in this way; and some or all of the novels of Gaskell, the BRONTËS, TROLLOPE; even as cynical a novelist as THACKERAY writes sentimental deaths (as with the death of Colonel Newcombe at the end of *The Newcombes*, 1853–5). But 'sentimentalism' was not limited to the novel. For many Victorians the greatness of classic literature such as Homer or Attic Tragedy lay in its sentiment.

TENNYSON's *The Princess* (1847) describes 'a classic lecture' (which is to say, a lecture on the classics):

> A classic lecture, rich in sentiment,
> With scraps of thunderous epic lilted out
> By violet-hooded Doctors, elegies
> And quoted odes.

(Tennyson, *The Princess*, Part 2, ll. 352–5)

In the words of Fred Kaplan

> CARLYLE believed, as did Dickens and Thackeray, that the greatest danger to the human community was the increasing devaluation of human nature, either in mechanical, secular, or biological forms. . . . The Victorian Sentimentalists affirmed the fragile hope that human beings, in their instinctive natures, innately know right from wrong, and that at the level of innate response they take pleasure in the triumph of goodness and the defeat of evil in literature. These Victorian sentimentalists trusted that the source of 'sacred tears' was the moral spring of human nature.

(Kaplan, 1987: 143)

Further reading

Sacred Tears: Sentimentality in Victorian Literature (1987) by Fred Kaplan.

Serialisation   This mode of publishing was most closely associated with DICKENS, all of whose novels, excepting only his Christmas Books, were first issued in either monthly serial instalments (as with *The Pickwick Papers* (1836–7), *David Copperfield* (1849–50) and *Our Mutual Friend* (1864–5), amongst others) or weekly serial instalments (*Hard Times* (1854) and *Great Expectations* (1860–1) were first published weekly in HOUSEHOLD WORDS and ALL THE YEAR ROUND respectively). Most Dickens novels, and a number of imitators (such as THACKERAY's *Vanity Fair* (1847–8) first appeared as a succession of pamphlets made up of 32 pages of text and two engraved illustrations, with an illustrated cover-wrapper and a variable number of pages of advertisements at the end. A novel issued in 20 such serial parts would in fact appear over 19 months, the last issue being of double length. Purchasers would collect all of these and then have them bound together into a volume. Single-volume editions of Dickens' novels sometimes appeared before the serialisation had run its course. However successful Dickens was with this form of publication, other mainstream Victorian novelists found the task of holding the public's attention over this period harder: to quote John Sutherland, 'the novel in monthly numbers was a bow of Ulysses which only Dickens could draw with consistent success' (quoted in Schlicke, 1999: 417). PENNY DREADFULS, 'bloods' and other populist narratives were very successfully issued in serialised form:

Edward Viles (1842–91) issued his highwayman romance *Black Bess; or, the Knight of the Road* in an astonishing 254 illustrated monthly parts (the bound volume runs to 2028 pages). Other forms of serialisation included part-publication in magazines and journals: many magazines serialised fiction over the period. Some works were published in serially issued bound volumes: Browning's THE RING AND THE BOOK was published in four bound monthly parts (November 1868 to February 1689) and George Eliot issued MIDDLEMARCH in eight monthly bound volumes from 1871 to 1872. By the 1860s and 1870s, however, serialisation was no longer as important a mode of publication. Disliked by the LIBRARIES, who preferred bound volumes, and rendered less financially attractive by generally lower publishing costs, monthly serials became more or less extinct by the later 1870s.

Further reading

The Victorian Serial (1991) by Linda Hughes and Michael Lund.

Servants Most upper-, middle- and lower-middle-class Victorians employed servants, or at least a servant. In an age before the widespread labour-saving devices of today, assistance was virtually a necessity. At the top end of the scale, wealthy families would maintain a veritable army of servants of all sorts, dressed in specially provided uniforms (or 'livery'). At the bottom end, many lower-middle class Victorian families would at the very least employ a 'maid of all works' to help with cooking, cleaning and child care.

The 'servant problem', as it was known, was confined to the wealthier members, since it expressed the anxiety of finding and keeping trustworthy men and women. It was a frequent complaint that servants could not be trusted; they stole food and drink from their employers, slacked from their work, were rude, and so on. DAVID COPPERFIELD, in Dickens' novel, finds himself unable to manage his servants during the time of his first marriage. 'The house kept itself,' he relates, 'and we kept a page. The principle function of this retainer was to quarrel with the cook ... He appears to me to have lived in a hail of saucepan-lids' (Chapter 48). This 'servant' steals Dora's watch, and 'converting it into money, spent the produce ... in incessantly riding up and down between London and Uxbridge outside the coach', and conspires burglary with the pot-boy. Henry Mayhew (1812–87) published a comic novel called *The Greatest Plague of Life: or, the Adventures of a Lady in Search of a Good Servant* (1847), in which the narrator (identified as 'One Who Has Been "Almost Worried to Death"') experienced all manner of shiftless, dishonest or parasitic servants.

The highest-ranking servants were head butlers or steward; they had managerial responsibilities for the many servants under them. A butler's duties, strictly, were confined to waiting on the family during breakfast, luncheon and dinner, and overseeing the running of the kitchen. A valet acted as a sort of personal assistant to a gentleman, cleaning his clothes, helping him dress, perhaps shaving him, and generally making himself useful; his duties brought him into close contact with his master, a fact recognised in the famous dictum of Madame Cornuel (1605–94) that 'no man is a hero to his valet' (Partington, 1992: 219). Women might have a lady's maid to undertake similar duties for them; cleaning clothes and helping dress her mistress, brushing hair, and so on.

Lower servants had more menial jobs. The footman was expected to rise early and clean boots, knives, furniture and plate. He would answer the door and deal with callers, and might be expected to carry messages. Housemaids were generally concerned with cleaning, scrubbing and dusting. The number of housemaids employed by a house, and their respective duties, would depend upon the size and nature of the place. Large families might assign a valet to each of their sons, and a waiting-maid to each daughter, to keep their rooms in order.

Early in the century most wealthier families would employ laundry-maids to clean and press all family clothing and linen; later in the century laundry-maids became less common in the larger cities, their work being taken over by professional laundries. Larger houses might keep a stables, so as to have horses for their carriages. In such cases, a coachman, groom and stableboy would be required; the first to drive the carriage, the latter two to care for the horses and the stables.

Two other forms of domestic servant that appear frequently in Victorian fiction were rarer in actual life. One is the figure of the governess, hired personally to supervise the educational development of children in a wealthy-enough house. There was a relative paucity of employment opportunities for women from backgrounds of good breeding but little money, and working as a governess was one possibility. The post demonstrates the anxieties of class that issues of the servant's position entailed: governesses were women of educational attainment and were mostly drawn from a higher class than ordinary domestic servants, but they were not therefore guaranteed to be granted a higher status by households. Anne Brontë's *Agnes Grey* (1847) works governess in several houses, and hopes to find an employer 'who would treat his governess with due consideration as a respectable, well-educated lady, the instructor and guide of his children, and not a mere upper servant'. But her employers treat her as if she does not exist, and 'seeing in what little estimation the governess was held by both parents and children' the other servants treat her poorly and she feels 'degraded' (Brontë, *Agnes Grey*: 54, 69). Governesses are frequent in literature, but were a small portion of the servant population of the country in real life. The other literary type is the faithful manservant, Sam Weller to Mr Pickwick (in Dickens' *Pickwick Papers*, 1836–7), or Mark Tapley to Martin Chuzzlewit (in *Martin Chuzzlewit*, 1842–4), the sort who stays with his master out of sheer human affection rather than salary, advises him, and sees him through scrapes and dangers: a type that finds its most enduring expression in P.G. Wodehouse's (1881–1975) Jeeves and Wooster. Whilst there presumably were genuinely loyal servants in the nineteenth century, this literary archetype owes more to the model established by Miguel de Cervantes Saavedra (1547–1616), whose Don Quixote and his servant Sancho Panza were immortalised in *Don Quixote* (1605–15).

Sex   In one of those rare occasions where a single work of scholarship overturns an entire climate of opinion, the first volume of Michel Foucault's (1926–84) *The History of Sexuality* (1976) has very largely redefined the way scholars think of the discourse of 'sex' in Victorian culture. Foucault notes that for many years 'Victorianism' was seen as an aberrantly sexually repressed and restricted age, in which 'sex' was something not spoken of in society except as a marginal medical discourse and even then coded in Latin terminology and euphemism. But Foucault notes that the Victorian period was not 'repressive' in this blanket, caricature manner: on the contrary, Victorian society (and modern culture) 'speaks verbosely of its own silence, takes great pains to relate in detail things it does not say, denounces the powers it exercises, and promises to liberate itself from the very laws that have made it function' (Foucault, 1990: 8). He explores the apparently 'repressive' nature of Victorian sexual discourse, uncovering the various ways that the Victorians nonetheless obsessively ('the ways in which sex is put into discourse' (Foucault, 1990: 11)) talked about and made public these sexual fascinations.

There was, it is true, a code of repression with respect to sex amongst many of the middle classes. But sexual bawdy was a consistent and enormously popular form of culture in the working classes throughout the century. In 1852 Henry Mayhew (1812–87) noted (with middle-class disgust) attending a 'penny gaff', or popular theatre, in which was performed a singing act 'perfect in its wickedness. A ballet began between a man dressed up as a woman, and a country clown. The most disgusting attitudes were struck, the most immoral acts represented, without one dissenting voice' (Mayhew (1849–62) 1985: 40). A PENNY DREADFUL such as *Reynolds's Miscellany of Romance, General Literature, Science and Art* – enormously popular amongst poorer readers – often carried very racy illustrations on its cover. The number (26 December 1846) that carried the SERIALISED Chapter 19 of 'Wagner: the Wehr-Wolf' portrays four topless woman beating one another with whips. This sort of publication is distinct from the underworld literature of Victorian pornography, which was very extensive and highly explicit.

Matters were different in the higher echelons of society, but not entirely so. Lord Acton's bizarre assertion that 'as a general rule, a modest woman seldom desires any sexual gratification for herself … [indeed] the married woman has no wish to be placed on the footing of a mistress' (Acton, quoted in Vicinus, 1973: 83) is sometimes quoted by scholars as evidence of a broad climate of opinion, although the eccentric Acton (1834–1902) is by no means a representative figure. It is true that, in Joan Perkin's words,

> sex was not a fit discussion in polite society, among women friends or between parent and daughter. There was no talk of pubic hair, the clitoris, or orgasm. The words were never spoken, let alone understood by most people, Methods of contraception were little known, and not considered respectable.

> (Perkin, 1993: 51)

But various groups could, and did, talk about sex in one mode or another. Francis Newman, for instance, commented upon (male) Oxford undergraduates in 1869:

> on the whole, they did not approve of seduction. A man could not exactly put the woman back where she had been. It was really a shame to spoil a girl's after-chances. But as to Fornication, that was quite another thing. A man found a woman already spoiled; he did not do her any harm, poor creature!

> (Newman, 1869: 275)

This sexual double-standard does not, of course, express 'repression' as such.

The social pressures to avoid even the mildest consideration of sexual matters, especially on women, were extreme. Elizabeth Gaskell's *Ruth* (1853), for instance, tells the tale – in what seems to modern sensibilities an extremely circumspect, delicate and unshocking manner – of a woman who bears a child out of wedlock. Yet a contemporary reader later recalled the shock that it occasioned in Oxford University circles:

> A moral lapse in a woman was spoken of as an immensely worse thing than in a man; there was no comparison to be formed between them. A pure woman, it was reiterated, should be absolutely ignorant of a certain class of evils in the world . . . silence was thought to be the great duty of all on such subjects.

> (Quoted in Flint, 1993: 213)

The most severe reaction to Regency laxness of morals was observable in the 1840s and 1850s, but, to quote David Newsome,

> the fact that as late as 1877 Charles Bradlaugh and Annie Besant were prosecuted for obscene libel (and acquitted only on a technicality) for proselytising birth-control, is a reminder that late Victorian society was still watchful, even irrationally so, over matters of sexual morality.

> (Newsome, 1997: 254)

This climate was heightened by a number of sexual *causes célèbres* in the later century. William Stead (1849–1912), editor of the *Pall Mall Gazette*, achieved sensational notoriety when he went 'undercover' to expose the sexual vice trade, particularly in very young girls. His articles 'Maiden Tribute of Modern Babylon' (1885), and the furore they created, led directly to Parliament raising the age of sexual consent to 16.

Further reading

The Making of Victorian Sexuality (1994) by Michael Mason.

Shakespeare   The eighteenth century was the age in which Shakespeare was elevated to the status of immortal literary figure, a process continued through the nineteenth;

the *Realm* (9 March 1869) talked of 'these days of Shakespearolatry'; Shakespeare formed the backbone of theatrical performance through the century, and significant scholarship was also performed. When William Macready (1793–1873) took over the management of the Covent Garden Theatre in 1837 he embarked upon a series of revivals of Shakespearean plays, sometimes restoring the text after many decades of performance in altered and 'improved' versions: his *King Lear* was the first since Shakespeare's day to restore the unhappy ending. A group of scholars including Alexander Dyce (1798–1869), Charles Knight (1791–1873) and James Orchard Halliwell (1820–89) established a Shakespeare Society in 1840; J. Payne Collier (1789–1883), an antiquarian whose enthusiasm for Shakespeare sometimes led him into forgery, was the society's first chairman. Shakespeare is a ubiquitous intertextual presence in most writers of the period, especially in DICKENS, ELIOT, BROWNING and HARDY. The establishment of a National Shakespeare Fund in 1861 caused the *Saturday Review* (30 November 1861) to declare that 'the national pulse beats Shakespeareanly'. A quest for 'authenticity' prompted the New Shakspere Society, formed in 1874, to include in its title what it believed to be the true spelling and pro-nunciation of the playwright's name, although this caused some derision. Oscar WILDE published a sensitive fictionalisation of the lengths to which Shakespearolatry took some people, which included an ingenious critical reading of Shakespeare's sonnets, in *The Portrait of Mr W.H.* (1889).

Further reading

Shakespeare's Lives (1991) by Samuel Schoenbaum.

Shaw, George Bernard (1856–1950)   Born in Dublin, Shaw grew up the child of a dysfunctional marriage. He left school at 15 and worked in a land agent's office. He moved to London in 1876. Shaw is by temperament as well as chronol-ogy more a twentieth-century writer than a nineteenth-century one, although he wrote prolifically from his arrival in London, composing five novels (including *An Unsocial Socialist* in 1884, and a novel about boxing, *Cashel Byron's Profession*, in 1885–6). He also wrote music reviews, and from 1895–8 he wrote many drama reviews, later collected as *Our Theatre in the Nineties* (1932). His political radical-ism was reflected in his engagement with the socialist Fabian Society, and in his authorship of many left-wing political tracts, amongst them *Fabian Essays in Socialism* (1889). His true genius was as a playwright; although his first play *Widowers' Houses* (performed 1892) was not a success, his next *Arms and the Man* (performed 1894) established his reputation. Many other plays followed, including – in the Victorian period – the daring analysis of high-class prostitution, *Mrs Warren's Profession* (published 1898, performed 1902) and *You Never Can Tell* (performed 1899). He went on to write over 50 plays, laying a plausible claim to the title of greatest dramatist of the twentieth century.

Silver-fork novels   The vogue for 'fashionable novels' (as they were sometimes also called) ran from the mid-1820s through to the 1840s: fiction concentrating on aristocratic characters, high life, elevated manners, gentlemen falling in love with ladies and all the paraphernalia of upper-class existence. According to John Sutherland, the publisher Henry Colburn (?1780–1855) conceived of the genre 'when the book trade was prostrated by recession' in 1824, and 'embarked on a saturation campaign of publishing short-life bestsellers, exploiting post-Regency fascinations with high life' (Sutherland, 1988: 577). He had great success with *Sayings and Doings* (1824) by Theodore Hook (1788–1841), *Tremaine, or The Man of Refinement* (1825) by Robert Plumer Ward (1765–1846) and the young DISRAELI's *Vivian Grey* (1826). These successes inaugurated a vogue for such novels amongst mostly middle-class readers excited at the supposed insight they granted into aristocratic life; Sutherland estimates that there were as many as 500 novels published in this genre alone. The most celebrated silver-forker was Catherine Gore (1799–1861), who claimed in a preface to her novel *Pin Money* (1831) to be moving 'the familiar narrative of Miss Austen to a higher sphere of society'. Mrs Gore's most celebrated novel, *Cecil* (1841), follows a high-born dandy and gentleman through the brilliant world of Regency London society to his redemption as a warrior-hero at Waterloo. By the 1840s the genre was starting to pall on a Victorian reading public more interested in domestic middle-class fiction; it probably did not require THACKERAY's witty, pinpoint satire to demolish it, but his burlesque *Dukes and Dejuners, Hearts and Diamonds, Marchionesses and Milliners, Loves and Liveries etc.* (1847) did just that anyway.

Further reading

Silver Fork Society: Fashionable life and literature from 1814 to 1840 (1983) by Alison Adburgham.

Slavery   Britain abolished its slave trade in 1808 after a vigorous eighteenth-century anti-slavery campaign (and, it should be added, after enriching itself enormously throughout the century on the proceeds of that trade); France abolished slavery in 1815 largely at the insistence of the British. Slavery, however, continued in many other countries including British dominions, and anti-slavery movements were common throughout the Victorian period. The Anti-Slavery Society was formed in 1823 and published *The Anti-Slavery Reporter* as well as putting forward numerous petitions to Parliament. A major slave rebellion in Jamaica in 1831 was followed by savage reprisals by the masters, and galvanised public opinion against slavery: in 1834 slavery was abolished throughout British colonies. The Emancipation Act of that year in fact replaced 'slavery' with a restrictive scheme of 'apprenticeships' binding former slaves to their masters, a move resented by many as slavery in all but name; and responding to continuing pressure Parliament abolished the apprenticeship scheme in 1838.

Focus now shifted to other slave-owning countries, especially in North and South America. The World Anti-Slavery Convention met in London in 1840, and prominent figures lent their voice to calls for global abolition. Nor was anti-slavery the domain only of private citizens. Successive British governments expressed disapproval of what PALMERSTON called 'this foul and detestable crime' (quoted in Porter, 1999: 107). The British aggressively targeted the slave trade; regularly intercepting slave ships sailing to Brazil, for instance, or bombarding slave-trading centres on the West Coast of Africa. An Anglo-Zanzibar anti-slave treaty was signed in 1840, addressing the widespread trade in slaves by Arabs working from Zanzibar across Africa and the Middle East, but it was not until another Anglo-Zanzibar treaty of 1871 that the slave trade was effectively ended. Indeed, anti-slavery seems to have lost momentum throughout the 1840s and 1850s. As many as two millions slaves were shipped across the Atlantic across the century as a whole, many of them to America, Cuba and Brazil. Although slavery was abolished in French colonial possessions in 1848, and in Dutch ones in 1863, it was the freeing of the very large population of slaves in the United States in 1865 (after a lengthy, bloody civil war fought primarily on this issue) that constituted the major breakthrough. Although anti-black RACISM continued as an oppressive and virulent fact of life in the USA for another hundred years, this abolition was the breakthrough for the world anti-slavery movement.

Smiles, Samuel. See *Self-Help*.

Smoking   Smoking, though a popular habit, continued throughout the century to be associated with idleness and shiftlessness, such that the *Pall Mall Gazette* (29 September 1890) could talk of 'the lazy, the drunken, the smoking, the thriftless'. Working for comic effect against this stiff moral climate, Robert Louis STEVENSON could propose his 'golden rule' for marriage, 'no woman should marry a teetotaller, or a man who does not smoke' (*Virginibus Puerisque*, 1881), and Oscar WILDE has his seemingly severe Lady Bracknell asking Jack 'Do you smoke?', only to subvert our expectation of her disapproval at Jack's reply 'Well, yes, I must admit I smoke': 'I am glad to hear it. A man should always have an occupation of some kind. There are far too many idle men in London as it is' (Act 1). On the other hand, DECADENT and FIN-DE-SIÈCLE writers exploited the shock value of smoking; Arthur Machen (1863–1947) published his *Anatomy of Tobacco* (1884) in imitation of Burton's *Anatomy of Melancholy*, praising the drug for its various psychotropic effects.

Socialism   Before the 1830s, adherents of political views that advocated social equality and justice were known as 'radicals', or (following the French Revolution) as 'Jacobins' or 'revolutionaries'. The distinction between LIBERALS and socialists was not a watertight one in the first decades of the century, although 'socialism' became increasingly closely defined as the century went on. The word 'socialist' was first used in a French newspaper in 1832; and followers of Robert OWEN began using the phrase in the later 1830s to express the view that the wealth of society should be held in

211

common rather than by individuals. An anti-Owenite book by John Mather, published in 1839 and entitled *Socialism Exposed*, subjected the fledgling movement to swingeing criticism. Indeed, this sort of widespread hostility was common in the 1840s: it is unsurprising, for instance, that the Tory Quarterly Review (December 1840: 180) identified 'the two great demons in morals and politics' to be 'Socialism and Chartism'. Perhaps the most significant intervention into the field of developing socialist theories came with Karl Marx and Frederick Engels (1820–95), whose populist *Communist Manifesto* (1848), backed by Marx's imposing edifice of theoretical analysis and ideological justification (culminating in the monumental *Das Kapital* of 1867) gave the various socialist movements a new focus. Marx and Engels in fact dismissed many of the century's earlier socialist thinkers, including two influential French thinkers, Saint-Simon (1760–1825) and Charles Fourier (1772–1837) as well as Owen, as 'utopian socialists' – by which they meant impracticable, insufficiently 'scientific' thinkers. In his pamphlet *Socialism: Utopian and Scientific* (1880) Engels attempted to establish Marxist 'communist' socialism as the only realistic form of the belief by denigrating other socialist thinkers with the 'utopian' tag. This Marxist belief in the necessity of revolution to bring about socialism was opposed by a raft of thinkers who proposed an evolutionary socialism. The former movement gained in influence as the century progressed, until the formation of the 'Second International' movement in Paris in 1889. The latter concentrated its energies on working within the existing constitutional framework. A Democratic Federation, formed in 1881, helped resuscitate the ailing culture of popular socialism in Britain; its name was changed to the Social Democratic Federation in 1884. The 'Fabian Society' was formed the same year, an association of upper-class intellectuals sympathetic to socialist ideals who were not prepared to go as far as Marx required. This new movement of popular support and intellectual respectability culminated in the formation of the Labour Party in 1893.

Social problem novel   Like the term INDUSTRIAL NOVEL this is a loose and rather unsatisfactory catch-all descriptor for a number of different sorts of fictional engagements with contemporary social and political issues. Works such as Frances Trollope's (1780–1863) *Michael Armstrong: the Factory Boy* (1839) and Charlotte Tonna's (1790–1846) *Helen Fleetwood* (1839) concentrated on particular abuses of factory workers; Dickens' early works similarly focused on specific social wrongs: the practice of the new Poor Laws in *Oliver Twist* (1837–9), or unlicensed schools in *Nicholas Nickleby* (1838–9). In the 1840s, social problem novels tended to take a broader view. Disraeli's *Sybil* (1845), for instance, blends analysis of INDUSTRIAL and Chartist phenomena with a broader manifesto for addressing 'social inequality' via a one-nation, pseudo-feudal Tory political agenda. The three novels in Disraeli's Young England trilogy, *Coningsby* (1844), *Sybil* (1845) and *Tancred* (1847), attempt with partial success to anatomise the whole nation from this Tory perspective. Charles Kingsley's *Alton Locke* (1848) attempts a similar broad view. This form of panoramic 'social' vision reaches an apogee in some of Dickens' later works, especially *Bleak House* (1852–3), but also *Little Dorrit* (1855–7) and *Our Mutual Friend* (1864–5), in which characters from every social class, and representing every social problem, are woven together into a large, complex canvas. The painted canvases of William Frith (1819–1909) provide a visual correlative to this inclusive approach. TROLLOPE's *The Way We Live Now* (1874–5) is a similarly capacious and powerful analysis of social problems, although not handled with the extraordinary aplomb of Dickens. Later in the century this form of 'social' novel was superseded by works written under the influence of French REALIST fiction; George Gissing (1857–1903) dissected social problems in grim studies of social deprivation such as *Demos* (1886) and *The Nether World* (1889).

Sonnet   A sonnet is a 14-line poem, often conforming to a set rhyme scheme and usually about love; it is especially associated with Italian medieval and English Renaissance literature, at which time Petrarch (1304–74) and Shakespeare (1564–1616) wrote enduring poems in the form. It is too-little noticed, but the Victorian period was one of the great eras of sonnet-writing in English literary history. Although several Romantic poets experimented with the sonnet format – notably Wordsworth (1770–1850) – the form remained out of fashion until the mid-nineteenth century. But from 1850 onwards the sonnet and particularly the sonnet-sequence (the focus for this study) increases in popularity exponentially, to the extent where the passion for sonnets and sonnet-sequences becomes a phenomenon. A key work was Elizabeth Barrett BROWNING's *Sonnets from the Portuguese* (1850), a sequence of seemingly intimate love poems whose success seems to have opened the floodgates. In 1867 Leigh Hunt published a collection of English and American sonnets, *The Book of the Sonnet*, itself an index to a growing sonnet vogue. As we might expect from a living remnant of Romanticism, Hunt was only half-convinced of the merit of the form he was anthologising:

> Some will think [that] we might have done better than confine ourselves to a species of composition not yet associated in the general mind with the idea of anything very marked or characteristic.

> (Hunt and Adams Lee, 1867: xii)

Nonetheless, Hunt's pre-emptive 'not *yet* associated' was prescient. The 1860s and 1870s saw a steadily increasing fascination with, and more prolific production of, sonnets of all kinds, and in particular, the composition of elaborate sonnet sequences. George Meredith (1828–1909) published a complex sequence of modern love sonnets, *Modern Love*, in 1862; the sonnets comprising ROSSETTI's *House of Life* began appearing in 1869, with expanded versions of the sequence published in 1870 and 1881; TENNYSON's brother, Charles Tennyson Turner (1808–79), published volumes comprised almost solely of sonnets in 1864 and 1873; Christina ROSSETTI's 14-sonnet sequence, *Monna Innominata*, begun perhaps as early as 1866, was not published until 1881; her brother, William Michael Rossetti (1829–1919), worked on his large-scale sequence *Democratic Sonnets* throughout the later 1870s, and Gerard Manley HOPKINS was fashioning his intricate religious sonnets in the same decade. When SPASMODIC poets Alexander Smith (1829–67) and Sydney Dobell (1824–74) wished to write poetry about the Crimean War they created a sonnet sequence (*Sonnets on the War*, 1855); when SWINBURNE was moved to memorialise the greats of world literature in the 1880s he turned out sonnets by the hundred. Anthologists suddenly seemed to discover the delights of the English sonnet, filling their works with the copious outpourings of nineteenth-century writers, some famous, many now forgotten. In terms of sheer numbers, more sonnets and sonnet-sequences were written in English between 1850 and 1890 than at any time since the 1590s.

Spasmodic literature   'Spasmodic' was a term of satirical abuse coined by William Aytoun (1813–65) to characterise a particular sort of psychological, intense and morbid style of poetry. The classic 'spasmodics' are Alexander Smith (1830–67), Philip James Bailey (1816–1902) and Sydney Dobell (1824–74), although some of BROWNING's poetry from the 1830s and 1840s is sometimes spoken of as sharing some of these characteristics. As we might expect from the provenance of the word ('spasmodic' was originally a medical term, meaning 'pertaining to cramp or convulsion, or hauling of the sinews') these characteristics included: stylistic abruptness and infelicity, bathos and inflated diction, repetition and *non-sequiturs*. In terms of subject, a typical spasmodic poem concerned the inner life or psychological profile of an intense, self-absorbed young man, often a poet or thinker, agonising over various issues. Robert Chambers (1802–71), in his 1860 *Cyclopedia of English Literature*, described such poets in the following terms: 'they heap up images and sentiments, the ornaments of poetry, without aiming at order, consistency, and the natural development of passion or feeling' (Chambers, Vol. 2, 1860: 609). The great error of spasmodic poetry, according to Chambers, is 'want of simplicity and nature'. Many spasmodic techniques, however, are fairly in tune with more recent poetic theories, and much spasmodic poetry can appear very beautiful to present-day readers. The following, for instance, is from Smith's *A Life Drama* (1852):

> Unrest! Unrest! The passion-panting sea
> Watches the unveiled beauty of the stars
> Like a great hungry soul. The unquiet clouds
> Break and dissolve, then gather in a mass,
> And float like mighty icebergs through the blue.
> Summers, like blushes, sweep the face of earth;
> Heaven yearns in stars. Down comes the frantic rain;
> We hear the wail of the remorseful winds

In their strange penance. And this wretched orb
Knows not the taste of rest; a maniac world,
Homeless and sobbing through the deep she goes.

Stevenson, Robert Louis (1850–1894) Born Robert Lewis Balfour Stevenson, the son of an Edinburgh engineer. Stevenson's precarious childhood health prevented him from following his father, and although he studied law he had determined to be a writer. In 1868, at 18, he was exhibiting a taste for bohemian life, in reaction to the stricter Scottish views of his father; he changed his middle name to 'Louis' and in the 1870s he visited a number of artist's communities at Graz and Fontainebleau. In 1875 he met William Henley (1849–1903) who was to become his friend and mentor. His health was never good; a chronic and debilitating bronchial condition, possibly tubercular, plagued him throughout his life. Nevertheless he travelled and wrote a great deal – four plays in collaboration with Henley, and the entertaining travel books *An Inland Voyage* (1878) and *Travels with a Donkey in the Cevennes* (1879). In 1880 he married Fanny Osbourne with whom he had conducted an affair since 1876. The two travelled extensively in America, an experience recorded by Stevenson in *The Silverado Squatters* (1883). A series of witty and penetrating essays, mostly written for the *Cornhill* magazine, was collected as *Virginibus Puerisque* in 1881, and two collections of stories followed: *Familiar Stories of Men and Books* (1882) and *New Arabian Nights* (1882). Stevenson's health was getting worse, with severe asthma and blood being coughed up, but he was entering into his golden years as a writer. His novel *Treasure Island* (1883) brought him deserved and widespread fame: it remains one of the most enduring classics of CHILDREN'S LITERATURE. It was followed by the iconic and enduring SCIENCE FICTION fable *The Strange Case of Dr Jekyll and Mr Hyde* (1886). Perhaps his most sheerly enjoyable tale, *Kidnapped*, appeared in 1886 (a sequel, *Catriona*, followed in 1893): set in eighteenth-century Scotland it appeals equally to children and adults with its gripping adventure plotline and its superbly drawn characters. *The Master of Ballantrae: a Winter's Tale* (1889), another story of the 1745 Scottish Jacobite rebellion, was another success. He also published a number of collections of minor but charming poetry: *Underwoods* (1887), *Ballads* (1890) and *Songs of Travel* (1896). He, his wife and entourage travelled to the South Seas in 1888, settling on Samoa, where he acquired the nickname of 'Tusitala' or 'Tale-teller'. The climate helped Stevenson's health and he loved the island, although life was hard, financially and otherwise: his wife suffered a nervous breakdown in 1892, and Stevenson worked hard at the writing that paid for everything, publishing various travel books, a further though inferior historical romance for youngsters (*The Black Arrow*, 1888), *The Wrong Box* (co-written with his stepson, Lloyd Osbourne, 1894), and *The Ebb-Tide* (1894). He died suddenly of a stroke in 1892, and was buried on the island. A number of works were published posthumously, including two unfinished works, *The Weir of Hermiston* (1896) and *St Ives* (1897).

It may be that Stevenson's enduring and enormous popularity has unfairly prejudiced his critical reception, as if 'populist genius' were a contradiction in terms. But he remains one of the most significant and brilliant writers of the period.

Stones of Venice* (1851–1853), by John Ruskin   Ostensibly an architectural study of the Italian city in three volumes, in fact Ruskin's work is a deeply considered moral-aesthetic manifesto for the liberty and dignity of the workman. The first volume, 'The Foundations', establishes the difference between what Ruskin considers good and bad architectural styles; the second, 'The Sea Stories', surveys the city itself, insisting on a corrective to rose-tinted Romantic versions of the city by dwelling on the physical and aesthetic jumble and misery amongst which its inhabitants live; the third volume, 'The Fall', charts the degeneration of architecture across the history of the Renaissance. The most famous portion of the work is the chapter called 'The Nature of Gothic', in which the harmonious social relations of the older feudal model are contrasted with the alienated labouring practices of the nineteenth century, very much to the latter's disfavour:

> we have much studied and much perfected, of late, the great civilised intention
> of the division of labour; only we give it a false name. It is not, truly speaking,
> the labour that is divided; but the men – Divided into mere segments of men –
> broken into small fragments and crumbs of life . . . and the great cry that rises
> from all our manufacturing cities, louder than their furnace blasts, is all in
> very deed for this, – that we manufacture everything there except men.
>
> (Ruskin, Stones of Venice, Vol. 2, 1904: 196)

Ruskin's conclusion is that social integration must follow an aesthetic revival. William Morris later claimed that it was reading this chapter that inspired him to take up his mission to awaken his contemporaries to the aesthetic and therefore moral ugliness of the world in which they lived.

Swinburne, Algernon Charles (1837–1909)   Swinburne's aristocratic background (he was the son of an Admiral and went to Eton) helped shape his particular view of the world, although not in the ways we might necessarily expect. He himself thought the parallels between his own life and that of the Romantic poet and revolutionary Percy Bysshe Shelley (1792–1822) to be significant; both were schoolboys at Eton and students at Oxford, both considered poetry a passionate vocation. Indeed, in an important sense, Swinburne worked to refigure the poetry of Shelley for a FIN-DE-SIÈCLE aesthetic. He copied his idol's atheism, his republicanism, and strove in his own way to be as outrageous as Shelley had been. In particular, the young Swinburne picked up the habit of drinking to extremes. At Oxford, Swinburne became friendly with Gabriel Dante Rossetti and Edward Burne-Jones (1833–98), and after being sent down from university in 1860 he lived for a while in Rossetti's London house.

Swinburne first came to fame with the publication of *Atalanta in Calydon* in 1865, a verse-drama modelled on the forms of Greek Tragedy, but written with a vigour and energy that was in stark contrast to previous dull and solid works written in that form (such as Arnold's rather boring *Merope* of 1858). By contrast Swinburne's muscular rhythmic inventiveness and neo-pagan gusto brought with it a new approach to poetry.

> The hounds of spring are on winter's traces,
> The mother of months in meadow or plain
> Fills the shadows and windy places
> With lisp of leaves and ripple of rain;
> And the brown bright nightingale amorous
> Is half assuaged for Itylus,
> For the Thracian ships and the foreign faces,
> The tongueless vigil and all the pain.
>
> (*Atalanta in Calydon*, ll. 65–72)

A collection of short poems, entitled *Poems and Ballads*, followed in 1866 and caused no small storm of indignation and horror; there were calls for prosecution on grounds of obscenity, and horrified critical reactions to poems about sado-masochistic sexual encounters ('Dolores', 'Anactoria'), grisly fables of leprosy, sex and death ('The Leper') or energetically hostile attacks on Christianity:

> Thou hast conquered, O pale Galilean; the world has grown grey from Thy
>   breath;
> We have drunken of things Lethean, and fed on the fullness of death.
>
> ('Hymn to Proserpine', ll. 35–6)

Swinburne's paganism, his fascination with sexual sadism, hermaphroditism and disgusting disease, all reflected in the subject and style of these pieces. In setting out to *epater les bourgoise* Swinburne looks forward to the aestheticism of the fin de siècle. Swinburne's dissipated lifestyle, his drinking, his visiting a brothel in St John's Wood (where he paid a prostitute to beat him), his diminutive body, bright red hair and manic excitability – all this contributed to a certain mythos of the new school of poetry. Swinburne continued writing and publishing, composing two politically radical works (*Song for Italy* in 1868 and *Songs Before Sunrise* in 1871) and reiterating his paganism again in another verse-drama, *Erechtheus* (1876). He put out a second collection of short poems (*Poems and Ballads: Second Series*) in 1878.

What happened next marks the major change in Swinburne's life. By 1879 it was clear that he was drinking himself to death, and would not have lasted much longer. But a friend, Theodore Watts (later Watts-Dunton, 1832–1914) took him away to his Putney home, 'The Pines'. There he managed to wean Swinburne off the drink, and to provide a settled, regular environment. This meant that Swinburne was able to live (and write) through to the end of the century and even beyond, although many critics have detected a weakening in the later poetry, a tendency towards prolixity and the calcification of stylistic habits (excessive alliteration, rhetorical parallelism and a fondness for abstraction) into unyielding pastiche of his earlier, more fluent work. Nevertheless, many of the later poems are beautiful: many BALLADS written in brilliant imitation of northern English and Scottish traditional literature, and more considered poems such as 'A Nympholept' (1894) and 'The Lake of Gaube' (1899). He also published two longer ARTHURIAN poems of considerable interest and power: *Tristram of Lyonesse* (1882) and *The Tale of Balen* (1896). In addition, Swinburne wrote a large number of plays (none of which have been performed) and a significant body of prose criticism.

Sybil, or the Two Nations (1845), by Benjamin Disraeli   The second of Disraeli's three novels sometimes grouped together as the YOUNG ENGLAND trilogy (*Coningsby* (1844) and *Tancred* (1847) are the other two). The 'two nations' of the title are the rich and the poor, 'two nations between whom there is no intercourse and no sympathy; who are as ignorant of each other's habits, thoughts, and feelings as if they were dwellers in different zones, or inhabitants of different planets' (*Sybil*, Book 2, Chapter 5).

The novel begins with a (to modern sensibilities) interminable chapter on the political situation leading up to the REFORM ACT OF 1837, when the tale is set. The aristocratic Charles Egremont, younger brother of an Earl, the hard-hearted Lord Marney, decides to explore the poorer parts of England. Disguising himself as Mr Franklin he visits industrial towns and sees the misery of many working people. He befriends the working-class radical Walter Gerard, and falls in love with Gerard's beautiful young daughter Sybil. This inspires a terrible jealousy in Sybil's longtime admirer, Stephen Morley, a 'moral-force' CHARTIST; Morley attacks Egremont in the mist, but he survives the assault. Egremont tries to effect change through a recalcitrant House of Commons, and the situation in the country deteriorates over several years. Morley, now advocating 'physical force', becomes involved in a large Chartist riot with which the novel climaxes. He is killed, as is Walter Gerard, although Egremont rescues Sybil from the mob, and afterwards marries her. It transpires that Sybil is the true heir to lands now owned by the cruel Lord Marney. Marney dies in the riot, and his castle is burned down. The novel concludes with a peroration to the youth of the country: 'we live in an age when to be young and to be indifferent can no longer be synonymous.

We must prepare for the coming hour ... the Youth of a Nation are the trustees of Posterity' (Book 6, Chapter 13). Egremont and Sybil's marriage is meant to symbolise a union between the two nations, a fact rather undermined by the consideration that Sybil is as blue-blooded as her husband.

Critics have pointed out how thoroughly *Sybil* embodies Disraeli's ideological agenda; his nostalgic, rose-tinted and frankly fuzzy sense that the conflicts of 'the two nations' could best be resolved within a neo-medieval feudal framework of privilege, duty and responsibility. As Sybil herself put it: 'when I remember what the English people once was: the truest, the freest, and the bravest, the best-natured and the best looking, the happiest and most religious race upon the surface of the globe, and think of them now ...'

T

Technology   The INDUSTRIAL REVOLUTION provided nexus and motor for a century of accelerating technological advances. The invention of relatively efficient steam-powered engines in the eighteenth century led to enormous advances in two areas: industrial production and TRANSPORT. Thomas Newcomen (1663–1729) had invented the world's first successful atmospheric steam engine in 1712, although his design was not particularly efficient or high pressure; Scotsman James Watt (1736–1819) greatly improved this engine's efficiency, and his design, improved incrementally across the century, was the key to technological and industrial advances. Steam-driven pumps, hammers, pistons and looms enabled an enormous increase in industrial and factory production. Similarly, the first railway steam engine ran in 1814, and in 1819 the steamship *Savannah* became the first craft to cross the Atlantic using nothing but steam. Of the two mediums, land transport saw the first advances. George Stephenson (1781–1848), engineer on the first commercial railway line (which opened between Stockton and Darlington in northern England in 1821), helped create the Liverpool–Manchester and Manchester–Leeds rail lines in 1825. Steamships were limited by the use of side-mounted paddles; not until propeller technology and iron hulls became common in the 1840s did they supersede sailing ships. At the beginning of the century the sea voyage from London to Calcutta took several months; by the middle of the century the voyage time was six weeks, and at the end of the century it was two weeks.

Over the century, the technology of railway transport increased enormously in capacity and efficiency. DICKENS' *Dombey and Son* (1847–8) records the huge impact the railways were having on various aspects of Victorian life, from cityscapes and reduced transport times, to new livelihoods and new dangers (Dickens' Carker is the first character in literature to be killed by a train). In 1864 the Metropolitan Railway opened in London; part of this line was underground, and it was the first of the many underground railways built in the later nineteenth and twentieth centuries.

Another area of significant technological advance was medicine. The vital medical anaesthetic technologies of ether (1846) and chloroform (1847) not only made surgical intervention less painful, but much more survivable. Vaccination, understood vaguely in the eighteenth century, reached a new level in 1881 when Louis Pasteur (1822–95) vaccinated some sheep against anthrax in France; in 1885 he successfully vaccinated a young boy who had been bitten by a rabid dog, to widespread acclaim. Pasteur is also responsible for one of the most important developments of food science; he discovered in 1864 that gently heating wine killed the microbes that soured the beverage. His technique of 'pasteurisation' is widely used today, most notably to keep milk fresh and safe.

Other important technological advances included Fox Talbot's invention of Calotype PHOTOGRAPHY in 1840, one of a number of advances in this field. The opening of the first public telegraph line in 1844 heralded great things, but not until Scots-born American inventor Alexander Graham Bell (1847–1922) patented the telephone in 1877 did long-distance communication become a popular possibility. Electricity had been known about since the eighteenth century, but did not become a widespread technology until the work of the American inventor Thomas Edison (1847–1931); his electric light bulb (1879) eventually replaced gas-light as the chief means of lighting cities. Another Edison invention, the phonograph (invented 1877) was later to have significant cultural impact. After photography and the phonograph, moving pictures were being produced by the end of the century; the French Lumière brothers had developed cinematic shorts by 1895. Guglielmo Marconi (1874–1937) invented a wireless telegraph in 1896. Cinema and wireless, it goes without saying, were two Victorian technologies that were to have the greatest impact during the twentieth century. A third nineteenth-century technological innovation that has had a comparable impact on our lives was the invention, in 1878, of reinforced concrete beams by the French engineer Joseph Monier (1823–1906). It is not coincidental, however, that none of these last four mentioned figures was British.

A chronology such as is contained in this entry, however sketchy, gives the impression of continuous technological advance and progress. This is rather misleading. After an initial boom in technological advances associated with the first decades of the century, technology reached a plateau; the collapse of the railway bubble in the later 1840s cooled financial interest and therefore motivation. Through the 1850s and the 1860s, the (in many ways) core Victorian decades, technology advanced little; and the impulse to further technological advance during the 1870s and 1880s mostly came from non-British or expatriate inventors and engineers. The deep-rooted conservatism of much Victorian culture acted as a 'watt governor' on the pace of technological advance.

Tennyson, (Alfred, Lord) (from 1884, First Baron Tennyson) (1809–1892)

Tennyson was born at Somersby, Lincolnshire, the third son of the rector, George Tennyson. An introverted and gloomy youth, influenced by the melancholia (and eventual breakdown) of his alcoholic father, Tennyson went up to Trinity College, Cambridge, as an excessively shy undergraduate; he once, the story is told, ran away from a lecture hall because it was too full of people. His time at Cambridge saw him coming out of his shell, in large part due to the friendships he made there – most notably the intense connection he made with Arthur Hallam. Hallam swiftly became the poet's closest friend, and became engaged to Tennyson's sister Emily.

Tennyson won the university's chancellor's medal for English verse with a blank-verse poem on the subject of 'Timbuctoo' in 1829. His verses had already appeared in a volume entitled *Poems by Two Brothers* (1827), which actually contained three brothers' work (that of Alfred, Charles and Frederick Tennyson). More successful was the sole-authored 1830 collection, *Poems, Mostly Lyrical*, which contained some of his most enduring verses, amongst them 'Mariana'. The collection was, however, savagely reviewed by some influential critics. Tennyson was greatly discouraged (as his later autobiographical poem 'Merlin and the Gleam' makes plain). His 1832 collection, *Poems*, included masterpieces, many on mythic themes such as 'The Lotos Eaters', 'The Kraken' and 'The Lady of Shalott'. It is difficult, however, to avoid seeing all this as nothing more that a prelude to the event of the following year that was to constitute the central shaping incident of Tennyson's life. When visiting Italy in 1833, Arthur Hallam, aged 22, suddenly dropped dead. Tennyson was overwhelmed with grief.

The poetry Tennyson wrote in the aftermath of this bereavement was almost exclusively concerned with articulating his devastating sense of desolation and loss. Many of the lyrics that were later incorporated into In Memoriam date from this period, as well as 'Break, break, break', 'Tithonus', 'The Morte D'Arthur' and many others. All of these poems take the subject of the death of the loved man and weave heart-breaking lyric moods of despair around it. Tennyson did not publish another collection of poetry until *Poems* in 1842, and it was not until 1847, with the publication of *The Princess*, that Tennyson really began to achieve wide public prominence. This unusual long poem took as its topic the creation of a women-only university, and addressed a number of concerns that were pressing in the proto-feminist cultural idiom of the day; although the Romance trappings, fairy-tale plot and reductive conclusion (in which the formerly spirited women disband their university and take husbands instead) dilutes the possibilities of the whole. It was a popular verse-novel, however, and went a good way towards establishing Tennyson's reputation. During the 1830s, Tennyson had become engaged to Emily Sellwood, but the engagement had faltered, possibly because of fears that Tennyson might have inherited his father's tendency towards madness.

The breakthrough year for Tennyson was 1850. He finally published, as *In Memoriam A.H.H.*, the lengthy collection of elegiac lyrics occasioned by the loss of Arthur Hallam. This work struck an immediate chord with the Victorian reading public, and was almost universally praised. Queen Victoria, who would later turn to the work for consolation on the death of Albert, greatly admired it. Wordsworth having died earlier in the year, it was decided to make Tennyson Poet LAUREATE; 1850 was also the year that Tennyson finally married Emily Sellwood.

From here on, Tennyson's position as the chief poet of his age was unassailable. *MAUD* (1855) and the first four *Idylls of the King* (1859) sold in large quantities, and Tennyson enjoyed a wide circle of friends and admirers. A son, Hallam Tennyson, was born in 1852, and another, Lionel, in 1854. Tennyson wrote copiously, and to an increasingly admiring audience. The modern verse-novel *Enoch Arden* came out in 1864, and Tennyson put great effort into the completion of his vast Arthurian epic. *The Holy Grail and Other Poems* (1869) and *Gareth and Lynette, etc.* (1872) added to the collection of Arthurian idylls, and a collection of them was published as *Idylls of the King* in 1872. He was offered a Baronetcy in 1865, and in 1873, 1874 and 1880, but refused it each time, only eventually agreeing to the honour in 1884. By 1875, when Tennyson was 66, he decided to begin a career as a playwright. *Queen Mary* was published in 1875 and produced for the stage the following year. Other plays included *Harold* (1877), *The Falcon* (1879), *Beckett* (1884) and *The Foresters* (1892). His final illness and his death occurred in 1892, and he was buried at Westminster Abbey.

Tennyson's reputation has sunk and risen, but is currently high. Criticism has never really challenged the opinion that 'his genius was lyrical', and that he lacked the necessary narrative and architectonic powers to produce long and epic poetry. Yet his sensibility was, of all Victorian poets, the one most precisely attuned to the spirit (or spirits) of his age. His engagements with issues of doubt and faith, action and lassitude, duty and desire are rendered not only with technical virtuosity, but with a profound and often neglected dialecticism.

Further reading

Tennyson (1972; 2nd edn 1989) by Christopher Ricks; *Alfred Tennyson* (1986) by Alan Sinfield; *Poems* (edited by Adam Roberts 1999) by Alfred Tennyson.

Thackeray, William Makepeace (1811–1863)   Born in Calcutta, the son of an employee of the East India Company, Thackeray came to England following his father's death in 1817. He was educated at Charterhouse public school, and then at Trinity College, Cambridge, where he gambled away much of his inheritance. He left in 1830 without taking a degree. A talented artist, he attempted to make his living as an illustrator, but was unable to earn very much money; he also contemplated practising LAW, but decided against it. By 1833 all his inherited money was gone, and he moved form London to the cheaper Paris from 1834–7, where he made money inter-mittently as a journalist. But it was as a freelance writer that he eventually settled. In 1836 he married, improvidently in financial terms, a dowryless Irish woman called Isabella Shawe. The couple had three children together, two of whom survived, but by 1840 his wife's sanity had collapsed. Thackeray placed her first with a doctor, and then in an insane asylum, and sent his two daughters to live with his mother in Paris.

In the 1840s Thackeray built his reputation as a writer, with a wide range of comic works, squibs, parodies, sketches and other pieces. *The Yellowplush Papers* (serialised in *Fraser's Magazine*, 1837–8) is an accumulation of comical observations on society foibles, narrated by a footman; *Catherine* (1839–40) is a parodic satire on the vogue for NEWGATE NOVELS current at that time; *The Great Hoggarty Diamond* (1841) cata-logues the effect the apparently cursed jewel of the title has on a young clerk; *The Fitzboodle Papers* (1842–3) relates the amorous adventures of a gentleman-bachelor. Thackeray's first major fictional achievement was his comic novel *The Luck of Barry Lyndon* (serialised in *Fraser's* in 1844), in which the roguish Irish narrator's propensity to lying and exaggeration does not hide from the reader the bathetic and often sordid nature of his life and adventures.

Thackeray contributed to PUNCH from 1842 through to 1854, and several collections ensued, including *The Book of Snobs* (1846–7), a comic gallery of prose portraits accompanied by Thackeray's own illustrations. *Mr Punch's Prize Novelists* (1847) con-tains parodies of contemporary writers. The publishers of *Punch* encouraged Thackeray to write a more considered novel and, after several false-starts and delays, *Vanity Fair* began SERIALISATION in 1847. Once again, Thackeray illustrated his own work, and although the work was slow to catch on, from the fourth instalment onwards it became a great triumph. Although never as popular as DICKENS (a friend of Thackeray's, whose mode of novel writing and publication *Vanity Fair* apes), this novel marks Thackeray's emergence as a serious and feted literary figure. The novel was a turning point in his professional and personal lives. In John Sutherland's words, 'in 1847 he gave up his largely bohemian life and settled himself with his two daugh-ters in Kensington', living a more respectable life as a hit with 'the discriminating reader . . . the second novelist in Britain after Dickens' (Sutherland, 1988: 624–5).

Pendennis, an even longer novel, followed in instalments in 1848–50, and was a sim-ilar success. At this stage in his life Thackeray seems to have fallen in love with the wife of an old friend, an unhappy affair that added to the misery of a prolonged illness. His next novel, the somewhat cynical historical romance *Henry Esmond* (1852), reflects this more sombre mood; although his next large serialised novel *The Newcomes* (1853–5), a sentimental family saga with autobiographical elements, was his most popular yet. John Lothrop Motley described his physical appearance as follows in 1858:

he has the appearance of a colossal infant, smooth, white, shiny, ringlety hair, flaxen, alas, with advancing years, a roundish face with a little dab of a nose upon which it is a perpetual wonder how he keeps his spectacles, a sweet but rather piping voice, with something of the childish treble about it, and a very tall, slightly stooping figure.

(Quoted in Gross, 1998: 453)

His next novel, a prolix tale of the American Revolution called *The Virginians* (1857–9), did less well, and in 1860 he agreed to edit the new mainstream periodical the *Cornhill Magazine*. This was a success, attracting many readers and earning a great deal of money for Thackeray. He serialised his last novels, including the unfinished *Denis Duval*, in this publication. He gave up the editorship in 1862 and died prematurely in 1863.

For many present-day critics, Thackeray is the greatest Victorian novelist, more intelligent, more adult, and less sentimental than Dickens; a judgement so untenable as to be startling. Undeniably, he leavened the conventions of Victorian DOMESTIC fiction with an appealing sense of the sharpness of actual living, and his wit (only occasionally cynical) is excellent at puncturing the hypocrisies of middle-class existence. But his humour is corroded by a streak of fictive cruelty, as when in *Vanity Fair* the pleasant but insipid Amelia becomes fixed in her love for her utterly unworthy husband after his death on the battlefield at Waterloo. The man-of-the-world air that his novels often adopt flatters the reader with its manner of gentlemanly confidence ('Tis strange what a man may do and a woman yet think him an angel', he says in *Henry Esmond*, Book 1, Chapter 7), and a repeated theme is the way financial considerations underlay the practice of 'love': 'remember,' says a character in *Pendennis*, 'it is as easy to marry a rich woman as a poor woman' (Chapter 28). Similarly, the narrator of *Vanity Fair* observes that 'a woman with fair opportunities, and without a positive hump, may marry whom she likes' (Chapter 4). But this world-wisdom verges on the dishonest for all that, because it pretends to disguise the broad streak of sentimentality running through all the novels, a gush epitomised by one of Thackeray's most famous scenes, when the dying Colonel Newcome reverts to his schoolboy childhood on his deathbed: 'he lifted up his head a little, and quickly said, "Adsum!" ['Present!'] and fell back . . . he, whose heart was as that of a little child, had answered to his name, and stood in the presence of The Master' (*The Newcomes*, Chapter 80).

Theatre. *See* Drama.

(Thirty-nine) XXXIX Articles

The 39 articles of faith of the Church of England may be found at the back of the *Book of Common Prayer* in any Anglican Church. They begin with a statement of belief in God, and go on to assertions of the spiritual authority of the Church of England and the Archbishop of Canterbury, with the

British monarch as head of the Church. So, the ninth article ('man is very far gone from original righteousness') would be as acceptable to a Catholic or Noncomformist as an Anglican; but the thirty-seventh ('The Bishop of Rome hath no jurisdiction in this Realm of England') and the thirty-eighth ('the Riches and Goods of Christians are not Common ... as certain Anabaptists do falsely boast') specifically exclude Catholic and Anabaptist approaches to Christian faith.

In the nineteenth century adherence to all of these articles was not only a precondition of communion at an Anglican Church, but of taking a degree at Oxford or Cambridge Universities and of taking up a position as Member of Parliament. This fact excluded a variety of people from these organisations, including eminent Jews, Catholics and Nonconformist Protestants, and even – in the case of the Anglican Arthur Hugh CLOUGH, who forfeited an Oxford university post because of his disinclination to swear to the XXXIX Articles – Anglican individuals undergoing a process of spiritual questioning. London University was founded in 1825 in part to provide a forum of higher education for those who did not or would not accede to these articles. Many of John Henry NEWMAN's *Tracts for the Times* discuss the status of individual articles of faith; and Tract 90 announces his conversion to the Catholic Church in terms of the compatibility of that faith with the tenets of the XXXIX Articles (*see* OXFORD MOVEMENT).

Three-per-cents. *See* **Consols**.

Through the Looking-Glass and What Alice Found There* by Lewis Carroll (1871)**. *See **Alice's Adventures in Wonderland.

Times, The   The leading Victorian daily newspaper; it was founded in 1785 and is still on sale today (sometimes known as 'the Times of London' to distinguish it from the *New York Times* and other international imitators) although much reduced in cultural influence. The paper acquired its nineteenth-century reputation as 'The Thunderer' from concerted editorial policies aimed at establishing the organ as authoritative. It was, for instance, the first paper to employ specific foreign correspondents – Henry Crabbe Robinson (1775–1867) travelled to Germany in 1808 to report for the paper there. Editors included Thomas Barnes (1817–41) and Thaddeus Delane (1841–77), under whom the paper's political and cultural influence spread. Walter Bagheot (1826–77) could declare without irony in 1867 that 'the *Times* has made many ministries'.

The flipside of the paper's status as 'The Thunderer' or 'The Olympian' was a reputation for arrogance. In his *English Traits* (1856) American Ralph Waldo Emerson expressed his disapproval:

> was never such arrogancy as the tone of this paper ... one would think, the world was on its knees to the 'Times' Office, for its daily breakfast. But this

arrogance is calculated. Who would care for it, if it 'surmised' or 'dared to confess' or 'ventured to predict' &c. No; *it is so*, and so shall be.

(Quoted in Gross, 1998: 394)

Tory/Conservative   One of the two great political parties of the nineteenth century, opposed to the Whigs (later the Liberals). It is important to resist the temptation to map this political binary onto modern-day 'right-wing' and 'left-wing' assumptions. In some senses the Tories were of 'right-wing' political complexion (as we understand the term), but in many respects the nineteenth-century Tory Party was utterly different from the 'wealth-creation' laissez-faire contemporary UK Conservative or US Republican Parties. The division between 'Tories' and 'Whigs' goes back to the late seventeenth-century succession crisis: the question as to whether James Duke of York should become King as primogeniture dictated. Tories, who believed in respecting traditional authority above all things, thought he should; Whigs objected to the Duke's conversion to Catholicism. In 1688 the so-called 'Glorious Revolution' excluded James from the throne and established the Protestant succession by law, and for a while afterwards 'Tory' tended to be a religiously determined descriptor – for instance, throughout the eighteenth century it indicated a supporter of the 'Jacobite' rebellions to re-install the Catholic monarch. By the nineteenth century, however, the Tory Party had abandoned its Catholic roots, and instead upheld what it believed to be time-hallowed traditions by opposing any reform of traditional structures.

Royalist and aristocratic in predilection, the Victorian Tory Party strenuously upheld the established constitution of Church and state, and opposed reforms aimed at propagating religious freedoms on the one hand and parliamentary reform on the other. On occasion, a Tory premier might sponsor reformatory legislation – for example, with the Duke of Wellington's administration passing the act of Catholic Emancipation in 1828 (to the dissatisfaction of many of his supporters), or Derby and Disraeli passing the Reform Bill of 1867. But in general the Tory Party was dedicated to conserving the past, and its ideological ground was a respect for authority and tradition. As George Saintsbury observed in 1892, this set of beliefs meant that, in practice (and despite spending long periods in government), the Tories were defined throughout the nineteenth century chiefly in terms of opposition:

I define a Tory as a person who would at the respective times and in the respective circumstances have been opposed to Catholic Emancipation, [electoral] Reform, the Repeal of the Corn Laws and the whole Irish legislation of Mr Gladstone.

(Saintsbury, 1892: 5)

In more positive mode, there was a self-conscious attempt by Disraeli to configure the Tory Party as a paternalist, 'Young England' grouping.

From the 1830s the term 'Conservative' was increasingly used to describe the party; and in 1886 the name was changed officially to 'Conservative and Unionist Party', an alteration that reflected the defection of many Liberals to the Tories, alienated by Gladstone's support for Irish Home Rule. This Conservative Party was still known (and continues to be known) as 'Tory'. But there was a strong current of suspicion throughout the nineteenth century that 'the good old days' valorised by Tory ideology were not so good after all. In a poem published in the *Examiner* for 7 August 1841, Charles DICKENS satirised precisely this:

> The good old laws were garnished well with gibbets, whips and chains,
> With fine old English penalties, and fine old English pains,
> With rebel heads, and seas of blood once hot in rebel veins;
> For all these things were requisite to guard the rich old gains
> Of the Fine old English Tory times!

Tractarianism. *See* **Oxford Movement.**

Trade unions   Unions are groups of workers who have banded together the better to further their interests. Such groups, starting out in sporadic and localised fashion, began to combine in larger and therefore more powerful groups in the later eighteenth century. This is worth mentioning at the beginning of this entry, because as Richard Brown points out, 'the impression that trade unionism developed as a consequence of industrialisation has, until recently, led to the neglect of the existence of unionism among many groups of skilled workers in the eighteenth-century' (Brown, 1991: 329). The roots of the British trades union movement run deep. Indeed, it was in response to the success of union action, including many strikes, that the government passed two pieces of anti-union legislation at the beginning of the century. The Combination Acts of 1799 and 1800 rendered trades union action liable to criminal prosecution, and opened the organisations themselves to possible prosecution as criminal conspiracies. The Acts required workers and employers in dispute to settle under the arbitration for one (later two) magistrates. This legislation was fiercely resented by trades unionists, and in 1824 it was repealed after a campaign led by Francis Place. Without the Combination Act, union activity boomed during 1824–5, and anxious employers were successful in persuading parliament to restore the act in 1825. The 1825 Combination Act recognised the rights of workers to form unions, and to negotiate wages and conditions of labour collectively, but it restored the compulsion for arbitration, made strike action liable to prosecution and made picketing illegal.

Attempts at organising unions on a national level (as with Robert OWEN's short-lived Grand National Consolidated Trades Union in the 1830s) had been made before, but only later in the century did they become effective. Through the 1850s, unions were mostly organisations of skilled workers; not until the 1890s did trades unions penetrate into the mass of unskilled workers. The Trades Union Congress, a national confederation of unions, was formed in 1868. Legislation finally recognising the legality of unions was passed in 1871 (this was modified in 1875); according to this new law unions could act as associations and go on strike without being liable for damages (a court ruling in the so-called 'Taff Vale Case' in 1902 overturned this last principle).

Despite occasional examples of collective action, trades unions did not make a significant impact on British society until the end of the century. A range of new unions were formed in the later 1880s, and a widespread strike at London Docks in 1889 ushered in what is sometimes called the 'New Unionism'. Some 100,000 dockworkers and stevedores went on strike, processing in orderly fashion through London to air their grievances. Well organised and well disciplined, the strike resulted in capitulation by the initially hard-line employers. This success resulted in a number of other strikes – by gas workers, transport workers and other labourers – and union membership expanded. By 1890 some 350,000 workers were unionised; although economic hardship in the 1890s and renewed resistance by employers damaged the effectiveness of the movement (membership had dropped to 140,000 by 1893).

Further reading

Labour and Reform: Working-Class Movements 1815–1914 (1991) by Clive Behagg.

Translation   The public school system in Victorian times (and for a long period into modern times as well) was based upon the study of classical languages and the translation from and into Ancient Greek and Latin. Generations of educated writers and thinkers throughout the nineteenth century accordingly took for granted both the cultural centrality of 'the classics', and the importance and relevance of translation. University presses at both Oxford and Cambridge published collections of translations of famous English poetry into Latin and Greek throughout the century, to great success; and the older tradition of composing poetry in these dead languages persisted. Neither was this seen as a peripheral or only scholarly matter. The lack of an adequate national translation of Homer was described in 1862 by John Reynolds as a subject 'of really national importance' (*Westminster Review* 77, 1862: 151), and the *London Quarterly Review* insisted that 'the subject of Homeric translation is one of national importance to a highly civilized country such as our own' ('Homer's Iliad in Translation', 1874: 375). This importance was allied with a new belief that translation be as literal as could be managed: 'the old notion of translation,' announced John Conington, 'that which aims at substituting a pleasing English poem for an admired original – has been well nigh abandoned' (*Quarterly Review* 110, 1861: 93–4). In place of the distinctively eighteenth-century timbre of, for instance, Pope's Homer, Victorian culture produced works such as Browning's 'transcriptions' of Aeschylus's *Agamemnon* (1877) and Euripides' *Herakles* (1875) – 'literal,' Browning boasted, 'at every cost save actual violence to the language'. David Masson in 1851 had linked 'literalness' to moral character with striking but not unusual vehemence:

> Not the slightest deviation from the ipissima verba [the words themselves] of the original text ought, by rule, to be permitted. We cannot insist too strongly upon this. To us what are called free translations are an abomination. So-called 'freedom' of translation we regard as in most cases proceeding from nothing else but a defect of conscientiousness, a weakness of moral principle.

> (Masson, 1851: 261)

The most famous intervention into this lively and ubiquitous debate came from Matthew ARNOLD, whose lectures 'On Translating Homer' (1861) discuss various renderings of the *Iliad* and *Odyssey* in terms not of literal accuracy, but in how well the various translators capture what he calls 'the Grand Style' of Homer himself.

The implications of this huge cultural fact, the primacy of translation in Victorian poetics, has yet to be properly explored by critics. It is of pressing interest from at least two perspectives; one is the development of an acute sense of mediation in verse, the awareness of language as one code among many, that a habituation to translation develops in the poetic consciousness; the other is the way this potent tradition of schooling surreptitiously inculcated a belief in English itself as inferior. Ruskin's advice to translators of the Bible in *Fors Clavigera* (1873), for instance, betrays his belief that, compared to Greek, English is 'vulgar':

> you must learn to make a translation retaining as many as possible of the words in their Greek form, which you may easily learn, and yet which will be quit of the danger of being debased by any vulgar English use.

> Ruskin, *Works*, Vol. 27: 490)

Transportation: railways   The rise of the railways has been taken by some commentators as being the most representative emblem of the Victorian period as a whole. From not existing at all in the earliest years of the century the railway network grew rapidly over a few decades, transforming the speed and convenience of travel by the 1850s and 1860s, as well as materially altering the landscape. It is as a confluence of classically Victorian tropes that the railways have the greatest resonance: the application of new TECHNOLOGIES of metallurgy and steam; the large-scale engineering works involved in laying track and building such marvels as the Menai and Forth Bridges (1849 and 1890), the rapid cultural change involved, and an underlining brutality in the forms of death and injury that sometimes attended the railways (something often focused on by writers) – all these function eloquently as indices of their age.

James Watt (1736–1819) had brought the steam engine to industrial levels of efficiency by 1790, and George Stephenson (1781–1848) produced a working rail-running locomotive (to carry coals at the Killingworth mines, north of Newcastle) in 1814. The first commercial railway, also engineered by Stephenson, linked the northern English towns of Stockton and Darlington in 1825. The early years of the new technology were not auspicious. Stephenson's 'Rocket', a locomotive with a top speed of the then-unprecedented 28 mph, ran on the Manchester–Liverpool line from 1830. But a passenger alighting on the very first journey panicked to discover the machine still moving, ran stupidly onto the tracks and was fatally run over. Accounts of railways from the 1830s tend to stress the novelty of the transport. The great period of railway expansion was the 1840s. A number of companies were formed, important lines laid between cities and stations built. Isambard Kingdom Brunel was appointed chief engineer of the Great Western Railway company in March 1833, and constructed the line linking London to Bristol by 1844: impressive engineering achievements on the route included the viaducts at Hanwell and Chippenham, the Maidenhead Bridge, the Box Tunnel and Bristol Temple Meads Station. Many similar engineering feats were undertaken throughout the country. In 1849 John Ruskin described the new network of railway connection in heated terms, capturing both the sense of vigour and national health that the new transport implied, and also the underlying sense of threat.

> All along the iron veins that traverse the frame of our country, beat and flow the fiery pulses of its exertions, hotter and faster every hour. All vitality is concentrated throughout those throbbing arteries into the central cities; the country is passed over like a green sea by narrow bridges, and we are thrown back in continually closer crowds upon the city gates.
>
> (Ruskin, *Seven Lamps of Architecture*)

Through the remainder of the century, railway use and consequent development increased enormously. In 1845, 33,391,253 journeys were taken by train; over a mere four years this number doubled, and by 1880 it had risen to 587,230,641 (Newsome, 1997: 30). Dickens' *Dombey and Son* (1846–8) is the one Victorian novel that captures the sense of the physical and cultural changes that this 'railwayisation' of Britain involved.

Transportation: roads Prior to the nineteenth century road technology had changed little (and in some respects had declined) since Roman times. Most British roads were dirt trails; a few were paved or cobbled, although this was an expensive process and such road surfaces were usually restricted to major towns. The eighteenth-century establishment, by act of Parliament, of turnpike trusts had been designed to remedy the situation. Turnpikes were toll gates, users of the turnpike being charged a fee that was supposed to go towards road improvement and maintenance. But many turnpike trusts were inept, or corrupt, and relatively few roads were being properly engineered. Thomas Telford (1757–1834) did build a number of roads for turnpike trusts, and constructed a road from London to Holyhead in North Wales for the government. His roads had a stone base and were topped with gravel; they were expensive but better than previous roads.

The engineer John Loudon Macadam (1756–1836) was responsible for a revolution in road technology. His pamphlet, *Remarks on the Present System of Road-Making* (1822), advocated the creation of a smooth road surface by laying down layers of stone broken into pieces of similar sizes, each layer being bedded down by the pressure of traffic over it before the laying of another layer. Macadam himself opposed the use of sand or gravel as a binding agent and the use of heavy rollers to settle the stones, although these practices are now thought of as part of macadamising. The use of tar as a matrix for the broken stones – which is to say the use of 'tarmacadam' or 'tarmac' as a road surface – is a later development, emerging in the 1870s and 1880s.

But the macadamisation of the nation's road networks proceeded only slowly. Even by 1860 the general state of the roads was very poor. 'How comes it?' asked *Chambers's Journal* in 1859

> that our roads are cut up everywhere into ruts, and the surface is here and there sinking below the level? – for which the existing remedy is to lay on cart-loads of metal [i.e. broken stones] at a great outlay, and to the detriment of horses and conveyances. Why are the roads in wet weather covered with mud, which must be scraped off and carted away at great expense?

> ('Road Draining', *Chambers's Journal*, 1859: 288)

Macadamised roads were (and are) hard on horses' hooves, and for many Victorians this practice was not as desirable as a properly drained mud or gravel road.

The expense of turnpike roads, and the often poor quality of those roads, led to much bad feeling, especially in rural areas. The so-called Rebecca Riots between 1839 and 1844 involved disaffected countrymen, sometimes dressed in women's clothing as disguise, attacking and destroying turnpike toll gates. In 1844 the Turnpike Act was passed, bringing all the turnpike trusts under consolidated control.

Travel literature   The Victorian period was the first golden age of books about travel to other countries: the advances in forms of TRANSPORTATION, the expansion of EMPIRE, and a burgeoning cultural interest in foreign lands and cultures provided a market for a great many works of travel literature. Frances Trollope (1780–1863) enjoyed success with her critical account of America, *Domestic Manners of the Americans* (1832); George Borrow lived amongst Gypsy communities before writing a number of books based on his experience, including *The Zincali, or an account of the Gipsies in Spain* (1841). DICKENS published two travel books: *Pictures of Italy* (1846) and *American Notes* (1842), the latter an account of one of his reading tours around North America.

Some of the biggest commercial successes in the genre were enjoyed by two travellers into lands previously unknown to Europeans, or 'explorers'. Richard Burton (1821–90) travelled to the forbidden city of Mecca, avoiding death by disguising himself effectively as a Muslim pilgrim. His account of his adventures, *Personal Narrative of a Pilgrimage to El-Medinah and Meccah* (1855–6), was a great success. Burton spent much of the rest of his life travelling, through Africa and both Americas, and published over 40 books of his experiences. The most famous explorer of the age was the Scot David Livingstone (1813–73), who travelled widely in central and southern Africa. He was the first white man to encounter several natural features of this continent already well known to the locals (which is to say, the first to 'discover' these places), amongst them Lake Ngami, Lake Nyasa and the Victoria Falls. He published *Missionary Travels and Researches in South Africa* (1857) and *Narrative of an Expedition to the Zambesi and its Tributaries and the discovery of the Lakes of Sharwa and Nyassa* (1865).

Robert Louis STEVENSON was a dedicated traveller in more familiar lands, and wrote a number of evocative and entertaining travel books, including: *An Inland Voyage* (of a journey round Belgium and France by canoe) in 1878; *Travels with a Donkey in the Cevennes* (1879), and his account of California, *The Silverado Squatters* (1883). Charles Doughty (1843–1926) travelled in the Middle East 1876–8, and wrote a bizarre but beautiful account of his time in *Travels in Arabia Deserta* (1888); the work is mostly famous now for its eccentric prose style, deliberately archaic and Elizabethan, but the atmosphere of the Arabian peninsula is vividly evoked (T.E. Lawrence admired the book, and wrote an introduction for the 1921 re-issue).

Trollope, Anthony (1812–1882)   The prolific Victorian novelist was born in London. His childhood was overshadowed by family financial difficulties, on account of his father's failure as lawyer, and later as a farmer. After schooling in Harrow and Winchester, Trollope's family moved to Belgium, where the cost of living was cheaper; his father died there and his mother Frances Trollope (1780–1863) did her best to support the family with her own writing career. Trollope himself returned to London to take a job in the General Post Office as a junior clerk in 1834, later transferring to the Post Office in Ireland in 1841. His autobiography (written 1875–6 but only published after his death in 1883) records that this move coincided with career advancement and a new degree of personal happiness. He married Rose Heseltine there in 1844, and his first novel, *The Macdermots of Ballycloran* (1847), was an Irish tale. From then on he combined two careers: rising through the ranks of the Post Office to a senior position (he was responsible for introducing pillar boxes for posting letters to Britain), but also writing and publishing novels in a regular stream, 47 in all. He was able to combine these two careers by adhering to a strict routine. He paid a servant to rouse him at five in the morning, and then wrote for a set number of hours; when he reached the end of this period of time he stopped writing, even if he were in the middle of a sentence, and went off to his Post Office job. His pastimes were dominated by hunting-at-hounds, which he pursued with a near-fanaticism. He was also something of a politics junkie; after finally resigning from the Post Office in 1867 he stood, unsuccessfully, for Parliament as a Liberal candidate in the 1868 election. He edited the *St Paul's Magazine* from 1867 until 1870.

He is best known for two *romans-fleuves*, or series of interlinked works. The first of these is the 'Barchester' sequence, six novels beginning with *The Warden* (1855) and including *Barchester Towers* (1857), *Doctor Thorne* (1858), *Framley Parsonage* (1861), *The Small House at Allington* (1864) and *The Last Chronicles of Barset* (1867). Not originally planned as a sequence, Trollope returned to his imaginary English location of 'Barsetshire' many times with a genuine affection for the place and people, pioneering the novel-sequence in English. As well as a great many stand-alone novels, he also published six interlinked political novels that trace the parliamentary career of Plantagenet Palliser, an aristocratic GENTLEMAN of honourable and Liberal instincts, who becomes ennobled to the PEERAGE as the Duke of Omnium and is eventually made Prime Minister. His story, and a number of connected narratives, make up *Can You Forgive Her?* (1864), *Phineas Finn: the Irish Member* (1869), *The Eustace Diamonds* (1873), *Phineas Redux* (1876), *The Prime Minister* (1876) and *The Duke's Children* (1880). These 'Palliser' novels are, for many critics, Trollope's most interesting work, providing *inter alia* a densely worked flavour of political life in the later century. On the other hand, it misrepresents Trollope to see him as a 'political' novelist: the main engine in all his fiction, almost without exception, is a DOMESTIC-fictive fascination with love-leading-to-marriage. As he put it in his own autobiography, 'very much of a novelist's work must appertain to the intercourse between young men and young women. It is admitted that a novel can hardly be made interesting or successful without love' (Trollope (1875–6) 1999: 138). Even in the Palliser books, political affairs are secondary to the love stories. For some readers this means that Trollope's weighty oeuvre lacks heft when taken as a whole; it tends towards the predictable and the comfortable.

J. Hillis Miller argues that the heart of Trollope's fiction is 'the idea that a man's substance is his love for another person', and that 'falling in love is a spontaneous commitment of one self to another, a commitment in which the person comes into existence as himself once and for all' (Miller, 1981: 129). This 'love' ethic, however, only exists in a rigorously drawn context of Victorian bourgeois family life. The chief interest in the books is 'who will marry whom?'; such that the question posed by the novel *Can You Forgive Her?* refers to a female character's jilting of one man's proposal of marriage for another. A more positive perspective on this feature of his work would be that his sense of character is more sophisticated than that of many of his contemporaries. Stephen Wall points out that the effective source of authorial energy [in Trollope's novels] is not the impulse to make public statements, but the private desire to know his characters – those characters which the *Autobiography* insists the novelist must live with 'in the full reality of established intimacy'.

(Wall, 1988: 388)

Unitarianism   A Unitarian believes that the Christian Godhead is singular rather than tripartite. In place of the Trinitarian God of three aspects as Father, Son and Holy Spirit, Unitarians believe God to be one, and Jesus Christ to be no more than a human (though exalted) agent of God's. This belief goes back to the earliest days of Christianity itself, but modern Unitarianism is traced to a sect founded in Italy in the sixteenth century by two Italian Protestants, Laelius Socinus (1525–62) and his nephew Faustus Socinus (1539–1604). Accordingly Unitarians were sometimes called 'Socinians' by those hostile to their views. In the nineteenth century the Established Church of England was firmly Trinitarian and the Unitarian Church constituted one of the dominant 'dissenting' Protestant movements. Although the established Church sometimes expressed suspicion of Unitarianism (*Blackwoods Magazine* talked darkly of a 'clandestine plan to Socinianize the church' (Vol. 51, 1842: 166)), in general Unitarianism was one of the more respectable dissenting varieties of Protestant faith. Mrs GASKELL was a Unitarian, the wife of a Unitarian minister. DICKENS came close to Unitarian belief in the 1840s under the influence of Mr Edward Tagart, a Unitarian minister, although after a few years his faith settled back into broad-church Anglican currents. One reason why Dickens was drawn to Unitarianism is that it was associated in the nineteenth century with a practical and philanthropic practice. Victorian Unitarianism was also much less doctrinaire than mainstream Christianity; it did not espouse elaborate church rituals or a complicated church hierarchy, it did not tell its followers exactly what to believe, and it did not seek to advance to power or glory of its own doctrine.

Utilitarianism   John Stuart MILL found the word 'utilitarian' in a novel by John Galt (1779–1839) called *Annals of the Parish* (1821) and popularised it as a shorthand term for the ethical philosophy that had been developed largely by Mill's mentor Jeremy

Bentham (1748–1832) and continued by Mill himself. Bentham had published a number of books relating to law, politics and ethics, including *Introduction to Principles of Morals and Legislation* (1789). The 'principles' referred to in the titles were, roughly, that human beings should be treated as rational creatures who seek pleasure and avoid pain; and that the duty of government was to maximise the former and minimise the latter for the largest number: in Bentham's famous formulation 'the greatest happiness of the greatest number is the foundation of morals and legislation' (Partington, 1992: 64). Mill's influential interpretation of Bentham's philosophy shifted the 'principle' to usefulness – utility – partly in order to avoid the sense that Benthamism was a merely hedonistic or pleasure-seeking code ('to suppose that life has ... no higher end than pleasure' Mill conceded in 1861, is 'a doctrine worthy only of swine' (Mill, 1987: 278)). In fact, according to Mill, 'useful' knowledge was the only kind worth having, 'useful' ends were the only ones that a government could legitimately pursue. It seems a little odd to us, perhaps, that he was able to conflate this stern-sounding principle (satirised by the 'Facts! Facts! Facts!' educational establishment of DICKENS' anti-Utilitarian novel *Hard Times*, 1854) with the much less dutiful-sounding concept of 'happiness'; but this was precisely the equation at the heart of Mill's thinking.

> Utility, or the Greatest Happiness Principle, holds that actions are right in proportion as they tend to promote happiness, wrong as they tend to produce the reverse of happiness. By happiness is intended pleasure, and by unhappiness, pain.

> (Mill, 1987: 278)

That the serious, intellectual and rather dry Mill possessed a different sense of 'happiness' to many people has been held by some to be a flaw in his system. Nevertheless, Mill's writings on utilitarianism, particularly three articles on the subject he published in *Fraser's Magazine* in 1861 (published in one volume in 1863), constitute one of the most influential interventions into ethical philosophy of the century. The Cambridge philosopher Henry Sidgwick (1838–1900) elaborated the basic insights of Mill's *Utilitarianism* in *The Method of Ethics* (1874), in which he argues that the injunction to promote universal happiness should be considered a fundamental ethical obligation, with specific moral rules and legal codes expressing this underlying obligation.

Further reading

Utilitarianism, and Other Essays by John Stuart Mill and Jeremy Bentham (edited by Alan Ryan 1987).

Victoria   Victoria was born on 24 May 1819, the only daughter of Edward, Duke of Kent, and the Princess Victoria of Saxe-Coburg-Saalfeld. Her father died in 1820, and when her uncle William IV died without a direct heir on 20 June 1837, she succeeded to the throne. Her coronation took place on 28 June 1838. She married a distant relative, the handsome and polite German Albert of Saxe-Coburg-Gotha, on 10 February 1840; her love for him, and his for her, was pronounced. She had nine children. The first, Princess Victoria, the Princess Royal, was born on 21 November 1840; she went on to marry (in 1858) Prince Frederick of Prussia, who later became German Kaiser (Frederick III). She died a few months after her mother, 5 August 1901. Victoria's second child was Prince Albert Edward, Prince of Wales, born on 9 November 1841, who acceded to the throne as King Edward VII on his mother's death in 1901. He died in 1910. Subsequent children (in order) were: Princess Alice (born 25 April 1843, died 14 December 1878); Prince Alfred, Duke of Edinburgh (born 6 August 1844, died 30 July 1900); Princess Helena (born 25 May 1846, died 9 June 1923); Princess Louise (born 18 March 1848, died 3 December 1939); Prince Arthur, Duke of Connaught and Strathearn (born 1 May 1850, died 16 January 1942); Prince Leopold, Duke of Albany (born 7 April 1853, died 28 March 1884); Princess Beatrice (born 14 April 1857, died 26 October 1944). Apart from Alfred, who married Russian royalty, all these children married either German or British nobility.

This imposing list of offspring draws out a key feature of Victoria, as monarch and individual: her devotion to what she saw as her domestic duty. 'They say,' she wrote to her uncle Leopold in 1844, '*no* Sovereign was *more loved* than I am (I am bold enough to say), and *that*, from our *happy domestic home* – which gives such a good example.' Representations of the Queen mediated her official role as authority figure, monarch and head of state, with her domestic role as wife and mother, subordinate to her husband. Albert's foreign-ness, and his willingness to become involved in certain issues of the day, created a low level of hostility towards him, but his unstinting dedication to the domestic ideal eventually endeared him to the public.

Albert died on 14 December 1861, and Victoria's grief was so great that she came near to absolute collapse. For a while her uncle Leopold, the Belgian royal, exercised royal duties, and although Victoria resumed the throne she withdrew from as much of her public life as she could. Her friendship with John Brown, a gillie from Balmoral, began in 1864. The two became so close that some referred satirically to Victoria as 'Mrs Brown', although it seems unlikely that their relationship was sexual (Brown died in 1883). Through the 1860s and the first half of the 1870s Victoria's absence from public life was so complete as to erode her popularity. DISRAELI helped draw her back into the public spotlight to a certain extent. It was his idea to proclaim her Empress of India (1 May 1876), and by 1887 with the celebration of her Golden Jubilee the public was again enthusiastically pro-Victoria. Celebrations for the Diamond Jubilee in 1897 were even more widespread, and at her death (on 22 January 1901) she was unanimously seen as having been synonymous with the values and characteristics of her time. She is buried with Albert in Frogmore, a chapel in the grounds of Windsor Castle.

Further reading

Queen Victoria: Born to Succeed (1964) by Elizabeth Longford; *Royal Representations: Queen Victoria and British Culture 1837–1876* (1998) by Margaret Homans.

War of the Worlds, The (1897), by H.G. Wells   Wells' famous and enduring novel of invasion by extraterrestrial beings was originally serialised in *Pearson's Magazine* between April and December 1897, and issued in one volume at the end of the year. The effectiveness of this novel depends in the first instance upon Wells' skilful balancing of the ordinary and extraordinary. He takes a perfectly ordinary man, an especially ordinary place, Woking, and then he imagines the extraordinary erupting into it – a giant cylinder crashing to Earth from Mars; tentacled Martians climbing out and making war upon humanity from towering mechanical tripods, laying waste to the south-east of England before eventually succumbing to earthly bacteria against which they possess no natural defence, and dying. This is rendered all the more effective by Wells' impeccable sense of the interlinked beauties of the familiar and the strange. The early chapters of the book build an understated but brilliant sense of anticipation by stressing that very ordinariness.

> There were lights in the upper windows of the houses as the people went to bed. From the railway station in the distance came the sound of shunting trains, ringing and rumbling, softened almost to melody by the distance. . . . It seemed so safe and tranquil.

> (Wells, *War of the Worlds*: 189)

The same sort of poetry that Wells can find in the evening shuntings of trains at Woking, is evoked in the desolate beauty he evokes in a London emptied by the

Martian threat and over-run with the red weed they have brought across space. At this point in the book the last Martian is ceasing his weird call and dying.

> Abruptly as I crossed the bridge, the sound of 'Ulla, ulla, ulla, ulla' ceased. It was, as it were, cut off. The silence came like a thunder-clap.

> The dusky houses about me stood faint and tall and dim; the trees towards the park were growing black. All about me the red weed clambered among the ruins, writhing to get above me in the dimness. Night, the mother of fear and mystery was coming upon me. But while that voice sounded the solitude, the desolation, had been endurable; by virtue of it, London had still seemed alive, and the sense of life about me had upheld me. Then suddenly a change, the passing of something – I knew not what – and then a stillness that could be felt.

> (Wells, *War of the Worlds*: 309–10)

Wells' potently imagined novella symbolically distils the concerns of the age, published, as it was, during Victoria's Diamond Jubilee. His Martians are Imperialists with superior technology, invading a nation, England, which had been accumulating its own Empire in part because of a superior technological sophistication. In other words, the novel is not a narrow mapping of Imperialist anxieties onto a symbolic form, but rather a complex symbolic meditation of the paradoxes of Imperialist ideology.

Wells, Herbert George (H.G.) (1866–1946)   Born in Bromley (then Kent, now south-east London) into a lower-middle-class family. His father was a professional cricketer and unsuccessful tradesman; his mother was a housekeeper in an aristocratic Kentish country house, Uppark (a period of his life fictionalised brilliantly by Wells in *Tono-Bungay*, 1909). Young Wells was put into lower-middle-class career path, first as apprentice to a pharmacist, then as a draper's assistant. He escaped the dullness of this life by his own efforts, becoming assistant teacher at a grammar school in Midhurst, Kent. Largely autodidactic, studying at night, Wells won a scholarship in 1884 to study science in the Normal School, South Kensingston, where he heard lectures by Darwin's apostle, T.H. Huxley (1825–95). Inspired by the Darwinian view of the cosmos (which is crucially important to his writing), Wells went on to work as a teacher, although various health breakdowns put an end to this career. He started writing journalism and fiction in the 1880s. He married in 1891, but ran off with another woman a few years later, marrying for a second time in 1895.

Wells' literary career stretches, enormously, to the middle of the twentieth century; for a while in the 1930s he was, perhaps, one of the most famous 'sages', writers and thinkers, in the world, the author of conventional fiction, fantastic fiction, history, polemics, essays and much else. Although his Victorian writing career is only a small proportion of this whole, it represents his most significant and most lasting work. Above all, it is in the last five years of the nineteenth century that Wells wrote his most enduring and influential SCIENCE FICTION works. The first was *The Time Machine* (1895), in which an unnamed Victorian scientist uses his time machine to travel to the year 802,701 to discover that mankind has 'degenerated' into two races, the infantile Eloi on the surface and the monstrous, Eloi-devouring Morlocks in their subterranean caverns. This short novel remains one of the most powerful works in all science fiction, engaging on its own terms, but working also as a symbolic commentary upon the ineffectual aristocracy and the increasingly buried industrial working class of Wells' own day. In *The Island of Doctor Moreau* (1896) another scientist has practised painful vivisection on animals to create, Frankenstein-like, a race of semi-sentient beings; although their violent impulses cannot be restrained for long. The scientist in *The Invisible Man* (1897), whose title is self-explanatory, is a thoroughly unpleasant individual who tries to use his transparency to rob and cheat. *The War of the Worlds* (1898), in which alien Martians invade Earth, is his most all-round accomplished work. *The First Men in the Moon* (1901) imagines a spaceship built from an anti-gravity metal that flies to the moon, and the strange world its two occupants discover. As John Sutherland puts it, 'only a small portion of Wells' prodigious literary activity is located in the Victorian era. But it represents an achievement equivalent to the whole literary career of lesser authors' (Sutherland, 1988: 350)

Westminster Review   A journal founded by John Stuart Mill in 1824 specifically as an organ for writers of radical and liberal political affiliation, to counter the dominance of the two great serious periodicals, the Tory *Quarterly Review* and the Whig *Edinburgh Review*. These more highbrow quarterly journals, priced expensively at 6/-, contained lengthy review-articles by the eminent writers of the day. For much of the century (1851–94) it was edited by John Chapman (1821–94), who published George Eliot (who was assistant editor for a while in the 1850s), James Froude (1818–94), Walter Pater and others.

Whig   By the middle of the century this political descriptor had largely been superseded by Liberal, except as an term with archaic flavour. The original seventeenth- and eighteenth-century Whigs (opposed to the original Tories) had opposed the accession to the throne of James III on account of his conversion to Catholicism, and the term was sometimes used as a religiously significant political term: Disraeli's fictional Coningsby, for instance, declares 'I look upon an Orangeman [an Ulster Protestant] . . . as a pure Whig' (Disraeli, *Coningsby*, 1844, Vol. 6, Chapter 3). Mid-century Liberals might use the term 'whig' to indicate an old-fashioned, nostalgic or 'conservative' Liberalism. By the 1880s it was merely a historical term.

Widowhood   From Queen Victoria (after 1861) down, the Victorian age was filled with widows. Relatively high mortality rates for the period meant that nearly 20 per cent of marriages contracted in the 1850s had been broken by the death of one or other party within ten years. Pat Jalland points out that 'the majority of these widowed people were women, because of the mortality differential favouring women and the higher rates of remarriage for married men' (Jalland, 1996: 230). There were, approximately, twice as many widows as widowers. In a culture in which female status was largely tied to marriage, the death of a husband could leave a woman in a precarious position: status and income lost at a stroke. The conventions of mourning-dress were, to modern eyes, extremely strict. A widow was expected to wear nothing but black for the first two years of bereavement; a non-reflective black cloth such as paramatta and crape for the first year (during which time she was not allowed to accept invitations to social engagements); then for nine months the widow could wear black silk, trimmed with crape, and then three months in which the crape could be discarded. After this lengthy period a widow was permitted to change into the colours of half-mourning (grey, lavender or black and white) for six months.

Wilde, Oscar (1854–1900)   Wilde was born in Dublin, the son of an Irish Protestant doctor (his full name attests to his Irishness: Oscar Fingal Flahertie Wills Wilde). He studied at Trinity College, Dublin, and afterwards read classics at Magdalen, Oxford, where he won the Newgate prize for his poem 'Ravenna'. Tutors admired his prodigious scholarly talents, but despaired of his insouciant, apparently lazy, personal manner. Yet, as we now know, Wilde's personal style – witty, debonair, provocative and brilliant – was as significant a work as any of his writing. His witticisms have greater currency today than anything he wrote: 'I have nothing to declare but my genius' (at a custom house in New York); 'Work is the curse of the drinking classes'; 'ah well then, I suppose I shall have to die beyond my means' (on hearing of a large medical fee near the end of his life). He declared himself a disciple of PATER, a DECADENT in art, and practised what he preached. He married in 1884, and wrote a brilliant CHILDREN's story, *The Happy Prince and Other Tales* (1888), for his two sons. He wrote poetry more when younger, and some of these verses (collected in *Poems*, 1892) seem egregiously fin-de-siècle today:

> Against these turbid turquoise skies
> The light and luminous balloons
> Dip and drift like satin moons,
> Drift like silken butterflies

> ('Fantaisies Décoratives: les Ballons')

But his heartfelt *Ballad of Reading Gaol* (1897, written after his time in prison) retains its power today.

Wilde's greatest achievements in literature were theatrical. Although his first play, *Vera* (performed New York 1883), was not a success, later dramas became immensely celebrated for their polish, wit and bite. *Lady Windermere's Fan* (1892), *A Woman of No Importance* (1893) and *The IMPORTANCE OF BEING EARNEST* (1895) are all masterpieces, and breathed a new, sparkling life into the more lumpish traditions of British nine-teenth-century DRAMA. His decadent, openly sexual and rather morbid play *Salomé*, written in French, was refused a licence for British performance (although it was staged in Paris in 1896, and turned into an opera by Richard Strauss). *Salomé* was translated into English by Lord Alfred Douglas (1870–1945), the eldest son of the Marquess of Queensberry, a beautiful young man who had become Wilde's intimate friend. Aubrey Beardsley (1872–98) drew some striking illustrations for this edition. Wilde's prose also included some major achievements, notably the short novel *The Picture of Dorian Grey* (1890), in which the titular character remains unnaturally young whilst his portrait, hidden in an attic, ages and decays with sin. His essay 'The Soul of Man Under Socialism' (1891), pleading for individual liberty and artistic free-dom, was written after hearing SHAW speak about socialist ideals.

Wilde's bisexuality caused a certain degree of scandal, although this was a discrete matter until the choleric Marquess of Queensberry took angry offence to Wilde's friendship with his son, Lord Alfred Douglas. He handed Wilde a card calling him a 'sodomite', and Wilde – imprudently, as it turned out – sued him for libel. At the libel trial Queensberry was acquitted after evidence of Wilde's homosexual practices was brought before the court; and afterwards Wilde was prosecuted for homosexuality (still illegal in Britain at this time). Eventually he was convicted, and sent to prison with hard labour in 1895, an unusually degrading punishment for a man of Wilde's class and unfamiliarity with hard work. After two years Wilde was released, but he was a broken man. He left Britain never to return, living in France, sometimes under the assumed name Sebastian Melmoth ('Sebastian' from the beautiful youth cruelly mar-tyred by arrows – in reference to the arrows on Wilde's prison uniform – and 'Melmoth' after Charles Maturin's (1782–1824) GOTHIC romance of exile *Melmoth the Wanderer*, 1820). He died in Paris in 1900.

For many years Wilde's genius was obscured by the scandal of his last years; and then, obscured in a different manner by the enthusiastic adoption of Wilde as an iconic figure, a sort of Gay Christ persecuted to death for his sexuality by a puritani-cal establishment. This 'hero' Wilde played a valuable role in various movements for gay liberation in the latter decades of the twentieth century, but tends to misrepresent Wilde's own work – which, generally, is rather unconcerned with sex and sexuality as such, and much more interested in 'beauty', conceived not as erotically male or eroti-cally female but as a universal principle that dissolves all such categories.

Work   Work represents one of the most interesting problematics of nineteenth-cen-tury society. It was a widely held belief during the period that work ennobled and structured life, with various forms of employment being acceptable for men, and women expected to 'work' in the domestic sphere, managing a home and raising chil-dren. But a significant proportion of Victorians did no work at all, and for those with wealth a life of leisure was a perfectly respectable and desirable state of affairs. At the other end of the scale, most working-class women were compelled to take jobs by necessity, and for many workers work was neither ennobling nor dignified, but grinding, demeaning, relentless and poorly paid.

In other words a divide that can be thought of as ideological runs through the middle of Victorian culture. On the one hand there was what might be thought of as the school of Thomas CARLYLE, the Victorian sage most committed to a gospel of work: 'produce! Produce!' he exhorted in *Sartor Resartus* (1834), 'were it but the pitifullest infinitesimal fraction of a product, produce it in God's name! 'Tis the utmost thou hast in thee: out with it, then' (Book 2, Chapter 9). RUSKIN, another of the great Victorian sages, agreed with this gospel: 'life without industry is guilt,' he declared in 1870 (*Lectures on Art*, Vol. 3: 95), although he also understood that work in the Victorian world was intimately tied to class. 'Which of us . . .,' he asked in *Sesames and Lilies* (1865: 77) 'is to do the hard and dirty work for the rest – and for what pay? Who is to do the pleasant and clean work, and for what pay?'

For many Victorians, work was a necessary discipline. Matthew ARNOLD had the money to live an idle life had he so wanted; but he deliberately chose labour, doing arduous work as a Government Inspector of Schools, a job that involved a great deal of travelling, and that contributed directly to his early death. Charles Dickens was another Victorian whose punishing personal routine of work killed him early, and in Dickens' novels the idle are almost always portrayed negatively, especially if (like Harold Skimpole in *Bleak House*, 1852–3) their idleness depends upon the explicit or tacit exploitation of the labour of others. Dickens' heroes are all honest workers, although they tend to labour at middle-class, respectable occupations such as medicine, enterprise, the law or education. A painting such as Ford Madox Brown's epic *Work* (1852–65) celebrates the beauty as well as the merit of labour. In the centre of the composition, six 'navvies', or labouring workmen, are digging up a London street to lay drainage. They are watched by two of the brain-workers whose labour is intellectual: the Reverend Frederick Maurice (1805–72), a CHRISTIAN SOCIALIST, and Thomas Carlyle, who is the chief intellectual inspiration for Brown's painting. Myriad examples of London life crowd around this central scene, giving a colourful and vivid sense of the diversity of Victorian work. The size of the canvas (two metres by nearly one and a half) and the extraordinary detail link subject and theme, for Brown worked lengthily and minutely at the composition over more than a decade, such that the painting embodies what it celebrates. William Bell Scott (1811–90), a friend of Brown's, produced a similar painting, entitled *Iron and Coal* (1861), celebrating Tyneside ironworkers.

It was not always easy maintaining a sincere belief in the dignity of labour, given that the bulk of workers in Victorian Britain endured hard, demeaning and health-destroying working conditions. Thomas Hood's (1799–1845) poem 'The Song of the Shirt' appeared in *Punch* (November 1843); it evokes the miserable conditions that seamstresses endured:

With fingers weary and worn,
With eyelids heavy and red,
A woman sat, in unwomanly rags,
Plying her needle and thread –
Stitch! stitch! stitch!
In poverty, hunger and dirt,
And still with a voice of dolorous pitch
She sang the 'Song of the Shirt'.
'Work! work! work!
While the cock is crowing aloof!'

SOCIALIST revolutionary Friedrich Engels (1820–95) disliked the popularity of this poem (he said it 'wrung many compassionate but ineffectual tears from the daughters of the bourgeoisie, *The Condition of the Working Class in England in 1844*), and later Marxist critics have expressed similar reservations about the popularity of 'Condition of England' or INDUSTRIAL novels such as Mrs GASKELL's *Mary Barton* (1848) or DICKENS' *Hard Times* (1854): although the genre represents the miserable grind of work for the lowest paid, it also avoids any systematic critique of the circumstances that brought about this miserable situation. Henry Mayhew's *London Labour and the London Poor* (1852–65) details the grinding, poorly remunerated work most people undertook.

On the other hand, and despite this near 'official' doctrine of work as a duty and a virtue, there is a persistent strain in Victorian culture in praise of idleness. In a letter to his friend Bernard Barton (11 September 1822), Charles Lamb (1775–1834) versified:

Who first invented work – and tied the free
And holy day rejoicing spirit down
To the ever-haunting importunity
Of business?

(Quoted in Harper, 1905: Vol. 4)

Idleness, because associated with aristocratic manners (which remained middle-class aspirations throughout the century) acquired a certain sparkle. The essays collected in Jerome K. Jerome's (1859–1927) *Idle Thoughts of an Idle Fellow* (1886) depend, for their wit and charm, upon an assumption of work as middle-class drudgery: 'it is impossible to enjoy idling thoroughly,' he declares in 'On Being Idle', 'unless one has plenty of work to do'. Oscar WILDE's epigram, inverting conventional pieties about proletarian delinquency, amuses us because it aligns us, the reader, with the idle rather than the laborious: 'Work is the curse of the drinking classes.' The seeds of twentieth- and twenty-first-century animadversion against work, and our thorough-going passion for 'labour-saving' and 'leisure', were laid in the Victorian period.

The following figures are derived from the 1851 census (*Parliamentary Papers* 88: 1852–3), and give a sense of the numbers of different sorts of workers. They include neither 'gentlemanly' occupations nor military careers.

	Men	Women
Total population	10,224,000	10,736,000
Population over ten years of age	7,616,000	8,155,000
Agricultural worker	1,563,000	227,000
Fisherman	37,000	1,000
Domestic servant	134,000	905,000
Coal-miner	216,000	3,000
Copper, tin, lead-miner	53,000	7000
Iron-miner	27,000	910
Building worker (incl. carpenter bricklayer, mason, plumber etc.	442,000	1,000
Blacksmith	112,000	592
Ironworker	79,000	590
Machine-maker, boiler-maker	63,000	647
Miller	37,000	562
Earthenware worker	25,000	11,000
Sawyer	35,000	23
Nailer	25,000	10,000
Unskilled labourer	367,000	9,000
Milliner, dressmakers, seamstress	494	340,000
Cotton workers, incl. printers/dyers	255,000	272,000
Tailor	135,000	18,000
Silk worker	53,000	80,000
Linen, flax-worker	47,000	56,000
Hosiery worker	35,000	30,000
Lace worker	10,000	54,000
Wool-worker	171,000	113,000
Shoemaker	243,000	31,000
Straw-plait worker	4,000	28,000
Glover	4,500	25,000
Tanner, currier	25,000	276
Washerwoman		145,000
Charwoman		55,000
Merchant seaman	144,000	
Shipwright, boat-builder	32,000	28
Carter, coach-driver, cabman	83,000	1,000
Worker on railways	65,000	54
Wheelwright	30,000	106
Baker	56,000	7000
Commercial clerk	44,000	19
Printer	22,000	222

***Wuthering Heights* (1847), Emily Brontë** Emily BRONTË's only novel was published under the pseudonym 'Ellis Bell' in 1847. Its plot is rather involved: Lockwood, the novel's narrator, has come to Yorkshire and is renting a house, Thrushcross Grange. He visits his near-neighbour, the surly and misanthropic Heathcliff who lives at Wuthering Heights. Curious as to the history of the man, Lockwood learns it from his housekeeper Nelly Dean. Nelly recalls the area 40 years earlier, when the Heights had been occupied by the Earnshaw family, and Thrushcross Grange had housed the genteel Linton family. One day Mr Earnshaw returned from a trip to Liverpool having adopted a homeless Gypsy boy, later called Heathcliff. Heathcliff grew up largely running wild on the moors in the company of Earnshaw's daughter Catherine; but on old Mr Earnshaw's death his son Hindley became head of the family and began persecuting Heathcliff, humiliating him at every chance and reducing him to the level of a menial in the house. Catherine, meanwhile, was taken in by the Lintons, and her manners were cultivated and raised. Heathcliff was in love with Catherine, but after overhearing her confide to Nelly that it would 'degrade' her to marry him, he ran away. Three years later he returned rich to find Catherine married to Edgar Linton, and Hindley widowed with a son, Hareton. Heathcliff, always a passionate and destructive individual, now unleashed a drawn-out process of revenge, wrecking the peace of the Heights and the Grange both. Catherine's true love was for Heathcliff all along, and not for her husband ('my love for Linton is like the foliage in the woods; time will change it, I'm well aware, as winter changes the trees – My love for Heathcliff resembles the eternal rocks beneath', Chapter 9), and Heathcliff knew this. But he married Isabella Linton, who had fallen in love with him. He did not love her, and indeed abused her cruelly. She bore his son, young Linton. Heathcliff, meanwhile, did his best to come between Catherine and her feeble husband, precipitating her death in childbirth; her daughter (also called Catherine, and known as 'Cathy' to distinguish her from her mother) survived the birth. Heathcliff wormed his way into Hindley's affections and manipulated the latter's hopeless addiction to gambling, eventually buying Wuthering Heights from him and becoming its master. He tried to further wreck the happiness of the Lintons by marrying his degenerate son, Linton, to Cathy, thereby securing the property rights to Thrushcross Grange as well. Young Linton was not hale, and he died leaving Cathy a widow; she was now virtually a prisoner in the Heights, and cultivated a friendship with young Hareton, who had been brutalised by Heathcliff's treatment of him, and whom she attempts to educate. The novel concludes with Heathcliff being haunted by the ghost of Catherine, his love, and of his own yearning for the death that will reunite them. After he does die, apparently of starvation, Cathy marries Hareton, uniting the Heights and the Grange.

The novel's quite astonishing popularity (John Sutherland (1988) aptly describes it as 'the twentieth century's favourite nineteenth-century novel') can only partly be explained by the passionate erotic-romantic gush of the central sections. Despite a certain gaucheness there is a truly remarkable, gnawing, tempestuous power in the book, centred on the near-demonic GOTHIC figure of Heathcliff himself, but spreading throughout the conception of the whole.

Year of Revolutions (1848)   Political and social revolutions occurred across the whole of Europe with remarkable vigour in this one year; a striking focus of popular dissatisfaction. Unrest gathered throughout the 1840s, as millions suffered the consequences of widespread economic depression and poor harvests. The French government banned a demonstration for electoral reform in Paris, on 22 February 1848, which led to riots and a spiral of violence, with the army deployed in the streets to break up barricades. News of Paris (22–24 February) spread through Europe: riots followed in Vienna (13 March), and in Milan, Venice and Berlin later in the month. Revolt spread across Germany and Austro-Hungary, and through the Italian states. The revolutionaries were composed of many discrete groups: dissatisfied middle classes, desperate proletarians, people hoping for constitutional reform, the abolition of serfdom (in eastern Europe), or socialists wanting a complete reorganisation of the state. Only Britain avoided the spread of revolutionary activity, for reasons that are not entirely clear: either the British working classes were more inertial, more conservative, or (as some historians have argued) the successes of CHARTISM had defused much of the popular discontent.

By the end of the year, armies had regained control in Germany and Austro-Hungary; in October as many as 5000 revolutionaries died in Vienna as troops retook the city. In France, elections were called and NAPOLEON III took power as popular President. By the 1850s the revolutionary impulse had largely been contained, although many of the resentments continued to ferment. MARX saw the Revolutions of 1848 as the 'first great battle' between 'the two classes that split modern society'.

Yellow Book, The   A beautifully produced periodical devoted to literature and art, *The Yellow Book* was short-lived (1894–7), but it was extremely influential as a repository for FIN-DE-SIÈCLE art and literature. Edited by Henry Harland (1861–1905), with the assistance of Aubrey Beardsley (1872–98) as art editor, it created a deal of scandal in its short life with its often DECADENT content and manifesto. Many major writers were published in the *Book*, including Henry James (1843–1916), Edmund Gosse

(1849–1928), Ernest Dowson (1867–1900) and Henry Max Beerbohm (1872–1956). In a sense, *The Yellow Book* looks forward to the Modernist 'little magazine', a self-consciously elite, avant-garde and deliberately shocking medium, as opposed to the 'yellow press' of mass-market newspapers like the *Daily Mail* or the *Pall-Mall Gazette*.

Young England   A subset of Tory political belief, formalised by DISRAELI in 1842. Initially the term meant, as Terence Jenkins points out, 'as far as Disraeli was concerned, simply that: a party of Conservative youth, without any specific commitment to a programme of social measures' (Jenkins, 1996: 20–1). But it quickly acquired specific ideological connotations, a colourful but reactionary affection for an imagined English past and a belief that rich and poor could best to reconciled to one another in the framework of traditional social structures. The closest the movement came to a specific manifesto is to be found in Disraeli's three novels *Coningsby* (1844), *Sybil* (1845) and *Tancred* (1847), in which idealistic heroes search for solutions to contemporary malaises. *Sybil*, for instance, contrasts the miserable state of many working-class people in the 1840s with a rose-tinted and sentimentalised vision of England in medieval times, when feudalism guaranteed stability and happiness to rich and poor alike. 'Young England' meant a dislike of the 1688 Whig 'glorious revolution' (dismissively known as the 'Dutch settlement'), of utilitarianism and industrialisation, and an active support for traditional loyalties and organisations, a sympathy towards the Anglo-Catholic drift of the Tractarians, and – more sentimentally – a fascination with the notion of medieval chivalry (John Sutherland suggests that the Young England 'Bible' was 'Digby's *The Broad Stone of Honour, or the True Sense and Practice of Chivalry* (1822)', Sutherland, 1988: 687). Disraeli's idealistic young aristocrat Coningsby yearns for a politics capable of 'appealing to high sentiments', which would 'render government an object of national affection, which would terminate sectional anomalies, assuage religious hearts and extinguish CHARTISM' (*Coningsby*, Book 7, Chapter 2). Always susceptible to charges of mere sentimentalism, not to say puerility, Young England had ceased to be a genuine political force by the later 1840s.

Bibliography

Adburgham, Alison, *Silver Fork Society: Fashionable life and literature from 1814 to 1840* (London: Constable 1983).

Allott, Miriam (ed.), *The Brontës: the Critical Heritage* (London: Routledge 1974).

Altick, Richard, *Victorian People and Ideas* (New York: Norton 1973).

Armstrong, Isobel, *Victorian Poetry: Poetry, Poetics and Politics* (London: Routledge 1993).

Arnold, Matthew, 'On Translating Homer', in R.H. Super (ed.), *Arnold on the Classical Tradition* (Ann Arbor: Harvard University Press 1960).

Arnold, Matthew, *Culture and Anarchy: an Essay in Political and Social Criticism* (ed. Samuel Lipman, commentary by Maurice Cowling, Gerald Graff, Samuel Lipman and Steven Marcus; Hew Haven: Yale University Press 1994).

Ashton, Rosemary, *G.H. Lewes: An Unconventional Victorian* (Oxford: Oxford University Press 1991).

Baker, J.H., *An Introduction to English Legal History* (3rd edn, London: Butterworths 1990).

Baldrick, Chris (ed.), *Gothic Tales* (Oxford: Oxford University Press 1992).

Beer, Gillian, *Darwin's Plots: Evolutionary Narrative in Darwin, George Eliot and Nineteenth-Century Fiction* (1983; London: Ark Paperbacks 1985).

Beeton, Isabella, *Mrs Beeton's Book of Household Management* (1859–61; ed. and abridged by Nicola Humble, Oxford: Oxford University Press 2000).

Behagg, Clive, *Labour and Reform: Working-Class Movements 1815–1914* (London 1991).

Belchem, John and Richard Price (eds), *The Penguin Dictionary of Nineteenth-Century History* (Harmondsworth: Penguin 1994).

Bloom, Harold, *The Ringers in the Tower: Studies in Romantic Tradition* (Chicago: University of Chicago Press 1971).

Bloom, Harold (ed.) *Thomas Carlyle: Modern Critical Views* (New York: Chelsea House Publishers, 1986).

Boehmer, Elleke, (ed.), *Empire Writing: an Anthology of Colonial Literature 1870–1918* (Oxford: Oxford University Press 1998).

Booth, Michael, *Theatre in the Victorian Age* (Cambridge: Cambridge University Press 1991).

Briggs, Asa, *Victorian Cities* (1963; Harmondsworth: Pelican 1968).

Briggs, Asa, *Victorian Things* (Harmondsworth: Penguin 1990).

Brooks, Peter, *The Melodramatic Imagination: Balzac, James, Melodrama and the Mode of Excess* (rev. edn, New Haven and London: Yale University Press 1995).

Brown, Richard, *Society and Economy in Modern Britain 1700–1850* (London: Routledge 1991).

Browning, Robert, *Poems* (ed. Adam Roberts and Daniel Karlin; Oxford: Oxford University Press, 'The Oxford Authors' series 1995).

Brumberg, Joan Jacobs, 'The Appetite as Voice', in Caroline Counihan and Penny Van Esterik (eds), *Food and Culture: a Reader* (London: Routledge 1997), 159–79.

Buckley, Matthew, 'Sensations of Celebrity: *Jack Sheppard* and the Mass Audience', *Victorian Studies* 44(3), 2002, 423–63.

Carlyle, Thomas, Sartor Resartus, ed. Kerry McSweeney and Peter Sabor (Oxford: Oxford University Press 1987).

Carlyle, Thomas, *Reminiscences* (1881, ed. Kenneth Fielding and Ian Campbell, Oxford University Press 1997).

Carroll, Lewis (Charles Dodgson), *Alice's Adventures in Wonderland and Through the Looking-Glass* (1865, 1871: ed. Hugh Haughton, 'The Centenary Edition', Harmondsworth: Penguin 1998).

Chambers, Robert, *Cyclopedia of English Literature. A History, Critical and Biographical, of British Authors from the Earliest to the Present Times* (two vols, London 1860).

Chase, Karen and Michael Levinson, 'On the Parapets of Privacy', in Herbert F. Tucker (ed.), *A Companion to Victorian Literature and Culture* (Oxford: Blackwell 1999), 425–37.

Claeys, Gregory, *Citizens and Saints: Politics and Anti-Politics in Early British Socialism* (Cambridge: Cambridge University Press 2002).

Clute, John and Peter Nicholls (eds), *Encyclopedia of Science Fiction* (2nd edn, London: Orbit 1993).

Cockshut, Arthur O.J., 'Faith and Doubt in the Victorian Age', in Arthur Pollard (ed.), *The Penguin History of Literature, Vol 6: the Victorians* (Harmondsworth: Penguin 1993), 25–49.

Connor, Steven (ed.), *The Adventures of Oliver Twist*, by Charles Dickens (London: Dent (Everyman) 1994).

Cosslett, Tess (ed.), *Victorian Women Poets* (London: Longman 1996).

Cowling, Maurice, *1867: Disraeli, Gladstone and Revolution: the Passing of the Second Reform Bill* (Cambridge: Cambridge University Press 1967).

Creaton, Victoria (ed.), *Victorian Diaries: the Daily Lives of Victorian Men and Women* (London: Mitchell Beazley 2001).

Cunningham, Valentine, *The Victorians: an Anthology of Poetry and Poetics* (Oxford: Blackwell 2000).

Curtis, L.P., *Apes and Angels: The Irishman in Victorian Caricature* (Newton Abbot: David and Charles 1971).

Darwin, Charles, *On The Origin of Species* (1859; ed. J.W. Burrow, Harmondsworth: Penguin 1985).

Desmond, Adrian and James Moore, *Darwin* (London: Michael Joseph 1991).

Dickens, Charles, *The Adventures of Oliver Twist* (ed. Steven Connor; London: Dent (Everyman) 1994).

Dickens, Charles, *The Christmas Books* (ed. Sally Ledger, London: Everyman 1999).

Doody, Margaret Anne, *The True Story of the Novel* (New Brunswick, New Jersey: Rutgers University Press 1996).

Eliot, Thomas Sternes, 'In Memoriam' (1936), in Frank Kermode (ed.) *Selected Prose of T.S. Eliot* (London: Faber 1987).

Epstein, James, and Dorothy Thompson (eds), *The Chartist Experience* (London: Macmillan 1982).

Faas, Ekbert, *Retreat into the Mind: Victorian Poetry and the Rise of Psychiatry* (Princeton, New Jersey: Princeton University Press 1988).

Feltes, Norman N., *Modes of Production of Victorian Novels* (Chicago: University of Chicago Press 1986).

Feuchtwanger, E.J., *Democracy and Empire: Britain 1865–1914* (London: Arnold 1985).

Fitzpatrick, David, 'Ireland and Empire', in Andrew Porter (ed.), *The Oxford History of the British Empire: Volume III, The Nineteenth-Century* (Oxford: Oxford University Press 1999), 494–521.

Flint, Kate, *The Woman Reader 1837–1914* (Oxford: Clarendon Press 1993).

Foucault, Michel, *The History of Sexuality: Volume 1, an Introduction* (1976; trans. Robert Hurley, Harmondsworth: Penguin 1990).

Francis, Emma, 'Is Emily Brontë a Woman?': Femininity, Feminism and the Paranoid Critical Subject', in Philip Shaw and Peter Stockwell (eds), *Subjectivity and Literature from the Romantics to the Present Day* (London: Pinter 1991).

Freud, Sigmund, 'A Difficulty in the Path of Psychoanalysis' in *Standard Edition of the Complete Psychological Works* ed. James Strachey (London: Hogarth Press 1953–6), Vol. 17.

Friedman. Albert, 'The Ballad' and 'Ballad Metre', in Alex Preminger, Frank Warnke and O.B. Hardison (eds), *The Princeton Encyclopedia of Poetry and Poetics* (enlarged edition; Princeton: Princeton University Press 1974).

Gallagher, Catherine, *The Industrial Reformation of English Fiction 1832–1867* (Chicago: University of Chicago Press 1985).

Gammond, Peter, *The Oxford Companion to Popular Music* (Oxford: Oxford University Press 1991).

Gash, Norman, *Aristocracy and People: Britain 1815–1865* (London: Arnold 1983).

Gérin, Winifred, *Emily Brontë* (Oxford: Clarendon 1971).

Gilmour, Robin, *The Victorian Period: the Intellectual and Cultural Context of English Literature 1830–1880* (Harlow: Longman 1993).

Goldman, Paul, *Victorian Illustrated Books 1850–1870; the Heyday of Wood-Engraving* (London: British Museum Press 1994).

Green-Lewis, Jennifer, *Framing the Victorians: Photography and the Culture of Realism* (Ithaca: Cornell University Press 1981).

Griest, Guinevere, *Mudie's Circulating Library and the Victorian Novel* (Bloomington: Indiana University Press 1970).

Gross, John, *The New Oxford Book of English Prose* (Oxford University Press 1998).

Haight, Gordon, *Selections from George Eliot's Letters* (New Haven: Yale University Press 1985).

Hamilton, Susan, *'Criminals, Idiots, Women and Minors': Victorian Writing by Women on Women* (Peterborough, Ontario: Broadview Press 1995).

Harker, Margaret, *Julia Margaret Cameron* (London: Collins 1983).

Harper, Henry (ed.), *The Letters of Charles Lamb* (1905).

Harper, Marjory, 'British Migration and the Peopling of the Empire', in Andrew Porter (ed.), *The Oxford History of the British Empire: Vol III, the Nineteenth Century* (Oxford: Oxford University Press 1999), 75-87.

Hayes, Carlton J.H., *A Generation of Materialism, 1871–1900* (New York: Harper and Row 1963).

Heffer, Simon, *Moral Desperado: A Life of Thomas Carlyle* (London: Weidenfeld and Nicolson 1995).

Hennock, E.P., 'Philanthropy', in John Belchem and Richard Price (eds), *The Penguin Dictionary of Nineteenth-Century History* (Harmondsworth: Penguin 1994), 468–70.

Hilton, Boyd, *Corn, Cash and Commerce: the Economic Policies of the Tory Government 1815–1830* (Oxford: Oxford University Press 1977).

Hilton, Tim, *John Ruskin* (two vols, New Haven: Yale University Press 1985–2000).

Himmelfarb, Gertrude, *The Idea of Poverty: England in the Early Industrial Age* (New York: Alfred A. Knopf 1984).

Hinde, Wendy, *Catholic Emancipation: A Shake to Men's Minds* (Oxford: Oxford University Press 1992).

Hollingsworth, Keith, *The Newgate Novel, 1830–1847. Bulwer, Ainsworth, Dickens and Thackeray* (Detroit: Wayne State University Press 1963).

Homans, Margaret, *Royal Representations: Queen Victoria and British Culture 1837–1876* (Chicago: University of Chicago Press 1998).

Horn, Pamela, *Pleasures and Pastimes in Victorian Britain* (Stroud: Sutton 1999).

Horsman, Alan, *The Victorian Novel* (Oxford: Clarendon Press 1990).

Hughes, Linda, '1870' in Herbert Tucker (ed.), *A Companion to Victorian Literature and Culture* (Oxford: Blackwell 1999), 35–50.

Hughes, Linda and Michael Lund, *The Victorian Serial* (Charlottesville: University Press of Virginia 1991).

Hunt, John Dixon, *The Pre-Raphaelite Imagination: 1848–1900* (London: Routledge 1968).

Hunt, Leigh and S. Adams Lee (eds), *The Book of the Sonnet* (Boston, Mass.: Roberts Brothers 1867).

Irvine, William and Park Honan, *The Book, the Ring and the Poet: a Biography of Robert Browning* (London: Bodley Head 1974).

Jack, Ian and Robert Inglesfield (eds), *Men and Women. The Poetical Works of Robert Browning Volume 5* (Oxford: Oxford University Press 1995).

Jalland, Pat, *Death in the Victorian Family* (Oxford: Oxford University Press 1996).

James, Lawrence, *Raj: the Making and Unmaking of British India* (London: Abacus 1997).

Janowitz, Anne, *Lyric and Labour in the Romantic Tradition* (Cambridge: Cambridge University Press 1998).

Jay, Martin, *Downcast Eyes: the Denigration of Vision in Twentieth-Century Thought* (Berkeley: University of California Press 1993).

Jeffrey, Ian, *Photography: a Concise History* (London: Thames and Hudson 1981).

Jenkins, Terence, *Disraeli and Victorian Conservatism* (Basingstoke: Macmillan 1996).

Jenkyns, Richard, *The Victorians and Ancient Greece* (Oxford: Blackwell 1980).

Joseph, Gerhard and Herbert F. Tucker, 'Passing On: Death', in Herbert F. Tucker (ed.), *A Companion to Victorian Literature and Culture* (Oxford: Blackwell 1999), 110–24.

Judd, Dens, *Empire* (London: HarperCollins 1996).

Kaplan, Fred, *Sacred Tears: Sentimentality in Victorian Literature* (Princeton: Princeton University Press 1987).

Karlin, Daniel, *Browning's Hatreds* (Oxford: Clarendon Press 1993).

Kingsley, Fanny, *Charles Kingsley: his Letters and Memories of his Life* (two vols, 1876, one-vol. digest London: Macmillan 1883).

Kitson Clark, George, *The Making of Victorian England* (London: Methuen 1962).

Langbaum, Robert, *The Poetry of Experience* (1957; reprinted New York: Norton 1963).

Leavis, Q.D., *Fiction and the Reading Public* (1932; London: Chatto & Windus 1939).

Lightman, Bernard (ed.), *Victorian Science in Context* (Chicago and London: University of Chicago Press 1997).

Longford, Elizabeth, *Queen Victoria: Born to Succeed* (New York: Harper and Row 1964).

Maas, Jeremy, *Victorian Painting* (London: Barrie & Jenkins 1988).

Mackinnon, Frank, 'Notes on the History of English Copyright', in Margaret Drabble (ed.), *Oxford Companion to English Literature* (5th edn, Oxford: Oxford University Press 1985).

Maitland, F.W., *The Life and Letters of Leslie Stephen* (London: Duckworth & Co. 1906).

Marks, Shula, 'Southern Africa 1867–1886' and 'Southern and Central Africa 1886–1910', in Roland Oliver and G.N. Sanderson (eds), *The Cambridge History of Africa: Volume VI, From 1870–1905* (Cambridge: Cambridge University Press 1985).

Martin, Loy D., *Browning's Dramatic Monologues and the Post-Romantic Subject* (Baltimore: Johns Hopkins University Press 1985).

Mason, Michael *The Making of Victorian Sexuality* (New York: Oxford University Press 1994).

Masson, David, 'Translations from the Classics', *North British Review* 16 (1851).

Matthew, Colin (ed.), *The Nineteenth-Century: The British Isles: 1815–1901* (Oxford: Oxford University Press 2000).

Maunder, Samuel, *The Scientific and Literary Treasury: a new and popular Encyclopaedia of the Belles Lettres, etc.* (5th edn, London: 1848).

Mayhew, Henry, *London Labour and the London Poor* (1849–62; selected and introduced by Victor Neuberg, Harmondsworth: Penguin 1985).

Mill, John Stuart and Jeremy Bentham, *Utilitarianism, and Other Essays* (ed. Alan Ryan; Harmondsworth: Penguin 1987).

Mill, John Stuart, *On Liberty and Other Essays* (1859; ed. John Gray, Oxford: Oxford University Press 1991).

Miller, J. Hillis, 'Self and Community' in N. John Hall (ed.), *The Trollope Critics* (London: Macmillan 1981).

Miller, J. Hillis, *Illustration* (Cambridge, Mass.: Harvard University Press 1992).

Moore, Robin J., 'Imperial India 1858–1914', in Andrew Porter (ed.), *The Oxford History of the British Empire: Volume III, The Nineteenth-Century* (Oxford: Oxford University Press 1999), 395–446.

Moorman, John, *A History of the Church in England* (3rd edn, London: A&C Black 1973).

Mukherjee, Rudrangshu, *Awadh in Revolt 1857–58: a Study in Popular Resistance* (Delhi: Oxford University Press 1984).

Neuburg, Victor, *Popular Literature: A History and Guide* (Harmondsworth: Penguin 1977).

Newman, Francis, 'Remedies for the Great Social Evil', in *Miscellanies* 3 (1869).

Newsome, David, *The Victorian World Picture* (London: John Murray 1997).

Otis, Laura (ed.), *Literature and Science in the Nineteenth-Century* (Oxford: Oxford University Press 2002).

Palmer, J.A.B., *The Mutiny Outbreak at Meerut in 1857* (Cambridge: Cambridge University Press 1966).

Partington, Angela (ed.), *The Oxford Dictionary of Quotations* (4th edn, Oxford: Oxford University Press 1992).

Pearce, Lynne, *Women Image Text: Readings in Pre-Raphaelite Art and Literature* (London: Harvester Wheatsheaf 1991).

Perkin, Joan, *Victorian Women* (London: John Murray 1993).

Petch, Simon, 'Legal', in Herbert Tucker (ed.), *A Companion to Victorian Literature and Culture* (Oxford: Blackwell 1999), 155–69.

Phillips, John and Charles Wetherell, 'The Great Reform Act of 1832 and the Political Modernization of England', *American Historical Review* 100 (1995), 411–36.

Porter, Andrew (ed.), *The Oxford History of the British Empire: Volume III, The Nineteenth-Century* (five vols, Oxford: Oxford University Press 1999).

Porter, Andrew, 'Religion, Missionary Enthusiasm, and Empire', in Andrew Porter (ed.), *The Oxford History of the British Empire: Volume III, The Nineteenth-Century* (Oxford: Oxford University Press 1999), 222–46.

Poston, Lawrence, '1832', in Herbert Tucker (ed.), *A Companion to Victorian Literature and Culture* (Oxford: Blackwell 1999), 3–18.

Preminger, Alex, Frank Warnke and O.B. Hardison (eds), *The Princeton Encyclopedia of Poetry and Poetics* (2nd edition, Princeton: Princeton University Press 1974).

Proust, Marcel, *Sodom and Gomorrah* (trans. C.K. Scott Moncrieff, Terence Kilmartin and D.J. Enright; London: Vintage 1996).

Reed, John R., 'Educational', in Herbert Tucker (ed.), *A Companion to Victorian Literature and Culture* (Oxford: Blackwell 1999), 194–211.

Rich, Norman, *Why the Crimean War?* (New York: St Martin's Press 1985).

Ricks, Christopher, *Tennyson* (London: Macmillan 1972; 2nd edn, Macmillan 1989).

Ridley, Mark, (ed.) *A Darwin Selection* (London: Fontana 1994).

Roberts, Adam, *Romantic and Victorian Long Poems* (Aldershot: Ashgate 1999).

Robinson, Henry Crabb, *On Books and their Writers* (1765–1867; ed. Edith Morley; three vols paginated as one, London: Dent 1938).

Rose, Hilary and Steven Rose, *Science and Society* (Harmondsworth: Penguin 1969).

Royle, Trevor, *Crimea: the Great Crimean War 1854–1856* (London: Little, Brown 1999).

Ruskin, John *The Stones of Venice* (three vols), in E.T. Cook and Alexander Wedderburn (eds) *The Works of John Ruskin* (London: George Allen 1904), Vols 9–11.

Ruskin, John, *Ariadne Florentina* (1872), in E.T Cook and Alexander Wedderburn (eds) *The Works of John Ruskin* (New York 1906), Vol. 22.

Saintsbury, George, *Life of the Earl of Derby* (London 1892).

Sanders, Andrew, 'The Court of Chancery', in Sanders (ed.) *Charles Dickens: Bleak House* (London: Everyman 1994).

Saunders, Christopher and Iain R. Smith, 'Southern Africa 1795–1910' in Andrew Porter (ed.), *The Oxford History of the British Empire: Volume III, The Nineteenth-Century* (Oxford: Oxford University Press 1999).

Savile, J., *1848: The British State and the Chartist Movement* (London: 1987).

Scheckner, Peter (ed.), *An Anthology of Chartist Poetry: Poetry of the British Working Class 1830s–1850s* (London and Toronto: Fairleigh Dickinson University Press 1989).

Schlicke Paul (ed.), *The Oxford Reader's Companion to Dickens* (rev. edn, Oxford: Oxford University Press 1999).

Schoenbaum, Samuel, *Shakespeare's Lives* (Oxford: Oxford University Press 1991).

Shannon, Richard, *Gladstone 1: Peel's Inheritor 1809–1865* (Harmondsworth: Penguin 1999); *Gladstone 2: Heroic Minister 1865–1898* (London: Allen Lane 1999).

Shaw, Albert Thompson, 'Hymn', in Alex Preminger, Frank Warnke and O.B. Hardison (eds), *The Princeton Encyclopedia of Poetry and Poetics* (2nd edn; Princeton NJ: Princeton University Press 1974), 356–8.

Shaw, David, 'Browning's Murder Mystery. *The Ring and the Book* and Modern Theory', *Victorian Poetry* 27, 1989, 79–98.

Shaw, Marion, '*In Memoriam* and Popular Religious Poetry', *Victorian Poetry* 15 (1977), 1–8.

Shaw, Philip and Peter Stockwell (eds), *Subjectivity and Literature from the Romantics to the Present Day* (London: Pinter 1991).

Simpson, Roger, *Camelot Regained: the Arthurian Revival and Tennyson 1800–1849* (Woodbridge Suffolk: Brewer 1990).

Sinfield, Alan, *Alfred Tennyson* ('Rereading Literature Series', Oxford: Blackwell 1986).

Smith, Helen R., *A Feast of Blood: Bloods and Penny Dreadfuls* (London: Jarndyce Catalogues 2002).

Smith, Lindsay, *Victorian Photography, Painting and Poetry: the Enigma of Visibility in Ruskin, Morris and the Pre-Raphaelites* (Cambridge: Cambridge University Press 1995).

Southgate, Donald, *The Passing of the Whigs, 1832–1886* (London: Macmillan 1962).

Stanley, Brian, 'Missionaries', in John Belchem and Richard Price (eds), *The Penguin Dictionary of Nineteenth-Century History* (Harmondsworth: Penguin 1994), 386–8.

Sugden, Philip, *The Complete History of Jack the Ripper* (London: Robinson 2002).

Sutherland, John, *The Longman Companion to Victorian Fiction* (Harlow: Longman 1988).

Tennyson, Alfred, *In Memoriam* (Shatto, Susan and Marion Shaw (eds); Oxford: Clarendon Press 1982).

Tennyson, Alfred, *Poems* (ed. Adam Roberts, 'The Oxford Authors' series, Oxford: Oxford University Press 1999).

Tennyson, G.B., *Victorian Devotional Poetry: the Tractarian Mode* (Cambridge, Mass.: Harvard University Press 1981).

Tennyson, Hallam, *Alfred, Lord Tennyson: A Memoir* (two vols, London 1897).

Thackeray, William Makepeace, *The Newcomes: Memoirs of a Most Respectable Family* (1853–5; London: Nelson and Sons 1900).

Thomas, William, *Mill* (Oxford: Oxford University Press 1985).

Thompson, Dorothy, *The Chartists: Popular Politics in the Industrial Revolution* (New York: Pantheon 1984).

Thompson, Edward P., *The Making of the English Working Class* (Harmondsworth: Penguin 1968).

Thompson, Edward P. and Eileen Yeo (eds), *The Unknown Mayhew: Selections from the Morning Chronicle 1849–1850* (Harmondsworth: Penguin 1971).

Trollope, Anthony, *An Autobiography* (1875–6; London: The Trollope Society 1999).

Tucker, Herbert (ed.), *Blackwell Companion to Victorian Literature and Culture* (Oxford: Blackwell 1999).

Tucker, Herbert, *Browning's Beginnings* (Minneapolis: University of Minnesota Press 1981).

Turner, Frank, *The Greek Heritage in Victorian Britain* (New Haven: Yale University Press 1981).

Vanden Bossche, Chris, 'Realism Versus Romance: the War of Cultural Codes in Tennyson's *Maud*, *Victorian Poetry* 24 (1986), 69–82.

Vicinus, Martha (ed.) *Suffer and Be Still: Women in the Victorian Age* (Bloomington and London: Indiana University Press 1973).

Walkowitz, Judith R., *City of Dreadful Delight: Narratives of Sexual Danger in Late-Victorian London* (London: Virago 1992).

Wall, Stephen, *Trollope and Character* (London: Faber and Faber 1988).

Warwick, P., *Black People and the South African War 1899–1902* (Cambridge: Cambridge University Press 1983).

Washbrook, D.A., 'India 1818–1860: the Two Faces of Colonisation', in Andrew Porter (ed.), *The Oxford History of the British Empire: Volume III, The Nineteenth-Century* (Oxford: Oxford University Press 1999), 395–446.

Webb, Richard, 'The Victorian Reading Public', in *From Dickens to Hardy: Pelican Guide to English Literature Vol. 6* (Harmondsworth: Penguin 1958).

Weinreb, Ben, and Christopher Hibbert, *The London Encyclopedia* (London: Papermac 1983; 2nd edn 1993).

Williams, Raymond, *Culture and Society 1780–1850* (Harmondsworth: Penguin 1958).

Williams, Raymond, *Keywords* (2nd edn, London, Fontana 1983).

Wilmer, Clive (ed.), *John Ruskin: Unto this Last and Other Writings* (Harmondsworth: Penguin 1985).

Wolf, R., *Gains and Losses: Novels of Faith and Doubt in Victorian England* (New York 1977).

Woods, Robert, 'The Population of Britain in the Nineteenth Century', in Michael Anderson (ed.), *British Population History from the Black Death to the Present Day* (Cambridge: Cambridge University Press 1996), 281–357.

Woolford, John, *Browning the Revisionary* (London: Macmillan 1988).

Index